T0320128

INSTITUTIONS AND TRADE POLICY

For my mother
Bernice M. Carle Finger
who taught me to be proud always of what I am,
and concerned always to be something more.

Institutions and Trade Policy

J. Michael Finger

American Enterprise Institute for Public Policy Research

Edward Elgar

Cheltenham, UK • Northampton, MA, USA

Published by
Edward Elgar Publishing Limited
Glensanda House
Montpellier Parade
Cheltenham
Glos GL50 1UA
UK

Edward Elgar Publishing, Inc.
136 West Street
Suite 202
Northampton
Massachusetts 01060
USA

A catalogue record for this book
is available from the British Library

Library of Congress Cataloguing in Publication Data

Finger, J. M.
        Institutions and trade policy / edited by J. Michael Finger,
        p. cm.
        Selection of 18 essays written by J. M. Finger.
        Includes index.
        1. Commercial policy. 2. Tariff. 3. Protectionism. 4. United States—Commercial
policy. 5. Developing countries—Commercial policy. 6. General Agreement on Tariffs
and Trade (Organization) 7. World Trade Organization. 8. United States—Foreign
economic relations—Developing countries. 9. Developing countries—Foreign economic
relations—United States. I. Title.

HF1411 .F525 2002
382'.3—dc21   2002020226

Printed on FSC approved paper
Printed and bound in Great Britain by Marston Book Services Ltd, Oxfordshire

ISBN 1 84064 984 4

Contents

Acknowledgements

The editor and publisher wish to thank the following who have kindly given permission for the use of copyright material.

American Economic Association for 'Trade and Domestic Effects of the Offshore Assembly Provision in the U.S. Tariff', *American Economic Review*, **66** (4), September 1976, 598–611; 'The Political Economy of Administered Protection' (with H.K. Hall and D.R. Nelson), *American Economic Review*, **72** (3), June 1982, 452–66.

American Enterprise Institute for Public Policy Research for 'Trade Liberalization: A Public Choice Perspective', in *Challenges to a Liberal International Economic Order*, R.C. Amacher, G. Haberler and T.D. Willett (eds), 1979, 421–53.

American Society of International Law for 'The Economics of Commodity Agreements: A Skeptical View', originally published as 'Comments' by J.M. Finger, *Proceedings of the 71st Annual Meeting of the American Society of International Law*, January 1978, pp. 136–41.

Blackwell Publishers Ltd for 'GATT Tariff Concessions and the Exports of Developing Countries – United States Concessions at the Dillon Round', *Economic Journal*, **84** (335), September 1974, 566–75; 'Tariff Provisions for Offshore Assembly and the Exports of Developing Countries', *Economic Journal*, **85** (338), June 1975, 365–71; 'Effects of the Kennedy Round Tariff Concessions on the Exports of Developing Countries', *Economic Journal*, **86** (341), March 1976, 87–95; 'Incorporating the Gains from Trade into Policy', *The World Economy*, **5** (4), December 1982, 367–77; 'Development Economics and the General Agreement on Tariffs and Trade', in *Trade Theory and Economic Reform: North, South and East*, J. de Melo and A. Sapir (eds), 1991, 203–23; 'Implementation of Uruguay Round Commitments: The Development Challenge' (with P. Schuler), *The World Economy*, **23** (4), April 2000, 511–25.

Kluwer Law International for 'The Compensatory Finance Facility and Export Instability' (with Dean A. DeRosa), *Journal of World Trade Law*, **14** (1), January/February 1980, 14–22.

Minnesota Journal of Global Trade for 'The Meaning of "Unfair" in United States Import Policy', *Minnesota Journal of Global Trade*, **1** (1), Fall 1992, 35–56.

Springer-Verlag for 'Protectionist Rules and Internationalist Discretion in the Making of National Trade Policy', in *New Institutional Arrangements for the World Economy*, H.J. Vosgerau (ed.), 1989, 310–23.

The University of Chicago Press for 'The Processing of Primary Commodities: Effects of Developed-Country Tariff Escalation and Developing-Country Export Taxes' (with S.S. Golub), *Journal of Political Economy*, **87** (3), May–June 1979, 559–77; 'Policy Research', *Journal of Political Economy*, **89** (6), December 1981, 1270–72; 'What Can the WTO Do for Developing Countries?' (with L.A. Winters), in *The WTO as an International Organization*, A.O. Kruger (ed.), 1998, 365–92.

The World Bank for 'Dumping and Antidumping: The Rhetoric and the Reality of Protection in Industrial Countries', *The World Bank Research Observer*, **7** (2), July 1992, 121–43; 'Should Developing Countries Introduce Antidumping? Never', *World Bank Country Economics Department Outreach*, May 1991, 1–4.

Introduction

I received a long while ago a letter from Edward Elgar Publishing inquiring if I would pull together a collection of my papers for publication in a single volume. It took me a long time to respond, a longer time still to pull together the collection presented here and to write this Introduction. This was not the first time that I had thought about pulling together such a collection, but for my 30-plus working years I have usually found the bird in the bush to be more interesting than the one in the hand. As my work went along, questions asked seemed always more engaging than questions answered.

Without the encouragement of several friends, particularly Jagdish Bhagwati, Bernard Hoekman, Douglas Irwin and Alan Winters, I would probably have let things slip again. I appreciate very much their encouragement and their kind words about the value of my work.

When I left graduate school in 1965, the market for university teachers was a sellers' market. At the Southern Economics Association meetings, recruiters from the less prestigious schools were buttonholing in the hotel registration line people who looked like they might be graduate students there to find a job. I recall part of a conversation with one of these recruiters. My question, 'How many economics courses do you offer?' Response: 'Three, but next year we hope to offer six, and you can teach all of them!'

I did not consider then a career other than a teaching career. Five years later I took leave to spend a year at the US Tariff Commission and while I was there someone offered me a job at the United Nations Conference on Trade and Development (UNCTAD) in Geneva. Several years and several jobs later I realized that I had spent more years as a bureaucrat than as an academic and I accepted what that told me – but not completely. Part of my strategy for maintaining space in which to work has been to have the bureaucrats think of me as an academic, the academics think of me as a bureaucrat.

In my few years of university teaching, I developed the impression that research was what one did to advance one's career, as calling on clients was what one did if one chose a career in sales – that one's ambition, not one's love of knowledge, was the motive behind one's work. In a governmental organization, I found, research was never particularly valued (it compromised options) and outside recognition was a liability; hence one could be confident that one's research motives were pure.

I recall at one time defending my place in the bureaucracy by asserting that I never wrote a research paper, I always wrote a policy paper. If it came out well, I sent it to a journal, if the journal accepted it then I listed it in my résumé as a research paper.

I have sorted the papers in this collection into five categories, categories that obviously overlap:

1. Tariffs and other instruments of import policy.
2. The New International Economic Order.
3. Administered protection.

4. How the GATT works.
5. Developing countries in the GATT/WTO.

A final paper, though published in 1981, provides a Conclusion that I still consider appropriate.

The papers were written more or less in the order in which they are presented in the volume. The first group of papers is what one might call straight economics – identifying and measuring the response of economic agents to changes of economic policy, such as the GATT tariff reductions. My interest has shifted over time from the effects of policy to its determinants; this shows in the essays.

The theme that this work has plotted follows more or less the intellectual history of developing countries in the trading system. My work began immersed in the presumption that developing countries needed special and differential treatment if they were to use trade as an effective vehicle for development. In time, my own work provided a small part of the accumulating evidence to demonstrate that the presumption was not valid, that developing country exporters were as dynamic as developed country exporters. Some of this work – Balassa, Bhagwati, Krueger among the major contributors – focused on the importance of developing countries getting their own policies right. My attention was on dimensions of the trading system, for example, the tariff preference scheme that UNCTAD promoted, how developing country exports responded to the multilateral tariff reductions negotiated under the General Agreement on Tariffs and Trade (GATT), various of the components of the New International Economic Order that gathered a lot of attention in the 1970s. In time my attention moved from analyzing the effect of existing or proposed institutions and policies to thinking about where such arrangements came from – the GATT system, in particular the place or role of developing countries in that system. In short, from concern that developing countries needed special and differential treatment in the trading system to worrying about how to fit them more effectively into the routine of the trading system.

Tariffs and other instruments of import policy
These four papers were written in the three years I worked at UNCTAD in Geneva. When I began to analyze the impact of GATT tariff cuts on exports of developing countries, I saw the work as part of UNCTAD's efforts to support and expand the Generalized System of Preferences (GSP). My initial hypothesis was that developing country exporters had been left at the starting gate when the larger countries reduced their tariffs – the more powerful enterprises in the developed countries would move briskly to exploit the new opportunities; export expansion by developing country enterprises required preferential access.

I found the opposite to be true. Developing country exports, where they were covered by the tariff cuts agreed in the Dillon and Kennedy Rounds, were already growing rapidly and continued to outpace the growth of developed country exports when MFN tariff cuts were made (Chapters 1 and 2). True, the negotiated cuts were concentrated on goods that the developed countries traded among themselves, but as a way to extend GATT concessions to products of export interest to developing countries, more active developing country participation in the reciprocal negotiations looked like a more workable alternative than preferences. My previously unquestioned acceptance that developing countries needed special and differential treatment in the trading system began to slip.

The other two papers in this group (Chapters 3 and 4) are about the economic effects of offshore assembly provisions (OAP), tariff provisions that allow for duty-free re-importation of components that have been assembled abroad. (The mechanics is that the tariff on the imported item is calculated on its total value less the value of re-imported components.) I became aware of such provisions when I spent 12 months in 1970–71 as visiting economist at the US Tariff Commission. The Commission had just completed a study of the use of such provisions in the USA. From the information that the Commission assembled it was evident that imports under such provisions were increasing rapidly, particularly from developing countries. It was not, however, obvious to me how to judge the impact of the provisions. The largest category of imports was automobiles, but the value of US components in these imports was minimal; limited as best I remember to a few items on which US standards were different from those in the exporting countries, for example seatbelts and safety glass. Hence the duty saved would be minimal, it was not likely that the provisions had much of an impact there. The incidence was more complex than a tariff rate multiplied by an elasticity.

The incidence of such OAPs boils down to the importer paying less customs duty *if* he or she imports goods put together from home-made rather than foreign-made components. The duty saving is conditioned on using components from a particular source – possibly another form of trade diversion. If home components cost more than foreign ones the efficiency effect might be negative.

On the other hand, use of the provision seemed an accommodation to the USA and other developed countries having comparative advantage in the more capital-intensive production of components. Assembly, presumed to be more labor intensive, was taking place in developing countries.

The UNCTAD Secretariat helped me to canvass the major developed countries for information; we located data that allowed me to analyze OAP imports of the USA, Germany and the Netherlands. The analysis indicated a positive welfare impact on both sides: the exporter and the importer of the finished goods.

To provide a sense of perspective I compared the impact on developing country exports of the US OAP provision with that of the European Economic Community's (EEC) tariff preference scheme. (When I did this work the USA had not yet implemented a GSP program.) I found that per dollar of imports to which they were applied, the US OAP and the European GSP saved importers roughly the same amount of customs duty. At the time (the early 1970s) the US OAP contributed as much to developing country export earnings as the EEC's GSP and OAP together. The major difference was that OAP trade was increasing much more rapidly. (I am aware of no recent comparisons.) GSP continues to be a political football; the OAPs, because they have powerful domestic constituencies, continue quietly to make their contribution.

Over the next few years, while I was working at the US Treasury Department, the US OAP came forward once or twice as a minor policy issue. One instance was a push by textile industry lobbyists to make OAP inapplicable to textile and clothing imports. The logic of this for the industry was, however, questionable. Multi Fiber

Arrangement (MFA) quotas were applied to physical amounts (square yards or square yard equivalents) of goods imported, with no allowance for US content. Hence imports of foreign assembly were fixed by the quotas; eliminating OAP would have the effect only of removing the incentive to use US-made components. Why then was the industry in favor? The impression I gained from talking to proponents was that they viewed the OAP as generally liberalizing, the industry lobbyists looked for any opportunity to trim away at anything that was liberalizing. (One of my later colleagues, Helen Hughes at the World Bank, advised that in such matters, 'Do not look for complex explanations when plain stupidity will do.')

The New International Economic Order
The OPEC price increase of 1974 prompted many proposals for new arrangements in favor of developing countries in the international economic system. The price increase's suggestion of unexploited developing country economic power prompted the developed countries to pay attention to these proposals. The New International Economic Order's (NIEO) elements included: (a) expanded and preferential access by developing countries to developed country markets; (b) changes in international markets for primary commodities to reduce the volatility of prices and to raise their level; (c) increased foreign aid; (d) technology transfer; and (e) revision of the international monetary system to finance the recurring deficits that the Prebisch view saw as a recurring part of underdevelopment. By the time the NIEO issues heated up I had moved from UNCTAD to the US Treasury Department, Office of the Assistant Secretary for International Affairs. My NIEO-related work there was primarily on trade and commodities issues.

On trade, I was already convinced that preferences were not necessary; my work looked for ways that developing countries might move into the mainstream of the GATT process of reducing import restrictions through reciprocal negotiations. The paper with Stephen S. Golub (Chapter 5) is an example. Developed countries, in order to attract the processing activity, escalated their tariffs with stage of processing. Developing countries' export restrictions on primary commodities had the same intent. ('Value adding', 'beneficiation'; there were a number of phrases to convey the idea of what would be gained by locating the processing activity at home.) If these restrictions could be reciprocally reduced, our thinking was, the two sides could share in the market expansion that came with lower prices of finished goods. Positive-sum mercantilism, we reasoned.

A companion paper that the trade group at the Treasury commissioned looked into the scope for GATT-type principal supplier trade exchanges between the USA and developing countries. The analytical focus here was to find principal supplier exchanges between the USA and developing countries with no more of a free-rider problem than previous GATT exchanges among developed countries had overcome (see Lage and Kiang, 1979).

Commodities policy was perhaps a hotter issue than trade, and seemed to offer some possibility for a market-oriented economist to find the possibility of a defensible governmental intervention. (Market-oriented economists like to think of themselves as doing something *actively* for the market, not just defensively insisting that the market be left alone.) Instability, one might hypothesize, was a symptom of market imperfection, stabilization therefore an efficiency-improving policy. Commodity agreements that aimed to stabilize might therefore be considered.

Gordon Smith led the Treasury's analytical work on commodity price stabilization, my role was more to carry the economics into the policy debate. Our principal research findings were:

1. Market cycles were longer than proposals for agreements had presumed.
2. Trends were hard to identify prospectively, hence it was difficult to determine at the time a transaction was made if a buffer stock should be buying or selling.

The major policy implications of these findings were:

1. Buffer stocks would have to be much larger than any proposed; for example, for tin, 120,000 metric tonnes versus the actual stock committed to the International Tin Agreement of 20,000.
2. Commodity agreements, the political tradition was, had a life of five years, then were renegotiated. Analysis indicated that an agreement would sometimes have to stay on the same side of the market (always buying or always selling) for longer than that. The possibility that international politics would be strong enough to support such action was unlikely.

I participated in several policy discussion groups in those years, the presentation from an annual meeting of the American Society of International Law (Chapter 7) is representative of how we attempted to bring sound economic analysis into policy discussion. We built not just on sound economic reasoning; in many instances our view was different from that of other participants in large part because we had an appreciation for the magnitudes involved as well as the ideas.

The paper with Dean DeRosa on the Compensatory Finance Facility (CFF) (Chapter 6) began as a cost–benefit analysis. The CFF, an International Monetary Fund (IMF) facility, exists to help countries with widely-fluctuating export receipts. The idea is that the CFF lends in lean years, the country repays in rich years and the facility thus provides a degree of stability for foreign exchange earnings. Part of our interest in the research was that we had some ideas on how we might conceptualize and quantify the benefits of stabilization. The elements of our analysis were to be: (a) the degree to which the facility stabilized export receipts; (b) quantification of the benefit of such; (c) the amount of capital tied up in the facility; and (d) the opportunity cost of that capital.

We never got to an analysis of the benefits from stabilization; we found that the CFF did not stabilize. The historical record showed that foreign exchange earnings net of CFF borrowings and repayments were *less* stable than 'raw' earnings. When we looked behind this finding, we found a familiar explanation: the difficulty of knowing *ex ante* if the current year was above or below trend. More than half of the borrowings were in years in which foreign exchange earnings were above trend. A second part of the explanation was that borrowers almost always kept the money for the maximum five years that the facility allowed. The interest rate was below market rate, it made sense for them to do so – provided that in the borrower's view the value of stabilization was minimal.

Looking back today, I see that the CFF was not about stabilization, it was the administrative cover for lending more IMF money to countries already judged to be 'worthy' or 'needy'. (It was this instrument's misdirection and its obfuscation. I will come back to these concepts in the section on administered protection.) NIEO proposals for reform of the CFF confirm this view. They were not about the degree of stabilization the facility contributed but about making more countries eligible for more money, for example, by making countries eligible on the basis of the instability of their earnings from particular commodities when the degree of instability of their overall foreign exchange earnings did not qualify them.

Administered protection

My analytical work on the topic began when in 1979 Malcolm Gillis asked me to prepare a paper for an upcoming National Bureau of Economic Research (NBER) conference in Sao Paulo. He suggested that the paper explain to Latin American exporters how to deal with the antidumping and countervailing duty laws of the USA. The Treasury Department (where I still worked) was involved with enforcement, but antidumping and countervailing duties had not become important issues in international relations. This low international profile stemmed in good part from the Treasury Department's reluctance to rule in the affirmative – a reluctance that already had made enforcement a hot issue inside the USA.

That paper is not included here. The useful parts of it looked into two questions:

1. Can I sort out the simultaneity between imports attracting antidumping cases and antidumping cases retarding imports?
2. The harassment effect: does the initiation of cases – apart from the imposition of antidumping duties – cause imports to decline?

The analysis found that beneath the simultaneity, antidumping cases did retard imports. This answer was no surprise. Its value in the research was mostly that it uncovered the second question – did the impact come from the harassment effect of initiating cases or from the antidumping duties that resulted from some of them? I found that the major impact on imports was from the filing of cases – the harassment effect – and not from imposition of antidumping duties. Thus every case was a winner for protection.

That paper was regular economics, an identification and quantification of economic effects of changing policy parameters. My second look at administered protection, the paper with Douglas Nelson and Keith Hall (Chapter 8), was more about how the administrative protection process worked than about its effects. In my view, our most useful results were the following:

1. *Analytically, we categorized decision processes as either technical or political.* The paper explains what we meant and demonstrates how we used the concepts. Later, in my work on the GATT/WTO system, I used a synonymous sorting – rules at one extreme, discretion at the other. This I found more useful than to think of 'power' as the obverse of rules – as much GATT/WTO analysis does.
2. *We found that the escape clause and antidumping are both about injury*, though one is a less technical process. Process differs, the economic cause and effect is

the same – but the rules of one are about injury, as is the greater degree of discretion applied in the other.

3. *We introduced deliberate misuse of information into the analysis*, the importance of misdirection and obfuscation in and by the technical process. Zero-sum decisions are difficult for political entities to make, the losers may not go away quietly. It is easier for a political entity accountable to both sides to make a decision if it can do so in isolation from some of the interests at play. Basing import relief mechanisms on 'injury' to domestic producers who are displaced by imports has the effect both of defining an entitlement for one side and of leaving out the other domestic interests – users/consumers of imports and their domestic substitutes. Misdirection is to cast the problem forward as a conflict between domestic interests versus foreign; obfuscation is the mass of technical information that provides both the appearance of objective inquiry and an almost impenetrable screen that the casual analyst will not fight through. Transparency and other procedural virtues in this context are corrupted; the wealth of information made available on the side that is enfranchised helps to distract attention away from the realization that there are other, disenfranchised, domestic interests as well. This is how to do the wrong thing (economics) the right way (procedure). As with the Compensatory Finance Facility, the cause that justifies a policy intervention is often far removed from the motives that propel its advocates.

In the paper on the rhetoric versus the reality of antidumping (Chapter 9) I looked further into how the veneer of antidumping is different from its true economics. Antidumping, even at its beginning, was only in rhetoric about competition policy. The prose in this chapter is rather inflamed, it reflects perhaps my frustration at finding out not only how venal this part of policy making is, but how dishonest – in the misdirection and obfuscation sense of dishonest, none of it is illegal.

Looking back at the first paper I wrote on administered protection – that I chose not to include here – I am embarrassed at how much space I devoted to the question 'Is antidumping protection?' (That is why I decided not to include it here.) Soon after I lost patience with that question. Of course antidumping is protection. It has the intent and the effect of restricting imports. Many times – in academic circles as well as in political –when I spoke of antidumping as protection someone would object, 'But antidumping is GATT-legal.' 'Yes', my stock reply became, 'so are tariffs and no one hesitates to categorize them as protection.'

My work-a-day attitude toward antidumping soon became that it was perfectly legal but did not make economic sense. Buttressing this position was a decade of research, to which I contributed little, demonstrating that antidumping compromised the national economic interest. As competition policy, antidumping cases simply would not have been cases. There is also an extensive literature that competently documents various 'biases' in the application of antidumping – again I contributed little. I interpret these findings not as evidence that antidumping measures are illegal, but as evidence that the antidumping process had been captured.

As I look back, perhaps the most informative thing I have said about antidumping is the following: *Antidumping is ordinary protection with a good public relations program*. The phrase popped to mind in 1992 as I drove into the parking lot of a Canberra radio station where I was about to be interviewed.

When I moved to the World Bank, my work on antidumping was shaped by the many times someone asked me if a particular country should introduce an antidumping law. My stock response became to shift the discussion to the question of a pressure valve: *Is antidumping a good pressure valve, a way to allow a spot or two of protection for a powerful interest that might otherwise wreck an entire liberalization program?* My answer to the question was 'No' because:

1. Antidumping's unfair trade rhetoric tends to inflame the political debate in favor of protection – it worsens rather than strengthens the government's position for defending a liberalization program.
2. The obvious economic question is to look into the benefits and the costs of the proposed restriction – which domestic interests win, which domestic interests lose, by how much? The 'gains from trade' do not argue that imports will not inconvenience some domestic interests. The concept argues that trade's benefits to other domestic interests (users) will be even larger.

Chapter 10, the note titled, 'Should Developing Countries Introduce Antidumping? Never' was my summary advice on the matter. It explains why antidumping is inappropriate and offers guidelines for an appropriate safeguard mechanism. English and Spanish versions have been widely circulated.

Chapter 11, on incorporating the gains from trade into policy, is another attempt to make a simple point: GATT-sanctioned trade remedies consider only the inconveniences trade brings, not the benefits.

How the GATT works
I begin this section with a warning. Once upon a seminar Robert Hudec commented that Michael Finger knows a lot about the GATT, but he learned most of it studying antidumping. That, Professor Hudec added, is like a student presenting himself for the final exam in a course on Marriage and the Family when the only lecture he attended was the one on domestic violence.

Chapter 12 lays out a basic part of my view of what the GATT is and how it works. GATT is a contract. One part of the contract is the paperwork for an exchange of market access among countries – giving access to one's market buys access to another. The specifics of who gives and who gets what are listed in the schedules of tariff bindings 'attached' to the document. Other parts of the contract specify the rights to impose new import restrictions that the parties to the contract have reserved. Some of these require negotiation with the other contracting parties; some require that compensation be made. Some provisions allow unilateral, uncompensated action, for example, antidumping.

Another important point is that GATT was a contract among *governments*, the GATT acknowledged the authority to restrict imports as the property of governments.

Domestic trade remedy laws have the effect of transferring control over exercise of these rights to protection-seeking private parties. For example, a US company can petition the US government to investigate dumping-injury, if the resulting determination is affirmative the US government must take antidumping action. (Regulations in many other countries allow the government discretion not to act even if the determination is affirmative.)

As economics, the conditions for activating the trade remedies are broad. Their basic concept is injury to domestic producers from import competition and this condition is likely to be met in any instance in which it is worth a company's while to ask for protection, any instance in which having imports restricted would make for better business.

The dumping test is the operational counterpart to the rhetoric of foreign unfairness – it serves thus as the base for antidumping's anti-imports politics. It does not, however, serve to screen who gets protection from who does not; the scope of its legal/operational meaning is so broad that virtually every investigation returns a positive determination.

In GATT's early years, domestic trade remedies were infrequently applied because:

- the governments that administered them did not want to take action against foreign exports; and
- domestic trade remedy regulations provided sufficient discretion for the government to overcome the strong likelihood that the technicalities would return an affirmative determination – either formal discretion to treat the technical determination as a recommendation, or informal discretion, that is, sufficient wiggle room that the government could find a loophole or an ambiguity that allowed a negative determination.

The title of the paper is clumsy, 'Protectionist Rules and Internationalist Discretion ...', but it conveys a good deal of what I wanted to say in the paper. 'Internationalist' was a reminder that US trade policy in the early GATT days was dominated by foreign policy concerns, and those suggested that the US market be kept open. The internationalist/free-trade result of administration of the trade remedies depended on the exploitation of the discretion the law allowed – the informal discretion perhaps more than the formal. When I worked at the US Treasury Department we prided ourselves in running an *honest* antidumping system, that is, we looked for every possible way to avoid restricting imports, including never finishing investigations if the law did not impose a time limit. Had we been loyal to the spirit and the letter of the rules, we would have restricted imports a lot more than we did.

As long as protection-seeking industries were unsure of the content of the rules and the government retained discretionary authority over their application, a free-trade-oriented government could use GATT rules as a *political* crutch. Trade lawyers in time educated potential clients as to the possibilities; the Congress in eliminating the loopholes transferred authority over import restrictions to the particular interests that would benefit from them.

Chapter 13 provides a detailed look at outcomes of reciprocal negotiations, its analytical focus is the free-rider problem. Not all countries, not even all those that were 'members' of GATT, were active participants in the tariff-reductions negotiations. Because all GATT tariff concessions had to be applied MFN, the non-participants would be free riders. But negotiating parties did have means to reduce free riding; principally by selecting products on which concessions were made, even redefining tariff categories, so that concessions were made only on products imported in large part from other participants. Besides looking into how the negotiations controlled the free-rider problem, I wanted also to find out how much spillover had been tolerable in successful Rounds. This was part of my effort to identify possibilities for positive-sum mercantilism; possible principal supplier reciprocal negotiations between the USA and major developing countries.

The results did show a clear concern to eliminate spillover to free riders, and a growing sophistication among negotiators to do so. Before the Kennedy Round, though concessions were applied on an MFN basis to all GATT contracting parties, negotiations were bilateral. (A v. B and C v. D, then A v. C and B v. D, etc.) In early Rounds the elimination of spillover was accomplished mainly in the bilateral negotiations – no spillover from a bilateral deal to other countries, even to those active in the Round with which the negotiating pair would eventually negotiate. Later, perhaps under pressure to increase the coverage of the liberalization, product selection seemed to be based on imports from all participating countries and not just the immediate bilateral partner. In the language of the paper, the multilateral dimension of the negotiations became an increasingly important part in the control of spillover, or of expanding coverage of the negotiations to a larger share of trade without the free-rider problem becoming intolerable.

The Kennedy Round formula approach did allow much larger coverage and accepted a larger degree of spillover. But there was still an obvious attempt to cut into free riding – the chapter explains the point and documents the magnitudes involved.

In writing the paper I took the opportunity to look through US government files for information on what concessions the USA had exchanged with which countries in the earlier GATT Rounds, from the first in 1947 through the Kennedy Round of 1964–67. My editors were quite generous in allowing me to pass that information along in several tables that do not bear directly on the analysis I reported in the paper.

Chapter 14, 'The Meaning of "Unfair" in United States Import Policy', is a comparison of the standards of fairness in the rhetoric of protection versus in the economics. The thesis is that an objective definition of 'unfair' neither is nor ever has been the basis for determining when the US government will act against imports. The politics of import restrictions define the economic meaning of 'unfair', not the other way around. The chapter ends on a pessimistic note, a story to suggest that the trade policy process in the USA cannot even envision there being a better outcome, much less find a way to get to one.

Developing countries in the GATT/WTO

In 1986, Martin Wolf, then Director of Studies at the Trade Policy Research Center, invited me to be discussant of a paper prepared by Robert E. Hudec, a paper that Professor Hudec expanded in time into the history section of his book, *Developing Countries in the GATT Legal System* (see Hudec 1987). At its seminars, the TPRC asked the *discussants*, not the authors, to present the papers. Had I not been under the burden to do an honest job of presenting Professor Hudec's ideas I might not have worked so hard as I did to understand them. As it was, reading that paper and preparing that presentation probably expanded the scope of my thinking more than any other piece I have ever studied.

The message I took from Professor Hudec's paper I lay out in Chapter 15. The gist of it is in the following two points:

1. The spirit of the GATT negotiations (the negotiating framework and moral perception) was *individual sacrifice for the common good*. This was mercantilist economics – exports are good, imports are bad – plus a strong sense that an open trading system was needed to ensure the security as well as the prosperity of all.
2. In such a setting, it is difficult to ask the weaker members for the same sacrifice as the stronger members, hence weaker disciplines and lesser commitment to liberalize by the developing countries was an expression of the spirit of the undertaking.

As the place of developing countries in the negotiations settled into the conception that exempting them from GATT disciplines was a *concession* to them, developing country negotiators gauged their success by how effective they were in winning such exemptions. For developed country negotiators, exemption from legal discipline was cheap to give – no budget appropriations needed. In short, if granting such exemption bought the loyalties of the developing countries in the Cold War, it was exemption well spent. Economic principle – that developing countries' economic interests might be better served by liberalizing – was open to the accusation that it was crass mercantilism.

Besides laying out these ideas, Chapter 15 contrasts this evolution of the GATT as a political–legal system with the evidence that was building up at the same time that developing countries were not well served by their own, import substitution, trade policies. The GATT system actively ignored such information, for example, when brought forward by the Haberler Report of 1958 (see Campos, Haberler, Meade and Tinbergen 1958).

Work at the World Bank involved *unilateral* liberalization in which the focus is on eliminating trade restrictions because their impact on the domestic economy is more cost than benefit. The number of times I heard import restrictions defended as allowed by GATT rules brought home to me that GATT trade remedies rules are bad policy advice. They do not separate restrictions that augment the national interest of the country that imposes them from ordinary protection. They are at best about *more import restrictions versus less*, but the parts of the GATT that permit import restrictions are generous. Constrained only by these rules a country can maintain a high level of protection.

Chapter 16 (with Alan Winters) looks at a long list of GATT and World Trade Organization (WTO) provisions as economic advice, for example, on safeguards and on regional arrangements. Our perspective is that of the World Bank: do GATT/WTO obligations push developing countries toward policies that make economic sense? Our conclusions are critical of GATT/WTO obligations as policy advice. Sometimes, as with antidumping and safeguards, the economics is wrong. Sometimes, as with regional arrangements, the economics is incomplete – you can get the economics right or wrong and in either case be within GATT/WTO obligations.

Alan Winters and I were both at the World Bank when we wrote the paper. For us, a significant part of the context of the paper was the ongoing discussion of World Bank–WTO *coherence*. The initiative for this discussion came from the WTO; its initial thrust was more or less that the World Bank should spend its money and influence to help developing countries meet their WTO obligations. World Bank management at the time was inclined to let the WTO lead on trade. Alan's and my motivation in preparing the paper was in considerable part to arm ourselves for an internal discussion of a passive versus an active role for the Bank on trade. We did not see leaving trade to the WTO as a way to guide our clients toward good policy.

The last paper in this section, written with Philip Schuler, was another part of our consideration at the Bank of coherence and cooperation with the WTO. It began simply as an attempt to use Bank project experience in the areas the WTO was newly regulating as a basis for determining how much it would cost a developing country to get up to speed in these areas.

Our canvass covered only three of the WTO's 'new areas' – customs reform, intellectual property, and sanitary and phyto-sanitary standards – and we learned more than we set out to learn. Re our initial objective, we found that the cost would be considerable. Including, for example, the laboratories, staff training, and so on needed to establish a modern system for standards, the computers, software systems and physical equipment for a modern customs system could cost a lot – $150 million per country, or for many of the least developed countries, more than a year's development budget.

If this sort of money is to be spent, an economist should be concerned that it be productively spent. Thus our second look at Bank lending experience in these areas was to ascertain whether WTO obligations were good development advice. Did they, in the areas they covered, help to identify relevant problems, and did they offer workable solutions? We concluded that the answer was more often negative than positive.

Conclusion

If pressed for a conclusion about the impact of this work, I would say that in policy making the truth matters, but is not definitive. The last chapter, which was my valedictory address when I left the US Treasury Department in 1980, elaborates such a conclusion. When I delivered the address, the first comment a colleague offered was, 'Who told you *you* could be the valedictorian?'. That comment portrays the irreverence of my colleagues that I have long cherished, and though I have likely not communicated such in this book, something of the fun that doing this work has been.

References

Campos, R., G. Haberler, J. Meade and J. Tinbergen (1958), *Trends in International Trade*, Geneva: GATT.

Hudec, R.E. (1987), *Developing Countries in the GATT Legal System*, London: Gower, for the Trade Policy Research Center.

Lage, G.M. and F. F. Kiang (1979), 'The Potential for Mutually Beneficial Trade Negotiations between the United States and Advanced LDCs', *Weltwirtschaftliches Archiv*, Band 115, Heft 2, pp. 297–314.

PART ONE

TARIFFS AND OTHER INSTRUMENTS OF IMPORT POLICY

[1]

GATT TARIFF CONCESSIONS AND THE EXPORTS OF DEVELOPING COUNTRIES – UNITED STATES CONCESSIONS AT THE DILLON ROUND[1]

I. Introduction

AT the 1960–61 GATT tariff conference (The Dillon Round) the United States negotiated with the European Economic Community and 11 other developed countries (DC) as well as with six less developed countries (LDC) (Cambodia, Haiti, India, Israel, Pakistan and Peru) and agreed to reduce its duties on products covering some $2 billion of imports in 1960. While this 20 % reduction of tariffs on some 20 % of dutiable imports was small compared with the 35 % cut on almost 55 % of dutiable imports achieved in the more recent Kennedy Round, they were more extensive, both in terms of the magnitude of the reductions and extent of import coverage, than the reductions achieved in any of the previous five GATT rounds except the first, in Geneva in 1947.

II. Purpose and Method

In this paper I present estimates of the effects of these concessions on United States imports, with separate figures for imports from developed countries and from the less developed countries.

Method

An extension of the "Reduced Group, Non-Reduced Group" method of analysis introduced by Krause and also used by Kreinin to investigate the effects of United States concessions at earlier GATT rounds has been employed here. The method involves the selection of a sample of products on which tariff cuts were made (the reduced group), and a corresponding sample of similar products with approximately equal values of imports on which tariffs were not changed (the non-reduced group). The reduced and non-reduced groups are then interpreted as samples from the population of products on which tariffs were reduced and from a population of products similar in every respect except that they were not subject to tariff cuts. The import statistics for 1960 and 1965 are then compared, so as to obtain the percentage movement in value, quantity and unit value for each group, and the difference between the two percentages for each of these is taken as an estimate of the effect of the tariff cuts. Standard z and t tests were used to test whether or not the observed differences between the groups were statistically significant.

[1] An earlier version was presented at the Econometric Society Meetings, New York, 28 December 1973. I am grateful for helpful comments from R. E. Baldwin, W. B. Reddaway, and an anonymous referee. They are not responsible for any remaining shortcomings.

Data

A complete revision of United States tariff nomenclature which went into effect in mid-1963 made the collection of "before" (1960) and "after" (1965) data extremely difficult.[1] Though considerable effort was expended in collecting data, the sample included only 9 % of the trade on the concessions list (see line 1, Table I).[2]

Quantity and value of imports data were taken from the United States Census Bureau publications cited in the references, and tariff rates from the State Department report. Changes in value, quantity and unit value for each item were expressed as percentages of the average of their 1960 and 1965 levels, and average changes for the reduced and non-reduced groups were then computed using 1960 plus 1965 value of imports as weights.[3]

III. Extent of the Concessions

Not only were the concessions concentrated on manufactures, where the LDCs are relatively small suppliers, but within both the materials and manufactured goods categories the cuts were concentrated on products imported from DCs. Indeed, the cuts affected 11 % of United States imports of materials from DCs but only 2 % of materials imports from LDCs. For manufactures, comparable figures are 28 % and 21 %.

As United States bargaining at the Dillon Round was on a bilateral, item by item basis, it is not surprising that more than 70 % of United States imports of concession items originated in the country with whom the concession was negotiated. However, "spillover" (imports of concession items from other countries) accounted for 93 % of concessions on imports from LDCs— indicating that the major part of benefits to the LDCs resulting from these GATT concessions accrued to them as bystanders rather than as participants.

While this spillover was large relative to concessions granted directly to

---

[1] Details of such problems are given in a longer version available from the author.

[2] Automobiles and five other large items which could not be traced across the changes in data nomenclature accounted for over half of imports on which concessions were granted. Because the results in Tables I and II which are statistically significant are significant at very high confidence levels, and those which are not significant would not have been significant even if the sample size were several times larger (assuming that the values of the test statistics would be the same), the possibility that my conclusions are based on sampling error rather than on fact does not seem abnormally high.

[3] While there were a total of 189 products in the reduced group, for a number of these there were no imports from LDCs and for a few others none from DCs. But as changes of unit value could be calculated only for observations for which both 1960 and 1965 imports were non-zero (so that unit value could be determined each year), the number of observations usable for calculating changes of this variable was considerably reduced, especially for imports from LDCs. While the numbers of observations thus excluded from the reduced and non-reduced groups were roughly equal in most cases, elimination of a product from one group was not usually accompanied by elimination of its "partner" from the other group, and as a result the reduced and non-reduced groups used to calculate changes of unit value for the country subgroups were not as closely matched as to composition as the complete groups.

the LDCs it amounted to only 3 % of United States imports from them not directly affected by concessions. In contrast, spillover accruing to DCs amounted to almost 8 % of United States imports from these countries which were not directly affected by concessions, reflecting again the understandable fact that the cuts, which were in the main negotiated *with* DCs, were concentrated on products imported for the most part *from* DCs.

TABLE I

Effects of United States Dillon Round Concessions, 1960–1965

(Changes in per cent)

	Materials (SITC 0–4 plus 67, 68)			Manufactures (SITC 5–8 less 67, 68)		
	From all countries	From developed countries	From developing countries	From all countries	From developed countries	From developing countries
1. Value of Imports, 1960 ($ millions)						
(a) Concession list	550	432	118	1,446	1,350	96
(b) Included in sample	28	18	10	145	116	29
2. Change of value of total imports	22·6	42·4	4·7	50·0	47·6	72·1
3. Average change of value for sampled items						
(a) Reduced group	118·3 (49)	132·9 (45)	69·2 (25)	47·5 (140)	40·0 (140)	71·5 (64)
(b) Non-reduced group	43·9 (46)	38·5 (42)	48·7 (27)	28·1 (140)	21·7 (140)	74·2 (69)
(c) Difference	74·4*	94·4*	20·5	19·4*	18·2*	−2·7
4. Average change of quantity for sampled items						
(a) Reduced group	117·2 (49)	134·2 (45)	46·0 (25)	33·5 (140)	24·1 (140)	57·3 (64)
(b) Non-reduced group	39·6 (46)	51·4 (42)	26·7 (27)	14·6 (140)	7·4 (140)	52·6 (69)
(c) Difference	77·6*	82·8*	19·3	18·9*	16·7*	4·7
5. Change of tariff (as % of foreign price)	−2·1	−1·4	−4·1	−2·5	−2·5	−2·3
6. Average change of unit value (foreign price)						
(a) Reduced group	3·2 (49)	−1·2 (43)	39·2 (22)	14·9 (140)	16·6 (139)	16·6 (36)
(b) Non-reduced group	2·8 (46)	−17·7 (42)	22·9 (22)	14·1 (140)	15·3 (139)	27·0 (33)
(c) Difference	0·4	16·5	16·3	0·8	1·3	−10·4
7. Implicit change of domestic price	−1·4	15·1	12·5	−1·5	−1·0	−12·5

Numbers in parentheses are numbers of observations included in each calculation.
* Indicates that the difference between the means is significant at the 99 % confidence level.

IV. Effects of the Concessions on Total Imports

As was the case with the GATT concessions implemented in the mid-50s and examined by Kreinin (1961), the Dillon Round concessions had a significant effect on United States imports. Lines 3 and 4 of Table I show a much bigger percentage rise for imports of the reduced group than for the control group, whether the calculation is done in terms of value or quantity. In contrast, Krause, in his examination of the effects of the earlier Torquay and Annecy Rounds found that only the few cuts in excess of 30 % of the existing tariff levels had a significant impact on imports.

By the mid-50s and especially by the time of the implementation of the Dillon Round cuts, the erosion of specific and compound duties by price inflation as well as the concessions granted at earlier GATT rounds seemed to have taken almost all of the excess protection out of the United States tariff. And by the early 60s Europe and Japan had become competitive with the United States on a wide range of industrial goods, both in terms of comparative costs and in terms of capacity to supply exports on the scale of the United States market. This interpretation is borne out by the significant effects of the concessions on imports of both materials and of manufactures, and also by the small proportion of the tariff cuts which accrued to exporters in the form of higher f.o.b. prices. Calculations in this field are inevitably precarious, but line 6 of Table I shows that unit values rose on average by a rather bigger percentage for the reduced group than for the control group, and the small difference provides a rough estimate of the effects of the concessions on the price charged by the foreign exporter. Comparison of this with the cut in the tariff, expressed as a percentage of the foreign price (line 5) suggests that the f.o.b. price of manufactures rose, because of the tariff cuts, by about one-third of the magnitude of the cuts, while about one-fifth of the 2·1 percentage points reductions in the price of materials went to the foreign suppliers. By contrast, Kreinin (1961, p. 317) found a proportion of about half for the mid-50s concessions. In addition, while the 1955–59 cuts examined by Kreinin were of roughly equal magnitude with the Dillon Round cuts, they caused increases of quantity of imports of 12 %, while the Dillon Round cuts produced increases of nearly 80 % for materials and of nearly 20 % for manufactures.

V. Developed vs. Less-Developed Countries

Materials

In value terms, imports of materials from the LDCs lagged behind imports of materials from DCs in two respects. First, disregarding the effects of the tariff cuts, imports from LDCs did not increase as rapidly as imports from DCs, either in total (line 2 of Table I), or on the sort of products on the concession list (lines 3 (a) and (b)). Second, the effects of the tariff concessions (lines 3 (c), 4 (c)) were less on imports from LDCs than on imports from DCs in terms of import value and of import quantity. This, and the observation that the unit value of imports from the LDCs rose more than the unit value of imports from DCs suggest that the elasticity of supply of materials exports is lower in the LDCs than in the DCs.

This lower elasticity of supply could be explained by two factors: (1) specialisation by LDCs in products for which the elasticity of supply is low, wherever they are produced, or (2) less responsiveness on the part of LDC exporters to expanding markets and/or relative price changes.

Additional calculations,[1] some of which are reported in Table II[2] suggest that the first of these factors is much more important than the second. When the average change of unit value of imports from all countries was recalculated, using imports from LDCs and from DCs as weights, we found that the average change of unit value when weighted by imports from LDCs is much larger than when weighted by imports from DCs, both for the reduced and for the non-reduced group. That is, regardless of their origin, unit value rose more on the sort of products in which the exports of the LDCs are concentrated. Also (Table II, lines 2, 4) calculations of average changes of quantity of imports of materials from each of the country groups indicate that the quantity increase for both groups was less for the products in which developing countries exports are concentrated. Finally, LDC exports of materials responded to the tariff cuts more strongly than did DC exports, for both the LDC and DC baskets. This suggests no lack of supply response on the part of LDC exports.

Viewed another way, comparing rows 1 and 2 with rows 3 and 4 of Table II we see that imports of products in the developed country basket were more responsive to the Dillon Round cuts than imports of products in the developing country basket of exports to the United States. But column *vs.* column we see that basket by basket the supply response of the developing countries to the concessions was at least as strong as the developed countries'.

---

[1] Let subscript i (= 1, 2, 3) represent the country groups, *i.e.* all countries, DC, LDC, respectively, and the subscript j represent individual products. The weight W_{ij} is equal to the share of product j in total value of imports from country group i. X represents any one of the three variables' change of value of imports, change of quantity of imports, or change of unit value of imports. The averages in Table II were computed from the formula $X_{0i} = \sum_j W_{ij} X_{ij}$. In these calculations, the average change of a variable for a country group is weighted by own imports, *i.e.* imports from that country group. Additional calculations were made using the formulae

$$X_{1i} = \sum_j W_{1j} X_{ij} \quad (i = 1, 3), \quad X_{2i} = \sum_j W_{2j} X_{ij} \quad (i = 1, 3), \quad X_{3i} = \sum_j W_{3j} X_{ij} \quad (i = 1, 3).$$

Of course $X_{ki} = X_{0i}$ when $k = i$. The X_{2i}, X_{3i} for value and quantity are reported in Table II, and the other calculations are available on request.

[2] Row *vs.* row, Table II compares a country group's performance on one basket with that group's performance on the other basket. Column *vs.* column, Table II compares the relative supply responses of the country groups on the same basket of goods.

Manufactures

In contrast with imports of materials, line 1 of Table I shows that United States imports of manufactures from LDCs increased more rapidly than total imports of manufactures.[1] For manufactures of the type on the concession list, lines 3 and 4 show that imports from LDCs grew more rapidly, both in value and in quantity. But the tariff cuts seem to have had a significant impact

Table II

Average Changes of Value and Quantity of United States Imports, 1960–1965,
Weighted by Imports from Developed Countries and by Imports from
Developing Countries

(Per cent)

	Materials			Manufactures		
	From all countries (A)	From developed countries (B)	From developing countries (C)	From all countries (D)	From developed countries (E)	From developing countries (F)
Developed country basket†						
1. Average change of value						
(a) Reduced group	131·8	132·9	151·1	48·4	40·0	92·3
(b) Non-reduced group	40·0	38·5	18·9	27·2	21·8	78·5
(c) Difference	91·8*	94·4*	132·2*	21·2*	18·2*	13·8**
2. Average change of quantity						
(a) Reduced group	133·8	134·2	149·4	34·0	24·1	84·8
(b) Non-reduced group	53·9	51·4	35·0	13·5	7·4	44·7
(c) Difference	79·9*	82·8*	114·4*	20·5*	16·7*	40·1*
Developing country basket‡						
3. Average change of value						
(a) Reduced group	73·2	−7·8	69·2	44·9	14·3	71·5
(b) Non-reduced group	47·4	150·0	48·7	35·1	−28·9	74·2
(c) Difference	25·8*	−157·8	20·5	9·8**	43·2*	−2·7
4. Average change of quantity						
(a) Reduced group	61·3	−19·1	46·0	32·0	1·3	57·3
(b) Non-reduced group	26·9	133·0	26·7	22·9	−48·2	52·6
(c) Difference	34·4*	−152·1	19·3	9·1	49·5*	4·7

* Denotes significance at the 99% confidence level.
** Denotes significance at the 95% confidence level.
† Averages computed using imports, by product, from developed countries as weights, *i.e.* the averages are X_{2i}.
‡ Averages computed using imports, by product, from developing countries as weights, *i.e.* X_{3i}.

only on imports from DCs. Imports from the LDCs of products in the reduced and in the non-reduced groups increased by roughly equal percentages.

Cause of Rapid Growth of Imports from LDCs. A detailed look at the results presented in Table II allows us to be confident that the relative increase of United States imports from LDCs resulted from supply increasing more

[1] This trend has continued through 1972. See GATT, *International Trade* 1972, Appendix Table A.

rapidly there than in the DCs, rather than from a disproportionate increase in United States import demand for products in which the LDCs specialise. When the export performances of the two country groups are compared over the same basket of goods—whether the DC or the LDC basket—we see that exports of the LDCs to the United States increased more than exports of the DCs. Also, we note that United States imports of the DC basket from all countries increased in parallel with United States imports of the LDC basket from all countries—ruling out the hypothesis of relative increase of import demand for the LDC basket.

In addition, we note that LDC exporters did much better competing with the strength of DC exporters (the DC basket) than did DC exporters competing with the strength of LDC exporters. Comparing the figures in rows 1 and 2, column F—LDC exports of the DC basket—with those in rows 3 and 4, column E—DC exports of the LDC basket—confirms this. In fact, not only did LDC exports of the LDC basket expand more rapidly than DC exports of that basket of goods, but LDC exports to the United States expanded even more rapidly for the DC basket than for the LDC basket.

Effects of the Tariff Reductions. As to the effects of the tariff reductions, DC exports to the United States of products on the concession list were significantly affected by the tariff concessions: the average increase of imports from the DC of the reduced group is significantly larger than the average increase for the non-reduced group, for both baskets of goods.

The effect of the concessions on manufactured exports from LDCs seems to be a little more complicated. We see that while LDC exports of the LDC basket of goods to the United States were not significantly influenced by the tariff concessions, their exports of the other basket did respond in a significant fashion. This is consistent with the supposition that LDC exports to the United States are concentrated on products in which the cost difference between the United States and the LDC supplier is so large that a tariff concession equivalent to 2·5 % of f.o.b. price is not a significant *additional* export incentive.[1] The large increases of supply of exports from LDCs which account for the increase of exports both of the reduced and non-reduced groups are perhaps responses to the existence of this cost differential rather than to marginal changes of one or more exogenous factors.

But on products which might be called atypical LDC exports (the DC basket) we observe not only a significant increase of supply from the LDC, but also a significant response (especially in terms of quantity) to the marginal incentive of the tariff reductions. This could be explained in several ways. It is possible that production of these products for export from the LDCs is

[1] A study by the United States Tariff Commission revealed that unit labour cost in the LDC in the assembly of many products imported by the United States averaged about 32 % of unit labour costs in the United States in the production of wearing apparel; about 14 % of United States unit labour costs in the assembly of such articles as radios, phonographs, television receivers and related sub-assemblies; and about 27 % in the assembly of various manufactures, ranging from baseballs (7 %) to scientific instruments (46 %).

dominated by multi-national firms, who switch their global pattern of production in response to marginal signals such as that provided by the Dillon Round tariff concessions. Or it is possible that the cost difference between the United States and the LDCs on these products is not as large as on the others, so that an opportunity of the magnitude offered by the tariff concessions is not swamped by other incentives to export.

VI. APART FROM THE EFFECTS OF THE CONCESSIONS

With the advantage of hindsight, it is interesting to speculate on the constellation of political forces and objectives which determined the make-up of the United States concessions list. The supposition that the pre-concession screening process had as an objective the minimisation of the effect of each concession on United States imports appears to be too simple a view.

Apart from the effects of the concessions, we find that the sorts of materials on which concessions were made were products of which United States imports were increasing *more rapidly* than total imports of materials. For materials, the mean increase of import value from 1960 to 1965 of both the reduced and non-reduced groups was significantly larger (at the 99 % confidence level) than the increase of the total of United States imports.

Again, apart from the effects of the concessions, the opposite pattern seems to apply to imports of manufactures—the hypothesis that the products on which concessions were offered were not those experiencing strong import competition seems to be valid. Imports of products in the non-reduced group (*i.e.* products similar to those on which concessions were made, but on which themselves no concessions were made) increased significantly less than total imports.

Thus it is possible that the concessions on materials, at least to some extent, were on materials falling into relatively short supply in the United States, and that in reducing duties on these materials the United States was reducing the cost squeeze on the manufacturing sectors which use them as inputs.

The net increase of imports, or increase attributable to the concession (value and quantity), was considerably larger for materials (75–80 %) than for manufactures (20 %). This again is consistent with the proposition that concessions on imported materials were granted on products the domestic supplies of which were becoming bottlenecks to more advanced stages of domestic manufacturing. The opportunity for a small cost saving seems to have caused a number of users to switch away from domestic sources of supply.

VII. SUMMARY

If we apply the median estimates of the percentage effect of the tariff cuts (Table I, line 3 c) to the volume of trade affected, we estimate that in 1965 imports were about $700 million higher than they would have been had the

United States Dillon Round concessions not been made. Although over 70 % of the imports affected by the concessions were manufactured products, 65 % of the imports which resulted from these concessions were imports of materials: the explanation is that the percentage effect of the cuts was larger on materials imports than on manufactures.

Almost all of the "additional" imports came from DCs. Using the median percentage figures[1] we estimate that United States imports in 1965 from LDCs were only about $24 million larger than they would have been without the concessions—this amount being about 3 % of the increase of imports 1960–65 from developing countries, or less than one half of 1 % of the level of United States imports from these countries in 1965.[2]

There seem to be three reasons for the small impact of United States Dillon Round concessions on LDC exports:

First, these concessions were negotiated primarily with other industrial countries on goods traded primarily among industrial countries.

Second, there is evidence to suggest that the sort of materials on which concessions were made to LDCs are products with relatively inelastic supply in the short run both in the LDCs and in DCs (*e.g.* bauxite, wooden timbers, and various unprocessed minerals such as talc, graphite and kaolin).

Third, although LDC exports of some manufactured goods included in the concessions have been expanding rapidly, this expansion seems to be based on cost differences between the LDCs and the United States which are so large that a tariff concession equivalent to a $2\frac{1}{2}$ % increase of f.o.b. price is no significant *additional* export incentive.

Finally, the results reported here indicate that in those instances in which concessions did apply to them, LDC suppliers responded at least as strongly as their DC competitors, and thus that further concessions negotiated with the LDCs would contribute significantly to the expansion of their exports.

J. M. FINGER

United Nations Conference on Trade and Development.

Date of receipt of final typescript: March 1974.

REFERENCES

Hunsberger, W. S. (1959). "Discussions of Krause," *American Economic Review Papers and Proceedings,*
     May, Vol. 49, pp. 555–8.
Krause, L. B. (1959). "United States Imports and the Tariff," *American Economic Review Papers and
     Proceedings,* May, Vol. 49, pp. 542–51.

[1] Because the estimate of the percentage effect on imports of manufactures from LDCs is negative, that median volume estimate was taken to be zero.

[2] If 95 % confidence interval estimates of the percentage effects are used, the value estimate for 1965 from all countries is $400 million. The estimate of the percentage effect and hence the value estimate for LDC exports is not significantly greater than zero at the 95 % confidence level.

Kreinin, M. E. (1961). "Effect of Tariff Changes on the Prices and Volumes of Imports," *American Economic Review*, June, Vol. 51, pp. 310–24.

United States Bureau of the Census (1961). *United States Imports of Merchandise for Consumption, Calendar Year 1960* (Report No. FT 110), Washington.

—— (1966). *US Imports, TSUSA Commodity by Country*, 1965 Annual (FT 246), Washington.

United States Tariff Commission (1972). *Economic Factors Affecting the Use of Items 807.00 and 806.30 of the Tariff Schedule of the United States* (T.C. Pub. No. 339), Washington.

The Economic Journal, **86** *(March* 1976), 87–95
Printed in Great Britain

EFFECTS OF THE KENNEDY ROUND TARIFF CONCESSIONS ON THE EXPORTS OF DEVELOPING COUNTRIES[1]

I

At the Kennedy Round the major industrial countries agreed to tariff reductions of about one-third of the initial level on about one-third of their total or two-thirds of their dutiable imports – the largest set of concessions negotiated at any of the six completed GATT rounds.

This paper summarises the results of a study of the effects on manufactured imports (SITC 5–8 less 67, 68) of the Kennedy Round tariff concessions implemented by the United States, the EEC and Japan. In particular it is concerned with the supply-lag hypothesis that developing-country exports will not respond as strongly as developed-country exports to the marginal profit incentive of the tariff cuts.

The methodology of the study was to compare the change of industrial-country imports of a random sample of products on which large tariff reductions were made with the record of another sample of similar imports on which tariffs were changed by smaller amounts. The extension of the familiar "reduced group, non-reduced group" methodology[2] to allow for tariff changes in the "control group" was made necessary by the inclusiveness of the Kennedy Round cuts.

Although the last stage of the Kennedy Round reductions went into effect in 1972, the data used were for 1967 and 1970, and hence include the effects of only three of the five stages by which the Kennedy Round tariff concessions went into effect. The year 1970 was chosen as the end period in order to avoid the very difficult if not impossible task of modifying the estimating procedure to take into account such institutional changes as the "Nixon shock" of 1971, the implementation in 1971 of tariff preferences by the EEC and Japan, as well as the expansion of the EEC in 1972 and the accompanying negotiation of special arrangements between the EEC and many other countries, both developed and developing.

In sections II and III the formulae used are derived and the selection of the samples of products used in the calculations is explained. In the following two sections we examine problems which might arise from the assumptions on which the method is based not being strictly true. The results of the calculations performed for this study are presented in section VI, and their implications are discussed in the final section.

[1] This study was conducted while the author was on the staff of the Research Division, UNCTAD, Geneva. The assistance of L. Leonetti, P. Zogeb and D. de Carvalho in assembling the data is gratefully acknowledged, as are helpful comments by W. B. Reddaway and an anonymous referee. Only the author is responsible for the contents of this report.

[2] The "reduced group, non-reduced group" method was introduced by Krause (1959) and used by Kreinin (1964) and Finger (1974).

II. THE ASSUMPTIONS AND THE FORMULAE

A. *Assumptions*

There are three assumptions critical to the method used in this paper. They are:

(*a*) We assume that the "big reduction" and "small reduction" samples are chosen so that the elasticities of import demand for and supply of the products in one group are equal to those for the other group.[1] Related to this is the further assumption.

(*b*) That all exogenous factors *other than the tariff change* apply with equal intensity to the products in the two groups.

(*c*) We assume no substitutability between the products in the small reduction group (SRG) and those in the big reduction group (BRG).

The restrictiveness of these assumptions and the effects on the interpretation of the results of their not being strictly valid will be discussed below.

B. *Notation and Derivations*

Only the derivation of the effects of the tariff cuts on the *value* of imports will be explained – the derivations for quantity and price being closely parallel.

The effect of a tariff change can be derived analytically by taking the derivative of the supply–demand equilibrium condition. Other factors being constant, the proportional effect on the value (at foreign prices) of imports, V^* ($= dV/V$), is related to the proportional change of price which would be caused by the change of the *ad valorem* rate if supply were perfectly elastic,[2] T^* $[= dT/(1 + T)]$, by

$$V^* = \frac{-D(S+1)}{D-S} T^*, \qquad (1)$$

D and S being the elasticities of demand for and supply of imports.[3] As we assume that the elasticities are the same for the two groups, the expression will apply to either the SRG or the BRG, or to the two groups combined, when the appropriate measure of the proportional tariff change is introduced.

When we consider the changes in the actual trade figures we know they will be influenced by many factors other than the tariff changes. Thus, the observed, or measured proportional changes of the import figures can be expressed

$$V_{bm}^* = V_{bt}^* + V_{bi}^* \qquad (2)$$

and

$$V_{sm}^* = V_{st}^* + V_{si}^*. \qquad (3)$$

In expressions (2) and (3) the first subscript distinguishes between the SRG and the BRG. The second subscript distinguishes among the "measured" (*m*) change of the import figures and the parts (designated by *t* and *i*) of this change which result from the tariff changes and from "incidental" or other factors.

---

[1] Implicit is the presumption common to all cross-section (or aggregated) studies that it is meaningful to group the individual products covered. As the big and small reduction samples each cover all of manufactured goods, we are talking about the import demand for and supply of manufactured goods.

[2] Henceforth called the "the proportional tariff change".

[3] As defined, D will be negative.

Table 1

Effects of Kennedy Round Tariff Concessions

Imports of	Average proportional tariff change* (expressed as a percentage)	Estimated tariff elasticity of imports†	
		Value	Quantity
1. European Economic Community			
(a) From developing countries	−4·3	−3·9	−3·5
(b) From developed countries	−4·0	−5·4	−4·3
2. United States			
(a) From developing countries	−4·7	−14·8	−10·6
(b) From developed countries	−4·2	−9·5	−7·0
3. Japan			
(a) From developing countries	−5·3	−11·9	−11·9
(b) From developed countries	−5·8	−8·0	−6·4

* Source, UNCTAD (1968), p. 208. Proportional change is defined as $100\, dT/(1 + T)$. The figures are the average over all manufactured goods (not just those in the samples) and cover all five stages of the reduction (not just the three stages used in estimating the elasticities).

† The proportional change of import value (or quantity) caused by the tariff reductions divided by the proportional change of the *ad valorem* tariff rate.

The selection (explained below) of the BRG and the SRG was done in such a way as to give reasonable assurance that the other, or "incidental", factors will have equal impacts on the BRG and the SRG. We therefore have

$$V_{bi}^* = V_{si}^*. \tag{4}$$

From equation (1) and the assumption that the import demand and supply elasticities are the same for the BRG and the SRG, we derive

$$V_{bt}^*/T_b^* = V_{st}^*/T_s^*, \tag{5}$$

V_{bt}^* and V_{st}^* being the proportional changes of value of imports of the BRG and of the SRG caused by the tariff changes, while T_b^* and T_s^* are the average (proportional) *ad valorem* tariff changes for the two groups.

The tariff changes and the "measured" changes of the import values can, of course, be calculated from the tariff and trade statistics. Our objective then is to rearrange the information in equations (2) through (5) in such a way that the trade and tariffs figures may be used to estimate V_{bt}^* or V_{st}^*, the effects of the tariff changes on the value of imports.

Subtracting (3) from (2) and substituting from (4) we arrive at

$$V_{bm}^* - V_{sm}^* = V_{bt}^* - V_{st}^*.$$

When we substitute (5) into this expression and rearrange terms we have

$$V_{bt}^* = [V_{bm}^* - V_{sm}^*]\, [T_b^*/(T_b^* - T_s^*)] \tag{6}$$

or

$$V_{st}^* = [V_{sm}^* - V_{bm}^*]\, [T_s^*/(T_s^* - T_b^*)]. \tag{7}$$

By an identical procedure, with Q's or P's in the places of the V's (the subscripts being unchanged), we could derive equivalent expressions for the effects of the tariff changes on the quantities or prices of imports.[1]

The results are presented in Table 1 in tariff elasticity form – the proportional changes of the value and quantity of imports *caused by* the tariff changes have been divided through by the proportional change of the tariff. As equation (5) shows, the same estimate would result if we used equation (6) or equation (7). The assumptions imply that the *tariff elasticity* estimate is the same for the SRG as for the BRG, and therefore is the tariff elasticity estimate for the two groups combined, i.e. for all manufactured imports.

III. THE DATA

The samples of products from which the effects of the Kennedy Round cuts were estimated were based on a random sample of tariff line (7-digit code) items drawn by the UNCTAD Secretariat to estimate pre- and post-Kennedy Round tariff averages. In constructing the UNCTAD sample care had been taken to make the sample comparable across countries, i.e. though lack of compatibility at the tariff line level had made it necessary to define a separate sample for each country, in terms of that country's tariff nomenclature, in constructing the UNCTAD samples for each country care had been taken to make them as compatible as possible.[2]

For each of the EEC, the United States and Japan, the UNCTAD sample was divided into a BRG and a SRG, based on the median of the proportional tariff change, $dT/(1 + T)$, of tariff lines in the sample. We then found that for some SITC 3-digit groups the value of imports covered by the SRG was larger than the value covered by the BRG, and vice versa. We then expanded the original sample by randomly selecting tariff lines (with big or small tariff reductions, as was appropriate) until for each 3-digit group the value of imports covered by the SRG and the BRG did not differ by more than 15 % (10 % in most cases).[3]

In short, while the "observations" in the BRG and the SRG samples were defined at the 7-digit tariff line (e.g. black and white television receivers with 11-inch or smaller screens), an attempt was made to keep the distributions of the two samples parallel at the SITC 3-digit level (e.g. telecommunications apparatus).

The BRG sample for each importer included about 200 tariff lines, the SRG group sample slightly more tariff lines, but approximately the same value of

---

[1] In the reduced group, non-reduced group case, the proportional change of V which results from the tariff change is estimated by subtracting the observed (total) change for the non-reduced group from the observed (total) change for the reduced group. If T^* in equations (6) and (7) is set equal to zero, so that we have a non-reduced group rather than a SRG, equation (7) states, as it should, that there is no tariff induced change in the non-reduced group, and equation (6) reduces to the appropriate expression for the reduced, non-reduced group case.

[2] The UNCTAD sample was drawn using probability weights based on total imports of OECD countries. It is described in UNCTAD (1968), pp. 10 f., 44 f.

[3] As the BRG derived from the original sample included a larger value of imports than did the SRG, most of the additions were to the SRG. Because the tariff cuts were not identical for the EEC, the U.S. and Japan, the make-ups of the BRGs and consequently of the SRGs were different from one country to another.

imports. For each of the United States and Japan the two samples together covered about 15 % of the items on which concessions were made; for the EEC, slightly more.[1]

For each tariff line, 1967 and 1970 figures for the value and quantity of imports were taken from national sources, and tariff rates were taken from the GATT report on the Kennedy Round.[2] Proportional changes of value and quantity of imports, and of the *ad valorem* tariff rate were calculated for each tariff line, and average changes were then computed for the BRG sample and for the SRG sample. In calculating these averages, the tariff line changes were weighted by 1967 plus 1970 value of imports for each tariff line.

IV. THE PROBLEM OF SUBSTITUTION BETWEEN THE TEST AND CONTROL GROUPS

It is well known that in practice the "control" and "test" groups of products used in studies such as this one will to some extent be substitutes, and hence that the resulting estimates of the response of imports to tariff reductions will be overstatements. But while this means that the method will overstate the magnitude of the response of imports to the tariff cuts, it does not mean that the method will indicate such a response when there is none. That is, while the method may not answer correctly the question "By how much do tariffs matter?", it should adequately answer the simpler question "Do tariffs matter? "

If imports were not affected by the tariff cuts, imports of the BRG and SRG would increase equally. If the tariff cuts did cause imports to rise, then each observation in the BRG will be larger and each observation in the SRG smaller than they would be if the effects of substitution were netted out. This will amplify the estimate of the difference between the mean changes of imports of the BRG and SRG, but it will very likely also amplify the estimated variance of this difference and if so will not seriously affect tests of the significance of difference of the average changes.

If we assume that within 7-digit categories, buyers are indifferent to the country source of imports, we are, at the same time, assuming that substitution between the BRG and the SRG is the same for imports from developing as for imports from developed countries. Under these conditions the tariff reductions (which apply on a most favoured nation basis) will have the same effect on the price of imports from developing countries as from developed countries, and hence comparing the quantity tariff elasticities of imports between country groups is equivalent to comparing their supply elasticities.[3]

---

[1] There are fewer lines in the EEC tariff than in those of the U.S. and Japan.
[2] Sources are listed after the references. For *each* importer the import figures were for imports from all countries – EEC imports included imports from the U.S. and Japan, etc.
[3] See footnote 1, p. 93.

V. THE ASSUMPTION OF EQUAL ELASTICITIES FOR THE TWO GROUPS

The assumption that the import demand and supply elasticities are the same for the SRG as for the BRG is essentially the assumption that products with large and with small tariff reductions were randomly drawn from the same population, i.e. that there was no systematic tendency to include or exclude products with particularly high elasticities from the group on which significant concessions were made. If the negotiating procedure was "biased", it probably tended toward small or no reductions on products with high import demand and supply elasticities. If so, the observed changes of imports of the SRG are larger than they would be if the assumption of equal elasticities were true, and the effects of tariff concessions are understated.

If the results had indicated that the tariff cuts had no effect, i.e. that imports of the BRG and SRG increased by equal amounts, this bias would be a cause for concern, but as reported below, this is not the case.

VI. RESULTS

To test whether the Kennedy Round tariff cuts had a statistically identifiable impact on imports, tests were made of the hypothesis that the mean changes of imports (value and quantity) were the same for the SRG as for the BRG. These tests showed that the tariff cuts of each importer (EEC, United States, Japan) caused a significant increase of imports, from developing and from other developed countries.[1]

The change of foreign price (actually unit value) caused by the tariff changes was also estimated. For each importing country the increase of foreign unit value (of imports from all countries) absorbed about two-thirds of the tariff reduction. However, the estimated variances of the mean changes of unit value were very large, so that the difference between the BRG and SRG of the mean change of unit value was not significant for any of the three importers. Further, the hypothesis that the effect was the same on unit value of imports from developed as from developing countries cannot be rejected.

In Table 1 are presented estimates of the tariff elasticities of imports, i.e. of the proportional change of the value (quantity) of imports which results from the tariff change, divided by that proportional tariff change.

Comparing the tariff elasticities of imports from developed with those for imports from developing countries, we observe that the export supply response of developing country exporters was apparently larger than that of developed country exporters when one looks at imports of the United States and Japan, and apparently smaller when one looks at EEC imports. However, while the differences of import changes between the test and control groups are statistically significant, it is not possible to show that one of these is significantly different from another – i.e. we cannot show that the responses to the tariff cuts

---

[1] All statements of statistical significance refer to a one-tail test of the difference of two means, at a 95 % confidence level.

by developed as compared with developing country exporters were significantly different.[1]

Another pattern which shows up in the table is that imports of the EEC were less affected by the tariff changes than imports of the United States and Japan. If this is an accurate measure of relative tariff elasticities, it indicates that the EEC "gained" more from the Kennedy Round as an exporter than it "lost" as an importer.

However, this pattern may be, to some extent, a reflection of the relative level of aggregation of the EEC tariff rather than a true measure of the relative response of EEC imports. There are fewer 7-digit lines in the EEC than in the United States and Japan tariffs. As a result the BRG and SRG may be less close substitutes in the EEC case than in the U.S. and Japanese cases. For example, the more detailed tariffs allow the possibility that "black and white television receivers, 11 inch and smaller" may be in one group and "black and white television receivers, larger than 11 inches" in the other group. A tariff with fewer lines may allow only the separation of "black and white television receivers" from "colour television receivers". The larger the degree of substitutability between the BRG and the SRG (other things constant), the larger will be the observed difference between the increases of imports of the two groups, and hence the greater the overestimation of the tariff elasticity.[2]

VII. CONCLUSIONS

The findings of this study lend support to two points: (a) tariffs matter and (b) the supply response on the part of developing country exporters was substantial.

Previous studies have determined that the Dillon Round and the mid-1950s rounds had a significant effect on U.S. imports, and this study extends that finding through the Kennedy Round, for the EEC and Japan as well as the United States.[3]

Examination of the results of U.S. concessions at the Dillon Round indicated that these had little effect on the developing countries' "basket" of exports (i.e. those products in which affected developing country exports are con-

---

[1] Estimates of the export supply elasticities are implicit in information already given. If we use foreign unit value as foreign price, the elasticity of supply, Es, is related to the quantity tariff elasticity, Et, from Table 1, as follows:

$$Es = Q_{bt}^*/P_{bt}^* = Et \cdot T_b^*/P_{bt}^*.$$

The denominator, P_{bt}^*, as estimated from an expression similar to (6), was equal to about $\frac{2}{3}$ the observed tariff change, T_b, hence Es is roughly equal to 1·5 times the quantity tariff elasticity from Table 1. The estimate of the standard deviation of the mean P_{bt}^* was, for the U.S. and the EEC, about as large as the estimate of the mean, and for Japan was approximately twice as large as the estimate of the mean. Hence, even without taking the variability of Q_{bt}^* into account, we know that the supply elasticity estimates are very imprecise.

[2] Another possible explanation might be the preferential arrangements which existed in the period covered between the EEC and the former French colonies in Africa. But EEC imports in 1970 from these countries were less than 5% of EEC manufactured imports from LDCs, and if this were the explanation it should have affected only imports from LDCs and not imports from developed countries as well.

[3] Kreinin (1961) and Finger (1974). Krause's (1959) examination of the earliest GATT rounds found that only the few cuts in excess of 30% of then existing levels had a significant impact on imports.

centrated).[1] But when examined in detail these results did not support the assertion that developing country exports are not responsive to "marginal" incentives. Developing country exports, both of products on which concessions were made and of similar products on which no concessions were made, increased more rapidly than developed country exports, and developing country exports of the developed country basket were significantly affected by the tariff cuts. This is consistent with the supposition that developing country manufactured exports to industrial countries were concentrated in products in which the cost difference between the recipient country and the developing country supplier was so large at that time that a tariff concession equivalent to 2% to 3% of f.o.b. price was not a significant *additional* export incentive. The large increases of supply of exports from developing countries which accounted for the increases of exports both of the reduced and non-reduced groups were perhaps responses to the existence of this cost differential rather than to marginal changes of one or more exogenous factors.

But on products which might be called atypical developing country exports (the developed country basket) we observed not only a significant increase of supply from the developing countries, but also a significant response to the marginal incentive of the tariff reductions.

The Kennedy Round results were much more straightforward. Developing country exports to the EEC, the United States and to Japan of both the developed and developing country baskets[2] responded significantly and as strongly as developed country exports,[3] on those products on which tariffs were reduced.

It is, however, well documented that tariff cuts negotiated under the GATT have been concentrated on products which the industrial countries import from each other rather than from the LDCs. For example, at the 1960–1 Dillon Round, the last GATT round at which the "bilateral bargaining" negotiating technique was used, United States concessions affected 11% of U.S. imports of materials from other developed countries but only 2% of materials imports from LDCs. For manufactured imports the figures were 28% and 21% (Finger, 1974, p. 567).

While the Kennedy Round followed an "across the board" tariff cutting technique, the Kennedy Round cuts, like those of previous rounds, were concentrated away from materials (which account for more than 80% of LDC exports). Within manufactures the larger concessions were concentrated on finished manufactures more than on semi-processed goods. As a result the cuts amounted to about 45% of their initial level on manufactured products for which the industrial countries dominate world trade, but to only 33% of the initial level on other manufactured products (UNCTAD, p. 15).

[1] To examine the developed and developing country "baskets," the item by item changes in the test and control groups were weighted by imports from developed and developing countries. See Finger (1974).

[2] These comparisons are not shown in the table.

[3] These results, of course, describe the response of the twelve or so countries which account for 80% of developing country manufactured exports.

The "exceptions" to the across the board cuts on manufactures were mainly simply processed goods such as wood products on which LDCs tend to have comparative advantage.

The Kennedy Round did, however, produce tariff reductions on products for which LDC exports in 1964 to the EEC, the United States, the United Kingdom and Japan came to well over $2 billion (UNCTAD, p. 19). This, plus the results of this study, which indicate that tariff concessions which did apply to the exports of LDCs did lead to increases of these exports, suggest that the developing countries derived considerable benefits from the Kennedy Round tariff reductions of the industrial countries – concessions for which the developing countries were not required to provide a *quid pro quo*. These countries may then be required to play a more active role in the Tokyo Round.

Of perhaps more significance, the relative response of the LDCs suggests that *they would benefit* from a more active role.

The findings also suggest that in pushing for tariff preferences the developing countries may be seeking an advantage they do not need. It seems likely that they would benefit from a general (m.f.n.) reduction of trade barriers, and it is possible that the establishment of a precedent of separate treatment of developing countries may not be in their long-run interest.

Methodologically, these results tend to justify the use of supply–demand models by economists´ working to predict the effects on developing country exports of alternative sets of tariff concessions which may be negotiated at the Tokyo Round.

J. M. FINGER

Department of the Treasury, Washington

Date of receipt of final typescript: September 1975

REFERENCES

Finger, J. M. (1974). "GATT Tariff Concessions and the Exports of Developing Countries: United States Concessions at the Dillon Round." ECONOMIC JOURNAL, vol. 84 (Sept.), pp. 566–75.
Krause, L. (1959). "United States Imports and the Tariff." *American Economic Review Papers and Proceedings*, vol. 49 (May), pp. 542–51.
Kreinin, M. E. (1961). "Effects of Tariff Changes on the Prices and Volumes of Imports." *American Economic Review*, vol. 51 (June), pp. 310–24.
UNCTAD Secretariat (1968). *The Kennedy Round, Estimated Effects on Tariff Barriers.* New York (Doc. no. TD/6/Rev. 1.)

DATA SOURCES

GATT Secretariat, *Legal Instruments Embodying the Results of the 1964–67 Tariff Conference*, vols. 2, 4.
Japanese Tariff Association, *Japanese Exports and Imports, Commodity by Country*, 1967 and 1970.
Office Statistique des Communautés Européennes, *Commerce Exterieur, Tableaux Analytiques-CST, Import* 1967 and 1970.
U.S. Bureau of the Census, *U.S. Imports, TSUSA Commodity by Country* (FT246), 1967 and 1970.

[3]

TARIFF PROVISIONS FOR OFFSHORE ASSEMBLY AND THE EXPORTS OF DEVELOPING COUNTRIES[1]

I. Introduction

THE assembly for re-export of components produced in industrial countries constitutes a large and very rapidly growing part of the manufactured exports of the less developed countries (LDC), and of Eastern European trade with Western Europe.[2] This activity is encouraged by the existence of provisions in the tariffs of nearly all industrial countries which provide for duty-free re-entry of domestically produced components which have been assembled abroad, i.e. whereby the tariff on an assembled product is applied only to the value added in the assembly process, if domestically produced components are used.

The details of this offshore assembly provision (OAP) vary slightly between Western European Countries and the United States.[3] To fall within the OAP of Western European countries[4] the imported products must be made from components exported by a domestic enterprise on its own account, they must be processed abroad on account for that enterprise, and they must be imported by that enterprise on its own account. The provision applies to all kinds of products, and to all forms of processing as well as to simple assembly.

The United States' provisions for offshore assembly are in one respect more and in another respect less liberal. US tariff item 807.00 (which accounts for over 90 % of United States OAP imports) provides for duty-free re-entry only of components which do not lose their physical identity in the assembled article. On the other hand, the provision is available to foreign firms who buy US components for assembly into products for sale in the United States, i.e. it is not limited to domestic firms.[5] US tariff item 806.30, which provides for the offshore processing of certain metal products, is similar to the European OAPs, except that it is limited to products which are returned for further processing in the United States.

---

[1] The helpful comments of an anonymous referee are gratefully acknowledged. I wish to thank Miss L. Cholumpi and Mr. F. Usmani for their assistance in organising the data for this study.

[2] For a general discussion of assembly specialisation within vertically integrated industries see Helleiner (1973).

[3] A survey of the OAPs in effect in a number of countries is given in the Tariff Commission report (1970).

[4] This refers in particular to the Netherlands and West Germany.

[5] In 1969 some 60% of US imports under item 807.00 were from foreign concerns, which, on their own account, obtained US components for assembly into products they export to the United States (Tariff Commission 1970, p. 6).

II. Recent Expansion of OAP Imports

As shown in Table 1, OAP imports of the Netherlands, West Germany, and the United States[1] increased considerably more rapidly than imports of other manufactures over the period 1966–72. As the figures show, the increase of OAP imports from LDCs has been especially rapid, as has the increase of Netherlands and West German OAP imports from Eastern Europe. And OAP imports in 1972 already made up a substantial part of US and West German manufactured imports from developing countries (22 % and 10 %, respectively) and of West German and Netherlands imports of manufactures from Eastern Europe (17 % for each).[2]

Almost all of West German OAP imports from LDCs are from Yugoslavia, while over 20 different countries each provided over $1 million of US OAP

Table I

Imports under Offshore Assembly Provisions of the Netherlands, West Germany and the United States: Values, 1972, and Recent Rates of Increase

Importing country and origin of imports	OAP imports			Annual compound rate of increase of non-OAP manufactured imports
	Value, 1972 ($ million)	As % of manufactured imports, 1972	Annual compound rate of increase 1966–72*	
Netherlands				
From all non-EEC countries	101	3	28	8
From Eastern Europe	31	17	72	10
From all non-European countries	16	2	39	2
West Germany				
From all non-EEC countries	451	4	19	11
From Eastern Europe	126	17	84	19
From developing countries	156	10	36	11
From Yugoslavia	139	30	35	12
United States				
From all countries	3,409	9	24	17
From developed countries	2,377	8	18	17
From developing countries	1,032	22	60	12

Sources:
Netherlands Central Bureau of Statistics, *Maandstatistiek van de Buitenlandse Handel*, January 1969 and January 1973.

W. German Statistisches Bundesamt, *Aussenhandel, Zusammenfassende Übersichten*: Fachserie G, Reihe 1, 1966, 1972.

United States Tariff Commission, *Economic Factors Affecting the Use of items 807.00 and 806.30 of the Tariff Schedules of the United States*. Tables 4 and 21, and other tabulations by the US Tariff Commission.

      * 1968–72 for the Netherlands.

[1] Data for OAP imports are available only for these countries.

[2] In 1972 manufactures as a percentage of total imports from developing countries were about 33 %, 20 % and 10 % for the United States, West Germany, and the Netherlands, respectively. About half of West Germany's and one-third of the Netherlands' imports from Eastern Europe were manufactured.

imports in 1972.[1] The largest single source country was Mexico, which was the origin of 43 % of US OAP imports. About 49 % of US OAP imports came from Taiwan, Hong Kong, Singapore, and S. Korea, and 6 % from Caribbean countries.

Though product-by-product data for the OAP imports from LDCs of West Germany and the Netherlands are not available, some idea of the composition of OAP imports can be gained from Table II. Textiles are a much smaller part and electronic products a much larger part of US OAP imports than of West German and Netherlands OAP imports. Netherlands OAP imports from Eastern Europe are made up almost entirely of textile products, which suggests that Western European imports from lower wage countries tend to be heavily concentrated on textiles.

TABLE II

Industry Distribution of OAP Imports, United States,
Netherlands and West Germany, 1972

(Per cent)

Industry	United States		Netherlands		W. Germany from all countries
	From all countries	From developing countries	From all countries	From Eastern Europe	
Processed foods, beverages	—	—	1	—	1
Chemicals, rubber, plastic materials	—	—	4	—	2
Textile products	3	8	41	95	49
Electronic products	18	56	—	—	—
Machinery	27	13	29	—	29
Motor vehicles including aircraft	39	—	4	—	6
Scientific, precision instruments	1	2	5	—	2
Misc. metal products	9	11	9	—	3
Other manufactures	3	10	7	5	8

Source: Tabulated from data from sources cited in Table I.

III. OAP vs. GSP

It is interesting to compare the value of LDC trade under the seldom-discussed provisions for offshore assembly with the values of trade under the EEC's general system of tariff preferences (GSP) for LDCs. UNCTAD tabulations (1973, table I) indicate that in 1972 the EEC's GSP covered about $825 million of imports, as compared with about $1032 million of US imports from LDCs under the OAP.[2]

This comparison should not be overstressed, because the values of imports under the GSP and under the OAP are not appropriate measures of

[1] A more detailed breakdown of Netherlands' OAP imports by country of origin than is given in Table I is not available.

[2] In 1972 West Germany took 43 % of the EEC's manufactured imports from LDCs. If we assume that the $156 million of West German OAP imports from LDCs was also 43 % of the EEC's OAP imports from LDCs, we estimate that total OAP imports from LDCs were about $360 million in 1972. This is probably an overestimate.

the net export earnings of LDCs attributable to the two policies. First, not all of the $825 million of LDC exports to the EEC are attributable to the existence of tariff preferences—if there were no tariff preferences not all of this trade would disappear.

Likewise, the contribution of the West German and US OAPs to the net exports of LDCs is not equal to the values of West German and US OAP imports. A part of this value is domestically produced components—about 49 % of the total value for the United States and about 70 % for West Germany and the Netherlands. Furthermore, because an OAP allows the tariff liability on an imported article to be calculated on the value added in the assembly process rather than on the total value of the assembled article, it reduces the effective rate of protection of domestic assembly. But, as this tariff break is allowed only if domestic components are used, the OAP tends to switch demand from foreign components to domestic components at the same time that it reduces the disadvantage of foreign assembly *vis à vis* domestic assembly. Hence the net impact of the OAP on the LDC trade balance is the attributable increase of LDC assembly activity for export, less the attributable reduction of exports of LDC components.[1]

With educated guesses[2] as to the values of the relevant elasticities of domestic and foreign supply of assembly and of components as well as to the product distribution of West German OAP imports from LDCs we were able to estimate that some $96–130 million of net exports by LDCs result from the US OAP and some $12–18 million from the West German OAP.[3]

To estimate the impact of the EEC's GSP we multiplied the UNCTAD (1973, table 1) tabulation of its product coverage by Clague's (1972, p. 387) estimate of the proportionate impact of the scheme. The United States, of course, has not implemented a preference scheme. We thus estimated that in 1972 the EEC's GSP increased LDC export earnings by about $107 million, or roughly the same amount as the US OAP.

But there are two reasons to believe that this comparison understates the relative importance of OAPs. First, Clague's estimates are not discounted for the import content of LDC exports, i.e. it is possible that part of the $107 million of additional export receipts is offset by increased imports needed to produce them.

Furthermore, these are comparisons based on 1972 data and as OAP imports have been increasing rapidly, while the quotas in the EEC's GSP will prevent imports under the scheme from increasing rapidly,[4] comparison at a

---

[1] The theory of the incidence of an OAP is spelled out mathematically in Finger (1974). Copies are available from the author on request.
[2] Which are simply arbitrary assumptions.
[3] Details of these estimates are given in a longer version of this paper which is available on request. Experimenting with various sets of elasticity values indicated that the results were not sensitive to the particular values used. Likewise, because most of the other parameters (such as tariff rates) needed in the calculations do not differ greatly between industries, the results are not greatly influenced by the assumed product distribution of West German OAP imports from LDCs.
[4] On this point see Cooper (1972) and Murray (1973).

later point in time would probably favour the OAP. It is also possible that the West German OAP will soon generate larger export earnings for LDCs than the West German "part" of the EEC's GSP.

IV. OAPs AND THE POLICIES OF INDUSTRIAL COUNTRIES TOWARD DEVELOPING COUNTRIES

There are generally two ways in which the tariff liability of an OAP can be defined.

(*a*) The tariff rate is applied to the value of assembly or processing performed abroad, as is the case with the Netherlands and West German OAPs and item 806.30 of the US tariff.

(*b*) The tariff rate is applied to the total value of the imported good, less the value of domestic components contained therein, as is the case with item 807.00 of the US tariff.

An OAP of the first type provides for the processing offshore and return of components, but in so doing effectively limits the offshore operation to processing or assembly. But an OAP of the second type does not limit the foreign 'stage' of the production process to processing or assembly. As the tax liability is defined as the value of the finished good *less* the value of domestic components, the foreign value adding process can take place in many 'stages', and can consist of foreign production of components which are then assembled, along with some domestic components, into the finished good.[1]

Such a provision allows a labour-rich country to perform the parts of the production process in which it has comparative advantage (including production of those components which require labour intensive methods) without subjecting the country to the higher effective rates of protection it would face if forced to bear the duty on the imported components, in production of which it does not have comparative advantage. Thus this sort of OAP treatment is not drastically different from a tariff reduction, whether preferential or not.

Of course, to qualify for OAP treatment, the value adding country must use components from the country which will import the final good. This gives these components an edge over similar components produced in the value adding country or in third countries. Inefficiencies will result when components from the importing country are not the cheapest, and the displacement of local components reduces the net impact on the exchange earnings of the value adding country.

But this qualification does not eliminate the benefits just estimated to

---

[1] According to the US Tariff Commission report (1970) most of the products imported by the United States from developed countries under item 807.00 are foreign goods in which only a part of the components used are of US origin (p. 60). A related advantage is that a provision of this type can readily be extended to firms from the value adding country which incorporate some importing country components into products made for export. As noted above (p. 365, n. 5), in 1969 about 60% of US imports under item 807.00 were the exports of foreign concerns.

LDCs of the OAPs of industrial countries—it means only that the benefits would be larger if the duty were applied only to the value added in the LDCs, whatever the source of components.

Furthermore, there are also inefficiencies associated with tariff preferences. Labour intensive products on which LDCs have comparative advantage are often excluded from preferential treatment, and resources of the LDCs are thus attracted by advantageous tariff treatment into activities in which they are less efficient. And country of origin requirements[1] can force LDCs to use components produced domestically at high cost in order to qualify for preferential tariff treatment.

Finally, the qualification that components from the importing country be used is an important source of political support for OAPs within industrial countries. This domestic political support from the producing sector means that an OAP is more likely to attact sufficient political push for enactment and expansion than a tariff preference scheme, which has only widely diffused consumer interests and good will to back it. Perhaps this is, in part, why we observe tight restrictions placed on imports under those preference schemes in operation (and no preference scheme yet implemented by the United States) while OAP imports continue to increase rapidly. This suggests that efforts to liberalise OAP treatment of articles from LDCs could produce considerably greater benefits to the LDCs than have resulted from attempts to negotiate tariff preferences.

J. M. FINGER

Department of Treasury, Washington.

Date of receipt of final typescript: September 1974.

REFERENCES

Clague, C. C. (1972). "The Trade Effects of Tariff Preferences," *Southern Economic Journal*, Vol. 38 (January), pp. 379–89.
Cooper, R. N. (1972). "The European Economic Community's System of Generalized Tariff Preferences: A Critique," *Journal of Development Studies*, Vol. 8 (July), pp. 379–94.
Finger, J. M. (1974). "Trade and Domestic Effects of the Offshore Assembly Provision in the United States Tariff." UNCTAD Research Division, mimeographed.
Helleiner, G. K. (1973). "Manufactured Exports from Less Developed Countries and Multinational Firms," ECONOMIC JOURNAL (March), pp. 21–47.
Murray, T. (1973). "Preferential Tariffs for the LDCs," *Southern Economic Journal* (July), pp. 35–46.
Netherlands Central Bureau of Statistics (1969, 1973). *Maandstatistiek van de Buitenlandse Handel*, jaargang 20, 24 (January).
UN Conference on Trade and Development (1972). "The Generalized System of Preferences: A Comparative Study of the Rules of Origin in Force" (30 November), Doc. No. TD/B/C.5/2.
UNCTAD (1973). "General Report on the Implementation of the Generalized System of Preferences" (9 March), Doc. No. TD/B/C.5/9.
US Bureau of the Census (1973). *US Imports of Merchandise for Consumption and General Imports of Merchandise*, Report No. I A 245-A, Washington.
US Tariff Commission (1970). *Economic Factors Affecting the Use of Items 807.00 and 806.30 of the Tariff Schedules of the United States* (TC Publication 339), Washington.
West German Statistisches Bundesamt (1967, 1973). *Aussenhandel, Zusammenfassende Übersichten*, Fachserie G, Reihe 1.

---

[1] See UNCTAD (1972).

ANNEX TABLE 1

*Values of Offshore Assembly and Directly Competitive Imports from
LDCs and Eastern Europe, 1972: and Estimates of the Effects on
Imports from LDCs of Removing the Offshore Assembly Provision*

($ million)

	USA imports from LDCs	Netherlands imports from Eastern Europe	W. Germany's imports*	
			From LDCs	From Eastern Europe
OAP imports from LDCs	1,032	31	156	126
Directly competitive imports	868	29	165	133
Value of components/total value	0·49	0·69	0·73	0·73
Estimated changes of value of assembly and of value of components exported by LDCs and E. Europe†				
(1) Efa, Efc = ∞; Eda = 1, Edc = 3‡				
Assembly	−217	−4·7	−29	−23
Components	121	3·7	11	9
Net	−96	−1·0	−18	−15
(2) Efa = 40, Efc = 10, Eda = 1, Edc = 3; D = 0·75				
Assembly	−231	−4·8	−31	−25
Components	97	3·0	10	8
Net	−134	−1·8	−21	−17
(3) Efa = 72, Efc = 24; Eda = 1·2, Edc = 6; D = 0·75				
Assembly	−268	−5·1	−34	−27
Components	135	4·8	15	12
Net	−133	−0·3	−19	−15

  * Based on the assumption that W. Germany's OAP imports from LDCs and E. Europe have the same product distribution as her imports from all countries.
  † Elasticities of import supplies of textiles assumed constrained to zero by quotas.
  ‡ Efa, Efc; Eda, Edc are the assumed values for the elasticities of supply of foreign (f) and domestic (d) assembly (a) and components (c): D is the assumed value for elasticity of demand.

ANNEX TABLE 2

Summary of Estimates of Effects on Trade Balances of OAP and GSP

($ million)

	GSP imports		OAP imports from LDC		OAP imports from E. Europe	
	Total value	Estimated net impact on LDC trade balance	Total value	Estimated net impact on LDC trade balance	Total value	Estimated net impact on E. Europe trade balance
USA	0	0	1.032	96–130	0	0
EEC	793–871	102–112	(361)*	(28–42)*	n.a.	n.a.
W. Germany	(342–376)†	(44–48)†	156	12–18	126	10–16
Netherlands	(63–69)‡	(8–9)‡	n.a.	n.a.	31	0·3–1·8

  * W. German estimate divided by share specified in footnote †.
  † EEC estimate multiplied by the share of W. Germany in EEC imports of manufactures from LDCs.
  ‡ EEC estimate multiplied by the share of the Netherlands in EEC imports of manufactures from LDCs.

Trade and Domestic Effects of the Offshore Assembly Provision in the U.S. Tariff

By J. M. FINGER*

The *U.S.* tariff contains an offshore assembly provision, (*OAP*). The tariff on certain imported goods is charged on the value of such goods *less* the value of incorporated domestically produced components, i.e., the tariff on an assembled product is applied only to the value-added in foreign assembly or processing if domestically produced components are used. Such provisions were included in the 1930 *U.S.* tariff,[1] and they are the subject of continuing controversy. Clauses to repeal the offshore assembly provisions[2] in the *U.S.* tariff were included in the recent Mills and Burke-Hartke trade bills (which were not passed by the Congress), and an unsuccessful attempt was made to include such a repeal clause in the recently passed Trade Reform Act of 1974. The AFL-CIO is actively pursuing the repeal of these provisions.

With an *OAP*, the tariff on an imported good is applied only to the value-added in assembly, *if* domestic components are used. One of its effects then is to reduce the effective rate of protection of the assembly activity, and hence to shift demand from domestic to foreign assemblers. Opponents of the provisions stress the associated displacement of domestic assembly activity and the accompanying negative balance-of-trade impact.[3] They frequently cite the rapid rate of increase of *OAP* imports from developing countries (*LDC*); 60 percent per year over the period 1966–72 as compared with 12 percent for other manufactured imports from *LDC*.[4]

But this "tariff break" is available only if domestic components are used—implying a simultaneous shift of demand from foreign to domestic components. Defenders of the *OAP* stress the associated positive effects on domestic activity and on the balance of payments.

The object of this paper is to estimate the static impact of the *OAP* on domestic economic activity (in assembly and in production of components) and on the balance of trade. Estimates of the effect on domestic economic welfare of the *OAP* will also be presented. The effect on investment flows will be taken into account indirectly by the supply parameters of the model, but will not be explicitly estimated. To measure balance of payments rather than simply the balance-of-trade impact, an

---

* U.S. Treasury Department.
[1] A history of such provisions is included in the Tariff Commission report.
[2] Item 806.30 of the *U.S.* tariff allows such tariff treatment on metal articles exported by *U.S.* firms for processing abroad by a subsidiary or foreign subcontractor, and returned for further processing by the *U.S.* firm. Item 807.00 allows such tariff treatment on any imported article which contains *U.S.* components, regardless of whether the foreign operation is performed by a *U.S.* subsidiary, a foreign subcontractor, or a foreign firm which purchases *U.S.* components for inclusion in products exported to the United States. Over 90 percent of *OAP* imports enter under item 807.00. There are limits to the sort of processing allowed abroad. For de-

tails, see the Tariff Commission report, pp. 9 ff.
[3] Throughout, the "balance-of-payments impact" is understood to be a pressure on the exchange rate under a regime of flexible rates.
[4] For imports from all countries, comparable rates of increase are 24 and 17 percent. *OAP* imports from all countries were \$3.4 billion in 1972—about 9 percent of manufactured imports; *OAP* imports from *LDC* were \$1 billion—22 percent of manufactured imports.

estimate of the effect of OAP trade on the profit remittances of foreign subsidiaries would also be required.

In Sections II, III, and IV a comparative statics theory of the incidence of OAP is formulated, and expressions for the various effects of their repeal are derived. In Section V the effects are estimated by substituting parameter values into the formulae.

I. The Model and Assumptions

The model is essentially the fixed coefficients, partial equilibrium, effective protection model with less than perfectly elastic import supplies. In order that the shifts from domestic to foreign assembly and from foreign to domestic components may be analyzed, it must incorporate foreign and domestic assembly and foreign and domestic production of components. It thus consists of five equations: the demand for the finished good,[5] supply functions of foreign and of domestic components, and supply functions of foreign and domestic assembly. The model is completed by aggregating across countries to determine the total supplies of assembly and of components, which are then aggregated vertically to determine the supply of the finished good. The intersection of this curve with the demand function defines market equilibrium.

In analyzing the OAP we are looking at final goods which are imported by the United States and contain components exported by the United States. In the language of the model, this makes the United States an exporter of components and an importer of assembly.

Operationally, the distinction between "assembly" and "components" is based on the separation of the dutiable from the duty free value of a finished good imported under the OAP. This distinction is then used to specify what is defined as assembly and as components in import replacements (domestic assembly of domestic components) and in non-OAP imports of the same final good (foreign assembly of foreign components).[6] OAP and non-OAP imports and domestic import replacements are assumed perfect substitutes for each other.

For example, suppose shirts imported under OAP are made from parts which are cut in the United States from $U.S.$ fabric. The parts are then shipped outside of the United States, where they are sewn with foreign thread into shirts. Upon entry into the United States, the tariff is charged on the "final" value of the shirts, less the value of the $U.S.$-made parts. Thus the dutiable value includes foreign-made components as well as assembly cost, in the strict sense of the term. Components therefore refers to the shirt parts and assembly to the thread and the sewing. Because we assume fixed coefficients, and because the same tariff rate (the rate for the finished good) is applied to all segments of the foreign value, it is not necessary to distinguish in the model the thread from the sewing. Imported shirts sewn from foreign cloth (and thus ineligible for OAP treatment) contain foreign components (the parts) and foreign assembly (the thread and the sewing). We distinguish in the same way the components from the assembly of domestically produced import replacement shirts.

The "quantity of assembly" is defined as the quantity of finished goods produced (assembled), and the "supply of assembly" relates this quantity to the rate of payment for the assembly process, i.e., to the "piece rate" received by a contract assembler or the difference between the price

---

[5] "Finished" of course is relative to the process being studied. Whether these are consumption, intermediate, or capital goods is irrelevant for our purposes.

[6] The reason for not assuming that all imports of the finished good contain $U.S.$ components (i.e., are OAP imports) is empirical. For virtually every 7-digit product for which there are OAP imports, there are also non-OAP imports.

received for finished articles and the price paid for components by an assembler who works for his own account.[7] Supplies of components are supply functions in the usual sense and the demand for the finished good is a demand function in the usual sense.

The foreign supply functions are defined as export functions—the foreign supply of assembly refers to assembly for export, and the foreign supply of components to the foreign supply net of demand for production for the foreign market.[8]

A. Notation

The notation has been made mnemonic as far as possible. The P, Q, and V represent prices, quantities, and values, while T is the ad valorem tariff rate applicable to the finished good. The subscripts d, f, and t distinguish domestic, foreign, and total (sum of foreign and domestic), while a and c identify assembly and components. The subscript j refers to the finished good. Elasticities of supply are represented by Φ; Γ is the elasticity of domestic demand for the finished good, defined so as to be negative; C is the component's input-output coefficient, evaluated at foreign prices, i.e., $C = P_{fc}/(P_{fa}+P_{fc})$. The R_{fa} and R_{fc} are shares of imports in total assembly and in total production of components for the U.S. market. Starred variables refer to proportionate changes (for example, $V^* = dV/V$) for all variables except $T(T^* = dT/(1+T))$.

B. Equations of the Model

In the case in question, in which domestic components (DC) are reimported after assembly abroad, the foreign assembler

(or a foreign exporter who buys components and has them assembled into goods for export) can choose between DC and foreign components (FC).

If there is no OAP, the foreign assembler will always choose the components with the lower price, hence at equilibrium

$$(1) \qquad P_{dc} = P_{fc}$$

Because of the domestic economy's tariff on J,

$$(2) \qquad P_{dj} = (1 + T)(P_{fa} + P_{fc})$$

By definition,

$$(3) \qquad P_{da} = P_{dj} - P_{dc}$$

and combining the three equations, we have

$$(4) \qquad P_{da} = P_{fa} + T(P_{fa} + P_{fc})$$

If, however, there is an OAP, the foreign assembler can avoid ·a tariff liability of $T \cdot P_{fc}$ by using DC. Hence, at equilibrium (1) is replaced by

$$(5) \qquad P_{dc} = (1 + T)P_{fc}$$

while (2) and (3) remain relevant, so we have

$$(6) \qquad P_{da} = (1 + T)P_{fa}$$

Thus the effect of removing the OAP is to "shift" the term $T \cdot P_{fc}$ from the difference between the domestic and foreign prices of components to the difference between the domestic and foreign prices of assembly. This can be treated algebraically by introducing the term X, which measures the proportion to which the tariff is a simple tariff on imports of J rather than a tariff with an OAP. At one extreme, when $X = 1$, the tariff is a "pure" tariff on imports of J without an OAP, while at the other extreme when $X = 0$, the OAP is in effect. We can thus write

$$(7) \qquad P_{dc} = (1 + (1 - X)T)P_{fc}$$

$$(8) \qquad P_{da} = (1 + T)P_{fa} + X \cdot T \cdot P_{fc}$$

which with (2) express the equilibrium

---

[7] The concept of a value-added product basic to such a supply function is explored by Chulsoon Khang.

[8] An equivalent procedure for analytical purposes would be to assume that all production is for U.S. consumption, i.e., that products of the type imported under OAP are consumed only in the United States.

price relationships of the model, and allow the removal of the *OAP* (i.e., the comparative statics shift from the "with *OAP*" to the "without *OAP*" case) to be handled by taking the derivative of the model with respect to X (T held constant) and setting $\Delta X = 1$.

The behavioral relations of the model are $Hd(P_{da})$ and $Hf(P_{fa})$, the domestic and foreign supplies of assembly; $Gd(P_{dc})$ and $Gf(P_{fc})$, the domestic and foreign supplies of components; and $K(P_j)$, the domestic demand for the finished good.

The total supplies of assembly and components, expressed by substituting for P_{da} and P_{dc} from (7) and (8) as functions of foreign prices are

(9) $Q_t = G_d[(1 + (1 - X)T)P_{fc}] + G_f[P_{fc}]$

(10) $Q_t = H_d[(1 + T)P_{fa} + XTP_{fc}]$
$\quad\quad + H_f[P_{fa}]$

Note that in (9) and (10) we do not distinguish between the total quantities of assembly and of components. This means that (9) and (10) incorporate the equilibrium condition that these two quantities are equal. Further $Q_t = K(P_j)$ is the equilibrium condition that quantity supplied of J equals quantity demanded.

By definition, $P_j = P_{da} + P_{dc}$. When we substitute for P_{da} and P_{dc} from the equilibrium price relations (7) and (8), we have

(11) $P_j = (1 + T)(P_{fa} + P_{fc})$

When (11) is substituted into the demand function, we have

(12) $Q_t = K[(1 + T)(P_{fa} + P_{fc})]$

The initial system contains five behavioral relations (the two H, two G, and K), three definitions (of P_{da}, and of the total quantities supplied of assembly and of components), and four equilibrium conditions (equations (7) and (8), plus the implicit equality of the quantity demanded of J with the total quantities supplied of assembly and of components). The variables in this system are P_{da}, Q_{da}, P_{dc}, Q_{dc}, P_{fa}, Q_{fa}, P_{fc}, Q_{fc}, P_j, the quantity demanded of J, and total quantities supplied of assembly and of components. In use this system is reduced to the three simultaneous equations (9), (10), and (12) in the variables P_{fa}, P_{fc}, and Q_t. Conceptually, after equilibrium values of these variables are solved for simultaneously, they can be substituted into (7), (8), (11) and the supply functions in order to determine equilibrium values of the other variables.

II. Effects of the Offshore Assembly Provision

In this model the effects of the *OAP* are the derivatives with respect to X (T held constant) of the system of equations. The resulting expressions will be evaluated for the case in which $X = 0$, initially, but $T > 0$. (An *OAP* cannot be defined when $T = 0$.)

After substituting (11) into (12), taking total derivatives of equations (9), (10), and (12), with T held constant, and converting to elasticity terms, we have[9]

(13) $Q_t^* = \Phi_{tc}P_{fc}^* - \Phi_{dc}R_{dc} \cdot T/(1 + T) \cdot dX$

(14) $Q_t^* = \Phi_{ta}P_{fa}^* + \Phi_{da}R_{da}(T/(1 + T))$
$\quad\quad \cdot (C/(1 - C)dX)$

(15) $Q_t^* = (1 - C)\Gamma P_{fa}^* + C\Gamma P_{fc}^*$

A. Effects on Prices and Outputs

The solutions for P_{fc}^* and P_{fa}^* are shown in (16) and (17). If we replace the dX by ΔX and let $\Delta X = 1$, these expressions measure the effects of removing the existing *OAP*, and the assumptions that the Φ are positive and that Γ is negative imply that

---

[9] From the total supply of components and of assembly functions (9) and (10) we can show that $\Phi_{ta} = R_{da} \cdot \Phi_{da} + R_{fa} \cdot \Phi_{fa}$, and $\Phi_{tc} = R_{dc} \cdot \Phi_{dc} + R_{fc} \cdot \Phi_{fc}$, where $R_{da} = Q_{da}/Q_t$, etc.

$$(16) \quad P_{fc}^* = \left[\frac{-\Gamma[C \cdot \Phi_{da} \cdot R_{da} + (1 - C)\Phi_{dc} \cdot R_{dc}] + \Phi_{la} \cdot \Phi_{dc} \cdot R_{dc}}{-\Gamma[C \cdot \Phi_{la} + (1 - C)\Phi_{lc}] + \Phi_{la} \cdot \Phi_{lc}} \right] \left(\frac{T}{1 + T} \right) dX$$

$$(17) \quad P_{fa}^* = \left[\frac{\Gamma[C \cdot \Phi_{da} \cdot R_{da} + (1 - C)\Phi_{dc} \cdot R_{dc}] - \Phi_{lc} \cdot \Phi_{da} \cdot R_{da}}{-\Gamma[C \cdot \Phi_{la} + (1 - C)\Phi_{lc}] + \Phi_{lc} \cdot \Phi_{la}} \right] \left(\frac{C}{1 - C} \right) \left(\frac{T}{1 + T} \right) dX$$

$P_{fc}^* > 0$ and $P_{fa}^* < 0$.

From equations (7), (8), and (11) we derive

$$(18) \quad P_{dc}^* = P_{fc}^* - \left(\frac{T}{1 + T} \right) dX$$

$$(19) \quad P_{da}^* = P_{fa}^* + \left(\frac{T}{1 + T} \right) \left(\frac{C}{1 - C} \right) dX$$

Comparing the numerator and the denominator in both (16) and (17), we see that term by term the numerator of the expression in the square brackets is less in absolute value than the denominator. (For example, $\Phi_{da} \cdot R_{da} < \Phi_{la}$, $\Phi_{dc} \cdot R_{dc} < \Phi_{lc}$, etc.) The expressions in square brackets in (16) and (17) are thus between 0 and 1 in absolute value, so (18) and (19) imply that $P_{dc}^* < 0$, and $P_{da}^* > 0$. The solutions for Q_{da}^*, Q_{dc}^*, Q_{fa}^*, Q_{fc}^*, have the same sign as the respective price changes, hence there remains only the question of the effect on P_j and Q_t of removing the *OAP*. The expression for the effect on Q_t^* is

$$(20) \quad Q_t^* = \Gamma \cdot C \left[\frac{\Phi_{la} \cdot \Phi_{dc} \cdot R_{dc} - \Phi_{lc} \cdot \Phi_{da} \cdot R_{da}}{den} \cdot \frac{T}{1 + T} \right] dX$$

The denominator inside the square brackets is the same as in equations (16) and (17).

On closer examination of this expression we find that it is positive or negative as

$$\left(\frac{\Phi_{fa}}{\Phi_{da}} \right) \cdot \left(\frac{R_{fa}}{R_{fc}} \right) \cdot \left(\frac{\Phi_{dc}}{\Phi_{fc}} \right) \cdot \left(\frac{R_{dc}}{R_{da}} \right)$$

is less than or greater than 1.

Because *OAP* imports contain domestic components and are assembled abroad, we know that $Q_{fc} < Q_{fa}$ and $Q_{da} < Q_{dc}$, i.e., $R_{fc} < R_{fa}$ and $R_{da} < R_{dc}$. This information about the relative positions of the domestic and foreign supply curves does not specify their relative elasticities. But because "assembly" is an activity with a relatively large input of unskilled labor, it seems reasonable to assume that expansion of assembly would require less bidding away of labor from higher paying activities if that expansion took place outside of the United States, i.e., to assume that $\Phi_{fa} > \Phi_{da}$. One is tempted to reason conversely that $\Phi_{fc} < \Phi_{dc}$. The foreign supply of components refers however not only to the labor-rich areas which might have comparative advantage in assembly, but also to industrial countries such as Japan and Germany, and the foreign supply curve is net of foreign demand, hence it is possible that $\Phi_{fc} > \Phi_{dc}$.

We cannot therefore conclude on a priori grounds that Q_t^* is either positive or negative. But because R_{fa}/R_{fc} and R_{dc}/R_{da} are definitely greater than 1, and Φ_{fa}/Φ_{da} is likely greater than 1, it seems likely that Q_t^*/dX will be negative and $P_t^*/dX = (1/\Gamma)$. (Q_j^*/dX) will be positive, i.e., that repeal of the *OAP* will raise the price and reduce domestic consumption of goods imported under the provisions.

B. Effect on the Trade Balance

The supply functions of the model all refer to production of the final good for sale in the U.S. This means that the net value of imports M is equal to $P_{fc}Q_{fc} + P_{fa}Q_{fa}$. From this,

$$(21) \quad M^* = A(1 + \Phi_{fa})P_{fa}^* + (1 - A)(1 + \Phi_{fc})P_{fc}^*$$

where A is the value of assembly as a proportion of net imports. The first term on the right-hand side of (21) measures the effect of the OAP on imports of FA, the second term its effect on imports of FC.

Because $P_{fa}^* < 0$ and $P_{fc}^* > 0$, it is clear that the change in the trade balance resulting from elimination of the OAP will not necessarily be positive—the change being larger (in a positive sense) as the elasticities of supply of assembly in the two countries are smaller and as the elasticities of supply of components are larger.

III. Welfare Effects

Following Harry Johnson's classic article, the net domestic welfare effect of a change in a trade policy variable is the sum of the change of consumers' surplus, the change of producers' surplus, and the transfers of wealth between the domestic and foreign economies associated with the collection of tariff revenue.

A. *Change of Consumers' Surplus*

The change of consumers' surplus resulting from a policy change is always measured by the change of the area under the demand curve which is above the price paid by the buyer. Thus the gain of consumers' surplus is measured by

$$(-dP_j)Q_t + 1/2(-dP_j)(dQ_t)$$

or in relative terms,

$$(22) \quad \frac{Gain \ of \ CS}{P_j Q_t} = -P_j^*(1 + 1/2\Gamma \cdot P_j^*)$$

where P_j, Q_t are the initial values of the variables and the dP_j, dQ_t are the results of the change in the policy variables in question.

B. *Change of Domestic Producers' Surplus*

As an OAP and tariffs with and without OAP will affect the level of DA and of production of DC, there will be changes of producers' surplus in each sector. In each

sector, the gain of producers' surplus will be equal to

$$(dP)Q + 1/2 \ (dP) \cdot (dQ)$$

or, in relative terms

$$(23) \quad \frac{Gain \ of \ PS}{PQ} = P^*(1 + 1/2 \ \Phi \cdot P^*)$$

where again P and Q represent initial values, and refer along with Φ to DC in one case and to DA in the other.

C. *Transfers Associated with Tariff Revenue*

Figures 1 and 2 will be used to isolate the wealth transfers between the domestic and foreign economies which are associated with the OAP. In these figures, the first subscript distinguishes among domestic, foreign, and total (the sum of domestic and foreign) while the second distinguishes among the three policy situations—free trade (o), a tariff with OAP (p), and a tariff without $OAP(t)$. To reduce the number of lines, the supplies of DC and of FC in Figure 1, and the supplies of DA and FA in Figure 2 have been assumed to be identical.

Because a tariff on J without OAP does not affect the relation between P_{dc} and P_{fc} (see equation (7) with $X=1$), such a tariff will not shift any of the curves in Figure 1. A tariff with an OAP (equation (7) with $X=0$) shifts the supply of FC and hence the total supply of components upwards.

The effects of removing the OAP (with the tariff rate constant) are thus shown by moving from policy "p" to policy "t." With the OAP, the prices in Figure 1 of DC and of FC are P_{dp}, and the tariff revenue collected on imports of components is represented by the area $ADFC$. When the OAP is eliminated, there is no longer any tariff revenue on components. The parts of former tariff revenue represented by rectangles $ADEB$ and $NEFM$ are transferred to other domestic uses (involving no change of welfare), while the part repre-

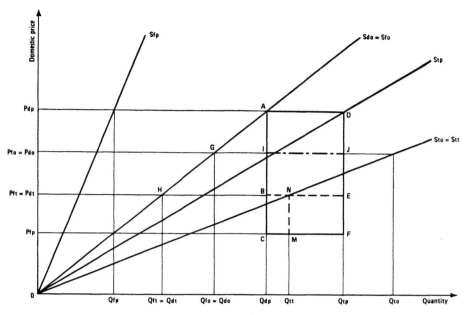

FIGURE 1. EFFECTS ON COMPONENTS

sented by $BNMC$ is transferred from tariff revenue to payment for imports—a loss of domestic welfare.

The vertical dimension of the area $BNMC$ is the change of the price of FC caused by eliminating the OAP, while the horizontal dimension is Q_{tt} less Q_{dp} which is equal to $Q_{ft}+Q_{dt}-Q_{dp}$. Changing the sign so that the change is defined as a gain rather than a loss, and converting to relative terms, we have

$$(24) \quad \frac{Gain}{V_{fc}} = \frac{R_{dc}}{R_{fc}} \left(\frac{1}{1+T} \right) P_{fc}^* Q_{dc}^*$$
$$- P_{fc}^*(1 + Q_{fc}^*)$$

In this expression V_{fc} is the value in the p instance, i.e., the instance for which we have observations.

Similarly, in Figure 2 the effects on DA of a tariff with and without an OAP have been sketched. As equation (8) shows, a tariff with an $OAP(X=0)$ shifts the supply of FA leftward, while a tariff without an $OAP(X=1)$ shifts it even further to the left. Tariff revenues in the t and p cases are represented by areas $ABCD$ and $EFGH$. When the OAP is eliminated, area $IJKL$ remains tariff revenue and hence does not involve a welfare change. Area $EILH$ is transferred from tariff revenue to suppliers of DA, area $EIHL$ is shifted from tariff revenue to suppliers of DA, area $ABJI$ from domestic consumers to tariff revenue and area $JFGK$ from tariff revenue to domestic consumers—involving in none of the three instances a change of the total wealth of the domestic

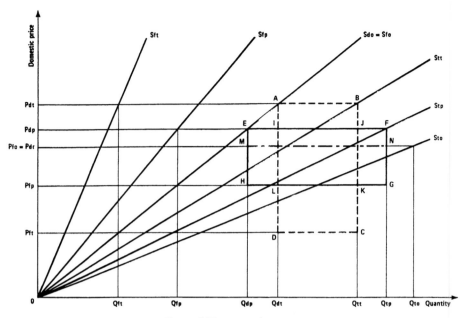

FIGURE 2. EFFECTS ON ASSEMBLY

economy.

Finally, *LKCD* is shifted from receipts of foreign assemblers in exchange for *FA* to tariff revenue—for which foreign assemblers receive no *quid pro quo*. Hence the area *LKCD* represents a welfare gain to the domestic economy. The horizontal and vertical dimensions of this area are Q_{fa} in the t case, and the change of P_{fa} caused by eliminating the *OAP*. Converted to relative terms, we have

$$(25) \qquad \frac{Gain}{V_{fa}} = - P_{fa}^*(1 + Q_{fa}^*)$$

in which V_{fa} is the value of *FA* in the p case.

IV. Data Inputs and Parameters

A. *Data*

The basic data used in the study were from the Census Bureau's report of the total and dutiable values of *OAP* imports. These data; plus data for "Directly Competitive Imports" (non-*OAP* imports in those 7-digit *TSUS* categories in which there were *OAP* imports)[10] provided the measures of imports of foreign assembly and of foreign components, and of *C*, the components' input-output coefficient.[11]

Components are identified in the data and therefore in the results only by the industry in which they are used, and not by the industry in which they are produced. It follows that labor-output coefficients could not be identified, and the

[10] I wish to thank the U.S. Tariff Commission and George N. Ecklund, Director of the Office of Economic Research at the Commission, for making these tabulations available.

[11] Tariff data were taken from a GATT tabulation, and import shares data (the parameters R_{da} and R_{fa}) were based on data tabulated by the Trade Relations Council. Details of how the data were fitted together are available on request.

estimates of output displacement could not be translated into employment displacement estimates.

B. *Parameters*

The selection of supply and demand elasticities began with estimates (from the literature) of the elasticity of import demand for finished goods (Γ_m). This elasticity was decomposed into consistent values for the elasticities of domestic demand (Γ) for and supply (Φ_s) of finished goods, and the value of Φ_s was then decomposed into consistent values of Φ_{da} and Φ_{dc}. Values for Φ_{fa} and Φ_{fc} were obtained by similar decomposition of the estimate of the foreign elasticity of export supply of finished goods used by Stephen Magee.[12]

The parameter values on which the results in Tables 1 and 2 are based are[13] $\Gamma = -0.75$, $\Phi_{da} = 1$, $\Phi_{dc} = 3$, $\Phi_{fa} = 40$, and $\Phi_{fc} = 10$. A sensitivity analysis indicated that the major conclusions reported below are quite robust with respect to assumed values for these parameters. The same values for these parameters were used for all industries, but the values for T, C, R_{da}, and R_{dc} were specific to the industry.

V. Results

The results shown in the tables are based on the assumption that Φ_{fa} and Φ_{fc}

[12] The reason for using indirect estimates is that more direct ones are not available. The relations involved are

$$\Phi_m = 1/M(\Gamma - \Phi_s) + \Phi_s$$

and

$$1/\Phi_s = ((1 - C)/\Phi_{da}) + C/\Phi_{dc}$$

The first of these is given by Magee and the derivation of the second is available from the author on request. The second expression, with the subscripts appropriately modified, relates Φ_{fa} and Φ_{fc} to the foreign elasticity of export supply of the finished good.

[13] This value for Γ was used by Magee. The values for Φ_{fa} and Φ_{fc} are consistent (by the expression in fn. 12) with Magee's value of 1.5 for Φ_s. The values of Φ_{fa} and Φ_{fc} imply a foreign export supply elasticity of the finished good equal to 16, which is slightly higher than the value of 14.4 used by Magee.

for textile products are restricted to zero by import quotas. Initial calculations using the same parameter values as for the other industries indicated that *OAP* removal would cause *U.S.* imports of foreign assembly of textile products to become negative—i.e., would cause the United States to become a reexporter of textile components produced abroad but assembled in the United States. This result seems to be inconsistent with the generally accepted pattern of *U.S.* comparative advantage and disadvantage, and might be the result of basing the estimates on a situation in which imports of assembly are less than they would be if all variables were at long-run equilibrium values, as the model assumes.

Comparison with the list of textile products subject to import quota[14] indicated an overlap with virtually every category of *OAP* imports, hence the assumption that Φ_{fa} and Φ_{fc} are zero for the textile industry. Because this assumption is somewhat tenuous, separate totals with and without textile products, which account for less than 3 percent of *OAP* imports, are given.

Because the ratio of duty-free value (i.e., domestic components) to total value, as given in the second column of Table 1, is very low for motor vehicles and household sewing machines, the tariff saving from the *OAP* is very low and hence the effects of the *OAP* on these industries is slight. In terms of gross value of trade involved, motor vehicles account for almost 40 percent of *OAP* imports. But in terms of the effects of the *OAP*, this industry is an almost insignificant part.

With motor vehicles and household sewing machines (on which the effects of the *OAP* are very slight) excluded, about half the value of imports affected by the *OAP* is assembly and half is foreign components. Thus the effects of the *OAP* on

[14] See U.S. Department of Commerce.

TABLE 1—VALUES OF IMPORTS AFFECTED BY THE OFFSHORE ASSEMBLY PROVISION, 1972, AND ESTIMATED EFFECTS ON THE TRADE BALANCE OF THE REMOVAL OF THE OFFSHORE ASSEMBLY PROVISION

(Values in millions of dollars)

Industry	OAP Imports		Tariff rate[a]	Directly competitive imports	Effects on imports of removing OAP		
	Total value	Duty free value as percent of total value			Assembly	Components	Total
Textile products	87	52	26	1202	−60	82	23
Lumber and paper products	9	63	7	217	−61	52	−9
Household sewing machines	31	1	6	79	−0.0	0.1	0.1
Office machinery	251	50	5	302	−98	62	−36
Electronic products	607	37	7	1093	−122	157	35
Motor vehicles	1310	2	4	3488	−24	19	−5
Aircraft	109	34	5	365	−86	50	−35
Other machinery	557	28	6	5355	−688	616	−72
Scientific instruments	17	43	9	156	−34	36	2
Sporting goods	45	38	14	207	−38	52	14
Miscellaneous manufactures	69	43	13	2638	−844	865	21
Metal products (item 806.30)	318	59	7	2247	−715	617	−98
Total	3409	25		17,350	−2768	2608	−160
Total excluding textiles	3322	25		16,148	−2709	2526	−183

Note: Parameter values are $\Gamma = -.75$, $\Phi_{da} = 1$, $\Phi_{dc} = 3$, $\Phi_{fa} = 40$, $\Phi_{fc} = 10$, for all except textile products. For these products, Φ_{fa} and Φ_{fc} were assumed restricted to zero by quotas.

[a] Shown in percent.

assembly and on components have a tendency to cancel each other.

A. *Balance of Trade*

It appears that the balance-of-trade effect of the OAP is rather slight. With the parameter values used in Table 1, I estimate that repeal of the OAP would have reduced net-imports by less than $200 million in 1972. The estimated increase of imports from repeal of the OAP is less than 2 percent of total affected imports (dutiable value of OAP imports plus directly competitive imports)—this small net effect resulting from the offsetting changes of imports of assembly and components. By contrast, Magee estimated that removal of the tariff on imports directly competive with U.S. production would cause these imports to increase by

65 percent.

The conclusion that repealing the OAP would not significantly improve the trade balance was confirmed by the results of the sensitivity analysis. When other "reasonable" parameter values were used, it was often estimated that removal of the OAP would increase net imports.

B. *Domestic Effects*

Estimates of the effects of removal of the OAP on domestic consumption and output, and on domestic economic welfare are given in Tables 2a and 2b. For perspective I have listed the value of domestic shipments and the implicit value of domestic output competitive with OAP imports,[15] calculated by dividing V_{fa} and V_{fc}

[15] Because the R_{fa} and R_{fc} values used were matched as

TABLE 2A—VALUE OF DOMESTIC PRODUCTION DIRECTLY COMPETITIVE WITH *OAP* IMPORTS

(Values in millions of dollars)

Industry	Value of domestic shipments 1971 (a)	Implicit value in 1972 of domestic output competitive with products imported under *OAP*		
		Total (b)	Assembly (c)	Components (d)
Textile products	27,973	4,707	2,037	2,670
Lumber and paper products	22,178	2,067	1,018	1,049
Household sewing machines	143	72	71	1
Office machinery	7,021	3,929	1,974	1,955
Electronic products	24,944	4,488	2,767	1,721
Motor vehicles	60,845	28,830	28,239	591
Aircraft	15,203	5,768	3,863	1,905
Other machinery	72,287	42,373	31,122	11,251
Scientific and precision instruments	12,311	967	576	391
Sporting goods, toys, games	2,786	829	534	295
Miscellaneous manufactures	21,470	19,363	11,729	7,634
Metal products (item 806.30)	42,026	20,970	8,887	12,083
Total	309,214	134,363	92,817	41,546
Total, excluding textiles	281,241	129,656	90,780	38,876

TABLE 2B—ESTIMATES OF THE EFFECTS ON THE DOMESTIC ECONOMY OF REMOVAL OF THE OFFSHORE ASSEMBLY PROVISION

Industry	Quantity of *J* consumed[a] (e)	Assembly		Components		Total		Net Welfare Gain[b] (l)
		Quantity[a] (f)	Value[b] (g)	Quantity[a] (h)	Value[b] (i)	Quantity[a] (j)	Value[b] (k)	
Textile products	0	0	0	0	0	0	0	−23.3
Lumber and paper products	−1.1	5.0	102	−6.0	−84	−0.6	18	−7.2
Household sewing machines	−0.01	0.05	0.1	−13.3	−0.1	−0.1	−0.1	−0.03
Office machinery	−1.1	3.9	155	−4.1	−108	−0.1	4.7	−12.9
Electronic products	−0.8	3.5	192	−9.9	−227	−1.6	−35	−36.6
Motor vehicles	−0.03	0.06	31	−3.0	−24	−0.00	8	−3.3
Aircraft	−0.06	1.6	127	−3.1	−80	0.05	47	−7.8
Other machinery	−0.5	1.7	1,042	−5.9	−883	−0.2	209	−95.4
Scientific and precision instruments	−1.1	4.9	57	−10.6	−55	−1.4	2	−5.6
Sporting goods, toys, games	−1.3	6.2	66	−19.9	−78	−3.1	−12	−8.7
Miscellaneous manufactures	−1.5	6.2	1,460	−13.4	−1359	−1.5	100	−128.7
Metal products (item 806.30)	−1.3	6.9	1,231	−6.4	−1032	−0.8	199	−88.6
Total	−0.7	2.4	4,464	−7.1	−3931	−0.5	533	−418.3
Total, excluding textiles	−1.0	2.5	4,464	−7.6	−3931	−0.5	533	−395.0

[a] Shown in percent.
[b] Values in millions of dollars.

closely as possible with the product composition of imports affected by the *OAP*, they were usually larger than such figures for the entire industry. For this reason, and because imports affected by the *OAP* do not include all imports, the implicit values of affected domestic production are smaller than the values of domestic shipments of each industry.

by R_{fa} and R_{fc}, respectively. The estimate for each industry of the effect on total domestic real output (col. (j)) is the average of the changes in real output of assembly and components, weighted by the input-output coefficients (measured at domestic prices) for assembly and components. The other estimates, of course, were made by substitution of values into the appropriate expressions from Sections III and IV. For the estimates of changes of real output (cols. (f), (h), (j)) the "Total" lines are averages of the industry estimates weighted by the corresponding values from columns (b), (c), or (d).

The estimates indicate rather strongly that if the *OAP* were repealed the output of components would decline sufficiently to more than offset the increase of domestic assembly, so that the net impact would be a slight reduction of real domestic economic activity. Among product groups, the estimated net impact on domestic activity of removal of the *OAP* is positive only for aircraft, and in this case the figure is very small, only 0.05 percent.[16]

The estimated percentage effects on domestic output are relative to the implicit value of domestic output in column (b) rather than to value of total domestic shipments, as given in column (a). The 0.5 percent reduction thus is 0.5 percent of $134 billion or about $672 million (at 1972 prices). By comparison, the total value of manufacturers' shipments in 1971 was about $671 billion.

Repeal of the *OAP* would reduce consumption of products affected by it by about 1 percent, and, as demand is assumed inelastic, would cause consumer expenditure on these products to increase by about $200 million.

Finally, the welfare calculation in the last column of Table 2b indicates that the *OAP* generated in 1972 a net welfare benefit of about $400 million. The net loss which would result from its repeal is made up of a $1,424 million loss of consumers' surplus and a $346 million transfer loss associated with tariff revenues, partly offset by a gain of producers' surplus of

$1,349 million. The sensitivity analysis again shows that the choice of parameters was not critical.

VI. Offshore Assembly Provisions as Development Incentives

One is on solid ground to conclude that the United States benefits in a welfare sense from the existence of the *OAP*. I have pointed out elsewhere that in 1972 the value of *U.S.* imports from less developed countries (*LDC*) under the *OAP* was as large as exports of these countries to the European Economic Community (*EEC*) under the *EEC*'s system of tariff preferences, and I have estimated that the *U.S. OAP* generated in 1972 net foreign exchange earnings for *LDC* equal to those generated by the preference system of the *EEC*. And, while *U.S. OAP* imports from the *LDC* have been increasing very rapidly, it has been pointed out frequently that the potential for growth of *LDC* preferential exports to the *EEC* is severely restricted by the ceilings and quotas built into the scheme.[17] Hence it is probable that the *OAP* scheme of the United States at present is a more important contributor to the foreign exchange earnings of the *LDC* than is the *EEC*'s preference scheme, and that the difference is increasing rapidly year by year.

Why then do we observe these tight restrictions placed on preferential imports (indeed, the United States has only recently implemented a limited preference scheme), while *OAP* imports into the United States continue to increase rapidly? To the exporting country, preferences or *OAP* treatment are similar incentives.[18] Tariff preferences allow the *LDC* to compete more effectively with domestic producers in the industrial countries on those

---

[16] The conclusion that *OAP* removal will reduce domestic activity is reinforced by the sensitivity analysis.

[17] See Richard Cooper and Tracy Murray.

[18] As the *EEC* preference scheme allows generally for 50 percent preferences, and the dutiable value of *U.S. OAP* imports is about 50 percent of total value, the tariff reductions allowed by the two schemes are about equal.

products in which the *LDC* have comparative advantage—provided that these products are not excluded from the preference scheme and that the *LDC* are not required to use components produced domestically at high cost in order to satisfy the "country of origin" requirements of the preference scheme.

As for an *OAP*, it allows the labor rich *LDC* to do the assembly jobs in which they have comparative advantage without subjecting them to the higher effective rates of protection they would face if forced to bear the duty on the value of components which they do not produce.

Of course, this "out" provided by the *OAP* has a catch in it. The *LDC* must use *U.S.* components in order to qualify for the tariff reduction. But the estimates of the impact of the *OAP* on *LDC* exports referred to above indicate that this out with a catch is better than no out at all.

The other side of the *OAP*—its negative impact on production of foreign components—is probably not extremely burdensome to *LDC*. The displacement of foreign components by *U.S.* components in the *LDC* assembling country will often be the replacement by *U.S.* components of Japanese or German components rather than the displacement of components produced by *LDC*. Hence the shifting of the assembly process to the *LDC* will often be a net as well as a gross gain to these countries.

The fact that the *OAP* shifts demand toward domestic components generates domestic political support in the producing sector, which means that an *OAP* is more likely to attract sufficient political push for enactment and expansion than a tariff preference scheme, which has only widely diffused consumer interests and good will to back it.[19]

[19] Additional support for an *OAP* comes from domestic firms who shift assembly operations to offshore affiliates, but these firms would also benefit from tariff reductions and hence would be expected to also support preferences.

This suggests that efforts to liberalize *OAP* treatment of articles assembled in *LDC* could produce considerably greater benefits to the *LDC* than have resulted from attempts to negotiate tariff preferences.

REFERENCES

R. N. Cooper, "The European Economic Community's System of Generalized- Tariff Preferences: A Critique," *J. Develop. Stud.*, July 1972, *8*, 379–94.

J. M. Finger, "Tariff Provisions for Offshore Assembly and the Exports of Developing Countries," *Econ. J.*, June 1975, *85*, 365–71.

H. G. Johnson, "The Cost of Protection and the Scientific Tariff," *J. Polit. Econ.*, Oct. 1960, *48*, 327–45.

C. Khang, "Factor Substitution in the Theory of Effective Protection," *J. Int. Econ.*, Aug. 1973, *3*, 227–46.

S. P. Magee, "The Welfare Effects of Restrictions on U.S. Trade," *Brookings Papers* Washington 1972, *3*, 645–707.

T. Murray, "Preferential Tariffs for the LDCs," *Southern Econ. J.*, July 1973, *40*, 35–46.

Economist Intelligence Unit, "Electronic Components," *Multinational Business*, No. 2, 1973, 23–31.

GATT, *Basic Documentation for Tariff Study, Summary Table No. 2—Tariff and Trade Profiles by Product Categories*, Geneva 1970.

Trade Relations Council of the United States, Inc., *Employment, Output, and Foreign Trade of U.S. Manufacturing Industries, 1958–71*, 5th ed., 3 vols., Geneva 1973.

U.N. Conference on Trade and Development, *Second General Report on the Implementa-*

Data are not available which would separate *OAP* imports among those assembled in offshore affiliates of *U.S.* firms, foreign assemblers who work under contract with *U.S.* importers, and foreign firms which buy *U.S.* components on their own account for assembly into product which will be marketed in the United States. The Tariff Commission's report, p. 94, does however state that two-fifths of *OAP* imports of apparel came from foreign establishments in which no financial interest was held by *U.S.* firms.

tion of the Generalized System of Preferences, Doc. No. TD/B/C.5/22, Apr. 17, 1974, Geneva.

U.S. Bureau of the Census, *U.S. Imports of Merchandise for Consumption and General Imports of Merchandise,* rept. no. IA 245-A, Washington 1973.

U.S. Department of Commerce, *Long Term International Cotton Textile Arrangement Categories,* Washington 1968.

U.S. Tariff Commission, *Economic Factors Affecting the Use of Items 807.00 and 806.30 of the Tariff Schedules of the United States.* TC publication 339, Washington 1970.

Reprinted from

THE AMERICAN ECONOMIC REVIEW

© The American Economic Association

PART TWO

THE NEW INTERNATIONAL
ECONOMIC ORDER

[5]

The Processing of Primary Commodities: Effects of Developed-Country Tariff Escalation and Developing-Country Export Taxes

Stephen S. Golub

Federal Reserve System

J. M. Finger

U.S. Department of the Treasury

Both DC (developed country) tariffs and LDC (developing country) export taxes are "escalated" to protect local processors of primary commodities. The paper develops an analytical model of north-south commodity trade which is used to estimate the effects of reciprocal elimination of these trade barriers for eight commodities. It is estimated that processing would increase by 9 percent in the LDCs and decline by less than 1 percent in the DCs. The LDC export revenue for the eight-commodity sample would increase by 11 percent, or just over $1 billion (based on 1973 trade flows), which is considerably more than the estimated effect of the Generalized System of Preferences.

I. Issue

It is often noted that developed countries (DCs) tend to have lower import duties on commodities which enter in raw form than on the processed products. This "tariff escalation" provides high rates of effective protection for the developed countries' processing sector, and hence inhibits the expansion of such activities in the developing countries (LDCs) (Balassa 1968; Yeats 1974, 1976). Reduction of

The authors would like to thank Lee F. Kolman and Raymond E. Oliver, Jr., for their valuable and efficient assistance. The order of the authors' names was determined by flipping a coin. The paper was completed while both authors were affiliated with the Treasury Department.

[*Journal of Political Economy*, 1979, vol. 87, no. 3]
© 1979 by The University of Chicago. 0022-3808/79/8703-0008$01.58

TABLE 1

AVERAGE LDC EXPORT TAXES AND DC TARIFFS

	LDC Export Tax	DC Tariffs
Copra	6.0	.0
Coconut oil	4.0	10.1
Natural rubber	6.3	.0
Rubber articles	.0	7.6
Cocoa beans	26.5	3.2
Cocoa butter and powder	5.6	10.2
Raw cotton	11.9	.7
Cotton yarn and fabric	.0	9.9
Raw wool	11.8	1.3
Wool yarn and fabric	.0	11.4
Hides and skins	23.4	.0
Leather	13.3	6.9
Logs	11.3	.0
Sawn logs	4.0	1.1
Coffee beans	30.0	3.3
Soluble coffee	6.0	8.9

SOURCES.—The average tariffs were in all but one case (coffee) calculated from Yeats's 1976 tabulation. For coffee, the tariffs were obtained from tariff tables for the EEC, United States, and Japan. The export-tax information was obtained from a U.S. government interagency report on export restrictions (U.S. Government 1976). Export taxes and tariffs were averaged across countries using weights based on 1973 trade flows.

these tariffs on processed goods is often proposed as a way to improve the economic lot of the LDCs, but little has been done to implement such proposals. When industrial country policymakers have to choose between expanding processing in LDCs and not reducing it in their own countries, they usually side with their own processors.

Less often noted is the extensive use of export taxes by developing countries for the same purpose. The first column of table 1 shows that LDC export taxes are higher if products are exported in the primary rather than the processed form and hence tend to protect the processing activity in the country which produces the primary product.

Thus export-tax and import-tariff escalation tend to offset one another as far as the division of the processing pie is concerned. But both cause the price of the processed good to increase in the importing country, which reduces the size of that pie. It should then be possible to simultaneously reduce LDC export taxes on primary goods and DC import tariffs on processed goods in such a way that processing will expand in the LDCs but not contract in the DCs—that is, to give DC policymakers an easier choice than is provided by suggestions that they unilaterally reduce their import duties.

II. Purpose of the Paper

In this paper we will estimate and compare the magnitudes and effects of LDC export taxes with those of DC import tariffs. Of particular interest are the effects on the amounts of processing performed in LDCs and DCs and on the levels of trade of primary and processed commodities.

In order to estimate such effects, it was necessary to construct a model capable of isolating them. While tariff escalation is usually studied by calculating effective rates of protection, the effective-rate concept breaks down when the small-country assumption is dropped. In the context of north-south trade in commodities such as cotton and coffee, it is clearly not tenable to assume that either side is too small to influence world prices. Thus the model we developed is capable of determining resource flows and trade patterns without assuming that either the DCs or the LDCs take world prices as given.

The point of this analysis is to suggest the possibility of the *simultaneous* reduction of LDC export taxes on primary commodities and DC import tariffs on processed commodities. Unfortunately, sympathy for improving the economic lot of the poorer countries has become almost synonymous with voicing demands for unilateral concessions by the developed world. But while this "confrontation" has produced an acrimonious north-south dialogue, few substantive changes in economic policy have resulted. If areas of common interest between LDCs and DCs can be found, and if their benefits can be shown to be large relative to the LDC gains from unilateral gifts, perhaps the north-south dialogue can be diverted toward a more constructive path. Reductions of DC tariffs and LDC export taxes on raw and processed commodities is one such avenue of mutual interest.

III. The Model

The analysis is intended to capture the effects of the export taxes and import tariffs on the levels of production and of processing in LDCs and in DCs and the effects on exports of primary and processed goods from the LDCs. The model we have constructed is similar to the fixed coefficient, partial-equilibrium model used by Finger (1976b) to analyze the offshore assembly provisions in the U.S. tariff. It is based on six behavioral relationships: demands in the DC and the LDC for the "finished" or "processed" good,[1] and supplies in the DC

---

[1] "Finished" is, of course, relative to the process being studied. Whether the processed good is demanded by final consumers or by manufacturers who use it as an input is irrelevant for our purposes.

and in the LDC of the primary good and of processing. The "quantity of processing" is defined conceptually as the quantity of primary goods processed, and the supply of processing relates this quantity to the unit rate of return to the processing activity—to the difference between the price paid for a unit of the primary good and the price received for that unit when it is sold in processed form.

Notation

As usual, P's are prices and Q's are quantities; T is one plus the ad valorem tariff rate in the importing (developed) country and X is one plus the ad valorem export tax rate in the exporting (developing) country; D's represent demand and S's supply, while Φ's are supply elasticities and Γ's are demand elasticities (defined so as to be negative for downward-sloping demand curves). Subscripts n (for north) and s (south) distinguish between the DC importer and the LDC exporter while b, c, and g distinguish among the primary good (e.g., beans), the processed good (e.g., coffee), and the processing activity (e.g., grinding).

The DC and LDC shares of consumption of the processed good are Rnc and Rsc, while Rsb, Rsg, Rnb, and Rng are DC and LDC shares of world output of the primary good and of processing and Vs is value added by processing as a porportion of the value of the processed good, evaluated in the LDC $[Vs = Psg/(Psg + Psb)]$. For convenience, define A as the reciprocal of V.

The production function for the processed good is assumed to be subject to fixed coefficients with the units defined in such a way that to produce one unit of the processed good requires one unit of the primary good and one unit of processing. The function may thus be written

$$Qc = \min(Qb, Qg). \tag{1}$$

The same production function is assumed to apply in the DC and in the LDC.

The specification of the supply and demand functions follows the usual partial-equilibrium practice of excluding all variables except own price. Hence, $Dnc = Dnc(Pnc)$, $Ssb = Ssb(Psb)$, etc.

When the DCs impose import duties and the LDCs impose export taxes on the primary and processed goods, the following relationships hold between prices:

$$Pnb = Tb \cdot Xb \cdot Psb, \tag{2}$$

$$Pnc = Tc \cdot Xc \cdot Psc. \tag{3}$$

By definition,

$$Psg = Psc - Psb, \tag{4}$$

and

$$Png = Pnc - Pnb. \tag{5}$$

At equilibrium, world (DC plus LDC) quantities demanded and supplied of the processed good are equal. With quantity units defined so that one unit of processing and one unit of the primary good are required per unit of the processed good, at equilibrium world quantities supplied of all three are equal. Thus equation (6) defines Q as world quantity demanded of the processed good and equations (7) and (8) express the equilibrium conditions:

$$Q = Dnc + Dsc \tag{6}$$

$$Q = Snb + Ssb \tag{7}$$

$$Q = Sng + Ssg \tag{8}$$

The complete model consists of the equilibrium conditions (7) and (8), the definitions (4), (5), (6), the price equations (2) and (3), two demand functions (for the processed good in DC and LDC), and four supply functions (of processing and of primary goods from both DC and LDC). The corresponding variables are Pnb, Pnc, Png, Psb, Psc, Psg, and their corresponding Q's, plus total quantity, Q, defined in equation (6).

When we substitute the demand and supply functions into (6), (7), and (8), and then use equations (2), (3), (4), and (5) to eliminate Pnb, Png, and Pnc, we can express the model as

$$Q = Dnc(Tc \cdot Xc \cdot Psc) + Dsc(Psc) \tag{9}$$

$$Q = Snb(Tb \cdot Xb \cdot Psb) + Ssb(Psb) \tag{10}$$

$$Q = Sng(Tc \cdot Xc \cdot Psc - Tb \cdot Xb \cdot Psb) + Ssg(Psc - Psb). \tag{11}$$

Conceptually, these three equations can be solved for equilibrium value of Q, Psb, and Psc. Substitution into (2), (3), (4), and (5) gives equilibrium values for the other price variables. Substitution of the prices into the demand and supply functions determines quantities consumed (of the finished good) and produced (of primary goods and of processing) in the DC and the LDC.

The LDCs export both the final and intermediate goods to the DCs. Let E represent quantity of exports and W value of exports. The price received by the exporting LDC includes the export tax, so the value of exports may be written

$$W = Wb + Wc = Eb \cdot Psb \cdot Xb + Ec \cdot Psc \cdot Xc. \tag{12}$$

IV. Comparative Statics

The following definitions will be used to simplify the expressions for the effects on the endogenous variables of changes of the policy parameters. (Asterisked variables represent proportional changes.)

$$\Gamma = Rnc \cdot \Gamma n + Rsc \cdot \Gamma s \tag{13}$$

$$\Phi b = Rnb \cdot \Phi nb + Rsb \cdot \Phi sb \tag{14}$$

$$\Phi g = Rng \cdot \Phi ng + Rsg \cdot \Phi sg \tag{15}$$

$$Z_c^* = T_c^* + X_c^* \tag{16}$$

$$Z_b^* = T_b^* + X_b^*. \tag{17}$$

In addition, we evaluate the expressions at the free trade equilibrium, that is, at the point at which $Tc = Xc = Tb = Xb = 0$. At this point A, the reciprocal of the value-added coefficient, is the same when measured in the exporting country (LDC) or in the importing country, that is,

$$A = As = An. \tag{18}$$

After totally differentiating, taking proportional changes, and substituting from (12) through (17),

$$Q^* = \Gamma \cdot P_{sc}^* + Rnc \cdot \Gamma n \cdot Z_c^* \tag{19}$$

$$Q^* = \Phi b \cdot P_{sb}^* + Rnb \cdot \Phi nb \cdot Z_b^* \tag{20}$$

$$Q^* = A \cdot \Phi g \cdot P_{sc}^* - (A - 1) \cdot \Phi g \cdot P_{sb}^* + A \cdot Rng \cdot \Phi ng \cdot Z_c^* \\ - (A - 1) \cdot Rng \cdot \Phi ng \cdot Z_b^*. \tag{21}$$

From (2) and (3) we know that

$$P_{nb}^* = P_{sb}^* + Z_b^* \tag{22}$$

$$P_{nc}^* = P_{sc}^* + Z_c^*. \tag{23}$$

Solution

When we solve (19)–(21) simultaneously, and substitute into (22) and (23), we obtain

$$Q^* = Z_c^* \cdot [\Phi ng Rng A \Gamma s Rsc - \Phi sg Rsg A \Gamma n Rnc] \Phi b / den \\ + Z_b^* \cdot [\Phi nb Rnb \Phi sg Rsg (A - 1) - \Phi sb Rsb \Phi ng Rng (A - 1)] \Gamma / den \tag{24}$$

$$P_{sc}^* = Z_c^* \cdot [\Phi b (-\Gamma n Rnc + \Phi ng Rng A) - \Phi g (A - 1) \Gamma n Rnc] / den \\ + Z_b^* \cdot [\Phi nb Rnb \Phi sg Rsg (A - 1) - \Phi sb Rsb \Phi ng Rng (A - 1)] / den \tag{25}$$

PROCESSING OF PRIMARY COMMODITIES 565

$$P_{sb}^* = Z_c^* \cdot [\Phi ngRngA\Gamma sRsc - \Phi sgRsgA\Gamma nRnc]/den$$
$$+ Z_b^* \cdot [-\Gamma(\Phi nbRnb + \Phi ngRng(A-1) + \Phi gA\,\Phi nbRnb]/den \qquad (26)$$

$$P_{nc}^* = Z_c^* \cdot [\Phi b(\Gamma sRsc - \Phi sgRsgA) + \Phi g(A-1)\Gamma sRsc]/den$$
$$+ Z_b^* \cdot [\Phi nbRnb\Phi sgRsg(A-1) - \Phi sbRsb\Phi ngRng(A-1)]/den \qquad (27)$$

$$P_{nb}^* = Z_c^* \cdot [\Phi ngRngA\Gamma sRsc - \Phi sgRsgA\Gamma nRnc]/den$$
$$+ Z_b^* \cdot [\Gamma(\Phi sbRsb + \Phi sgRsg(A-1) - \Phi gA\Phi sbRsb]/den \qquad (28)$$

where $den = -\Phi b\Phi gA + \Gamma\Phi g(A-1) + \Gamma\Phi b$.

Analogous expressions for P_{sg}^* and P_{ng}^* can be obtained by recalling that $Psg = Psc - Psb$ and $Png = Pnc - Pnb$, which implies

$$P_{sg}^* = A \cdot P_{sc}^* - (A-1) \cdot P_{sb}^* \qquad (29)$$

$$P_{ng}^* = A \cdot P_{nc}^* - (A-1) \cdot P_{nb}^*. \qquad (30)$$

Evaluation

We assume that supply curves slope upward (all Φ's positive) and demand curves slope downward (Γ's negative). (Note that *den* therefore is negative.) Downward-sloping demand curves imply that the sign of the effects on quantity consumed in the DCs and the LDCs will be the opposite of the sign of the effects on Pnc and Psc, respectively. Also, upward-sloping supply curves imply that the sign of the effects on output of the primary good or on the level of processing in each country will be the same as the sign of the effect on the appropriate price.

Prices and Quantities

As intuition suggests, export taxes and tariffs on the processed good (Zc) raise its price in the importing and lower its price in the exporting countries. Similarly, the export taxes and tariffs on the primary good (Zb) raise its price in the importing DCs and lower its price in the exporting LDCs. Also, taxes on international sales of the processed good protect processing in importing countries and retard it in exporting countries, while trade taxes on the primary good have the opposite effect.

The cross-effects and the effects on total consumption do not fall into place so readily. Intuitively, one would reason that a tax on international trade in the finished good would reduce its consumption. This would reduce (derived) demand for the primary good, forcing down its price, both in the LDCs and the DCs.[2] Likewise, we would expect a trade tax on the primary good to raise the overall cost and hence reduce consumption of the finished good. With less consumption of the finished good, demand for and hence the rate of return to processing are depressed.

While a priori knowledge suggests that these intuitive notions will probably be correct, it does not exclude the possibility of paradoxical results. Upon closer examination of equations (24), (26), and (28), we note that each of $\partial Q/\partial Zc$, $\partial Psb/\partial Zc$, and $\partial Pnb/\partial Zc$ will be negative, when

$$|\Phi sgRsgA\Gamma nRnc| > |\Phi ngRngA\Gamma sRsc|, \tag{31}$$

zero when the two terms are equal, and positive when the inequality is reversed. Thus the cross-effects will be paradoxical ($\partial Psb/\partial Zc$ and $\partial Pnb/\partial Zc$ positive) only when the consumption effect is paradoxical ($\partial Q/\partial Zc$ is positive).

While the signs of the elasticities do not assure that inequality (31) will hold, there is reason to presume that it will. As the DCs are importers of the processed good, not all of DC consumption is processed in the DCs, that is, $Sng/Dn < 1$. In the exporting LDCs, all of local consumption plus some goods for export are processed at home, that is, $Ssg/Dsc > 1$. From this we have $Dnc/Sng > Dsc/Ssg$ or $Dnc/Q \cdot Ssg/Q > Dsc/Q \cdot Sng/Q$, which means that $Rnc \cdot Rsg > Rsc \cdot Rng$. Thus, unless there is some basis for arguing that the elasticity of demand for the finished good is higher and/or the elasticity of supply of the processing activity is lower in LDCs than in DCs, the presumption would be that trade taxes on the finished good reduce total consumption and depress the price and output of the primary good in both the exporting and the importing country.

Similarly, the effect of primary-good trade taxes on total consumption "should" be negative and on the price of the finished good "should" be positive. Equations (24), (25), and (27) indicate that this will be the case if

$$\Phi sbRsb\Phi ngRng(A-1) > \Phi nbRnb\Phi sgRsg(A-1). \tag{32}$$

That LDCs export the primary good implies $Rng \cdot Rsb > Rsg \cdot Rnb$, hence, inequality (32) will hold unless the elasticity of supply of the primary good is considerably lower and/or the elasticity of supply of processing considerably higher in LDCs than in DCs.

---

[2] From eq. (2) we know that changing the trade tax on the finished good will have the same proportionate effect on Pnb as on Psb.

Value of LDC Exports

Equation (12), which specifies the value of LDC export receipts, can be rewritten as

$$W = (Ssb - Ssg)PsbXb + (Ssg - Dsc)PscXc. \tag{33}$$

The intention of an LDC export tax on a primary good is to increase earnings from raw materials exports by exploiting monopsony power in the market for the primary good and/or to earn more on processed exports by shifting foreign demand to processed forms of the good. While the results reported in table 2 indicate that $PsbXb$ will rise when Xb is imposed, the quantity exported will decline, especially if Φnb is large. Looking at the second term of the right side of equation (33), we note that while Xb will cause Ssg to increase, it could cause Psc to fall and Dsc to rise, and hence could reduce the value of exports of the finished good. Thus, while an export tax on the primary good will likely increase LDC export receipts, the perverse result is possible.

Similar analysis indicates that an export tax on the finished good might reduce LDC export earnings, both on exports of the finished and/or on exports of the primary good. Likewise import tariffs would probably, but not necessarily, reduce LDC export revenue.

V. Estimated Effects

Data

The calculation of the impact of export taxes and tariffs requires values for input coefficients, share parameters, and elasticities.[3] In addition, the trade and production effects use 1973 trade flows (OECD 1973) and production levels (FAO 1976) as the base. The share parameters are shares of production and consumption of the LDCs and DCs with these two comprising the world (i.e., the centrally planned bloc is excluded). The elasticity terms were in part based on estimates of commodity experts and in part are simply educated guesses. Estimated changes are expressed as proportions of the "with tariffs, with export taxes" values. The formulas used to make the

---

[3] We are indebted to A. J. Yeats for providing the input coefficients for all products except soluble coffee and cocoa butter. For these two, the coefficients were derived from the conversion factors used by the coffee and cocoa agreements. The share parameters were obtained from the FAO, which provided figures on production and consumption of the raw material. For the other stages of the process, the share parameters were obtained by adding or deducting trade flows from the raw-material figures. The elasticity estimates are $\Phi nb = \Phi sb = 0.5$; $\Phi sg = 10$ $\Phi ng = 1$; $\Gamma s = \Gamma n = 0.4$ for cocoa and copra; $\Gamma s = \Gamma n = 0.6$ for rubber, wood, leather, and soluble coffee; $\Gamma s = \Gamma n = 1$ for cotton and wool. Sensitivity analysis is reported in the Appendix.

TABLE 2

SUMMARY OF COMPARATIVE STATICS RESULTS

POLICY PARAMETER	VARIABLES					
	∂Pnc	∂Psc	∂Pnb	∂Psb	∂Png	∂Psg
∂Zc	+	−	Uncertain but probably negative*	Uncertain but probably negative*	+	−
∂Zb	Uncertain but probably positive†	Uncertain but probably positive†	+	−	−	+

* $\partial Pnb/\partial Zc$ and $\partial Psb/\partial Zc$ will have the same sign.
† $\partial Pnc/\partial Zb$ and $\partial Psc/\partial Zb$ will have the same sign.

calculations were similar to equations (24)–(30) but did not reflect the simplifying assumption that T's and X's were initially zero.

Results

Several experiments were performed: the DC import taxes were removed while holding the LDC export taxes constant, the export taxes were removed while holding the import taxes constant, and both trade taxes were eliminated simultaneously. The effects on production, consumption, and trade are presented in tables 3, 4, and 5. The sensitivity analysis reported in the Appendix shows that the results are quite robust with respect to variations in supply and demand elasticities.

The DC Tariffs

The DC tariffs are intended to protect DC processors, and removal of these tariffs would increase processing in the LDCs and reduce it in the DCs (table 3). Liberalization entails increased final consumption in the north, lower consumption in the south, but increased consumption overall and hence increased raw material production for both "countries." The "shifting" of processing from DCs to LDCs is much more pronounced than is the "market-expansion" effect. The LDC export earnings would increase especially sharply on cotton, wool, and leather, and over the eight commodities would increase by about 16 percent.

The LDC Export Taxes

Repeal of the LDC export taxes alone would retard LDC processing of each of the commodities except leather, in which case the export-tax escalation is not steep enough to protect leather tanning[4] (table 4).

Elimination of export taxes has the expected result of increasing LDC raw-material production and lowering DC raw-material production. For some commodities, liberalization causes world final consumption to decline (cotton, wool, and wood).[5] In most cases, LDC foreign exchange receipts fall after export-tax elimination.

Export and Import Taxes

Estimates presented in table 5 indicate that if LDC export and DC import taxes were simultaneously eliminated LDC processing of six of

[4] The export-tax escalation required to protect LDC value added depends on the input coefficient of the raw material in the finished good.
[5] The theoretical possibility of such counterintuitive results was discussed in Sec. III.

TABLE 3

CONSUMPTION, PRODUCTION, AND TRADE EFFECTS OF REMOVING DC TARIFFS

COMMODITY*	FINAL CONSUMPTION (% Change)			PRIMARY PRODUCTION (% Change)		PROCESSING (% Change)		LDC EXPORT REVENUE	
	World (LDC + DC)	LDC	DC	LDC	DC	LDC	DC	Value†	(% Change)
Copra	1.1	−.8	2.8	1.1	‡	16.9	−43.9	24.8	6.2
Rubber	1.7	−1.8	2.5	1.7	‡	28.1	−5.7	74.8	6.3
Cocoa	1.7	−1.5	2.1	1.7	‡	52.0	−16.0	103.6	11.3
Cotton	2.0	−3.5	5.5	2.1	1.8	23.1	−17.4	803.9	42.3
Wool	2.3	−6.5	3.7	2.8	2.2	75.6	−11.6	73.2	36.6
Leather	1.2	−1.2	2.6	1.2	1.2	17.9	−11.0	320.4	39.6
Wood	.1	−.5	.2	.1	.1	15.6	−1.0	129.0	4.0
Coffee	1.6	−3.3	1.7	1.6	‡	79.5	−5.2	85.8	6.9
Total§	.7	−2.2	1.2	1.3	.4	23.0	−3.8	1,615.5	16.3

* See table 1 for names of the primary and processed varieties.
† $ millions, 1973 base.
‡ No primary production in developed countries.
§ Except for the "value" column, these are averages of the product-by-product figures weighted by values of the variables listed in that row.

TABLE 4

CONSUMPTION, PRODUCTION, AND TRADE EFFECTS OF REMOVING DC EXPORT TAXES

COMMODITY*	FINAL CONSUMPTION (% Change)			PRIMARY PRODUCTION (% Change)		PROCESSING (% Change)		LDC EXPORT REVENUE	
	World (LDC + DC)	LDC	DC	LDC	DC	LDC	DC	Value†	(% Change)
Copra	.5	−.3	1.2	.5	‡	−.6	3.5	−11.0	−2.7
Rubber	.1	.1	.1	.1	‡	−2.8	.9	−64.3	−5.4
Cocoa	1.5	−.3	1.8	1.5	‡	−53.8	21.0	−178.9	−19.4
Cotton	−.7	−.7	−.7	1.1	−4.2	−15.0	12.4	−274.1	−14.4
Wool	−1.0	−1.0	−1.0	2.9	−2.3	−42.0	6.8	−7.4	−3.7
Leather	.8	−3.6	3.4	5.6	−3.9	7.0	−3.7	275.2	34.0
Wood	−.1	−2.3	.0	4.3	−.8	−29.2	2.1	29.9	.9
Coffee	2.8	−.6	2.9	2.8	‡	−42.0	6.7	−182.2	−14.7
Total§	.0	−1.6	.3	2.7	−1.3	−14.7	2.9	−412.7	−4.2

* See table 1 for names of the primary and processed varieties.
† $ millions, 1973 base.
‡ No primary production in developed countries.
§ Except for the "value" column, these are averages of the product-by-product figures weighted by values of the variables listed in that row.

57 [1]

TABLE 5

CONSUMPTION, PRODUCTION, AND TRADE EFFECTS OF REMOVING DC TARIFFS AND LDC EXPORT TAXES

COMMODITY*	FINAL CONSUMPTION (% Change)			PRIMARY PRODUCTION (% Change)		PROCESSING (% Change)		LDC EXPORT REVENUE	
	World (LDC + DC)	LDC	DC	LDC	DC	LDC	DC	Value†	(% Change)
Copra	1.5	-1.1	4.1	1.5	‡	16.3	-40.4	13.8	3.5
Rubber	1.9	-1.6	2.6	1.9	‡	25.4	-4.8	10.4	.9
Cocoa	3.2	-1.9	3.9	3.2	‡	-1.8	4.9	-75.3	-8.2
Cotton	1.3	-4.2	4.8	3.3	-2.4	8.1	-5.0	529.9	27.9
Wool	1.3	-7.6	2.6	5.7	-.2	33.6	-4.9	65.9	32.9
Leather	1.9	-4.8	6.1	6.8	-2.7	24.9	-14.7	595.5	73.5
Wood	.0	-2.8	.2	4.4	-.7	-13.6	1.1	158.9	4.9
Coffee	4.4	-3.8	4.5	4.4	‡	37.5	1.5	-96.4	-7.8
Total§	.7	-3.8	1.5	4.0	-.9	8.3	-.9	1,202.8	12.1

* See table 1 for names of the primary and processed varieties.
† $ millions, 1973 base.
‡ No primary production in developed countries.
§ Except for the "value" column, these are averages of the product-by-product figures weighted by values of the variables listed in that row.

the eight commodities would increase, while DC processing of five of the eight would decline. The striking declines of DC processing are in copra and leather—declines of 40 and 15 percent, respectively. But the value added in DC processing of hides and copra is unimportant relative to the processing of other commodities; hence, the aggregate result is a decline of processing in DCs of less than 1 percent. On the plus side, processing in the LDCs would increase by more than 8 percent—a substantially larger percentage increase than the less than 1 percent decline in the DCs. This is in part because LDC processing starts from a lower base (less than one-quarter of DC processing activity), so that a given shift of processing volume from north to south generates a small percentage loss in the DCs and a large percentage increase in the LDCs. More important, liberalization increases total world final consumption and, hence, the size of the processing pie. The DC loss of processing accounts for less than half of the LDC increase—the larger part coming from the expansion of the wor.d processing pie. If, instead, tariffs were unilaterally lowered, three-fourths of the LDC processing gain is a transfer from the DCs with only one-fourth due to expansion of the market.

Liberalization of export taxes and tariffs also stimulates raw-material production in the LDCs and retards it in the DCs.[6] As is the case for processing, the LDC gain exceeds the DC loss. The DCs do not produce four of the eight raw materials.

The 8 percent increase in the level of processing in the LDCs amounts, at 1973 prices and based on 1973 levels of activity, to about $1.2 billion. On the same basis, the 4 percent increase of production in the LDCs of these primary products comes to about $0.9 billion. Because "world" production and processing of commodities rise, the corresponding declines in the DCs are about one-third as large as the volume increases in the LDCs.

The effect of liberalization on LDC export earnings is not positive for all commodities, but overall the estimated increase is in excess of $1 billion. As policy alternatives to increase LDC export earnings go, this is a significant impact. Tariff preferences, by comparison, are estimated to have increased LDC exports (including trade diverted from DCs) by less than $500 million—and even under the most optimistic scenario of a Generalized System of Preferences (GSP) without value limits and with expanded product, coverage would expand LDC export earnings (again including exports diverted from DCs) by only $772 million (Baldwin and Murray 1977, p. 37).

The large increase in trade which would result from the liberaliza-

---

[6] Thus, the net effect of the LDC export and DC import taxes combined is to protect processing *and* primary production in the DCs.

tion considered here reflects the importance of primary and processed commodities in north-south trade and the high levels of tariffs
and export taxes. Furthermore, we have considered only eight commodities.[7] When extended to others, particularly minerals such as
phosphates and metals, the trade benefits would be much larger.

VI. Conclusion: The Case for Liberalization

The export taxes in the developing countries and the import taxes in
the developed countries are designed to protect local processors of
primary commodities. For the eight-commodity sample studied here,
the export and import taxes together have the effect of slightly increasing DC processing activity, but the main effect is to reduce the
size of the processing pie. In contrast to the effects of unilateral
reduction by the DCs of their import taxes, simultaneous elimination
of LDC export taxes and DC tariffs involves a minimal reduction of
DC processing activity and is hence more likely to be acceptable to DC
policymakers.

Such a reciprocal liberalization would involve gains to both north
and south. The gains to the DCs accrue in the form of lower consumer prices and increased consumption. For the LDCs, in addition
to increased processing, liberalization entails greater primary production and expanded foreign exchange receipts.

While the increases of the level of LDC processing and of export
earnings would be very attractive to LDC policymakers, the policy
move examined here would also reduce LDC consumption of processed goods and eliminate the revenue LDC governments collect
through export taxes. The decline of LDC consumption is not likely
to be weighted very heavily by most LDC governments relative to the
processing gain and increased foreign exchange receipts. But their
fiscal systems may not be sufficiently developed to provide them with
alternative sources of revenue. If this is a serious problem, negotiations might focus on other protective devices employed by LDCs.

Commodity trade, under steady multilateral rules and in open,
competitive markets, could provide LDCs with the benefits of economic efficiency while also advancing their objectives of national
self-determination and the avoidance of playing a dependent's role in
international relations (Diaz-Alejandro 1975, p. 225). More generally,
the liberalization of commodity trade is only one avenue of mutual
interest that developed and developing countries might explore. The
effects of the Dillon and Kennedy Rounds of tariff reductions dem-

[7] The eight, including their processed forms, accounted for 11.5 percent of LDC
export value in 1973.

TABLE A1

ESTIMATES OF EFFECTS OF REMOVING LDC EXPORT TAXES AND DC TARIFFS WITH VARIOUS SUPPLY AND DEMAND ELASTICITY VALUES

Scenario	Final Consumption (% Change)			Primary Production (% Change)		Processing (% Change)		LDC Export Revenue	
	World (LDC & DC)	LDC	DC	LDC	DC	LDC	DC	Value*	% Change
Base case†	.7	−3.8	1.5	4.0	−.9	8.3	−.9	1,202.8	12.1
$\Phi_{sg} = \Phi_{ng} = 1$‡	.4	−4.5	1.2	3.5	−1.0	4.2	−.3	915.8	9.2
Γ_{nc} & Γ_{sc} halved	.4	−1.7	.8	3.5	−1.0	7.4	−1.0	722.7	7.3
Γ_{nc} & Γ_{sc} doubled	.9	−8.3	2.5	4.6	−.8	9.4	−.8	2,003.4	20.2
$\Phi_{sb} = \Phi_{nb} = .3$	.5	−4.0	1.3	2.7	−.5	7.7	−.9	1,079.9	10.9
$\Phi_{sb} = \Phi_{nb} = .8$	.8	−3.5	1.6	5.8	−1.6	8.9	−.9	1,428.8	14.4

* $ millions, 1973 base.

† Base case $\Phi_{nb} = \Phi_{sb} = 0.5$, $\Phi_{ng} = 1$, $\Phi_{sg} = 10$, $\Gamma_c = 1$ (cotton, wool), $\Gamma_c = 0.6$ (coffee, rubber, leather, wood), $\Gamma_c = 0.4$ (cocoa, copra).

‡ Each scenario consists of varying the listed elasticities only, holding the others at their base case value.

onstrate that LDCs have benefited from trade liberalization aimed primarily at interdeveloped country trade (Finger 1974, 1976a). A conscious effort to locate and implement policies of mutual benefit to DCs and LDCs could make a far more important contribution to LDC development than futile demands for unilateral concessions. Substantive LDC involvement in multilateral negotiations can play a part in creating a more stable and less asymmetrical international economic order.

Appendix

Sensitivity Analysis of Elasticity Values

The parameter values on which the results in the text are based are those which we feel are the "central tendencies" of available estimates. Our primary source of information on the parameter values was the opinion of World Bank commodities experts and U.S. Treasury commodity desk officers. Several estimates of elasticities of primary product supply and of demand for the processed good are available, but we found no direct estimates of the elasticity of the supply of processing. Hence values for this parameter are more a matter of expert opinion.

Table A1 presents the effects of varying the supply and demand elasticities on the main conclusions of the paper. The rows of table A1 correspond to the last row of table 5, that is, they reveal the effects of removing both LDC export taxes and DC tariffs on all eight commodities. Five variations from the base case are reported. (1) The LDC processing supply elasticity is lowered from 10 to 1 (i.e., set equal to the DC processing supply elasticity), (2) the demand elasticities are halved, (3) the demand elasticities are doubled, (4) the common primary supply elasticity is lowered from 0.5 to 0.3, (5) the primary supply elasticity is raised to 0.8.

The results indicate that the main conclusions of the paper are quite robust. In all cases, simultaneous elimination of trade taxes increases the percentage rate of growth of LDC processing while causing a much smaller percentage decline in DC processing.

Halving the demand elasticities reduces the trade gains considerably, to $723 million, but even this figure exceeds, by over $200 million, Baldwin's and Murray's estimate of the trade expansion of GSP.

The other results are also intact. In each case, world final consumption increases, LDC consumption decreases, DC consumption increases, LDC primary production increases, and DC primary production decreases as a result of liberalization.

References

Balassa, Bela. "The Structure of Protection in Industrial Countries and Its Effects on the Exports of Processed Goods from the Developing Countries." In *Kennedy Round Estimated Effects on Tariff Barriers*, by Secretary General, UNCTAD. New York: United Nations, 1968.

Baldwin, R. E., and Murray, T. "MFN Tariff Reductions and Developing Country Trade Benefits under the GSP." *Econ. J.* 87 (March 1977): 30–46.

Diaz-Alejandro, Carlos F. "North-South Relations: The Economic Component." In *World Politics and International Economics*, edited by C. Fred Bergsten and Lawrence B. Krause. Washington: Brookings Inst., 1975.

Finger, J. M. "GATT Tariff Concessions and the Exports of Developing Countries." *Econ. J.* 84 (September 1974): 566–75.

―――. "Effects of the Kennedy Round Tariff Concessions on the Exports of Developing Countries." *Econ. J.* 86 (March 1976): 87–95. (*a*)

―――. "Trade and Domestic Effects of the Offshore Assembly Provision in the U.S. Tariff." *A.E.R.* 66 (September 1976): 598–611. (*b*)

Organization for Economic Cooperation and Development (OECD). *Statistics of Foreign Trade, Trade by Commodities, Market Summaries: Imports.* Ser. C. Paris: OECD, 1973.

United Nations Food and Agriculture Organization (FAO). *Commodity Review and Outlook.* Rome: United Nations, 1976.

United States Government. "Export Taxes." An interagency report on export restrictions prepared for submission to the GATT as a background paper for the ongoing Tokyo Round multilateral trade negotiations, pt. 4, sec. G. Mimeographed. Washington: Dept. Treasury, 1976.

Yeats, A. J. "Effective Tariff Protection in the United States, the European Economic Community, and Japan." *Q. Rev. Econ. and Bus.* 14 (Summer 1974): 41–50.

―――. "Effective Protection for Processed Agricultural Commodities: A Comparison of Industrial Countries." *J. Econ. and Bus.* 29 (Fall 1976): 31–39.

[6]

The Compensatory Finance Facility and Export Instability

J. M. FINGER and DEAN A. DEROSA

A FREQUENTLY heard complaint about the "old" economic order is that the export receipts of many developing countries are unstable, and that this instability involves significant economic costs.[1] Extensive negotiations have taken place about commodity agreements which might reduce this instability and about a common fund to finance buffer stocks for these agreements, but the major instrument now in place which deals directly with this problem is the International Monetary Fund's Compensatory Finance Facility (the CFF). Since 1977, outstanding drawings from the CFF have continuously exceeded four billion dollars. By comparison, no more than $500m. is likely to be contributed to the Common Fund, and buffer stock for commodity agreements now in existence or likely to be negotiated soon will have maximum possible sizes of about $500m. each for tin and natural rubber, and $700m. for cocoa.

The concept behind the CFF is simple—the facility will lend to countries in years in which their export receipts are "below trend," and the countries will repay when their receipts are above trend. If year-to-year disparities between trend values and actual values are correctly measured, a participating country's export receipts net of CFF transactions will be more stable than its "unadjusted" export receipts.

In practice, things are not so simple. To determine when and by how much a country's export receipts are "in shortfall" (i.e. below trend) the IMF compares the "shortfall year's" export receipts with average receipts over the five year period centered on the shortfall year. In order to make CFF funds available in or soon after the shortfall

[1] This paper will not go into the debate over the costs of export instability and its effect on economic growth. For recent reviews see papers by Stephen J. T. Turnofsky, Alexander A. Saris and Lance Taylor, Gordon W. Smith, and Edwin Burmeister, in Part II of F. Gerard Adams and Sonia A. Klein (eds.). *Stabilizing World Commodity Markets*, (D. C. Health Lexington Books) 1978, and M. E. Kreinin and J. M. Finger, "A Critical Survey of the New International Economic Order," *Journal of World Trade Law*, Vol. 10, No. 6 (Nov/Dec 1976), pp. 493–512.

Keith H. Hall, our research assistant, contributed much to this paper. Views expressed here are those of the authors, and should not be attributed to their employer, the U.S. Treasury Department.

year, it is thus necessary to forecast export receipts two years into the future. It is often also necessary to "estimate" current period receipts, or at best, to use preliminary data.

Thus a major part of the task of operating the CFF is the forecasting of export receipts, and this must be done for countries whose export receipts are the most difficult to forecast—those with high degrees of export instability. To the extent that such forecasts are incorrect, the CFF would lend the wrong amounts at the wrong times, and thus it is possible that CFF transactions have not stabilized export receipts.

When we began this study, our objectives were first to measure the impact of the CFF on the *stability* of participating countries' export receipts, and then to compare the benefits which might have resulted from this stabilization with the costs of providing that service. We found, however, in the first part of our study, that the CFF has not stabilized export receipts, and hence the second part of the study became an attempt to explain why there has been no export stabilization rather than to measure its costs and benefits.

Method and Data

Through January 1979, seventy-one countries have made purchases from the CFF. We took annual export data for each of these countries from the IMF's *International Financial Statistics*. For most of them the data covered 1961 through 1977. From the same source, we obtained year-by-year data for each country's drawings from and repayments to the CFF.

To measure instability, we first determined the trend line of export receipts by regressing the natural logarithm of export receipts against time. The standard error of this regression measures the deviation of the year-to-year figures from their trend values, and this statistic then is the measure of instability we have used. The instability calculation was made for export receipts without the CFF, and for export receipts plus (or minus) CFF transactions, and the difference in the instability index from the "without CFF" to the "with CFF" case measures the impact of the CFF on export instability.

Effect on Export Instability

In performing the instability calculations, CFF transactions were treated several different ways, but as Table 1 shows, no matter how they were handled, their effect on export instability was very slight. In our first calculations we added CFF borrowing to export receipts in the year in which the borrowed funds were actually received, and treated repayments similarly. In this case, we found CFF transactions have the perverse effect of increasing export instability for thirty-one of the sixty-two developing countries which have used the facility. (Likewise for five

TABLE 1

EFFECT OF COMPENSATORY FINANCE FACILITY TRANSACTIONS ON THE EXPORT INSTABILITY OF COUNTRIES WHICH HAVE USED THE FACILITY, 1963–1977 AND 1974–1977

(average percentage reduction[a] of the export instability index[b])

Country group and number of user countries	CFF purchases and repayments, 1963–1977		CFF purchases only 1963–1977		Distributed purchases only 1974–1977
	Undistributed purchases	Distributed purchases	Undistributed purchases	Distributed purchases	
	(1)	(2)	(3)	(4)	(5)
Developing countries (62)	−0·1	1·2	0·2	1·5	0·5
Developed countries (9)	−0·3	−0·8	−0·1	−0·6	−4·2
All countries (71)	−0·1	0·5	0·1	0·7	−1·1

[a] Cross country average changes weighted by each country's export receipts.
[b] See text for explanation as to how instability was measured.
[c] For exceptions to years of coverage, see Annex Table, available from the authors.

of nine developed country users.) The impact, however, was almost always minimal. For only eight LDC users (and for no DC user), did CFF transactions change export instability by as much as 5 per cent, and five of these eight "large" changes were in the wrong direction—toward more instability.[2] Averaged across users the impact was virtually nil—a net *increase* of instability of 0·1 per cent.

POSSIBLE EXPLANATIONS FOR MINIMAL EFFECTS

Discussions with persons familiar with the workings of the CFF suggested several possible explanations for its minimal impact on export instability. One of these is the administrative time lag between the occurrence of an export shortfall and the receipt of the associated CFF borrowing. Another is the schedule by which repayments are made. Finally, often mentioned is the IMF rule which limits the magnitude of CFF purchases, and hence the facility's ability to allow drawings to match estimated shortfalls in every case.

Time Lags and Repayments Schedules

CFF loans are made for a maximum of five years—usually half the borrowed amount must be repaid after four years and the remaining half after five. A borrowing country may, if it chooses, repay the drawing sooner, say, if it finds its export receipts to be considerably above trend before the term of the drawing has expired. But, the interest rate on CFF borrowings is below the market rate, and many of the countries which have used the CFF have only limited access to private capital markets, hence countries do not often choose to repay CFF drawings early. This suggests that other considerations outweigh export stabilization in determining when CFF repayments will be made.

With these two factors in mind, we measured (a) the stabilizing effect CFF transactions would have had if drawings had actually been received during the shortfall period, and (b) the stabilizing effect of CFF borrowings only.

To eliminate the effect of the time lapse between the shortfall and receipt of the drawings, we treated each CFF drawing as if receipt of the borrowed money had been evenly distributed over the actual twelve month shortfall period, which usually did not correspond to a calendar year. For example, if a shortfall period included the last four months of 1976 and the first eight months of 1977, we treated the associated CFF borrowing as if 1/3 of it had been received in 1976 and 2/3 in 1977. Thus one actual or "undistributed" drawing sometimes was treated as two separate drawings in our "distributed" drawings series.

[2] Country-by-country figures are given in an Annex table, available on request from the authors.

Using distributed purchases, and excluding the effects of repayments, we found that for forty-six of the sixty-two LDC users of the CFF, CFF transactions reduced export instability. The changes were again small, with only twelve of sixty-two exceeding 5 per cent in absolute value.[3] Overall, the average reduction of export instability over the sixty-two LDC users was 1-1/2 per cent, and for the DC users the net effect was an *increase* of export instability (Table 1, Column 4). Thus even when we ignore both the effect of repayments and the effect of the time lag between shortfalls and drawings, the inescapable conclusion is that the CFF has had almost no effect on export instability.

Size of the Facility v. *Forecasting Difficulties*

Every revision of the CFF has increased the amount of money a country may borrow through this facility—from 25 per cent of the country's IMF quota in 1963 to 100 per cent under present rules. This movement toward larger limits on CFF drawings suggests that the facility might have had a stronger stabilizing effect if it had been allowed to lend larger amounts.

The remaining possible explanation for the minimal impact of the CFF on export instability is the difficulty of determining, *ex ante*, when a country is in export shortfall, and by how much. The data sample we have used covered 127 country-year instances in which the IMF found that a compensable shortfall existed. (Seventy-one countries were covered, but several of them had compensable shortfalls in more than one year, giving us a total of 127 country-year compensable shortfalls.) Hindsight, however, now allows us to determine that in only sixty-two of these 127 country-year cases were export receipts actually below their trend value (fifty-six of 110 for LDC users, six of seventeen for DC users). Thus, apart from measuring correctly the magnitude of a shortfall, available forecasting techniques *were wrong half the times* they signaled just the *existence of a shortfall* (see Table 2, top half). This observation points to the present state of the forecasting art, not the quota limits on drawings, as the explanation for the CFF's failure to stabilize export receipts.

To further distinguish between forecasting problems and quota limits as explanations for our findings, we performed two additional tests. First, we restricted our measurement of the effects of the CFF to drawings since the 1975 revision and expansion of the facility came into effect.[4] If the quota limits were a significant factor, then the CFF should have done a better job of stabilization after the 1975 revision

---

[3] Eleven of these were improvements.
[4] There are limits both to the amount which may be drawn in a 12-month period and to the total amount which a country may have outstanding from the facility at any time. In 1975 these limits were changed from 25 per cent in 12 months and 50 per cent outstanding to 50 per cent in 12 months and 75 per cent outstanding.

TABLE 2

ANALYSIS OF APPROPRIATENESS OF COMPENSATORY FINANCE FACILITY TIMING AND MAGNITUDES

	Based on value of drawings by			Based on number of drawings by		
	Developing countries	Developed countries	All countries	Developing countries	Developed countries	All countries
Percentage of drawings when exports were *above* trend values						
Based on drawings as actually received[a]	71	86	75	49	65	51
Based on drawings with administrative time lag assumed away[b]	63	89	70	60	78	63
Percentage of drawings at quota limit which exceeded actual shortfall						
Based on drawings as actually received[a]	57	76	62	47	42	46
Based on drawings with administrative time lag assumed away[b]	45	94	59	42	72	47

[a] Undistributed drawings.
[b] Distributed drawings.

than before. We found, however, the opposite to be true. In this case, thirty countries' exports were destabilized (twenty-five LDC, five DC) as compared with twenty-one countries (sixteen LDC, five DC) when we measured stabilization over the entire 1963–78 period. As the fifth column in Table 1 shows, the average results also worsened when we restricted our stabilization calculations to drawings made after the 1975 expansion of the CFF.

Our other test of the influence of quota limits was to tabulate those CFF drawings which were at the drawing country's quota limit, and then subdivide these cases into those drawings which exceeded the true shortfall amount (as determined by hindsight) and those which did not. We found, as reported in the bottom half of Table 2, that more than half (by value) of CFF drawings restricted by quota limits already exceeded the true shortfall amounts. Had these drawings been larger (i.e. had they not been constrained by the quota limits) net export receipts (including CFF drawings) would have been *further from*, not closer to the trend line. Thus, without the quota limits, the CFF would very likely have had an even weaker stabilization effect, not a stronger one.

CONCLUSIONS

Could the capital tied up in the CFF have been better used in some other way? If the only benefit the borrowing countries received was the effect on export instability, the answer is clearly "Yes". Ignoring the assumptions which had to be made to arrive at the figure, the largest improvement in export instability we observed was 1·5 per cent for LDC users of the CFF, and 0·7 per cent over all users. Even so, when we combine these figures with estimates of the effect export instability has on the amount of monetary reserves a country will hold, we find that the reduction of instability by the CFF reduces the demand or need for monetary reserves by about one dollar for each ten dollars "tied up" in the facility.[5]

[5] The volume of outstanding CFF loans has increased almost continuously since 1963, hence it is hard to determine a figure for the amount of capital "tied up" in the facility over the period we have studied. We took, for our comparison, the 1978 figure of over four billion SDR's. One might criticize the 0·7 per cent figure for the effect on export instability as too low, and assert that if the CFF had had four billion SDR's outstanding over its entire history it would have had a larger effect on export instability. But results in the fifth column of Table 1 show that the effect of the CFF on instability has been less in recent years when the volume of lending was large, than it was earlier.

Published studies of the demand for reserves, such as Jacob Frenkel ("International Reserves: Pegged Exchange Rates and Managed Float," in K. Brunner and A. H. Meltzer (eds.), *Carnegie-Rochester Conference Series on Public Policy*, Vol. 9, 1978) indicate that the elasticity of reserve demand with respect to export instability is between 0·5 and 0·8. Our own estimates, restricted to the sample of countries which have used the CFF, fell within this range. Taking the elasticity figure, the 0·7 per cent figure for the reduction of export instability, and multiplying by the combined reserve levels in 1977 of the countries covered (something less than 40 billion SDR's) we get an estimated reduction of reserve demand or "need" of about 225 million SDR's, or considerably less than 1/10 of the capital tied up in the provision of this service.

THE COMPENSATORY FINANCE FACILITY 21

Of course, export stabilization is not the sole benefit borrowing countries received from these drawings.[6] Though administrative procedures are different than for "regular" IMF drawings, in substance CFF drawings are not different—medium term hard currency loans are made available, conditional for CFF drawings in excess of 50 per cent of quota on the IMF being satisfied that the country has been cooperating in an effort to find appropriate solutions for its balance of payments difficulties. The results we have presented here do not suggest that CFF drawings do not serve to fulfil a *useful* function, but only that they do not serve a *unique* function. The justification for making CFF drawings available is the same as the justification for making general IMF drawings available.

The function then of the CFF is to increase the amounts which countries may borrow from the IMF. Under present rules, which limit CFF drawings to 100 per cent of a member's quota, with the second 50 per cent being "conditional", the CFF expands the country's overall borrowing limit by a half (from 200 per cent to 300 per cent of quota) and trebles the country's reserve, or unconditional drawing tranche (from 25 per cent to 75 per cent of quota).[7]

In criticism of this paper, several colleagues have argued that we have mistakenly assumed that the purpose of the CFF is to "help with the export instability problems of developing countries", whereas its true purpose is to "help developing countries with export instability problems". If, however, administration of the CFF were consistent with this interpretation, there would be no CFF! Instead, export instability would be given more weight in the determination of IMF quotas, i.e. the IMF quotas, which determine borrowing limits, would be larger than they are for countries with historically unstable exports. Alternatively, quotas could be left as they are, but quota limits on borrowing made larger for countries with historically unstable exports. Lending would be based on general IMF criteria, on balance of payments need and the usefulness of the borrowing in promoting adjustment, and there would be no attempt to coordinate borrowing with the occurrence of (what apparently are unforecastable) "shortfalls".

It would, however, be politically difficult to gain approval for changes in the IMF which would allow some countries to borrow more (relative to quotas) than others. Enlarging some countries' quotas would also encounter tough political going—the countries whose quotas were enlarged would have to subscribe corresponding larger amounts, and

---

[6] That countries choose to hold CFF drawings as long as possible and not to make repayments in such a way as to increase export stability indicates that they do not consider stability a particularly important benefit.

[7] Our results show that the determination of "short-falls" is a very inexact science. This means that there is considerable potential for administrative discretion, and hence that CFF drawings up to the first 50 per cent are potentially subject to conditionality.

the countries whose quotas were not enlarged would have their relative voting power in the IMF proportionally reduced. By creating the CFF, sufficient administrative complication is provided so that the IMF can lend additional amounts to countries which are, by general IMF standards, deserving, and yet do so without encountering the political problems which would be encountered if this increase lending were provided for directly. This may seem odd to some, but those of us who work in bureaucracies know that our function is often to provide our political masters a way to enjoy the fruits of things to which they are, in principle, opposed.

[7]

The Economics of Commodity Agreements:
A Skeptical View

JOSEPH M. FINGER*

There is again concern about commodity markets and sympathy in the developed world for "doing something" about their unsatisfactory state or

* Director, Office of Policy Research, U.S. Department of the Treasury.

condition. These markets are important sources of income for many people in developing countries, people who are less fortunate than we. Hence, the concern about commodity markets is an offshoot of a more general concern about the plight of people in the developing countries. I share this concern, but I do not think that negotiating a series of commodity agreements along the lines proposed in the UNCTAD Secretariat's integrated program necessarily follows.

This, however, does not imply that I differ with the U.S. Government's willingness to discuss commodity agreements or financing arrangements for them. The Third World has brought up these subjects, and we could hardly maintain constructive contact with these countries by refusing to discuss them. But in my view, the UNCTAD Secretariat has baited the trap with a picture of cheese and we are now busily trying to find a picture of a mouse to push in.

The issue of commodity agreements can be separated into three general questions: How much would they cost? Would they work? If the proposed commodity agreements worked, what good would they do and could the money be better spent elsewhere? I will address primarily the first two questions.

In theory, the proposed commodity agreements would be more than expressions of concern; they would establish effective economic instruments the objectives of which would be to stabilize fluctuations in market prices and to transfer resources from industrial country consumers by maintaining prices at levels above the average that the free market would establish.

Two instruments would be established. The first is buffer stocks, which would buy as the market fell, and sell as it rose, thereby mitigating both upward and downward price movements. If buffer stocks, over the long run, bought as much as they sold and were not continuously provided with more money, they might stabilize price, but they would not change its average level. The second instrument is supply or export controls which, by restricting market supply, could prevent price declines. If "disastrous" price declines were so eliminated, producers that otherwise would shut down completely might still be in business when demand recovers. If so, their capacity would reduce the sharpness of the price upswing as demand picked up. If this should happen, and if the timing of export controls were correct, supply controls might reduce price fluctuations as well as raise the average level of prices.

How Much Would Buffer Stocks Cost?

Of current commodity agreements, only the tin agreement has operated a buffer stock. Econometric evaluations agree that the tin buffer stock has had little, if any, effect on the stability or the level of the price of tin. Further, these studies conclude that the buffer stock has been much too small to stabilize price effectively. Large-scale simulations of the world tin market indicate that to have kept price movements over 1956-73 to within ±15% per year, a buffer stock of some 120,000 metric tons, worth over $1 billion at present low prices, would have been necessary. By contrast, the tin agreement buffer stock has never reached 20,000 metric tons.

Simulations of the world copper market on a basis comparable to this analysis of the tin market also indicate that buffer stocks would have to be much larger than has been previously supposed. Such research indicates that to maintain price movements within the range ±15% per year over the period 1956-73, a copper buffer stock of nearly 4 million metric tons, worth well over $6 billion at present depressed prices, would have been necessary. These results suggest that buffer stocks for tin and copper alone would require some $9 billion, which is considerably more than the $3 billion to $6 billion proposed by the UNCTAD Secretariat to provide buffer stocks for ten to eighteen commodities.

Other studies have produced smaller estimates. Jere Behrman, in an extensive study of the UNCTAD Secretariat's proposal, estimates that buffer stocks for ten "core" commodities would require just over $10 billion. The analysis by Gordon Smith, upon which the larger estimates are based, indicates, however, that hindsight is a very valuable input into operating a buffer stock. The Behrman study, and a related one by the Commodities Research Unit, Limited, calculated the trend, or average price *after the fact*, and then simulated the behavior of a buffer stock as if the buffer stock manager knew beforehand what the future average price would be. Smith, however, makes the more realistic assumption that the buffer stock manager will have to guess each year, or estimate from past data, what the trend price really is. He found that, under such circumstances, buffer stocks would have to be quite large in order to be effective, and that under several "reasonable" decision rules, the buffer stock would not stabilize price. In fact, Smith finally abandoned his search for an operational decision rule, and exogeneously assigned his simulated buffer stock a target price. This choice of a target price certainly was affected by his knowledge of the behavior of the price of copper over the period simulated. Hence, I take with a grain of salt estimates of buffer stock size from experiments that assume hindsight.

Another reason to view Behrman's estimates of buffer stock size as minimal is that he simulated conditions over a relatively calm period (1963-72), which included neither the Korean War commodity boom, nor the 1973-74 commodity boom. His maximum size estimate for a tin buffer stock, given the objective of holding price movements within ±15% per year, is 19,000 metric tons. The U.S. strategic stockpile sold 47,300 metric tons of tin in 1974 and 1975, yet the price of tin rose as rapidly as prices of commodities for which there were no such sales from a public stock. Hence, it seems to me reasonable to conclude that effective buffer stocks for the ten core commodities would require considerably more than $10 billion.

Would Buffer Stocks Stabilize Price?

We know that the tin agreement buffer stock has not stabilized the price of tin, but would it have done so if it had been larger? The U.S. strategic tin stockpile is much larger, containing in 1975 over 200,000 metric tons of tin. While market stabilization is not the purpose of this stockpile, the U.S. Government has taken into account the stabilization objectives of the tin buffer stock in managing its strategic stockpile. As the U.S. stockpile has been reduced from 350,000 metric tons in the mid-fifties to about 200,000 metric tons now, it has been a larger net seller. Analysis of these sales indicates that their timing was such that, while over the period 1956-73 annual changes (absolute value) in the net price of tin averaged slightly less than 7%, without sales and purchases from the U.S. stockpile they would have averaged more than 10%.

This suggests that buffers stocks, if large enough, would be effective. On the other hand, Smith had difficulty, as discussed above, in finding effective operational rules for his simulated copper stock.

Would "Small" Buffer Stocks be Effective?

Even $10 billion is a lot of money. Hence, the most relevant issue is not "Would buffer stocks, *if large enough*, stabilize price?" but, "Would 'small' buffer stocks partially stabilize price or would they be disruptive?" The existence of a buffer stock which is too small to provide complete specialization might cause speculation to have a destabilizing effect. A buffer stock too small to prevent cyclical price movements would tend to provide speculators with a one-way bet, as is provided by a central bank which attempts to defend an exchange rate that the exchange market considers inappropriate. Half a buffer stock may be worse than none at all.

The Politics of Buffer Stocks

Even if the economics of buffer stocks might be consistent with their stabilizing prices, the politics of buffer stocks may not be. The tin and copper market simulations referred to above also indicate that stabilization would sometimes require that the buffer stock remain on the same side of the market for five to six years. The integrated program of ten buffer stocks studied by Behrman was a net purchaser in *each* of the ten years over which it was simulated. This does not constitute an economic argument against buffer stocks; it shows only that price cycles in these markets sometimes have unexpectedly long frequencies. It does suggest, however, that considerable political resolve will be necessary if buffer stocks are to perform their economic function—sufficient to allow the buffer stock to buy or sell continuously for long periods. If this economic necessity caused the commodity agreement to come apart politically, or if the politics of holding the agreement together dominated the economics of operating it effectively, the net effect could be destabilization rather than partial stabilization.

Supply Controls

A frequent reaction to findings such as those I have cited, which indicate that the buffer stocks needed to stabilize even a few commodity markets are much larger than those which have been proposed, is to suggest that "standby" supply controls will be provided to take care of those cases in which the buffer stock is inadequate. As a debating ploy, this response may score points, but as a negotiating technique, it may be a step backward.

While supply controls, if effective, would probably on average *raise* prices, it is not clear that they would stabilize them. The implementation or removal of export controls through the mechanisms of a commodity agreement is a time-consuming political process; hence, the use of this instrument cannot be varied on a day-to-day basis. Its use as an instrument of stabilization is thus dependent on accurate forecasts of market conditions at a considerable time in the future—forecasts which are not yet available.

The economics of export controls has not been researched, perhaps partly because of the conspiracy to pretend we are talking about stabilization, not income transfers. The difficulty of good timing is apparent in the statistic that over the first four tin agreements, 85% of buffer stock sales by the agreements took place while export controls were in effect, that is, while the two instruments were working at cross purposes.

In negotiating a commodity agreement, the presentation of supply controls as a "standby" instrument to a buffer stock suggests either a misunderstanding of what the effects of buffer stocks and of supply controls would be or an attempt to prevent other parties to the negotiations from realizing that price maintainance, rather than price stabilization, is the objective of the proposal. Either interpretation might cause one to ask how advocates of such a proposal would manage a buffer stock's resources once provided.

Just as discussions of commodity policy generally assume that buffer stocks would work as hoped, they seem also to assume that export controls, if established, would work in the interest of LDC producers. It is, however, doubtful that this is generally the case. The following example seems particularly appropriate to the world copper industry but may have wider applicability.

LDC copper exporters have already demonstrated that they cannot effectively police a system of export controls. Even if they could, they would have no interest in an agreement including importers. Hence, an effective system would have to be policed by importers, as is the case for the coffee agreement. The system would tend, in reality, to be a system of internationally sanctioned import controls.

Several major metals-importing countries, particularly the United States, are also major, and relatively high cost, producers. A widely circulated justification for policies to stimulate investments in commodity production in the LDC's emphasizes that at present, investment—especially for metals—is concentrated in the industrial world, where reserves are relatively "mined out" and costs relatively high.

There is a strong tendency for producer interests to dominate consumer interests when economic instruments are operated through a political mechanism, such as the regulatory agencies or tariff policy. Thus, an agreement which establishes an export control mechanism to advance the interests of relatively low cost producer-exporters, the LDC's, would probably mutate into a system of import controls to protect relatively high cost producers in countries which are importers, but in which domestic production fills a significant part of domestic usage.

Such an agreement sounds suspiciously like the textile agreement and not like the sort of cooperative arrangements favored by supporters of commodity agreements. This interpretation might help explain why the copper-exporting LDC's have not voiced strong support for the UNCTAD Secretariat's argument that a producer-consumer copper agreement is needed.

While I admit that my influence on policymakers has not been dominant, I think that my analysis helps explain why our policymakers are taking a cautious, but cooperative attitude toward commodity agreements. In commodities markets, LDC's may have a stronger economic than political position, and it would be unfortunate for their interests to create political instruments which would retard the emergence of that economic advantage. A picture of a mouse may be more in their long run interests than a real mouse that turns around and bites them.

Where could real progress be made? The obvious economic measure is the relaxation in the industrial world of protection for commodities processing against import competition. Trade liberalization is, however, unpopular now, so the politics of such policy advances requires more thought than the economics.

COMMENTS BY WILLIAM D. ROGERS*

It is important to understand the context of the current commodity discussions. In addition to commodities are issues of realigning the debt burden of the less developed countries, and of establishing a system of price indexation which would fix the prices of LDC exports to the developed countries to the manufactured imports of LDC's from the developed countries. These issues, together with those involving commodity agreements, have come to be seen in the LDC's as a fundamental test of the good will and good faith of the industrialized democracies towards them. It is within this context that the commodity debate has taken on such an inflamed character.

I am convinced that there are technical problems with the proposal put forward by the UNCTAD Secretariat. I would suggest that the LDC's have greatly misunderstood the significance of what they are seeking. They conceive the UNCTAD commodity scheme to be a fundamental change in the international economic system. The World Bank has estimated that, if trade barriers were eliminated in the MTN, earnings by 1985 would improve for Latin America, for example, by 29 billion constant

* Of the District of Columbia Bar and formerly Under Secretary of State for Economic Affairs.

PART THREE

ADMINISTERED PROTECTION

[8]

The Political Economy of Administered Protection

By J. M. Finger, H. Keith Hall, and Douglas R. Nelson*

Trade restrictions are hardly ever voted directly by Congress. Though the threat of direct congressional action is frequently present, pressure for protection is usually applied through the major instruments for the administrative regulation of imports: the antidumping and countervailing duty procedures and the escape clause mechanism.

In this paper, we will examine these instruments for the administrative regulation of imports—a theory of how these mechanisms work is developed, then operational implications of this theory are deduced and tested over the record of countervailing duty, antidumping, and escape clause cases decided from 1975 through 1979. This is the period over which the Trade Act of 1974 was in force. Because the nature of these mechanisms is relatively unfamiliar, a relatively large amount of institutional information is provided.[1]

I. Administrative Mechanisms

The distinction between "high" and "low" policy tracks is one which Richard Cooper has used in the international relations literature. The low, or technical, track is the "rules" track. Cases here are "determined,"

not "decided," according to criteria established by law, administrative regulations and precedent. Higher-track decisions are less circumscribed by rules and regulations, and require considerable attention by government officials entrusted with discretionary authority and subject to political accountability. Political influence is applied directly in high-track cases, but comes to bear on low-track cases only indirectly, through the shaping of the laws and regulations which define their technocratic nature.

The highest, most open, decision mechanism in trade matters is, of course, Congress. Here decisions are made in the light of public awareness by decision makers directly responsible to the voters. At this level, decision criteria are very open—any industry seeking protection may present any reasons which it feels will be convincing.

Both the escape clause and the less-than-fair value mechanism are delegations of Congress' authority to regulate trade. One might assume that the same forces which would have come to bear on Congress will influence the delegated decision. We will, however, argue that the delegation of such decisions to a technical track will significantly affect their substance.

A. *The Escape Clause*

The more political of the administrative tracks created by Congress is the escape clause (Section 201 of the 1974 Trade Act). Under this clause, an industry may petition the International Trade Commission (ITC) to conduct an investigation of "injury" from imports. The ITC's investigation is limited to whether or not there has been or is likely to be injury to "the domestic industry producing an article like or directly competitive with the imported article." The ITC reports its findings to the president, and if injury to the domestic industry has been found, the report includes the ITC's recommendation as

*World Bank, University of Rochester, and Rutgers University, respectively. The original draft of this paper was completed while we were with the U.S. Treasury Department, Office of Trade Research. The positions taken and opinions expressed in this paper are our sole responsibility.

[1] Various sorts of information have gone into the development of this theory, much of it derived from firsthand observation of how things are done. The reaction of several readers to earlier drafts suggests that trained economists find "institutional information" (such as what the antidumping law actually says) repugnant, and that they are unwilling to admit such information as evidence in the testing of theories. Their position, it would seem, is that reading what the law *says* will not help one understand what it *means*. This meaning they seem to assume can only be grasped by interpreting regression results.

to the import restriction and/or adjustment assistance necessary to prevent or remedy the injury. The president, however, is not legally constrained by the ITC's recommendation. He may, if the ITC determines injury, decline to provide import relief or adjustment assistance, may decide to provide one when the other was recommended, or may negotiate orderly marketing agreements with exporting countries. Thus, the ITC's function is like that of a grand jury, the commissioners being charged with examining only one side of the issue which the president must decide. The ITC decides not the outcome of the case, but whether or not the case should be taken up by the president.

B. Less-than-Fair Value Cases

Countervailing duty cases are concerned with the sale of subsidized exports in the U.S. market, and antidumping cases with sales in the United States at a price below the foreign producer's long-run costs, or below his home-market price. Such cases are described as "less-than-fair value (*LFV*) cases," because the trade practices they are intended to control involve, in legal terms, the sale of products at less than their "fair value." The imposition of dumping duties requires both a determination of *LFV* pricing and a determination of resulting injury to domestic producers. Over the period covered by this study, a countervailing duty case included an injury test only if the product involved was duty free in the U.S. tariff schedule. During this period, *LFV* investigations were the responsibility of the Treasury Department and injury investigations were the responsibility of ITC.[2]

The *LFV* criteria are, by law, more technically precise than escape clause criteria. Dumping, for example, is defined by 300 lines of text in the antidumping act plus 1,000 *Federal Register* lines of administrative

regulations. In contrast, the only criterion the Trade Act of 1974 imposed on the president's escape clause decisions was "the national economic interest of the United States," and the criteria by which the 1974 Trade Act charged the ITC with judging injury take up only 35 lines.

Further, the injury criteria are illustrative, while the dumping criteria are limiting. The Trade Act tells the ITC to take into account "all economic factors which it considers relevant, including (but not limited to)...[A list follows]." The antidumping act, in defining foreign value, specifies, for example, that "the amount for general expenses shall not be less than 10 percentum of the cost as defined in paragraph..., and the amount of profit shall not be less than 8 percentum of the sum of such general expenses and cost...."

That the technical criteria are followed is assured by the right of appeal. Any interested party can appeal a *LFV* determination into the federal courts. This right of court appeal does not apply to escape clause findings.

II. Nature of the Technical Track

A technical track is cheaper to operate than a political process. Discretion must be vested in relatively senior government officials, while a more tightly constrained process can be administered by a technically trained, as opposed to a broadly educated and politically astute, staff which could work out a political solution for their superior's signature.

A much more important characteristic of the technical track relates to the minimization of the *political* costs of making a decision. Protection involves large transfers of income—those from consumers to producers are typically eight to ten times the net costs of protection (Dale Larson). As Lester Thurow has pointed out, it is very difficult for democratic political systems to make such nearly zero-sum transfer decisions. Losses seem always to be more identifiable than gains; hence the optimal outcome is often to avoid a political decision.

---

[2]Since January 1, 1980, *LFV* investigations (in dumping and in countervailing duty cases) are done by the Commerce Department, and all countervailing duty cases include an injury test. Injury tests remain the responsibility of the ITC.

A. *Positive-Sum Decision*

When protection is the issue, the opposed interests are domestic producers, who want imports restricted, and domestic consumers or users, who want access to foreign sources of supply.[3] By specifying precisely how the interests of one group are to be taken into account, legal or technical criteria spare policy level officials from having to decide whose interests will be taken into account, and from having to explain why to those whose interests are left out. They provide solid reasons for the government's decision, and hence allow the government to point out to the losing side that no other decision was legally possible. This justification helps to diffuse the political costs of the decision without preventing the government from harvesting the gratitude of the winners.

In short, the technical track provides a way to decide between the courses of action which would be advocated by two directly opposed interest groups without facing up to the issue which divides them, that is, without weighing in comparable terms one side's interests against the other's. In terms of the interests *effectively* represented, the technical track turns a zero-sum situation into a positive-sum decision.

B. *Role of Misdirection and Obfuscation*

The key to the effectiveness of a technical track is that it disenfranchises one "side" with major interest in the decisions it makes. But the mechanism itself is established through democratic processes, hence, the disenfranchised "losers" from the decisions have the same right to shape its mechanisms as the "winners" do. That they do not is a reflection of their unawareness of what is going on. This unawareness in turn depends on two elements critical to an effective democratic decision mechanism—misdirection and obfuscation.

Misdirection has to do with the difference between the *LFV* mechanism's legal purpose and its economic function. In law, the mechanism is designed to impose import restrictions only in instances of "unfair" foreign pricing, for example, subsidized exports thereby priced below cost. (The *LFV* duties offset, in theory, the effects on import prices of unfair foreign practices.) But, as will be explained below, the economics of such mechanisms suggests that they will go "too far" and protect domestic producers from "fair" foreign competition as well.

As misdirection is the basis for establishing such mechanisms, obfuscation is what keeps them going. The *LFV* mechanism is an outlet for complaints by domestic producers, not domestic users or buyers, and hence at the initiation of each case, those who benefit from the possible import restriction will be better prepared than those who will lose. It is not likely that this discrepancy will disappear during the course of a case investigation. Lower-track procedures *are* technical, and thus incomprehensible without lengthy training. This means that such material is not likely to attract news media attention, and certainly not the attention which the more comprehensible political track events will receive. Thus technical procedures, whatever their purpose, tend to be obscure and the obfuscation they create allows the government to serve the advantaged interest group without being called to task by the disadvantaged.

C. *Nature of the Biases in the LFV Mechanism*

Our argument suggests that a low track will not function unless it is biased in favor of one or the other interest group in conflict. The direction of the bias in the *LFV* mechanism does not follow from the fact that it is technical, but simply from the fact that it is a channel for complaints about a surfeit of import competition, not a lack. Thus by design, it weighs domestic producers' interests more heavily than domestic users—it has the capacity to impose trade restrictions but not to remove them (other than those it imposes itself).

---

[3] This exposition assumes that the foreign exporter and/or government is not a major interest effectively involved in such decision mechanisms. This hypothesis will be tested below.

The characteristics of the *LFV* decision process come together in such a way as to suggest that the mechanism will be protectionist in more than the obvious sense just described. Control of the technocratic apparatus is ultimately political; hence the overall bias in the mechanism depends on how the political impacts of the disadvantaged interest's losses and of the advantaged interest's gains balance each other within it.

The existence itself of the mechanism demonstrates that one side has the advantage, and the obscure nature of its proceedings assures that that advantage can (to some degree) be exploited without generating opposition. Thus along whatever scale the *LFV* mechanism operates, it will be, as a central tendency, on the advantaged group's side of zero.[4]

The scale along which the *LFV* mechanism operates is the nature of the pricing practices which foreign sellers are allowed to employ in the U.S. market. Zero on this scale—the position accepted (as fair) by both conflicting interests, domestic producers and domestic consumers—is when foreign sellers are limited to the same pricing practices available to domestic sellers.[5] On the side of zero advantageous to domestic producers, foreigners will be more tightly restricted than U.S. sellers, that is, the *LFV* laws and mechanism will take pricing practices away from foreign sellers which the equivalent "domestic" law (for example, antitrust law) does not take away from domestic sellers. Thus our model predicts that the *LFV* mechanism imposes constraints on foreign sellers not imposed on domestic ones by equivalent domestic laws.

More than that, this approach suggests that protectionist pressure will bring about qualitative changes in the *LFV* mechanism and bring it to focus more on the question of comparative costs between domestic and foreign competitors for sales in the U.S. market than on the fairness of the foreigner's trade practices.

This argument is based on two propositions from social anthropology. The first of these is that the institutionalization of a social issue will attract, or cause to form, interest groups which stand to gain from that mechanism. The second is that institutional systems change over time, and that this change is significantly influenced by the interests of those groups which come to focus on it (Shmuel Eisenstadt, pp. 419–20; Walton Hamilton).

The legal objective of the *LFV* mechanism is to police the fairness of trade practices, and it pursues that objective by restricting imports (in design, from unfair exporters only). It is therefore an economic instrument with the power to restrict imports, and it will attract those with an interest in having imports restricted. This will include not only firms and industries beset by unfair competition, but more generally, those least favorably situated vis-à-vis their foreign competitors' costs. They will, the logic of social anthropology suggests, attempt to make their needs fit its scope, and its scope fit their needs. These tendencies, particularly the latter, suggest a convergence of the *economic* subject matter of *LFV* and escape clause (*EC*) cases—suggest that the *LFV* rules will tend toward protecting against the sort of injury from import competition which the escape clause goes at "officially."

III. Empirical Examination of *LFV* Determinations

A. *Empirical Questions*

In the most general sense, the purpose of our empirical examination of *LFV* and *EC* decisions is to demonstrate that the *LFV* system displays the characteristics of a technical track, and the *EC* mechanism those of a more political track. Several questions

---

[4] The logic of this paragraph applies to any delegation of authority to an administering agency. Hence OSHA is a good idea but we get too much of it. Likewise for Ralph Nader and factor-proportions model trade papers in this *Review*.

[5] The antitrust laws and enforcement mechanisms take up the general question of what trade practices are fair. Against this background, the *LFV* mechanisms deal only with the trade practices in the U.S. market of foreign sellers. The institutional basis for this separation may be that the mechanisms used to enforce the antitrust laws cannot be applied to foreign firms.

derived from the high-track, low-track model will be evaluated. The first and most obvious of these is that technical, not political, factors determine the outcome of cases on the lower track, and vice versa on the higher track.

The second point we want to make is that it is the relaxing of technical criteria rather than the direct specification of political criteria which allows political factors to influence a case outcome.

The difference between the *LFV* pricing and *LFV* injury determinations provide almost a controlled experiment for testing this hypothesis. Under the 1974 Trade Act, each dumping case and each countervailing duty case involving a duty-free product on which the Treasury Department's preliminary determination was affirmative then went to the ITC for an injury investigation. The decision environment of an injury investigation differed from that of a pricing determination in two important respects. First (as explained above), the technical criteria defining injury are much less precise than those defining *LFV* pricing. Second, the pricing, but not the injury determination, could be appealed in federal court—the pricing, but not the injury decision, is subject to a technical review which has the force of law behind it.

There is no formal political review of either determination. In form, the only difference is the relatively ambiguous technical definition of injury.

The third area we will examine is the nature of the bias in the *LFV* mechanism. We will take up two overlapping hypotheses. The first is that the technical rules which calibrate the mechanism not only prevent foreign sellers from using practices considered unfair (for all sellers) in the U.S. market, but spill over to protect U.S. producers against fair competition from foreigners. The second is that comparative costs have a major influence on *LFV* pricing decisions.

B. *Statistical Model*

The statistical objective of our data analysis is to determine the influence of political and economic variables on the likelihood of an affirmative determination in an *LFV* case. The dependent variable in this analysis was

the case decision (affirmative or negative). The *LFV* pricing tests covered every case decided during 1975–79 for which we could develop values for the independent variables —183 of 208 cases, or 96 percent of the value of imports covered by the 208 cases.[6] Analysis of *LFV* injury determinations covered 57 cases of 68 decided—again, all the cases for which we could assemble the relevant data.

C. *Independent Variables*

Political Influences: International. Two variables in our model represent international political influences. The first of these measures the proportion of total U.S. exports (1976) which are imported by the country against which the *LFV* case was filed. The hypothesis which this variable tests is that nations with which we experience a high level of economic interdependence exercise greater influence on *LFV* outcomes than nations with which we are less interdependent.

The second international political variable is a dichotomous variable which identifies those cases brought against less-developed countries (*LDCs*). The hypothesis here is that the *LFV* decision process is prejudiced against the *LDCs*. The basis for this hypothesis is the argument by some proponents of "dependency" analysis that the institutional and legal structure in the advanced capitalist countries is rigged against *LDCs*.[7] A less conspiratorial way of viewing such an expectation is that the *LDCs* are simply not as well equipped to apply political pressure on their own behalf as other more developed countries.

Political Influences: Domestic. Our model will test two hypotheses that relate to domestic political influence:

HYPOTHESIS 1: *Industry size is positively related to success in the LFV mechanism.*

[6] The product coverage of each *case* is defined in terms of the TSUSA seven-digit import categories covered by the petition. The *industry* affected by a case is the four-digit SIC category into which the relevant TSUSA categories are mapped by the U.S. Bureau of the Census classifications.
[7] See, for example, Andre Frank.

HYPOTHESIS 2: *Industrial concentration is positively related to success in the LFV mechanism.*

Both of these hypotheses are based on the assumption that, at least on economic issues, industry structure translates directly into political power.

In our statistical model, we have used three alternative measures of industry size: total employment, the value of the physical capital stock, and value-added in the industry. We have also included "case size"—the value of 1978 imports of products covered by the case —as an indicator of the political influence of size.

The widely suggested relationship between industry concentration and political influence is rooted in the theory of collective goods. This theory suggests that decision-making costs are low in groups with one or a few dominant actors, allowing relatively effective political action.

A final hypothesis about political influence refers to the administrator's instinct for self-preservation. On January 1, 1980, responsibility for enforcement of the dumping and countervailing duty laws was shifted from the Treasury to the Commerce Department. According to government officials directly affected by this transfer, the movement for trade reorganization began in earnest in January 1979, as markup of the Trade Agreements Act of 1979 was completed. Behind this shift of responsibility was the presumption that the Commerce Department would find affirmatively more often than the Treasury Department. If the frequently expressed assumption that defense and expansion of "turf" are important arguments in the objective function of bureaucrats and of bureaucratic agencies, and if the *LFV* decision mechanism allowed for discretionary response to political pressure, then there should have been a detectable shift in 1979 of the *LFV* decision function toward the affirmative. We test this hypothesis by introducing a dummy variable which identifies all cases decided in 1979.

Comparative Costs. Comparative costs are virtually impossible to measure directly. We have used instead "factor proportions," which an extensive body of theoretical and

empirical work argue are the determinants of comparative costs, as an indirect measure. The variables employed are the industry physical capital-labor ratio;[8] industry average wage per worker, as a proxy for human capital intensity; and the extent of economies of scale in the industry.[9] If our hypothesis about the bias in the mechanism is valid, then *LFV* decisions will be influenced toward the affirmative by the existence of a cost disadvantage for the American industry.

In addition to supporting our hypothesis about the protectionist bias of the mechanism, a significant influence for factor proportions on *LFV* decisions would be consistent with our general hypothesis that the *LFV* mechanism is a technical, not a political, track.

This interpretation is supported by logic and by fact. As to logic, the advantaged interest has two ways to get what it wants: 1) to have the rules changed (further) in its favor; 2) to have the rules relaxed, so as to allow a more open, more expensive political track procedure. The former is the more direct, less risky, and less expensive alternative. As to fact, we will cite below examples of specific rules which bring comparative costs into the *LFV* pricing determination.

Precision. Our remaining technical variable measures the number of different products covered by the case—in operational terms, the number of 7-digit TSUSA lines. The logic behind this variable is that less than fair value is a pricing concept, and thus more appropriately applied to individual products than to large aggregates. Because the rules specify precisely what *LFV* pricing is, our hypothesis is that determinations will tend toward the status quo (negative) when the technical criteria for a decision are less clearly met. Thus the technical track hy-

[8]The physical capital stock was estimated, for 1975, by the Branson-Monoyios method; as the gross book value of plant and equipment, plus the capitalized value of supply and materials inventories. Data for all industry variables are from the *U.S. Census of Manufactures.*

[9]Estimated by Hufbauer's method. His measure of economies of scale is the coefficient a in the regression equation $log\, v = k + a$ times $log\, n + e$, where v is the ratio between value-added per man in plants employing n persons and value-added per man for the entire four-digit industry, and k is a constant. We used 1972 data.

TABLE 1—LOGIT ANALYSIS OF INFLUENCES ON LESS-THAN-FAIR VALUE PRICING DETERMINATIONS, 1975–79

Hypothesis and Variable	Hypothe- sized Sign	Results—Estimated Coefficient (t-Statistic)					
		(1)	(2)	(3)	(4)	(5)	(6)
Political Track Hypothesis							
International Political Influences							
Proportion of U.S. Exports to Country	−	−9.1	76.2				
		(−0.03)	(0.25)				
Against a Developing Country	+	−28.	−.30				
		(−.61)	(−0.66)				
Domestic Political Influences							
Administrative Reorganization Threat	+	.69	.81	.80	.80		
		(1.27)	(1.53)	(1.52)	(1.52)		
Industry Concentration	+	−1.8	−2.3	−2.4	−2.4	−2.3	
		(−2.28)	(−3.07)	(−3.14)	(−3.16)	(−3.08)	
Case size	+	−.13					
		(−0.71)					
Industry Size							
Employment	+	2.9	−.13	−0.4			
		(1.05)	(−0.14)	(−0.04)			
Capital Stock	+	−0.3					
		(0.52)					
Value-Added	+	−.11					
		(−0.80)					
Technical Track Hypothesis							
Comparative Costs							
Capital-Labor Ratio	+	1.8	1.8	1.7	1.7	1.8	1.6
		(2.20)[a]	(2.36)[b]	(2.33)[b]	(2.37)[b]	(2.39)[b]	(2.28)[b]
Average Wage	−	−.19	−.29	−.28	−.28	−.28	−.31
		(−1.90)[a]	(−3.56)[b]	(−3.53)[b]	(−3.77)[b]	(−3.77)[b]	(−4.47)[b]
Scale Economies	−	−4.6	−5.2	−5.1	−5.1	−4.8	−3.5
		(−2.67)[b]	(−3.05)[b]	(−3.11)[b]	(−3.12)[b]	(−3.00)[b]	(−2.40)[b]
Technical Precision							
Number of Products	−	−.90	−.88	−1.0	−1.0	−1.0	−0.8
		(−1.54)	(−2.11)[a]	(−2.39)[b]	(−2.99)[b]	(−3.11)[b]	(−2.74)[b]
Constant		2.8	4.1	3.9	3.9	4.0	3.2
		(2.75)[b]	(4.57)[b]	(4.97)[b]	(5.11)[b]	(5.20)[b]	(4.75)[b]
Proportion of Outcomes Successfully Predicted		69	71	71	71	71	68
Chi-Squared		168[b]	172[b]	171[b]	171[b]	172[b]	178[b]
Number of Observations		183	183	183	183	183	183

[a]Indicates *rejection* of the null hypothesis that the sign is not the expected one, at the 95 percent level of confidence (one-tail test).
[b]Same as fn. a, but at the 99 percent level of confidence (one-tail test).

pothesis suggests a negative relation between the number of products covered by a case and the likelihood of an affirmative determination.

D. *Evaluation of Results*

LFV Pricing. The technical nature of the *LFV* pricing determinations is most di-rectly illustrated by the language of the law and the related administrative regulations— the sort of information presented in Section I above. Our statistical results, presented in Table 1, are also consistent with this hypothesis. In our examination of the influences on *LFV* pricing determinations, we found each technical factor to be statistically influential. And as we hypothesized, the significant test on each political variable is inconsistent with the political track hypothesis.

Most soundly rejected is the hypothesis of international political influence. The t-statistics on these two variables are much below unity (in absolute value) and the coefficient on the LDC variable has the wrong sign. Further, when these variables are removed from the equation (from col. 2 to col. 3), the coefficients and the t-statistics on the significant variables are virtually unaffected.

The domestic political influence variables fare only slightly better. Of the four size variables, only employment has the expected sign, and even it is a long way from statistically significant. The closest thing to a valid domestic political influence hypothesis seems to be the "turf defending" hypothesis about the administering agency. The coefficient on the administrative reorganization threat variable has the hypothesized sign, and though insignificant at the 95 percent confidence level, has a larger t-statistic than the other domestic political influence variables.

On the technical track side, there is not much to add to the message in the table. Each technical track variable has the expected sign and is significant, at the 99 percent level of confidence.

LFV Injury. When we deal with injury, where the technical rules are less precise, we expect political factors to be more influential. As tests of the impacts of the various factors, we expect the same signs on the coefficients as in the analysis of the *LFV* decision, with one exception. An affirmative *LFV injury* determination will become *more* likely as the number of products covered by the case increases. While price is a concept most readily made operational on an individual product basis, injury is more appropriately (for example, in the Escape Clause of the Trade Act) expressed in terms of capacity utilization, employment, or profits—concepts more readily made operational at the firm or industry level.

The results (Table 2) are consistent with our expectations. The political variables are much more significant here than they were in Table 1, and the technical variables much less. The hypothesized influence of the threat

of administrative reorganization is supported by our data, as is the hypothesized influence of the size of the petitioning industry's labor force.

International political influences again are not significant—it is domestic politics which counts.

John Odell obtained similar results in a study of twenty-five bilateral trade disputes between the United States and Latin American countries. He found that when the foreign country worked with common economic interests within the United States, the proportion of outcomes favorable to the foreign country was higher. But mobilizing the State Department or the National Security Council staff to make "foreign policy" arguments was not effective. Thus he found that foreign interests, to get what they want must work through allied domestic interests.

Protectionist Bias and Comparative Costs. In form, a LFV pricing investigation consists of observing the prices a foreign firm charges on home market sales and on sales in the United States, and then comparing the two. The details of the law and of the administrative regulations specify how the observations are to be made, and how one or the other is to be adjusted for different terms of sale (for example, lot size, payment terms, etc.), so as to make them comparable. William Dickey explains several ways in which these rules are more restrictive of foreign firms' than is comparable "domestic" law of domestic firms' sales practices in the U.S. market. For example, sales below full cost during periods of slack demand (i.e., sales which cover only variable costs) are normally not considered an unfair trade practice under the antitrust laws. But the antidumping law specifies that in determining the home market price charged by a foreign firm, observations of home market sales *below cost* must be disregarded.[10]

There are other, more direct illustrations that the *LFV* process now compares foreign and domestic costs. The administrative regulations for antidumping cases state that "Pe-

[10]See Dickey, p. 245. He provides several other, more complicated, examples.

TABLE 2—LOGIT ANALYSIS OF INFLUENCES ON ITC INJURY DETERMINATIONS IN LESS-THAN-FAIR VALUE CASES

Hypothesis and Variable	Expected Sign	Results—Estimated Coefficient (*t*-statistic)						
		(1)	(2)	(3)	(4)	(5)	(6)	(7)
Political Track Hypothesis								
International Political Influences								
Proportion of U.S. Exports to Country	−	−1276 (−1.64)	−1205 (−1.57)	−967 (−1.41)	−922 (−1.44)	−604 (−0.96)		
Against a Developing Country	+	−.5 (−0.44)						
Domestic Political Influences								
Administrative Reorganization Threat	+	2.5 (1.90)	2.6 (2.07)[a]		2.8 (2.30)[a]	2.7 (2.20)[a]	3.0 (2.49)[b]	2.9 (2.43)[b]
Industry Concentration	+	−5.9 (−2.22)	−6.1 (−2.44)	−5.6 (−2.39)	−3.9 (−2.05)	−5.5 (−2.34)	−5.6 (−2.35)	−5.6 (−2.34)
Case Size	+	2.3 (1.25)	2.5 (1.37)	2.2 (1.29)	1.7 (1.17)		1.0 (0.87)	
Industry Size								
Employment	+	36.1 (1.85)[a]	36.0 (1.98)[a]	27.5 (2.22)[a]	22.3 (2.22)[a]	27.9 (2.22)[a]	27.9 (2.07)[a]	28.4 (2.14)[a]
Capital Stock	+	−.57 (−1.87)	−.60 (−2.10)	−.47 (−2.45)	−.37 (−2.19)	−.42 (−2.27)	−.45 (−2.24)	−.43 (−2.19)
Value-Added	+	−0.7 (−0.12)						
Technical Track Hypothesis								
Comparative Costs								
Capital-Labor Ratio	+	1.5 (0.73)	1.5 (0.78)					
Average Wage	−	.35 (1.25)	.34 (1.48)	.39 (1.83)	.24 (1.39)	.38 (1.75)	.37 (1.67)	.37 (1.68)
Scale Economies	−	−2.2 (−0.64)	−2.2 (0.73)					
Technical Precision								
Number of Products	+	−55.6 (−1.86)	−54.3 (−1.82)	−49.8 (−1.84)		−46.7 (−1.73)	−50.0 (−1.80)	−48.3 (−1.76)
Constant		−.75 (−0.28)	−.71 (−0.34)	−1.2 (−0.61)	−1.2 (−0.67)	−1.2 (−0.63)	−1.4 (−0.70)	−1.4 (−0.72)
Proportion of Outcomes Successfully Predicted		84	81	81	79	79	83	83
Chi-Squared		127	126	130	84	129	149	145
Number of Observations		57	57	57	57	57	57	57

[a, b] See Table 1.

titioners unable to furnish information on foreign sales or costs may present information concerning US domestic producers' costs adjusted for differences in the foreign country in question... ."[11]

Our own analysis provides corroborating evidence. Each of the determinants of comparative advantage has the hypothesized sign and is significant at the 99 percent level of confidence.[12]

[11]*Federal Register*, No. 26, p. 8199, col. 1. This evolution continues. Matthew Marks (p. 432) points out that the shorter time limits put into effect by the Trade Agreements Act of 1979 will make the administering agency more dependent on such cost information supplied by the petitioner.

[12]We assume that scale economies and human capital intensity are positively related and physical capital intensity negatively related to U.S. comparative advantage. Virtually all relevant empirical work supports the assumed signs on the first two variables. As to our "Leontief paradox" assumption on the third variable, Robert Stern (pp. 86–90), reviewing recent cross-section studies of the trade position of U.S. industries, indicates that in each of them only when "resource intensive" industries are excluded does the relation between physical capital intensity and U.S. comparative advantage

E. *Anomalies*

The coefficients on several variables do not have the signs we expected. For example, we interpreted the concentration ratio as a reflection of political influence, and expected it to have a positive coefficient in Tables 1 and 2. It is, however, negative in both cases. This result might be consistent with a technical interpretation of the variable. According to the technical track hypothesis, the outcome of a case, once it is filed, depends on technical factors not affected by the petitioner's lobbying. Protection, from a successful petition, will add to the profitability of each domestic sale by the industry—not just to those sales by the petitioning firm or firms. But in a concentrated industry, a larger share of the benefits from a successful petition will be captured by the petitioner and a smaller share will spill over to firms which did not help finance it. Hence, a firm's filing a petition will make economic sense at a lower likelihood of success if the industry is concentrated.

As this paper examines influences on the *outcomes* of *LFV* cases (once they are filed), the negative coefficient on concentration can be consistent with the positive (but insignificant) cross-section relation Finger (forthcoming) found between concentration and the industry incidence of *LFV* complaints, and Robert Baldwin (1980) found between concentration and the depth of the tariff cut made by the United States at the Tokyo round. The Finger and the Baldwin results may indicate that the concentration ratio is not a reliable indicator of how well an industry is organized to take advantage of the avenues the government provides. And if the firms in concentrated industries tend to be multinational in scope, this weak result may simply indicate that restrictions on imports are not what they want from the government.

Several readers have suggested that the statistical significance of the wage variable might also be interpreted as evidence of political influence on *LFV* pricing decisions. One such interpretation is simply that the decision makers have sympathy for poor people, and will use the discretion the technical rules allow to protect them. A more cynical interpretation is that the politically sensitive decision makers "buy them off" by providing trade protection.

Serious questions can be raised about the analytical soundness of the latter proposition and about the validity of both.

If we accept the buy-them-off interpretation, then we are assuming that it is the votes of the poor, not their well-being, which is the politician's concern. If so, the critical variable is how *many* there are, not how *poor* they are. If so, the *number* of workers, not their wage rate, is the better representation.

Furthermore, higher-wage workers will more likely be able to afford political action and are more likely to be organized in such a way as to be politically effective. This would make the political association between affirmative decisions and the wage rate positive, not negative.

As to the evidence, if one looks at the entire pattern of statistical results, and not just at one *t*-statistic, a political interpretation of the average wage variable becomes untenable. All *three* comparative cost proxies are significant, and it is difficult to explain the other two in political terms. Economies of scale might lead to size and/or concentration, which would produce political power, but scale economies itself is not a political influence. Similarly, the number of workers in an industry or the industry's wealth (capital stock) might measure political power, but not the ratio of one to the other.

Even more to the point, the political interpretation of the average wage variable cannot assume that the law or the administrative regulations specify that the income or need of the affected workers be taken into account. They simply do not. Political influence slips in (if it slips in) because the technical specifications are ambiguous and allow it. If so, the more obvious and direct political influences represented by our list of political variables should be significant. They are not.

---

become positive. Our analysis included the resource intensive industries, and in this analysis, capital intensity is used only as a *forecaster* of comparative advantage. Correlation between physical capital and natural resource intensity, which muddles the analysis of *cause* of comparative advantage, is of no consequence to our analysis.

TABLE 3—CHARACTERISTICS OF HIGH AND LOW ADMINISTRATIVE DECISION TRACKS

Track	Functional Criterion	Scope of Decision	Decision Criteria	Decision Type
Low	Public Unawareness (political insignificance)	Parochial— Petitioner's Interests	Precise and Limiting	Positive Sum (easy)
High	Public Awareness (political significance)	National Interest	Open	Zero Sum (hard)

Finally, the technical criteria for injury *are* less precise than those of *LFV* pricing. The hypothesized influence of sympathy for the poor should therefore have a stronger influence on the injury determination. This is not the case. Results in Table 2 show that the domestic political factors *are* significant influences in *LFV* injury determinations, but the average wage variable's coefficient does not even have the sign which a political influences interpretation suggests.

IV. The Escape Clause (*EC*) Decision

A. *Determinants of where Cases will be Resolved*

From the petitioner's point of view, the distinction between a *LFV* case and an *EC* case is not a technical one. The technical criteria for demonstrating injury are not precise, hence a petitioner who feels that he has sufficient *political* influence to win has considerable latitude in putting together his supporting case. The technical criteria on *LFV* pricing are much more precise, but as our model suggests and our data demonstrate, they overlap considerably with comparative disadvantage, or the likelihood of injury from import competition. The other part of an *LFV* case *is* the ITC injury test, hence the *technical* criteria for good *LFV* cases and for good escape clause cases are much the same and do not serve to restrict a complaint to one track or the other.

The functional characteristic which separates the low from the high track is the political significance of the cases it handles. This characteristic will be closely related to the degree of public awareness of the cases being processed. If the public is unaware of a petition to the government for protection, then (as outlined in Table 3) the scope of the decision on the case can be limited to the interests of the petitioner, and a decision can be reached with dispatch. The technical criteria of the lower track will serve both to control the decision process and to keep it from becoming a public issue. They can therefore be designed to evaluate only the petitioner's interests. The decision then is easy. Those who will lose are not aware that the decision is being made.

A high degree of public awareness changes the game. It is impossible, in a democratic country, to define out of a public decision parties who are aware that their interests are at stake. Thus such a decision cannot be bounded by technical constraints, and it cannot be limited to considerations only of the petitioner's interests. Among the participants in such a decision, there will be losers as well as winners and, as Lester Thurow suggests, such decisions will be hard to achieve.

Within limits, the high track can create public awareness and the low track obscure it, but public awareness is more an exogenous factor than an endogeneous one. This factor has no obvious quantitive measure, but is likely closely related to case size. Case size thus should serve to distinguish between cases which the low track can and cannot process effectively. Table 4 shows that the average case filed in the *EC* mechanism was three times as large as the average *LFV* case. If we exclude antidumping petitions for steel and autos (disputes which we shall argue below did not "belong" in this mechanism

TABLE 4— *LFV* AND *EC* MECHANISMS: NUMBER OF CASES, 1975–79 AND IMPORT COVERAGE

	LFV Cases		EC Cases	
	All Cases	Excluding Steel and Autos	ITC Decision	Presidential Decision
Number of cases				
Filed	245	214	43	–
Decided	208	177	40	25
Affirmative	73	73	25	8
(Percent of Decided)	35	41	62	32
Orderly Marketing Arrangements	–	–	–	3
(Percent of Affirmative)	–	–	–	38
Import Coverage of Cases ($ million)[a]				
Filed	$25,948	$5,991	$14,224	–
Decided	$25,085	$5,079	$13,016	$8,968
Affirmative	$2,860	$2,860	$8,968	$4,992
(Percent of Decided)	11	56	69	56
Orderly Marketing Arrangements	–	–	–	$3,888
(Percent of Affirmative)	–	–	–	78
Average Case Size ($ million)[a]				
Filed	$106	$28	$331	–
Decided	$121	$29	$325	$359
Affirmative	$39	$39	$359	$624
Orderly Marketing Arrangements	–	–	–	$1,296

[a]In terms of 1978 import values.

and were not resolved there), *EC* cases were more than eleven times as large as *LFV* cases.

B. *The Presidential Decision*

Protection cases decided in the spotlight of national attention are close to zero-sum decisions. The political net gain (or minimal net loss) is not on either side of such decisions, but in avoiding them. This has two implications for the presidential decision. First, it will push the president toward saying no. Negative decisions will discourage further petitions and hence reduce the number of times the president will have to say anything. A minimal political gain from saying yes on one case may be undone by the loss from having to decide the four others this yes encourages. Second, it will push a presidential affirmative decision as far toward a nondecision as his legally defined options allow. The president cannot avoid public scrutiny or political accountability by ordering the negotiation of an orderly marketing arrangement (*OMA*), but he can cloud the public's view and diffuse accountability somewhat.

The details of an *OMA* can be made quite complex, or put off to be worked out in the future, when they will be announced at a high, but lower than presidential level (for example, the Special Trade Representative). The other affirmative options give consumer interests a more precise dimension on which to focus—several percentage points added to price by a tariff, or taken away from supply by a quota, or the budgetary cost of adjustment assistance. As Table 4 shows, the three *EC* cases in which the president recommended an orderly marketing arrangement covered 78 percent of the imports on which affirmative decisions were returned.[13] In effect, ordering the negotiation of an *OMA* is a step toward disenfranchising domestic consumers, and hence a movement toward a

[13]Virtually every line in the U.S. tariff has been "conceded" under the GATT. Import relief would therefore involve nullification or impairment of a GATT concession for which the countries to whom the concession had been made could demand compensation. Negotiation of an *OMA* with these trading partners would incorporate the question of compensation and thus avoid its becoming a separate issue.

positive-sum decision environment. If domestic and foreign producers are the only influences at play, a minimal amount of political craft should be needed to induce the competing producers to do what the antitrust laws attempt to prevent them from doing voluntarily.

On the high track, the clearest pressures are away from a decision, not toward either a yes or a no. Accepting this, and looking deeper for some political or economic basis of forecasting the president's decision when he must make one, we note that both the degree of injury to the domestic producer of import replacements and the "gains from trade" to domestic consumers will concentrate on those sectors in which the United States has comparative disadvantage. Hence, *net* losses to the national economic interest should not vary much between industries (see Larson, Table 1), and in cases which are big enough to overcome the relative dispersion of consumers and/or public enough so that consumers as well as producers will be aware of their stake in them, there is no basis for predicting that comparative costs will consistently push the decision in one direction or the other. As protection, except in unlikely "optimum tariff" situations, is a negative sum proposition, the "national economic interest" will always push toward a negative decision. But as this net loss to the economy comes to only 10 percent of the gross gain for protected producers (see Larson, Table 1), the net national interest is not likely to be a powerful influence.

The president's decision is made, therefore, at the razor's edge. The economic gains to those who want protection are only marginally smaller than its costs to those who oppose it, and this margin will not vary much from case to case. Because of the level at which the decision is made, consumers (potential losers from protection) will not be in the dark, but if there is a marginal difference in the degree of public awareness of a case and of its implications, it should favor the producer's side. Thus, the economics and the politics of the decision will each favor one side or the other only marginally, with economics tipped toward one side and politics toward the other.

The ITC's findings will not be definitive. Their role in the decision process will be more political than technical or economic, and more facilitating than decisive. Their major functions are to make sure a politically significant petitioner gets his day before the president; to occupy time during which resolution of the case may be achieved by less focused means than a presidential decision; to provide a focal point so that the president may observe how the sides are drawn before the mechanism focuses on him.

We thus find it difficult to say what will define operationally the "clout" needed to win an affirmative decision from the president. Baldwin, as we predict, did not find the ITC decision a significant factor. Our own *Logit* analysis was plagued by convergence problems, due in part, we suspect, to the smallness of the number of presidential decisions—this smallness being consistent with our predictions. The obvious, though gross, measure of political clout behaved in the obvious way. On eight "Big Cases" (over $400 million of imports), the president said yes five times (three *OMAs*). On seventeen "Small Cases," he said yes only three times (no *OMAs*).

Our and Baldwin's generally poor results with statistical decision rules illustrate perhaps the nature of the presidency. Those things which can be reduced to rules will be decided at a lower level.

V. Conclusions

We have presented and tested an interpretation of how the administrative import restraint mechanisms function. This interpretation differs in some respects from more or less "official" interpretations, but this difference is not an indictment of the mechanisms. Their function is to resolve or diffuse complaints about import competition, and all in all they seem to serve this function efficiently.

A major difference between our view and others' has to do with what the *LFV* and *EC* mechanisms actually do. In law, the escape clause deals with injury to U.S. producers from import competition and the *LFV* mechanism with the fairness of business practices

TABLE 5—PERCENTAGE OF IMPORTS OF MANUFACTURED GOODS
COVERED BY *LFV* AND *EC* CASES, 1975-79

	Antidumping and Countervailing Duty Cases		Escape Clause Cases	
Year[a]	Filed	Affirmative	Filed	Affirmative
1975	15.4	0.3	4.1	0.0
1976	0.8	0.9	2.3	0.5
1977	4.1	0.6	2.6	2.8
1978	0.6	0.4	1.0	0.4
1979	0.4	0.1	0.5	0.0
1975-79	21.3	2.2	10.4	3.8

[a]The trade coverage of each case was measured by 1978 imports of the products covered by the case, for example, *LFV* cases filed in 1975 covered products which in 1978 accounted for 15.4 percent of manufactured imports. The 1975-79 figures measure the percentage of 1978 manufactured imports covered by cases filed (or affirmatively decided) in the five-year period.

used in the U.S. market by foreigners. But in economics we find that they both deal with the same thing—injury from imports and the associated gains from trade. The functional difference between the cases which belong on one track or the other is the size and perhaps the degree of public awareness of the interests at stake, not the nature of those interests. Antidumping and countervailing duties are, functionally, the poor (or small) man's escape clause.[14]

The administrative mechanism is in part self-policing, but its effective function depends in part on the good citizenship of its users. It is not likely that a politically obscure case will be filed on the high track. It is less costly to provide data for technocrats to fit into their formulae than to establish the political basis for a presidential decision. Besides, the lower-track decision weighs the petitioner's interests more heavily than does the higher. In short, if you are politically obscure, the lower track will work *for* you. But if you are politically prominent, the lower track will not work. Highly visible petitions will attract political opposition which the technical rules of the track will not be able to depose, or even effectively express. Because they have no technical outlet, buyers must press their interests at the political level,

hence such cases will escalate into political issues.

The antidumping mechanism did not resolve the steel and auto cases. Though these antidumping cases were terminated, the conflicts they represented went on—autos became an escape clause case and finally an *OMA* with Japan, and the steel issue has led to high level administrative protection through the Trigger Price Mechanism. This is not to argue that the petitioner will not gain from such a filing. He will, through the news generated by such a petition and the opportunities it will create to complain about the ineffectiveness of the government and the bureaucracy, publicize his complaints about the "unfairness" of foreign competition. In so doing, he will be building the broad base of public support needed to win a favorable political decision at the national level.[15]

But using the mechanism to publicize a particular case will create public awareness of the mechanism, and hence reduce its capacity to process efficiently those cases for which it would have been appropriate. The recent trade reorganization act not only transferred administration of *LFV* cases from Treasury to Commerce, but made its procedures considerably more Byzantine—so

[14]And seems, in a way, to define having comparative advantage as an unfair trade practice.

[15]The uncertainty of the case outcome might slow foreign development of a market in the United States. For details and empirical tests, see Finger.

much so that its drafters describe it as a "Lawyer's Relief Act." The motive behind this might have been protectionist, but it may also have been to restore the degree of obscurity (and therefore effectiveness)[16] which use of the mechanism by the steel and auto industries took away.

Table 5 is presented to assure the reader that a cynical or despondent interpretation of the institutions we have described is not warranted. We have argued that in their central tendency these mechanisms are biased toward protectionism. But this bias is not large. In the five years, 1975–79, only 2.2 percent of U.S. manufactured imports have been granted relief under the *LFV* statutes, and only 3.8 percent under the escape clause.[17] The costs of gathering and disseminating information needed to reduce this bias would probably exceed the benefits. The dark side of the force is more protectionist than the light, that is, it is the openness of the system which keeps the bias as small as it is.

[16] Which suggests that the social value of lawyers lies in the confusion they create, not in that they dissolve.

[17] Of the imports subject to relief under the escape clause, 68 percent are covered by the *OMAs* for footwear and television receivers. Larson argues that these *OMAs* have had no effect on the trends of U.S. imports of footwear and television sets.

REFERENCES

Baldwin, Robert E., "U.S. Political Pressures Against Adjustment to Greater Imports," paper presented at the Eleventh Pacific Trade and Development Conference, Korean Development Institute, Seoul, September 1–5, 1980.

Branson, William H. and Monoyios, Nikolaos "Factor Inputs in U.S. Trade," *Journal of International Economics*, 7, May 1977, 111–31.

Cooper, Richard N., "Trade Policy is Foreign Policy," *Foreign Policy*, No. 9, Winter 1972–73, 18–36.

Dickey, William L., "The Pricing of Imports into the United States," *Journal of World Trade Law*, May–June 1979, *13*, 238–56.

Eisenstadt, Shmuel N., "Social Institutions" in *International Encyclopedia of the Social Sciences*, New York: Macmillan and the Free Press, 1968, *14*, 409–29.

Finger, J. M., "The Industry-Country Incidence of 'Less Than Fair Value' Cases in the United States Import Trade," in Malcolm Gillis and Werner Baer, eds., *Export Diversification and the New Protectionism*, National Bureau of Economic Research, forthcoming.

Frank, Andre G., *Capitalism and Underdevelopment in Latin America*, New York: Monthly Review Press, 1967.

Hamilton, Walton H., "Institution" in *Encyclopedia of the Social Sciences*, Vol. 8, New York: Macmillan, 1937, 84–89.

Hufbauer, Gary C., "The Impact of National Characteristics and Technology on the Commodity Composition of Trade in Manufactured Goods," in Raymond Vernon, ed., *The Technology Factor in International Trade*, National Bureau of Economic Research, New York: Columbia University Press, 1970.

Larson, Dale W., "The Cost of Import Protection in the United States," U.S. Treasury Department, processed, 1979.

Marks, Matthew J., "Recent Changes in American Law on Regulatory Trade Measures," *The World Economy*, July 1980, *2*, 427–40.

Odell, John S., "Latin American Trade Negotiations with the United States," *International Organization*, Spring 1980, *34*, 207–28.

Stern, Robert M., "Changes in U.S. Comparative Advantage: Issues for Research and Policy" in National Science Foundation, *International Economic Policy Research*, papers and proceedings of a colloquium held in Washington, D.C., October 3 and 4, 1980.

Thurow, Lester C., *The Zero Sum Society*, New York: Basic Books, 1980.

Federal Register, No. 26, Vol. 45.

U.S. Bureau of the Census, *Census of Manufactures*, Washington, various years.

DUMPING AND ANTIDUMPING: THE RHETORIC AND THE REALITY OF PROTECTION IN INDUSTRIAL COUNTRIES

J. Michael Finger

A wide gap separates the rhetoric from the reality of protection in industrial countries. Antidumping is the current reality of that protection. Protectionist interests stretch the definition of dumping as far as they may to shelter actions against imports under the antidumping umbrella.

This article is about antidumping, in particular about the history of anti-dumping regulation and its evolution under the GATT system into a major in-strument of protection. The thesis is straightforward: antidumping is the fox put in charge of the henhouse—ordinary protection with a good public relations program. There is little in its history to suggest that the scope of antidumping was ever more particular than protecting home producers from import compe-tition, and there is much to suggest that such protection was its intended scope.

The article has three sections. The first looks into the origins of antidumping regulation, the second examines contemporary regulation (antidumping under the GATT), and the third summarizes the significance of the first two.

Twenty years ago Bela Balassa began the preface to his path-breaking study, *The Structure of Protection in Developing Countries* (Balassa and associates 1971), by noting that import substitution was the rationale for the trade policies of many developing countries. But, Balassa noted, the gap between the rhetoric and the reality of developing country protection was large:

> The existing system of protection in many developing countries can be described as the historical result of actions taken at different

The World Bank Research Observer, vol. 7, no. 2 (July 1992), pp. 121–143
© 1992 The International Bank for Reconstruction and Development/THE WORLD BANK

times and for different reasons. These actions have been in response to the particular circumstances of the situation, and have often been conditioned by the demands of special interest groups. The authorities have generally assumed a permissive attitude toward requests for protection and failed to inquire into the impact of the measures applied on other industries and on the allocation of resources in the national economy. (p. xv)

The rhetoric of protection in developing countries was import substitution, the reality was ordinary protection. Recognizing the difference was an important step toward the many liberalization programs now under way in developing countries.

The gap between the rhetoric and the reality of contemporary protection is equally large in industrial countries. Antidumping is the current reality of that protection. According to Horlick and Oliver (1989, p. 5), two of Washington's top trade lawyers, such trade remedies "have become the usual first choice for industries seeking protection from imports into the United States."[1] The United States is not alone. Although the EC '92 program is carrying the European Community (EC) toward more liberal internal policies, antidumping actions are the principal face of its trade policy toward the rest of the world. Australia, for several years in the mid-1980s, had more antidumping cases than any other country and seems to have regained that position in 1990–91. In Canada, antidumping has been a major instrument of trade policy for almost a century. Although antidumping provides the legal avenue used by protectionist interests to force the government to act against imports, almost half of such cases reach a negotiated, out-of-court settlement—a voluntary export restraint or a voluntary export price minimum—rather than a formal legal end.

Foreign dumping is the rhetoric industrial countries use to excuse contemporary protection. This rhetoric gives antidumping the aura of being a special measure to undo a special problem—it suggests that somehow, although antidumping restricts or threatens to restrict imports, it is not really protection, but something that will, in the end, allow the world economy to function more effectively.

But the presence of dumping, objectively defined, does not determine when an antidumping action will or will not be taken, any more than the strictures of the import substitution development model determined when a developing country did or did not restrict imports. When the politics of the matter compel the government to take action against imports, the legal definition of dumping can be stretched to accommodate that action. In a practical sense, the word "dumping" has no meaning other than the one implicit in antidumping regulations. Its operational definition is the following: *dumping is whatever you can get the government to act against under the antidumping law.*

The Origins of Antidumping Regulation

Dumping, under one name or another, has been part of the rhetoric of political economy for a long time. Jacob Viner (1923), the first scholar to pull together previous writing on the subject, notes a sixteenth-century English writer who charged foreigners with selling paper at a loss to smother the infant paper industry in England. Viner also notes an instance in the seventeenth century in which the Dutch were accused of selling in the Baltic regions at ruinously low prices in order to drive out French merchants. Alexander Hamilton, in his *Report on Manufactures* of 1791 (cited in Viner 1923, p. 37), used much the same argument against English manufacturers who were exporting to America. But, as in the pre–twentieth-century incidents described by Viner, Hamilton was not arguing for action specifically against foreign dumping. He was arguing for a high and protective American tariff behind which the manufacturing industry could prosper in the new country.

The history of antidumping in Canada provides an explicit lesson as to what antidumping is—ordinary protection. Its history in the United States provides an explicit lesson as to what it is not—an extension of antitrust regulation.

The First Antidumping Law: Canada, 1904

The Liberal Party government in Canada was in a bind in 1904. Cursing the tariff was an important tactic for getting votes from farmers; keeping it high was an important way of obtaining contributions from manufacturers to carry the party's campaign to the public.[2] The Liberal Party owed its majority to the support of Canada's farmers, and its failure to reduce the tariff as promised was threatening to alienate that support, propelling a movement to break from the Liberal Party and create an independent farmers' party (Viner 1923, p. 193).

At the same time, Canadian steelmakers were pressing for higher tariffs on steel rails. As Canada's western plains were opened to immigrants, Canada's first transcontinental railroad, completed in 1885, was earning attractive profits, and railroad building began to surge. The U.S. Steel Corporation, recognizing an opportunity, set out aggressively to sell steel rails to Canadian railroaders. Canadian steelmakers alleged that U.S. Steel was unfairly aggressive and was dumping rails into the Canadian market (Easterbrook and Aitken 1988, pp. 438ff).

The Canadian government would have found it very hard to limit any tariff increase to steel rails alone. In Canada as in other countries, determining tariffs was not a discriminating process. Once the tariff was opened for revision, all producers to which the government owed a political debt would come forward; the increased tariff would spread to other iron and steel products, to textiles, to farm equipment, and on and on. (See Schattschneider's 1935 study of the log-rolling dynamic of setting tariffs in the United States.)

The Canadian minister of finance, W. S. Fielding, in presenting his proposed solution in June 1904, explained the situation as follows (quoted in U.S. Tariff Commission 1919, p. 22):

> We find today that the high tariff countries have adopted that method of trade which has now come to be known as slaughtering, or perhaps the word more frequently used is dumping; that is to say, that the trust or combine, having obtained command and control of its own market and finding that it will have a surplus of goods, sets out to obtain command of a neighboring market, and for the purpose of obtaining control of a neighboring market will put aside all reasonable considerations with regard to the cost or fair price of the goods; the only principle recognized is that the goods must be sold and the market obtained.... This dumping, then, is an evil, and we propose to deal with it.

Fielding's argument was not novel. Such alleged evildoing by foreigners, real or imagined, had for several centuries been a familiar justification for a higher tariff. It was a *target* of opportunity for interests seeking protection. The difference this time was that Mr. Fielding proposed to make antidumping an *instrument* of opportunity.

The substance of the proposed antidumping regulation, which is quoted in U.S. Tariff Commission (1919, p. 21), was contained in the proposal's first paragraph:

> Whenever it appears to the satisfaction of the minister of customs... that the export price...is less than the fair market value thereof, as determined according to the basis of value for duty provided in the Customs Act...such articles shall, in addition to the duty otherwise established, be subject to a special duty of customs equal to the difference between such fair market value and such selling price.

The invention of antidumping was not a signal departure from what was standard practice at the time. Canada had a long history of making clever changes in the procedures for customs valuation to achieve increased protection. McDiarmid (1946, pp. 8–9), in his history of Canadian commercial policy, concludes that "Canada's principal contribution to the technique of trade restrictions has been in giving the executive and administrative branches of government a wide measure of control over the effective rate of duties through artificial valuation of goods for duty purposes." Any pretext administrators could find to increase the customs value of a product would now have a double impact on the cost of importing the good. As with any trick of customs value, the regular tariff, assessed at an ad valorem rate, would be higher, and increases in the special antidumping duty would match dollar for dollar any increases in the customs value.

Canadian manufacturers at first opposed the antidumping law: making dumping illegal would vitiate one of their more effective arguments for a higher tariff. But as soon as the law was passed, U.S. Steel raised its prices in Canada by the amount required, and this example of the law's potential did not escape the attention of other manufacturers.[3] The government held hearings in 1905–06 at which Canadian manufacturers supported the antidumping law: "We heartily approve the principle embodied in the tariff legislation of 1904, but we are of the opinion that steps should be taken by the government to give more practical effect to the legislation" (quoted in U.S. Tariff Commission 1919, p. 25). They went on to offer suggestions for making enforcement more effective.

Soon afterwards Canada, Australia, and New Zealand passed antidumping laws, and a series of such laws was passed in the United States. By 1921, the United States, France, Great Britain, and most of the countries of the British Commonwealth had antidumping laws in place.

Dumping, of course, was not a new issue, so the explanation of why the time was ripe for passage of antidumping laws lies in several other factors.

HOSTILITY TOWARD GERMANY. Hostility toward Germany, combined with the popular conviction that German enterprises were particularly vicious dumpers, was certainly a factor. Viner (1923, p. 65) quotes a propagandist who insisted, as World War I neared its end, that "the German government was accumulating vast stocks of goods in order to dump them on the markets of the world... and regain in the field of economic warfare what she was losing on the military battlefield." Viner then comments that "these accusations have an interesting parallel in the similar charges brought against England after the Napoleonic Wars and the War of 1812, but they appear to have had even less basis."

THE HALO EFFECT OF TRUST-BUSTING. Trust-busting was in the political air at the end of the nineteenth century and the beginning of the twentieth. This provided a step up for any law that proposed to do something about the evil trusts. The emotion of trust-busting could be even more intense when directed at a foreigner. Frank Taussig, Harvard professor and first chairman of the U.S. Tariff Commission, once noted that "competition of any sort is unwelcome enough; competition from foreigners seems always to be regarded with particular dread" (Taussig and White 1931, p. 196).

Although emotion did lead to overstatement, the concern with regulating the evils of predatory trusts was not trivial, and price undercutting, employed just often enough to make its threat credible, was used by captains of industry to build and expand trusts. Driving the independent enterprise out of business was not, however, the trust's usual objective. Too much money would be lost and too many assets run down by price cuts severe and enduring enough for that purpose. A quick merger, profitable to both companies, would be better. John S. McGee (1958) explains the logic of this approach and documents that it was the way things usually went. Officers of the independent company usually became officers of the trust (see Yergin 1991, ch. 2, for examples).

HIGH TARIFFS EVERYWHERE. Every country except Great Britain had a high tariff in those days. These tariffs gave national firms the opportunity to price monopolistically at home and at the same time protected them from reimports of goods they sold competitively in world markets. In the United States, an important part of the populist argument against the tariff was that it allowed and protected domestic monopolies. Cordell Hull was Franklin Roosevelt's secretary of state and the father of the U.S. Reciprocal Trade Agreements Program. In his memoirs, Hull (1948, p. 52) writes about the first speech he made as a U.S. congressman:

> I made a vigorous attack on the high tariff and the monopolies and trusts that had grown up behind it. No kind of effort to curb and suppress trust violators [can] succeed unless such effort strikes at the main source of their constant creation—the protective tariff.

A NEW WAY TO DO IT. Canada had invented a new way to regulate foreign competition. The mechanics of enforcement under the Canadian law were seductively straightforward and familiar. Other high-tariff countries used valuation procedures similar to Canada's, and many of Canada's innovative uses of such procedures were soon copied by other countries. Where there is a way, there will soon be a political will.

The Evolution of U.S. Antidumping Law

In the early twentieth century the tariff was, for most countries, the major instrument for regulating imports. And in the United States, as in other countries, the evils of foreign trusts first entered trade politics as an argument for higher tariffs. But antidumping has a different history in the United States than in Canada. In Canada, policing the evils of monopoly power (trusts) was never more than rhetoric. In the United States at the early stages of antidumping regulation, the mechanics more closely matched the rhetoric—early U.S. antidumping regulations were, in substance, extensions of antitrust law. But these laws did not restrict imports, which is what the motivating politics demanded, and the pressure for change continued. The evolution of the U.S. antidumping law provides a graphic illustration of how different antidumping regulation is from antitrust law once antidumping has become a useful instrument for regulating imports.

THE SHERMAN ANTITRUST ACT OF 1890. The Sherman Antitrust Act of 1890 prohibits, under severe penalties, every contract or combination that restrains interstate or foreign commerce and every monopolization of or attempt to monopolize such commerce. Application of the act to sales of imports was severely limited by the Supreme Court, which refused to apply it to any sales contract that had been made in the exporting country rather than in the United States.

126

SECTION 73 OF THE WILSON TARIFF ACT OF 1894. The U.S. Congress, in section 73 of the tariff act of 1894, attempted to extend the scope of the Sherman act to imports by making unlawful every conspiracy or combination that was (a) engaged in importing and (b) intended to restrain trade or to increase the U.S. price of an imported article. Up until the time of Viner's writing (1923), the law had been invoked only once, against an association of U.S. bankers and importers plus the Brazilian state of São Paulo, to limit Brazilian exports and thereby rig the price of coffee on the U.S. market.

ANTIDUMPING LAW OF 1916. During World War I, the rise of anti-German sentiment and the widespread popular conviction that German enterprises were particularly vicious perpetrators of predatory dumping led to considerable pressure for revising the tariff upward. But the U.S. administration of President Woodrow Wilson, like the Canadian government in 1904, chose not to risk opening the tariff for revision and instead proposed legislation aimed specifically at foreign dumping. In line with the Wilson administration's recommendations, the U.S. Congress, in sections 800–801 of the revenue act of 1916, made it illegal to import goods at a price substantially below the "actual market value" in the producing country or in countries to which the goods were commonly exported providing there was an intent to injure, destroy, or prevent the establishment of an industry in the United States or to restrain competition.

This law is still on the books, but John J. Barcelo (1991), in his review of antidumping laws and actions, found that despite the attractive lure of triple damages, only one serious private suit had been brought under the law: a 1970 suit by Zenith Radio Corporation against Matsushita Electrical Industry Company. The suit was dismissed on summary judgment when Zenith did not provide facts to support a plausible theory of predatory dumping.

THE U.S. TARIFF COMMISSION STUDY OF 1919. In 1916, the U.S. Tariff Commission, at its own initiative, began investigating foreign competition in the U.S. market and Canada's experiences with its antidumping law. The key questions in its investigation of foreign competition sought "personal knowledge of unfair competition through the selling in the United States of articles of foreign origin at less than the fair market value when sold for home consumption in the country of origin" (U.S. Tariff Commission 1919, p. 12). The commission contacted 562 U.S. business enterprises directly. In addition, thirteen associations of producers or traders circulated the commission's questions to their membership. Thus, every enterprise in the United States against which imports provided some degree of competition was informed of the investigation and had the opportunity to respond.

The commission's survey of virtually every business enterprise in the United States found twenty-three that claimed knowledge of foreign dumping. Almost six times as many reported that they had no knowledge of unfair foreign competition or dumping. Of the complaints of foreign competition, the commission classified by far the largest share as "severe competition." An example demonstrates the tenor of these complaints (U.S. Tariff Commission, p. 15):

> *Patent leather.* After the enactment of the last tariff bill, Germany began to ship in grain-finished patent leathers made from cowhides and kid skins and these leathers were sold at a lower cost than we could produce the same article in our country, although we were the originators of grain-finished patent leathers.

Several of the complaints classified by the commission as dumping had a similar tone (U.S. Tariff Commission 1919, p. 14):

> *Japanese army equipment leather.* Our representative in the East reports the sale of Japanese leather at prices that barely cover the cost of the green hide, to say nothing of the cost of manufacture.

These statements are similar to those that Schattschneider (1935), in his study of the U.S. politics of protection in the 1920s and 1930s, quotes from statements made before tariff committees to justify a higher tariff rate. They are all based on the cost-equalization formula, the principle of protection that dominated the tariff politics of the day. (The 1908 Republican Party platform statement of the formula is quoted on page 140.)

We see, then, that advocates of antidumping regulation presented no singular reasons for this unique form of import protection. As in Canada in 1904, the voice that called for antidumping action was the voice of ordinary protection.

ANTIDUMPING LAW OF 1921. Where there is a way, there is a will. The 1916 antidumping act did little to diminish pressure for a Canadian-style antidumping law, and proposals for such a law were soon introduced before the Congress. And although most of the complaints about foreign competition brought forward by the 1919 U.S. Tariff Commission's study were not about foreigners selling at a lower price in the United States than in their home markets, the commission nonetheless recommended Canadian-style antidumping legislation.

Congress passed such an antidumping law in 1921, and the present law can be traced to it. The law empowered the secretary of the treasury (whose department included the customs service) to determine when a U.S. industry is being or is likely to be injured or prevented from being established by imports of a product at a price below its fair value in the exporting country or in other export markets. It also empowered the secretary to impose a special dumping duty in such a case. Congress has since reassigned the determination of injury to the U.S. International Trade Commission (originally the U.S. Tariff Commission) and pressed the president to assign the determination of dumping to the U.S. Department of Commerce. Numerous amendments have expanded its technicalities, but the form of the law has remained basically unchanged.

Changes in U.S. Law from 1890 to 1921

Initial U.S. regulations against "unfair imports" were, in substance, extensions of antitrust law. They brought forward the criteria and depended on the mode of enforcement and standards of proof of antitrust law. The sequence of revisions from 1890 to 1921 brought changes in both these dimensions. Trust-busting remained the rallying cry, but the object of the regulation shifted from trusts to imports, the instrument from law to bureaucracy.

CRITERIA FOR DEFINING THE OFFENSE. The major shift of criteria was from an antitrust standard to an injury-from-imports standard. The 1916 act, as table 1 shows, eliminated the need to identify a conspiracy or combination of sellers organized to commit some act toward some end. The offense under the 1916 act is simply to sell imports below the actual market value of the goods. The 1916 act states that this pricing is illegal if the intent is to restrain competition, but it also contains a second and more easily proven condition—the intent to injure a U.S. industry. The 1921 act completes the shift of criteria. Any mention of antitrust criteria—conspiracy, combination, or restraint of competition—is gone. Antitrust's injury-to-competition standard has been replaced by a diversion-of-business standard—the sort of diversion that is a normal part of the competitive process. A trade restriction is allowed if the pricing to win customers is undertaken by a foreign enterprise and the customers are domestic.

STANDARDS OF PROOF. The 1921 law differs from the 1916 law in two ways:

- The injury criterion of the 1921 law is not prefaced by the words "intent to."
- Enforcement is an administrative, not a legal, matter.

Proponents of antidumping action often point to the word "intent" to explain why the 1916 law has engendered no import restrictions. Intent, they argue, is difficult to prove: if the concept of effect had been used instead, the law would have worked.

Others, such as Barcelo (1991), argue that the lack of action against foreign predation under the 1916 and previous laws is a sound indicator that there was no such predation, or at least much less of it than the political rhetoric insisted. The 1916 antidumping act was, after all, the third attempt to legislate the basis for such prosecution, not counting proposals introduced but not passed into law. Technical glitches would have been worked out by then.

There are several other grounds for arguing that dropping the word "intent." was not a significant change. Like the 1921 antidumping act, section 316 of the tariff act of 1922 did not qualify its injury clause with the word "intent." The difference between the two was that enforcement of section 316 was in the strict legal tradition of antitrust laws. Viner (1923, p. 250), citing this aspect, concluded that section 316 would not be effective.

Table 1. *Elements in Early U.S. Laws to Regulate Unfairly Traded Imports, 1890–1922*

Act and date	Principal elements
Sherman Act, 1890	Conspiracy or combination Restraint, monopolization, or attempt to monopolize interstate or foreign commerce Criminal statute, strictly construed Fine, imprisonment; triple damages
Section 73, Wilson Tariff Act, 1894	Conspiracy or combination engaged in importing Intent to restrain trade, increase the price in the United States Criminal statute, strictly construed Fine, imprisonment; triple damages
Antidumping Act, 1916	Importing below actual market value Intent to restrain competition or to injure a U.S. industry Criminal statute, strictly construed Fine, imprisonment; triple damages
Antidumping Act, 1921	Importing below fair value Injury to a U.S. industry Administrative determination by the secretary of the treasury Special duty, equal to the difference between the fair value and the import price
Section 316, Fordney-McCumber Tariff Act, 1922	Unfair method of competition and unfair acts in importation Effect or tendency to destroy or substantially injure Tariff commission, with court review of questions of law only Additional duty to offset such act or method

Sources: Dale 1980, ch. 1; Viner 1923, ch. 13; U.S. Tariff Commission 1919, appendix.

Another argument is suggested by inserting (hypothetically) the word "intent" into the injury clause of the 1921 antidumping act. It seems unlikely that the additional word would change the way the clause is interpreted today. Anyone who offers goods for sale does so with the intent of winning the sale from someone else. So, in an administrative context, free from the precedents of the legal system, it is unlikely that the word "intent" would have limited the circumstances under which injury would be found.

We are left, then, with the conclusion that the limited effect of the 1916 law stemmed from its being a *legal* remedy, a part of criminal law and therefore subject to the strict rules of meaning and proof that apply to the law. The courts took antitrust law to be the relevant legal context for giving meaning to the terms in the law, and in this context the 1916 act was interpreted to demand the injury-to-competition standard.

Dissatisfaction with the 1916 act was political, not legal, and in politics, this dissatisfaction was relative to what a Canadian-style administrative remedy would provide. The rule of law, not any particular word in the law, was blocking action. Enlarging the scope for action against imports would require a shift from a legal to an administrative approach or, to use the pejorative synonym, a bureaucratic approach.

ANTIDUMPING AS A BUREAUCRATIC, NOT A LEGAL, PROCESS. The Australian antidumping law explicitly abandoned a legal for an administrative standard. When referring matters to the High Court, Australia's 1906 law stated that the court proceedings were to be informal and not subject to the rules of general jurisprudence or evidence (Viner 1923, p. 209). The United States and Canada made the same change by building antidumping regulation out of pieces—administrative functions—not subject to such standards.

Andreas F. Lowenfeld (1980, pp. 217–18), after comparing the standards of proof required for relief under the "fair" and "unfair" sections of U.S. trade law (both having administrative standards), concluded that there may be "a difference in the burdens of proof placed on the parties, although my impression is that burden of proof in the sense that lawyers are familiar with the term, in, say, determining the issue of contributory negligence in an automobile accident, simply does not exist in determinations of the kind we are talking about."

Perhaps the most straightforward expression of this soft standard of proof is the "facts available" or "best information available" clause, which is part of every country's antidumping regulations. In the GATT antidumping code (GATT 1990, par. 8), this clause reads as follows:

> In cases in which any interested party refuses access to, or otherwise
> does not provide, necessary information within a reasonable period
> or significantly impedes the investigation, [decisions], affirmative or
> negative, may be made on the basis of the facts available.

The import of this clause is that the threshold level of information necessary to open an investigation is sufficient to complete one. In almost every case, threshold information is provided by the party seeking import relief.[4]

The importance of the shift from a legal to an administrative standard of proof and evidence should not be underestimated. It not only broadened the scope of action against imports but also made the criteria for such action much more malleable. Under the softer standard of interpretation and proof, administration of the law could follow changing political pressures for protection much more quickly than a more rigorous, rule-of-law standard would allow. Thus it prepared the way for the eventual emergence of antidumping as the main vehicle for import-competing interests to press for protection—and for governments to respond to those pressures.

Early Use of Antidumping

The passage of antidumping laws did not mean that antidumping became a major instrument of import regulation right away. In the United States, the tariff remained the dominant instrument throughout the interwar period. The year after passing the 1921 antidumping bill, the U.S. Congress passed an extensive upward revision of tariff rates, the Fordney-McCumber Tariff. The tariff had been revised downward during the 1913–21 administration of President Woodrow Wilson—Wilson had vetoed the same bill that eventually became the 1921 antidumping bill—and the Fordney-McCumber Tariff pushed rates back up to or above the rates that had been in force at the end of the nineteenth century.

In Australia, South Africa, and especially Canada, antidumping actions soon became a prominent part of trade controls. Amendments to the Canadian antidumping clause adopted in 1921 and 1930 allowed the law to be interpreted with even greater flexibility, and Canadian administrators exploited that flexibility. The amendments established that fair market value would never be "less than the actual cost of production of similar goods...plus a reasonable advance for selling cost and profit" (quoted in McDiarmid 1946, p. 308). The minister of customs was able to find many degrees of freedom in both actual cost and reasonable profit, sufficient to bring McDiarmid to conclude that "the implication of this new conception of the potentialities of dumping duties is clear. The power of the executive to fix prices at which imports could be sold in Canada was practically unlimited.... The decision of the minister of customs and his civil service advisers became the final arbiter of 'fair market value'" (McDiarmid 1946, pp. 310–11).

Summing Up

The arguments made in this section can be summed up in three points:

- Antidumping has long been part of the rhetoric of protection.
- Manipulation of customs valuation has long been part of the arsenal of anti-import weapons.
- Antidumping is, in substance, another clever way to use customs valuation procedures as a weapon against imports. Antidumping preserves all the old tricks against the discipline that GATT brought to customs valuation. Actions that were once questionable practices of customs valuation are now routine antidumping calculations. Moreover, antidumping makes these tricks even more powerful. As increases of the dumping margin, they are fully added (at a rate of 100 percent) to import charges; as increases of the customs value, they would be added at the ad valorem tariff rate, which even in high-tariff countries is seldom as high as 100 percent.

The ingenuity and the magic of antidumping are how it harnesses the righteousness of trust-busting to propel the bureaucratics of customs administration in the service of restricting imports.

Contemporary Antidumping

The history of how antidumping expanded to become the principal means for controlling imports in four important trading entities—Australia, Canada, the European Community, and the United States—illustrates its inherent flexibility as a weapon against imports. Ultimately, antidumping regulations have come to label as dumping circumstances broad enough to encompass every instance in which domestic output is displaced by import competition—in the language of the regulation itself, any instance of "injury from imports."

Antidumping and the GATT

The accepted reading of the GATT's negotiating history is that no country delegation strongly insisted on including a provision for antidumping (see, for example, Barcelo 1991 and Jackson 1969). Nonetheless, despite concern that antidumping laws, if overused, might compromise the objectives of the agreement, the drafting committees concluded without controversy that provisions for antidumping and countervailing duties were needed.

During GATT's first two decades, antidumping was a minor issue. Although the GATT came into force in 1948, the contracting parties (as GATT member countries are called) did not canvass themselves about the use of antidumping until 1958. The resulting tally showed that, as of May 1958, thirty-seven antidumping decrees were in force across all GATT member countries, twenty-two of them in South Africa (GATT 1958, p. 14). At the end of December 1989, a comparable tally, covering only Australia, Canada, the United States, and the European Community, counted 530 such decrees (Low 1991, p. 22). The GATT report (1958, p. 14) notes, however, that "this table does not contain figures for Canada and New Zealand, since in those countries the customs authorities can take action without decree and therefore an enumeration comparable with that given by the other countries is impossible."

Antidumping first became a significant GATT issue at the Kennedy Round of 1964–67, perhaps more by dint of diplomatic manipulation than by clear intent. As Kenneth Dam (1970, p. 174) explains, "The United States, having introduced the subject of nontariff barriers into the negotiations, was chagrined to find that the nontariff barriers most often singled out by other countries for priority of action were those maintained by the United States, of which one of the most often mentioned was the U.S. antidumping statute." The attack on U.S. antidumping was clearly a strategy in which offense was considered to be the best defense of the European nontariff barriers that the United States had wanted brought to the negotiating table. From passage of the U.S. antidumping law in 1921 through 31 December 1967, the U.S. government conducted a total of 706 antidumping investigations, all but 75 of which ended with a negative determination (Seavey 1970, p. 65).

Nevertheless, the U.S. delegation to the Kennedy Round adopted a strategy of accommodation rather than of explanation or defense. When the administration realized that Congress would not legislate the changes required by the code, it insisted that the executive branch had the power to implement these changes by modifying investigation and enforcement procedures. Congress disagreed.

The resulting scrimmage between the administration and Congress was one of many through which the Congress reasserted its control over U.S. trade policy. Antidumping, countervailing duties, and safeguards—the major trade remedies—were often at the center of these affrays. Broadening and strengthening these trade remedies were, to Congress, much more than a means of taking control of trade policy back from the president. They were an important congressional objective on their own. Adding this or that technical amendment—tailor-made to fit the situation of a particular and powerful constituent—soon became another vehicle for constituent service, the lifeblood of congressional politics.

The reasons antidumping emerged as a major policy instrument in the EC were not all that different from those in the United States. Slower growth made European governments sensitive to the displacement of domestic production by emerging exporters from Asia. The EC antidumping mechanism—essentially the GATT Tokyo Round antidumping code translated into operational language (Eymann and Schuknecht 1991)—proved a doubly convenient means for responding to that challenge. As economics, it was flexible enough to cover all problems. As politics, it was a community instrument. The EC Commission, with the instinct of any organization for demonstrating its usefulness and thereby expanding its turf, pressed forward with antidumping action to preempt member state governments from serving the increased demand of industries for protection. Those who might have opposed either the illiberality of such actions or the shift of regulatory practice to Brussels were slow to see through the camouflage of propriety that cloaks antidumping actions.

The growth of unfair trade regulation in national policies is taken up elsewhere (for example, Finger and Messerlin 1989 and Low 1991). In this article I want to provide an overall sense of how antidumping came to expand. That story is, in essence, the cumulation of many small changes, each of which was made because antidumping, if expanded in a particular way, could fix a pressing political problem. The dominant question was always "How can antidumping be applied to this problem?" The question was never "Is this really a problem caused by *dumping?*"

In the end, dumping is just the cumulation of circumstances in which the politics of the immediate problem have exploited the flexibility of the underlying structure to rationalize taking action against imports. Dumping became, in law as well as in practice, anything you could get the government to act against under the antidumping law.

Extension to Pricing below Full Cost

Perhaps the most significant step transforming antidumping into a weapon to be used against all imports was its extension to imports not priced at full cost. This extension not only broadened the substantive scope of the instrument itself; it also brought its administrative focus in line with its political focus: keeping prices high enough to prevent injury to domestic companies. And, as has been true for many expansions of substantive scope, this extension significantly increased the administrative discretion needed to implement the standard. The extension to below-cost pricing also illustrates the role played by power politics, at both the national and international levels, in the emergence of antidumping as an all-purpose weapon against imports. Each of these effects is discussed in turn.

SUBSTANTIVE SCOPE. Competitive pricing does not always cover full costs. When demand surges, sellers can collect a premium, but when the market is sluggish, any order that pays enough to cover out-of-pocket (marginal) costs is welcome. As noted earlier, Canada, in amendments passed in 1921 and 1930, extended its antidumping regulations to cover sales priced below fully allocated costs plus a reasonable allowance for overhead and profit. Given the depressed markets of the 1930s, this meant that antidumping action could be taken against almost any import shipment—and, had the same standard been applied to national trade, to almost any sale. The fact that nowhere in the world did the exporter get a better price than in Canada did not matter: antidumping could be used to combat generally low prices, which the Canadian government perceived to be a major economic problem.

But business conditions do not have to be as severe as they were during the depression of the 1930s to activate the below-cost pricing provision. Gary Banks (1990) points out that the below-cost pricing provision in Australia's antidumping law was the basis for the expansion of Australian antidumping in the 1980s and that the government-commissioned inquiry into this expansion recommended repealing the provision in order to bring antidumping under control. Gary Horlick (1989, p. 136), once a high official in antidumping administration, estimates that some 60 percent of U.S. cases involve sales below cost.

POWER POLITICS: NATIONAL. Action against below-cost imports came into U.S. antidumping practice through the back door. Antidumping administrators found the necessary legal cover in the law's use of the phrase "in the ordinary course of trade": "The foreign market value of imported merchandise...shall be the price...at which such or similar merchandise is sold...in...the home country…in the ordinary course of trade" (U.S. Code 1677b). (The same phrase appears in GATT article VI.) Sales below full cost, the U.S. administrator interpreted, were not made in the ordinary course of trade. Before data on foreign price could be used, prices had to be compared with the exporter's cost, and prices below cost could be thrown out.

Action against import sales below full cost thus came into U.S. antidumping policy as a revision of administrative interpretation, not as a legislated change. When the administering agency (the U.S. Treasury Department at that time) first adopted this interpretation, it tried to limit application to instances that could not be explained as reductions of price to meet competition in a temporarily depressed market. But the agency had the bad judgment not to apply the below-cost standard in a case in which doing so was critical to an antidumping request made by a company with a powerful friend. The friend was Senator Russell Long of Louisiana who, as chairman of the Senate Finance Committee, probably wielded more power over trade legislation than any other person in Congress. Pending at the time was the 1974 trade bill, whose main purpose was to authorize U.S. participation in the Tokyo Round of GATT negotiations. Senator Long included in the bill an amendment to the antidumping law that required sales below cost to be considered dumping.

Current U.S. administrative practice for implementing this amendment is that if 10 percent or more of observed foreign sales are below estimated cost; such sales are not included in the calculation of foreign market value. This means that in any investigation, up to 90 percent of the U.S. government's information on foreign prices—the 90 percent most favorable to the exporter's case—may be thrown out.

POWER POLITICS: INTERNATIONAL. International sanction for taking antidumping actions against imports priced below fully allocated costs came about in a similarly arbitrary way. In November 1978, before the Tokyo Round antidumping code had reached the approval stage, Australia, Canada, the European Community, and the United States agreed to regard sales below costs as "not in the ordinary course of trade" and to exclude them from the determination of foreign market value. A document announcing this understanding was circulated in the manner in which negotiating proposals or comments on proposals were normally distributed (Koulen 1989, p. 366). Ever since, action against below-cost imports has been an integral part of antidumping policy in each of the parties to the understanding. The code itself does not address the matter.

Administrative Discretion

The story of how antidumping expanded to cover below-cost pricing shows that administrative discretion plays an important role not only in the enforcement of antidumping law but also in its expansion. In particular, three facets of administrative discretion have been influential:

- Adjustments (inferences), not observations, are the major input into an antidumping investigation.
- The detail of administrative regulation provides complexity, but not precision.
- Complexity camouflages opportunity for abuse.

Each is now examined in turn.

ADJUSTMENTS. Comparing home price with export price and then determining if any detected difference has injured an industry in the importing country appears at first glance to be a straightforward operation. But the simplicity disappears quickly under any kind of scrutiny. First of all, the GATT provides that the price of the exported good be compared with the price of a "like product" sold in the home market. The Korean electronics industry exports basic, no-frills television sets, while its home-market sales are concentrated in expensive, top-of-the-line models, with wooden cabinets and all the bells and whistles that can be installed. The intent of the investigation process is to compare apples with apples, not apples with pears, so the investigator must adjust for the different characteristics of the product to make the price of a fancy 27-inch set that retails in the neighborhood of $2,000 comparable to that of a 13-inch set in a metal cabinet that retails for $169.95.

Suppose that the antidumping investigation established from import documents that Sears paid $100 for the sets it retails for $169.95. In the case dealing with Korean televisions, the U.S. government found dumping margins to be about 15 percent, indicating that the "comparable" price of the sets sold in Korea was $115. This means that making adjustments for different characteristics of the product and for different ways of doing business in Korea and the United States reduced the $2,000 retail price to a comparable ex-factory price of $115. In other words, these administrative adjustments provide 95 percent of the information on which the eventual finding is based. The list of such examples is almost endless. Litan and Boltuck (1991) filled a book with them.

COMPLEXITY, NOT PRECISION. The increased scope of antidumping has brought a commensurate increase in administrative detail, but detail does not imply precision. William Carmichael (1986, p. 2), drawing on twelve years of experience as head of the staff of the Australian Industries Assistance Commission, concluded that "the procedures to be followed in antidumping investigations are not amenable to precise and consistent application. This means that the task of administering the legislation is not simply a task of following a set of unambiguous rules."

COMPLEXITY AS A COVER FOR ABUSE. Considerable expertise is needed even to see which technical alternatives exist, let alone exploit them. The general public and the news media do not possess this expertise: the result is an environment made to order for special-interest power politics. Extending the provision to cover pricing below full cost illustrates the typical sequence of events: first, pressure is applied to push administrative interpretation to the limit of existing law, then the extended interpretation is added to the law. Each time, the law becomes more detailed and its administration more complex—a medium more and more hospitable to power politics, more and more favorable to the home country petitioner's case over the exporter's, and more and more detached from the initial rationale for the regulation.

An Example of Skewed Procedures: Treatment of Selling Costs

Many writers have documented specific examples of changes in law or administrative practice that have worked in the petitioner's favor. Bierwagen (1990) provides an excellent tabulation; only one example is provided here.

As mentioned above, manufacturing companies often sell or transfer goods to a subsidiary sales company (for example, Sony to Sony-USA) so that the first arms-length transaction occurs when the sales company sells the product. To adjust costs to an ex-factory basis, the expenses of the sales company must be deducted. The following quotation (Bellis 1989, p. 83) relates specifically to practices in the European Community, but other countries treat selling costs the same way:

> A producer which sells a consumer branded product at exactly the same price in both domestic and export markets, a situation which to anybody outside an antidumping administration would appear to be a typical case of no dumping, will systematically be credited with a dumping margin corresponding to the indirect selling expenses of his domestic sales organization for which no allowances can be made.... Indirect selling expenses for consumer branded products are substantial, often in the order of 15 to 20 percent of the selling price.

The End Result

My conclusion borrows much from other analysts. N. David Palmeter (1991, p. 66), referring specifically to U.S. practice, describes the situation as follows:

> The standards of the day, the procedures it uses, and the implementation of these standards and procedures by the Department of Commerce increasingly ensure that, at the end of the day, an exporter determined to have been selling in the United States below fair value probably has been doing no such thing in any meaningful sense of the word "fair." On the contrary, rather than being a price discriminator, a dumper is more likely [to be] the victim of an anti-

dumping process that has become a legal and an administrative non-tariff barrier.

The European Community uses different procedures, but the end result is the same. As Angelika Eymann and Ludger Schuknecht (1991) point out, the United States applies protectionist rules, the European Community applies protectionist discretion. The result in both cases is protection. In Brian Hindley's (1988, p. 460) words, "From antidumping law, the Commission and the Council have fashioned a trade-policy weapon of great power. No legal process, either domestic or international, seems likely to place any substantial impediment in the way of the further development and deployment of that weapon."

Descriptions of worlds like that of antidumping are more often encountered in fiction—weird fiction—than in academic discourse. Note in the following passage by Douglas Adams (1980, pp. 38–39) the relationship between the *Hitchhiker's Guide to the Galaxy* and the galaxy. The relationship between antidumping law and dumping is the same.

> The *Hitchhiker's Guide to the Galaxy* is an indispensable companion to all those who are keen to make sense of life in an infinitely complex and confusing Universe, for though it cannot hope to be useful or informative on all matters, it does at least make the reassuring claim, that where it is inaccurate it is at least *definitively* inaccurate. In cases of major discrepancy it's always reality that's got it wrong.
>
> This was the gist of the notice. It said, "The *Guide* is definitive. Reality is frequently inaccurate."
>
> This has led to some interesting consequences. For instance, when the editors of the *Guide* were sued by the families of those who had died as a result of taking the entry on the planet Traal literally (it said "Ravenous Bugblatter Beasts often make a very good meal *for* visiting tourists" instead of "Ravenous Bugblatter Beasts often make a very good meal *of* visiting tourists"), they claimed that the first version of the sentence was the more aesthetically pleasing, summoned a qualified poet to testify under oath that beauty was truth, truth beauty, and hoped thereby to prove that the guilty party in this case was Life itself for failing to be either beautiful or true. The judges concurred, and in a moving speech held that Life itself was in contempt of court, and duly confiscated it from all those there present.

In Defense of Antidumping

Partly in response to criticism that dumping margins were frequently overstated by contemporary procedures, defenders of antidumping have pointed to what in EC practice is called the lesser-duty rule. The idea behind the rule is expressed in the GATT antidumping code: "It is desirable that the...

[antidumping] duty be less than the margin, if such lesser duty would be adequate to remove the injury to the domestic industry" (GATT 1980, art. VIII, par. 1).

EC Commissioner for External Relations Willy de Clercq, in defending the EC's antidumping policy as *"incontestably* by far the most liberal" (his emphasis), pointed out that "unlike U.S. authorities, the commission is not obliged to apply antidumping measures at rates which reflect the full margins of dumping established. On the contrary, under Community law the rate is restricted to that necessary to remove the injury caused" (de Clercq 1988, p. 29). Jean-François Bellis, a prominent Brussels lawyer and legal scholar—and sometimes critic of EC policy—is an outspoken advocate of the lesser-duty rule:

> The EEC justifiably prides itself on the fact that, unlike the U[nited] S[tates], it applies the "lesser duty rule," i.e., it limits antidumping duties to the level necessary to eliminate the injury. This practice should be multilateralized in GATT in the form of a binding obligation.[5] (Bellis 1989, p. 94)

Bellis also explains how to do it:

> In practice, the level of the duty is mainly determined by the level of price undercutting... or by the level of resale prices that would be required to cover the costs of Community producers and provide a reasonable profit. (pp. 84–85)

Compare that statement with the following (quoted in Taussig 1931, p. 363):

> In any protective legislation the true principle of protection is best maintained by the imposition of such duties as will equal the difference between the cost of production at home and abroad, together with a reasonable profit to American industries.

The second of these is the statement contained in the 1908 U.S. Republican Party platform of the cost-equalization formula, which the U.S. Congress followed in writing the Smoot-Hawley Tariff.

As to the usefulness of the formula as a guide to policy, E. E. Schattschneider (1935, pp. 84 and 284) argues emphatically that the formula has no operational meaning:

> Talk of tariffs written on the cost formula is no more than an elaborate sham and a bluff.... The committees did not generally determine rates according to the formula advertised, and they did not do so for the conclusive reason that they could not.... The difference of cost formula is to be classified more properly as a slogan belonging to the politics of gaining acceptance of [protection] than as a method of determining rates.

Frank Taussig (1931, p. 633) is equally critical of the lack of substance of the formula, but less scathing. He points out that anything can be made within any country if the producer is assured a price high enough to cover all costs of production together with a reasonable allowance for profits. "Yet," he adds, "little acumen is needed to see that, carried out consistently, it [the formula] means simple prohibition and complete stoppage of foreign trade."

Perhaps it is overkill to recall the wisdom of Schattschneider and Taussig to argue that contemporary antidumping is out of control. It should be sufficient to point out that its own defenders bring forward the economic philosophy of the Smoot-Hawley Tariff as its rationale.

Summing Up

The cause that justifies an action is often far removed from the motives that propel its advocates. When push comes to shove, the motives, not the cause, dictate the details of the action. And the details, in turn, dictate the substance. In trade policy, existence precedes essence.

Antidumping is not public policy, it is private policy. It is a harnessing of state power to serve a private interest: a means by which one competitor can use the power of the state to gain an edge over another competitor. Antidumping regulation was created by removing from antitrust law the checks and balances that limit it to disciplining only the competitive practices that compromise society's overall interests. Antitrust is in both theory and practice an instrument to defend the public interest. Antidumping is a different matter. Free from the constraints that the rule of law imposes on antitrust, antidumping is an instrument that one competitor can use against another—like advertising, product development, or price discounting. The only constraint is that the beneficiary interest must be domestic and the apparent victim must be foreign.

Antidumping puts the fox in charge of the henhouse: trade restrictions certified by GATT. The fox is clever enough not only to eat the hens, but also to convince the farmer that this is the way things ought to be. Antidumping is ordinary protection with a grand public relations program.

Notes

Michael Finger is lead economist in the Trade Policy Division of the Country Economics Department at the World Bank.

1. Horlick and Oliver were writing about both antidumping and antisubsidy (countervailing duty) measures. In the United States, the number of trade remedies cases is divided roughly equally between the two; in other countries, antidumping is by far the most popular instrument.

2. The Country Party practiced similar politics in Australia in the middle of the twentieth century. For one discussion, see Rattigan (1986).

3. The result brings to mind Frank Taussig's explanation of pricing strategy of a firm so situated: "The monopolist sells at high prices where he can, and accepts lower prices where he must" (Taussig and White 1931, p. 208). Taussig's quip reminds one to ask who came out ahead: Canada or U.S. Steel or U.K. exporters.

4. Palmeter (1991) explains that if the provision of best information available were not included, the respondent could block an investigation by refusing to cooperate. He points out that the provision was rarely used until recently. In recent cases, however, information requirements have been so complex that the respondents were either unable to comply or the estimated costs of complying were so high that they chose not to.

5. Bellis is, however, critical of how the EC has put the rule into practice.

References

The word "processed" describes informally reproduced works that may not be commonly available through libraries.

Adams, Douglas. 1980. *The Restaurant at the End of the Universe.* New York: Pocket Books.

Balassa, Bela, and associates. 1971. *The Structure of Protection in Developing Countries.* Published for the World Bank and the Inter-American Development Bank. Baltimore, Md.: Johns Hopkins University Press.

Banks, Gary. 1990. "Australia's Antidumping Experience." PRE Working Paper 551. World Bank, Country Economics Department, Washington, D.C. Processed.

Barcelo, John J., III. 1991. "An Analytical History of GATT Unfair Trade Remedy Law." In Brian Hindley, ed., *The Regulation of Trade.* London: Trade Policy Research Centre.

Bellis, Jean-François. 1989. "The EEC Antidumping System." In John H. Jackson and Edwin A. Vermulst, eds., *Antidumping Law and Practice.* Ann Arbor, Mich.: University of Michigan Press.

Bierwagen, Ranier M. 1990. GATT *Article VI and the Protectionist Bias in Antidumping Law.* Studies in Transnational Law 7. Boston, Mass.: Kluwer.

Carmichael, William B. 1986. "Review of the Customs Tariff (Antidumping) Act." Submitted to the *Gruen Review,* Canberra, Australia.

Dale, Richard. 1980. *Antidumping Law in a Liberal Trade Order.* New York: St. Martin's Press.

Dam, Kenneth W. 1970. *The GATT: Law and International Economic Organization.* Chicago: University of Chicago Press.

de Clercq, Willy. 1988. "Fair Practice, Not Protectionism." *Financial Times,* 21 November, p. 29.

Easterbrook, W. T., and Hugh G. J. Aitken. 1988. *Canadian Economic History.* Toronto: University of Toronto Press.

Eymann, Angelika, and Ludger Schuknecht. 1991. "Antidumping Enforcement in the European Community." PRE Working Paper 743. World Bank, Country Economics Department, Washington, D.C. Processed.

Finger, J. Michael, and Patrick A. Messerlin. 1989. *The Effects of Industrial Countries' Policies on Developing Countries.* Policy and Research Report 3. Washington, D.C.: World Bank.

GATT (General Agreement on Tariffs and Trade). 1958. *Antidumping and Countervailing Duties.* Geneva.

————. 1980. "Agreement on Implementation of Article VI of the General Agreement on Tariffs and Trade." In GATT, *Basic Instruments and Selected Documents.* 26th Supplement, Protocols, Decisions, Reports 1978–1979 and 35th Session. Geneva.

————. 1990. "Compendium of Drafting Proposals for Modifications to the Agreement on Implementation of Article VI of the General Agreement (Antidumping Code)." Attachment to MTN.GNG/NG8/W/83/ADD.5. Group of Negotiations on Goods, Multilateral Trade Negotiations. Geneva.

Hindley, Brian. 1988. "Dumping and the Far East Trade of the European Community." *The World Economy* 11 (December): 445–64.

Horlick, Gary N. 1989. "The United States Antidumping System." In John H. Jackson and Edwin A. Vermulst, eds., *Antidumping Law and Practice.* Ann Arbor, Mich.: University of Michigan Press.

Horlick, Gary N., and Geoffrey D. Oliver. 1989. "Antidumping and Countervailing Duty Law Provisions of the Omnibus Trade and Competitiveness Act of 1988." *Journal of World Trade* 23 (June): 5–49.

Hull, Cordell. 1948. *The Memoirs of Cordell Hull,* 2 vols. New York: Macmillan.

Jackson, John H. 1969. *World Trade and the Law of GATT.* Charlottesville, Va.: Michie.

Koulen, Mark. 1989. "Some Problems of Interpretation and Implementation of the GATT Antidumping Code." In John H. Jackson and Edwin A. Vermulst, eds., *Antidumping Law and Practice.* Ann Arbor, Mich.: University of Michigan Press.

Litan, Robert E., and Richard D. Boltuck, eds. 1991. *Down in the Dumps: Administration of the Unfair Trade Laws.* Washington, D.C.: Brookings Institution.

Low, Patrick. 1991. "The Impact of Industrial Countries' Trade, Agricultural, and Industrial Policies on Developing Countries." World Bank, International Economics Department, Washington, D.C. Processed.

Lowenfeld, Andreas F. 1980. "Fair or Unfair Trade: Does It Matter?" *Cornell International Law Journal* 13: 205–19.

McDiarmid, Orville John. 1946. *Commercial Policy in the Canadian Economy.* Cambridge, Mass.: Harvard University Press.

McGee, John S. 1958. "Predatory Price Cutting: The Standard Oil (N.J.) Case." *Journal of Law and Economics* 1 (October): 128–69.

Messerlin, Patrick A. 1991. "The Antidumping Law: A Legal and Administrative Trade Barrier." In Robert E. Litan and Richard D. Boltuck, eds., *Down in the Dumps: Administration of the Unfair Trade Laws.* Washington, D.C.: Brookings Institution.

Rattigan, Alf. 1986. *Industry Assistance, The Inside Story.* Melbourne: Melbourne University Press.

Schattschneider, E. E. 1935. *Politics, Pressures, and the Tariff.* New York: Prentice-Hall.

Seavey, William Arthur. 1970. "Dumping Since the War: The GATT and National Laws." Ph.D. thesis 205, Université de Genève, Institut Universitaire des Hautes Études, Geneva; Office Services Corporation, Oakland, Calif.

Taussig, Frank W. 1931. *The Tariff History of the United States.* 8th ed. New York: Putnam. Reprint, 1967. New York: Augustus M. Kelley.

Taussig, Frank W., and Harry Dexter White. 1931. *Some Aspects of the Tariff Question.* Cambridge, Mass.: Harvard University Press.

U.S. Tariff Commission. 1919. *Information Concerning Dumping and Unfair Foreign Competition in the United States and Canada's Antidumping Law.* Washington, D.C.: U.S. Government Printing Office.

Viner, Jacob. 1923. *Dumping: A Problem in International Trade.* Chicago: University of Chicago Press. Reprint, 1966. New York: Augustus M. Kelley.

Yergin, Daniel. 1991. *The Prize: The Epic Quest for Oil, Money, and Power.* New York: Simon and Schuster.

[10]

Should Developing Countries Introduce Antidumping? Never

Governments opening their economies to imports run afoul of local producers, who petition for exceptions to restore the protection they've long enjoyed. There is a right way to review these petitions. Adopting antidumping procedures is not it

There's a new vogue among developing countries— continuing the pernicious tradition of industrial countries—to introduce antidumping regulations in response to complaints from local firms about the competition from importing that liberalized trade brings. Brazil, Korea, and Mexico reported 34 cases to GATT in the late 1980s. Other developing countries have implemented antidumping regulations without reporting them to GATT—or have asked for technical assistance to establish such regulations. Costa Rica, Colombia, Chile, Morocco, and Indonesia are among them.

Any government pushing forward a program to deregulate industry— and remove import restrictions—can expect to come under pressure from various constituencies to give them special consideration. If that government is to maintain political support for the reforms—indeed, if it is to stay in office—it must have means to review what problems their constituents see as special and to decide whether such problems deserve at least temporary relief from the liberalization program.

But are antidumping regulations a good means for this? No. Accepted legal definitions of when imports are dumped can never be a guide for making economically sound decisions about when it is—or is not—in the national economic interest to restrict trade by granting exceptions to a liberalization program.

- *Identify the costs and the losers*

- *Be clear that the action is an exception*

- *Don't sanctify the criteria for the action*

Furthermore, the antidumping process can get out of hand and become a strong force against trade liberalization, as the politics of antidumping quickly dominate a country's trade policy (see the box).

Antidumping's apparent policing of predatory actions by foreigners is a major part of the emotional power of antidumping. In reality, however, antidumping does not police predatory actions. David Palmeter, a leading Washington expert and frequent counsel to developing country exporters beset by antidumping cases, concludes: "It probably is safe to predict that in none of the 767 affirmative antidumping determinations reached by Australia, Canada, the EC, and the U.S. between 1980 and 1986 was predatory pricing remotely present."

What then does antidumping do? It restricts imports. It is ordinary protection with a grand public relations program.

Antidumping and other concepts of unfair trade have reversed the post-World War II liberal momentum of U.S. trade politics. Except for Canada's and Mexico's leadership in engaging the United States in free trade area negotiations, there would be virtually nothing in U.S. trade politics except the momentum toward unfair trade restrictions. In like manner, the EC 1992 program is carrying the European Community toward more liberal policies internally. But toward the rest of the world, the Community's antidumping actions are the principal face of its trade policy. Self-seduced like Australia and the United States, the Community points to its consistency with the GATT in defending its antidumping regulations as "incontestably by far the most liberal."

If antidumping is not the way to go, how should a government meet its need for a means to evaluate requests for exceptions to liberalization? Here are some general guidelines:

• *Identify the costs and the losers.* Procedures should bring out the costs of the requested exception, and the identities of the persons or groups who will bear these costs. More expensive imports will cost somebody money and—if the imports are needed materials—eliminate somebody's job. These costs, and the people in the domestic economy who will bear them, should have the same standing in law and in administrative practice as the other side already enjoys. The process of considering the request for an exception should be used to help fortify the politics of not granting it.

• *Be clear that the action is an exception.* Procedures should also establish that the requested action would be an exception to the principles that underlay the liberalization program. Admitting to political weakness is better than admitting that the exception is a good idea.

• *Don't sanctify the criteria for the action.* Procedures should not presume that there is some good reason for granting exceptions—procedures that compare the situation of the petitioner with pre-established criteria for granting an exception should be avoided. Procedures should stress that the function of the review is to identify the benefits and the costs—and the domestic winners and the domestic losers—for the

But...

Pieter Bottelier agrees only partly with the message that Mike Finger articulates here. "Unless we can offer developing countries a GATT-consistent (that is, respectable) antidumping mechanism," Bottelier says, "trade liberalization adjustment loans are almost impossible to negotiate, especially for countries that are starting the process. This was true of the Mexico negotiations in the mid-1980s, and I've just experienced the same with Morocco."

"Mike's position," says Neil Roger, "is that just because antidumping procedures are GATT-consistent does not necessarily prevent them from being a recipe for disaster. His research has shown exhaustively how antidumping has been abused in industrial countries, and he is concerned that this not be repeated in developing countries."

"What is clear," Roger argues, "is that politicians sometimes see the promise of GATT-consistent antidumping procedures as a relatively cheap way of building support among industrialists for trade liberalization. But the tradeoff is not so simple, for if the industrialists capture the process, they may be able to use the back door of antidumping procedures to regain the protection they gave up through the front door of trade reform.

"Mike advocates some simple guidelines for governments to evaluate requests for exceptions to liberalizations," Roger continues. "Essentially these involve looking at economic costs and benefits, rather than legal definitions of dumping, material injury, and the like. It is important to note that Mike's guidelines are quite consistent with the GATT rules."

In Mexico, the current Salinas administration has put people committed to the liberalization program in charge of the antidumping procedures, and thus reduced the abuses of earlier administrations.

In Venezuela's negotiations, the practicality was that the Venezuelans wanted antidumping procedures. So, the Bank proposed GATT-consistent language and procedures, but also gave the Venezuelans the information and analysis to guide the design of those procedures—in a trade-friendly way. As negotiations proceeded, the Venezuelans backed off on the importance of antidumping—and they later undertook a major trade liberalization *without* any antidumping legislation. This legislation is only now (two years later) being put into place.

In short: You may have to give countries a bit of antidumping as a sweetener for launching a trade liberalization program. If so, beware the possible abuses—and ensure that the procedures examine the costs to the community as well as the benefits to the industrialists. But as the Venezuelan experience shows, you don't always have to accede to antidumping measures.

requested action.

The third guideline is more important than it might seem. The history of antidumping and other trade remedies shows that clever people will always be able to present their situation exactly as the criteria describe. If you start out to find just the few exporters who are being unfair to Australia or to the United States or to Mexico, you will soon be swamped by evidence that everyone is.

At the technical level, useful concepts for review procedures—such as transparency and automatic expiration for any exception that is granted (a sunset clause)—can be gleaned from procedural proposals made at the safeguards negotiations of the Uruguay Round.

J. Michael Finger ❖

Readings from the Working Paper Series:

"Australia's Antidumping Experience," Gary Banks, WPS 551.

"The Development of the Colombian Cut Flower Industry," Jose A. Mendez, WPS 660.

"Brazilian Frozen Concentrated Orange Juice: The Folly of Unfair Trade Cases," Carlos Alberto Primo Braga and Siamo Davis.

"Antidumping Enforcement in the European Community," Angelika Eymann and Ludger Schuknecht, WPS 743

"Stainless Steel in Sweden: Antidumping Attacks Good International Citizenship," Gunnar Fors, WPS 744.

"Enforcement of Canadian 'Unfair' Trade Laws: The Case for Competition Policies as an Antidote for Protection," Mark Dutz, WPS 776.

"The Korean Consumer Electronics Industry: Reaction to Antidumping Actions," Taeho Bark, WPS 781.

"The Economic Effects of Widespread Application of Antidumping Duties to Import Pricing," Patrick Conway and Sumana Dhar, WPS 782.

"The Origins and Evolution of Antidumping Regulation," J. Michael Finger, WPS 783.

"Chemicals from Poland: A Tempest in a Teacup," Andrzej Olechowski, WPS 784.

"The Meaning of 'Unfair' in U.S. Import Policy," J. Michael Finger, WPS 745.

For copies, call Nellie Artis at 38010.

Incorporating the Gains from Trade into Policy

J. M. Finger

THOSE who are convinced of the economic and political importance of maintaining an open international trading system face two challenges, namely to find a way to arrest the slippage towards protection which is occurring in the policies of industrial countries and to bring these countries and the developing countries, which are becoming significant elements in the world economy, to dismantle the restrictions on imports which they maintain. To an economic theorist, these would appear to be similar tasks, for trade liberalisation and protection are, in economic logic, opposite directions on the same scale.

But to a political theorist the differences are more evident than the similarities. Trade liberalisation and protection are, in government, completely different processes. Trade is liberalised through highly visible multilateral negotiations conducted under the auspices of the General Agreement on Tariffs and Trade (GATT), while trade restrictions are imposed through much less visible administrative mechanisms, such as anti-dumping and countervailing-duty procedures and safeguards or escape-clause mechanisms. These institutions have been much less extensively studied than the GATT negotiations, even though, as G. C. Hufbauer, a well-informed analyst and former trade official in the United States Treasury Department, has observed, 'administered protection has been the leading edge of trade policy at least since 1975'.[1]

Indeed, a major initiative of the United States in the Tokyo Round negotiations of 1973-79 was aimed at these administrative procedures. Codes were negotiated which specified in detail the way a country would undertake a countervailing-duty or anti-dumping investigation, grant import licences, assign values for customs purposes *et cetera*. It was hoped that making

J. M. FINGER: a Senior Economist on the Development Policy Staff, World Bank, Washington; formerly Director, Office of Trade Research, United States Department of the Treasury, 1974-79.

J. M. FINGER

national procedures consistent with these codes would reduce the degree by which they favour domestic sources over foreign ones; that is, reduce the degree of protection implicit in them. In like manner, systematic procedures for the settlement of disputes between countries were laid out and it was hoped that as cases passed through the dispute-settlement process a body of case law and precedent would be established which all countries would come to respect.

In effect the process of import regulation would be 'Americanised'. Each national government would codify its administrative procedures for deciding whether or not to approve petitions from its industries for protection from import competition. Procedures would be standardised and both importers and the complaining domestic industry would be assured access to the information on which the government would base its decision. As precedent built up, the government would have a painless means for handling pressures for protection. And if the effects of these decisions ever appeared to compromise the likewise codified interests of another country, a similarly constructed and therefore similarly painless international mechanism would resolve the dispute. This is a seductive idea, but not one likely to work. Not even Americans do things that way.

RULES AND TRANSPARENCY

The United States Administration's procedures for managing domestic pressures for protection include two different 'tracks', the technical and the political.

The anti-dumping and countervailing-duty mechanisms are technical procedures. Their determinations are defined by hundreds of lines of legislation and thousands of lines of administrative regulation. Furthermore, the decision whether or not to impose anti-dumping and countervailing duties is directly tied to those technical determinations. In order to assure that the rules are followed, a party to a case may appeal against the Administration's determination in the federal courts.

Examination of the record of such cases confirms that they are, indeed, technical not political determinations. John Odell, an American political scientist then at Harvard University, examined the outcomes of about two dozen such cases which involved Latin American countries.[2] He found that the proportion of cases 'won' by the Latin American countries was not affected by application of political pressure — either through the American Secretary of State or directly to the Treasury Department, the agency which administered such cases over the period studied by Professor Odell.

GAINS FROM INTERNATIONAL TRADE 369

Two colleagues and I recently studied the entire record of cases decided between 1975 and 1979, more than 200 cases.[3] We tested statistically for the influence of a number of non-technical or political factors, from the importance to American foreign policy of the country against which the case was filed to the threat that because the administering agency (then the Treasury Department) was not finding affirmatively often enough, responsibility for such cases should be shifted elsewhere. None of these political factors turned out to have any influence. Furthermore, a list of technical variables — the kind of economic and accounting factors one finds in rules and regulations — did have very significant explanatory power.

Escape-clause cases are a different matter. They involve an open political process, one in which the interested parties can effectively argue about the relevant criteria and not just about whether the predetermined criteria are satisfied. Each escape-clause case includes an injury investigation, which is conducted by the US International Trade Commission (ITC). If the ITC determines that import competition has brought injury to the complaining domestic producers they send the President their recommendation for the appropriate remedy.

But escape-clause cases differ from anti-dumping and countervailing duty-cases in two important ways: (i) the meaning of injury is much less precisely defined by law and regulation and (ii) the President's decision is not tied to the outcome of the injury investigation. He may refuse to restrict imports or grant other forms of relief even though the ITC found injury and, moreover, in the face of a 'no injury' determination, he may negotiate an agreement to limit imports, as was done in the recent motor car case. This is not a unique example. Robert E. Baldwin, of the University of Wisconsin, found insignificant association between the outcome of the ITC's injury determination and the decision which the President eventually made in the case.[4]

Here the record shows no tendency towards systematisation. Indeed, while the more technical or bureaucratic track tends towards regularity, the higher-level politically-accountable track tends towards singularity. Robert Walters, a political scientist at the University of Pittsburgh, analysing a series of recent trade cases, comes closest to this conclusion: 'It has proven almost impossible for the US political system to approach the steel crisis, Chrysler's collapse, the automobile crisis, and the difficulties of other industries as different manifestations of the same genre of challenge.' Although the United States Administration eventually reached decisions in each of these cases, Dr Walters described the decision process as a 'consensus of avoidance'.

The usefulness of the American proposal that more detailed rules be written can be boiled down to two questions:

370   J. M. FINGER

(a) Would elaboration of the rules make for more effective management of pressures for protection; that is, would it increase the number
of cases resolved (at either the domestic or the international level) 'by
the rules' and reduce the number of petitions for protection which
become open and political issues, requiring significant attention by
politically-accountable officials?

(b) Would more detailed rules increase the likelihood of negative
responses to pressures for protection and/or reduce the frequency of
such petitions?

Experience in the United States suggests that the answer to both questions is
'No'. In the recent motor car case the ITC followed the relevant rules and
determined that the American industry was not eligible for import relief.
Threats soon followed that the Congress would, by direct vote, limit imports
of motor cars. A more subtle, and perhaps more important, threat was that
unless the President took action, car-industry supporters in Congress would
hold hostage his tax-cut bill, the centrepiece of the Reagan Administration's
supply-side economic programme.

The lesson from this example is that whether or not pressure for protection leads to a rules-track case or becomes an open and political issue is not
determined by the existence of rules applicable to that case; it is determined
by the political significance (closely proxied by the economic size) of the
case.

This generalisation is strongly supported by the record of cases decided
under the Trade Act of 1974. The average technical track (anti-dumping or
countervailing-duty) case involved less than one tenth of the value of
imports of the average escape-clause case; and the 40 escape-clause cases
covered almost three times the value of imports of the 177 anti-dumping and
countervailing-duty cases. Furthermore, the escape-clause cases which ended
up as orderly marketing arrangements or 'voluntary' export-restraint agreements were four times as large as those resolved in accordance with the
ITC's interpretation of the relevant rules.[5]

Why do all the non-trivial cases evade the rules track and become open,
political issues? Perhaps it is because governments of the signatory countries
to the GATT have taken on the responsibility to maintain the openness of
their economies and yet they have outfitted themselves with the means and
procedures to manage domestic pressures for protection which capture the
discomforts of international competition, but not its benefits.

The ITC, for instance, in injury determinations, is required to investigate
injury to domestic producers of products which compete with imports. The
law, which is completely consistent with the GATT, allows no such investigation of gains to users of imports — either to other producers who use the
imported good as an input or to consumers of a finished good. These

interests may express their opinion as to whether or not the petitioners for protection have demonstrated injury to themselves from import competition, but the rules do not allow a demonstration of the gain, or saving, to the users of the imports. The pricing tests in anti-dumping and countervailing-duty procedures are similarly, although not so obviously, biased. In the United States, where the rules for these procedures are available for examination, they have been found to proscribe for foreign sellers a number of trade practices which parallel anti-trust law does not take away from domestic sellers. How this is done is explained in an article in the *Journal of World Trade Law* by William Dickey, who was formerly in charge of enforcing the American anti-dumping and countervailing-duty laws at the Treasury Department.[6]

Furthermore, only the *precision of the rules*, not their *economic subject matter*, changes as one moves from the technical to the more political decision mechanisms. The legal objective of the anti-dumping and countervailing-duty mechanism is to police the fairness of trade practices and it pursues that objective by restricting imports; in design, from unfair exporters only. It is therefore an economic instrument with the power to restrict imports and the simple idea of greed suggests that it will attract those with an interest in imports being restricted — not only firms and industries beset by unfair competition but also, more generally, those least favourably situated *vis-à-vis* their foreign competitors' costs. They will, the logic of economic anthropology suggests, attempt to make their needs fit its scope and its scope fit their needs. As this suggests, the details of American law and administrative regulations have been changed over time so that even the *pricing* investigation in such cases has come to turn on the same matters as does an escape-clause case. My colleagues and I have pointed out relevant specifics in our 1982 study. In corroboration, we found that among the technical factors examined those which related to comparative costs were the most powerful predictors of the outcome of anti-dumping and countervailing-duty cases.[7]

To meet its commitment to maintain openness, the government of a signatory country must rally interests to whom the rules track gives no voice. Likewise, interests that are harmed by the petitioned-for trade restrictions which come forward on their own must apply pressure directly on politicians. They are *excluded* from the rules track *by the rules*.

In minor cases a one-sided decision mechanism might work well. To quantify only one dimension of protection can be relatively inexpensive and if the rules and regulations for doing so are sufficiently complex, they might prevent the more widely dispersed consumer interests from being aware of their losses.

J. M. FINGER

West Europeans, I am told, seem generally less aware than Americans that protection has a cost to consumers and are also more respectful of the government's authority. Hence it is in the tradition of governments in Western Europe to operate relatively closed administrative mechanisms; that is, mechanisms for which the decision criteria are not specified and the information to be fed into a decision is not made public. In this view, elaborate procedures are the United States Administration's way to evade an accountability which West Europeans simply do not ask of their governments.

While the obfuscation provided by elaborate procedures can prevent a small case from becoming a public issue, it cannot transform an important case into an obscure one. So long as procedures do not provide channels for all the interests at play, transparency in decisions on industrial policy in the United States brings impotence and a search for a more obscure way, not unquestioning public acceptance to the decision. As the American public's awareness of the escape-clause mechanism grew, the United States Administration shifted towards using the anti-dumping and countervailing-duty procedures. (This shift has been noted by Rodney de C. Grey, a long-time Canadian trade official.[8])

In turn, attempting to use the anti-dumping or countervailing-duty provisions to manage the highly publicised pressures of the steel and motor car industries stripped them of much of their obscurity. The United States Administration has thus shifted to a different source of authority, namely the provisions on unfair trade practices in the Trade Agreements Act of 1979. These provisions, not the more familiar but exhausted parts of American trade law, provide the basis for 1980s-style 'reciprocity'.

Transparency is, to the present system, the antithesis. A responsive government cannot *openly* disenfranchise major interest groups and survive. That is why transparency does not make the management of trade policy easy for the United States and why West Europeans simply do not bother with it.

The problem is not that openness in decision making is bad. Rather the problem is that the philosophy behind the current set of decision-making rules is one-sided. Openness allows an importer to challenge a domestic industry's demonstration that imports are doing it harm. But it does not allow the importer to demonstrate that the *gains* to the importer and to his customers are at least as large. Rather than fixing this bias, openness makes it more obvious and hence *reduces* the likelihood that the question as to whether to protect an industry will be resolved within the rules-defined decision mechanism.

GAINS FROM INTERNATIONAL TRADE 373

BRINGING IN THE DEVELOPING COUNTRIES

International reciprocity has been the motive force in the series of GATT negotiations held in the post-World War II period, through which most industrial-country tariffs have been reduced to minimal levels. Although economic theory, supported by a long list of estimates of the costs of protection, demonstrates rather plainly that the user or consumer gains from unilateral removal of a trade restriction almost always exceed the costs to those displaced by import competition, the mercantilist tendency, to view imports as the cost of trade and exports as the gain, is strong. Countries have always excluded some products from their tariff reductions not necessarily because the costs (to competing domestic producers) would exceed the gains (to consumers); they have done so for fear that some displaced producers might make sufficient political trouble to block the negotiations. This has limited the exchange of concessions to products on which cost differences among the industrial countries were small and the result has been growth in intra-industry trade — a country's exports expanding in the same sectors as its imports. Such small cost differences, however, were observed over a wide range of products and, in consequence, the tariff reductions negotiated covered most of the industrial sector.

But the most labour-intensive industries, where cost differences between countries were large, experienced minimal tariff cuts. In spite of faster growth in the 1950s and early 1960s and fuller employment, reciprocity from Japan, then *the* major supplier, was not sufficient for the United States Administration and governments in Western Europe to overcome resistance from the producer interests that would lose in order to achieve the larger consumer gains.

Trade liberalisation by developing countries in the period since World War II has been primarily a matter of domestic evaluation of the domestic pluses and minuses, not of international negotiations. Even among the older industrial countries, the GATT negotiating process has not been effective where cost differences were large. Between developed and developing countries, the cost differences (one way or the other) are large in nearly all sectors and therefore not much can be expected from the old system of reciprocal concessions qualified by the understanding that no significant (or material) costs will be imposed on a domestic interest, no matter how large the accompanying savings to other domestic interests. Trade liberalisation by developing countries will continue to depend on a country's coming to realise that its *domestic* benefits exceed its *domestic* costs.

What can the present GATT system contribute to that realisation? The answer is very little. It institutionalises the idea that any move towards openness which meets with domestic resistance is to be avoided. What is needed is guidance as to how the domestic interests which would gain from that liberalisation might be organised and how their needs might be brought to bear on the relevant policy decisions.

Common sense and a very brief inquiry suggest that developing countries have regular procedures for responding to domestic pressures for protection. A preliminary investigation in one country, Indonesia, revealed a strong functional similarity with the procedures of the United States.[9] In Indonesia, a petition for a higher tariff or an import quota is addressed to a cabinet minister, usually the Minister of Industry. It is then referred to a trade policy team composed of staff from the trade, finance and industry ministries. This team then attempts to determine (i) Indonesian capacity and unit costs, (ii) Indonesian demand at a price which covers domestic costs and (iii) the tariff rate which would bring the world price up to the level of Indonesian costs or the equivalent import quota. As with an escape-clause case in the United States, the technical formality or precision which these steps suggest is more apparent than real. When Indonesian officials were asked if they always aimed protection at the observed level of the domestic industry's costs they replied that they do not. On the other hand, they were aware that a commitment to aim at the level of costs of exporters (from developed or developing countries) would usually not provide protection. Hence the practice in Indonesia preserves considerable discretion for officials to assess how deserving the petitioning industry may be and how likely the industry would be to become competitive on world terms if granted protection.

The formalised part of such a case deals only with the idling of domestic capacity and the policy response which would negate this injury — as would emergency protection applied under Article XIX of the GATT. Following the letter of the GATT might require that minutes be taken when the Indonesian team discusses with importers or domestic producers the information it has collected and perhaps that tables be prepared for a few additional variables. But their procedure captures the same spirit as do currently sanctioned procedures taken by industrial countries. Suggesting that import relief be provided only when there is a 'material' or 'substantial' amount of injury or idle domestic capacity would make Indonesian procedures more complex, but it would not change the economic sense of them.

The Indonesian Government is seriously considering tariff reform (liberalisation) and realises full well that before it can implement such reform it must make the case *in Indonesia* that the economic benefits *to Indonesia* will exceed the costs. It would be hard to advise them that strict adherence to the GATT can help them or even that the GATT demonstrates how the countries which promote it have realised and institutionalised the gains from international trade.

CONCLUSIONS AND RECOMMENDATIONS

The approach to trade embodied in the principles and rules of the GATT is based on a belief by the participating countries that the benefits of an open system of international trade would exceed the costs. But the GATT system does not bring participating countries to weigh all the benefits they derive from international trade against the costs. The record of the tariff negotiations and the administrative parts of the General Agreement certainly illustrate this.

It is not likely, then, that passing the same plough over the field again will till the soil any deeper. If progress is to be made towards controlling the administrative procedures through which trade restrictions come into being or towards dispelling the resistance of both industrial and developing countries to further liberalisation, some additional weight must be added to the plough. This weight should be the *gains* from international trade — the interests of those who *save* because of access to foreign products and markets and who bear the costs of government restrictions on that access. The aim should be to move beyond the mercantilist concept of the gains from international trade now built into national and international institutions which manage these matters and to move towards a more balanced concept which includes the beneficial side of imports, not just the harmful side.

I offer three suggestions for achieving this aim. They would probably rank 1-2-3 in terms of acceptability, but 3-2-1 in terms of usefulness. The third suggestion is critical to making the second effective; and the execution of those two would be the strongest expression of the first.

The first task for the leadership of the trade policy community is to recognise the instinct of policy makers to seek foreign scapegoats for the effects of domestic indecision or wrong decisions. Efforts should be made to publicise the simple truth of classical economics, namely that trade restrictions by one country, no matter what any other country does, has for that country larger costs than benefits.

Disputes over international trade almost always overlie *national* decisions with larger *domestic* costs than benefits. Dispute-settlement procedures that build on the same concepts as lead to the wrong domestic choice should not be expected to set things right, no matter how detailed they might be made. Good relations among countries cannot be based on an attempt to choose through international bargaining among options whose *domestic* effects make a *domestic* decision onerous.

One of the major accomplishments of the international monetary conferences held in the mid-1970s was that there emerged from them an international consensus that domestic stabilisation was necessary before international stabilisation could be achieved. A parallel consensus on trade matters is sorely needed.

A way must be found to build the gains from international trade into national decisions on trade matters. Under present national rules, sanctioned by the GATT, the national commissions and bureaus which evaluate trade matters take into account only the costs to domestic producers from import competition. Savings to other industries which use imported inputs, or to consumers, are not taken into account.

The economic sense of this change is obvious and the political sense is compelling. Now, those who bear the costs of trade interference by their government have no choice but to go over the heads of the formalised decision processes and apply pressure on politicians. If these pressures had a technical outlet, trade matters might escalate less quickly into political disputes.

The third task is to begin a process to create a greater public awareness of the domestic costs of protection, a process to educate the groups which bear the costs of their own government's protectionist policies, and thereby to help bring into the public mind a non-mercantilist sense of the gains from international trade.

It would be relatively easy to verify that procedures to measure the gains from international trade and to identify the gainers had been added in those countries which employ formal and open administrative mechanisms. But in the European Community, for example, two thirds of anti-dumping and countervailing-duty petitions result in 'undertakings' or 'arrangements' on which a minimal amount of information is released — either about the nature of the arrangement that the Community has reached with the exporter or about the way in which the Community calculated the domestic benefits and costs which that course of action would entail.[10]

It might therefore be necessary to harness again the mercantilist instinct for exports and allow trading partners to calculate and publicise the costs to a country of that country's trade policies. The Argentines would buy television time in Japan to show an Argentine family enjoying a big roast beef and to show Japanese families how much of that roast beef they would have after the Government of Japan took its slice. The United States would buy space in French newspapers to publicise how much the French Government spends to subsidise exports, perhaps under the headline 'Your government gave more money last year to international corporations than to the "x" poorest countries in the world'! In 1978 the South Koreans might have sponsored a television spot as follows:

As the first innings of the World Test Series ends, the television picture flicks to a scene of happy children dancing their way down the street to the shoe shop singing, 'New shoes for school, new shoes for school!' They gambol one by one into the shop, but as the twelfth one comes to the door, Uncle Sam, in striped trousers and white beard, steps forward and throws the child out, saying, 'No shoes for you this year, kid.'

The voice-over then explains: 'The US, Korean and Taiwanese governments have just concluded an agreement which will reduce the number of children's shoes available for sale in the US by one twelfth. That means somebody doesn't get any.' Then back to the ballgame.

This is perhaps inaccurate or one-sided. But for once let the other side calculate the welfare triangles and explain how domestic supply is perfectly elastic at a level really no higher than costs in exporting countries.

'Or, if it is not now it will be sometime in the future if the following investment schedule ...' 'Can we have the chart, please? Charlie, you've got it upside down, Charlie. Thanks, Charlie.' 'Anyway, you see on the chart ...'

This is the same exchange of information we usually get on such matters. But the modes of expression that the two sides usually employ have been switched.

Without domestic appreciation of their domestic benefits, 'standstill' arrangements on trade restrictions are soon outflanked by new forms of protection which escape the letter of the agreement. We should agree to harness the interests of the exporters to detect these flanking movements and to identify their costs. Eternal vigilance is the price of free trade and the profit motive is the most vigilant force afield.

---

1. G. C. Hufbauer, 'Analyzing the Effects of US Trade Policy Instruments', National Science Foundation, Washington, mimeograph, October 1981.

2. John S. Odell, 'Latin American Trade Negotiations with the United States', *International Organization*, Spring 1980.

3. J. M. Finger, H. Keith Hall and Douglas R. Nelson, 'The Political Economy of Administered Protection', *American Economic Review*, June 1982.

4. Robert E. Baldwin, 'The Political Economy of US Import Policy', draft manuscript, July 1981, ch. 4.

5. Finger, Hall and Nelson, *loc. cit.*

6. William L. Dickey, 'The Pricing of Imports into the United States', *Journal of World Trade Law*, May-June 1979.

7. Finger, Hall and Nelson, *loc. cit.*

8. Rodney de C. Grey, 'A Note on United States Trade Practices', paper prepared for a conference on Trade Policy in the Eighties, sponsored by the Institute for International Economics, held in Washington on 23-25 June 1982.

9. Finger, 'Administered Protection in the United States and Indonesia', World Bank, Washington, mimeograph, March 1982.

10. For details, see Nelson, *The Political Structure of the New Protectionism*, World Bank Staff Working Paper No. 471 (Washington: World Bank, 1981).

PART FOUR

HOW THE GATT WORKS

[12]

Protectionist Rules and Internationalist Discretion in the Making of National Trade Policy

J. Michael Finger

The post-World War II deliberations on institutional arrangements for the world economy were successful in leading to the establishment of the International Monetary Fund and the World Bank. However, the proposed International Trade Organization which would regulate international trade was not to be. There was a general reluctance among governments to accept institutionalized restrictions on the conduct of countries' national trade policies. At the same time the ITO negotiations over the "rules" of the trading system were unsuccessful, the community of nations reached agreement on a significant package of reciprocal tariff reductions. The document or contract which gave legal effect to the agreed reduction of tariffs included three functional parts. The first of these committed each participating country to allow other participants access to its market at least as favorable as the schedule of its import restrictions it annexed to the agreement. When agreement involved reductions of tariffs, the negotiated reductions over previous rates were reflected in this schedule. Each schedule, the parties agreed, would be subject to MFN treatment within the group.[1]

The second functional part of the agreement defined the circumstances under which a country might go back on the access it had guaranteed to its trading partners in the first part, e.g., restrictions to safeguard the balance of payments, antidumping and countervailing duties, etc. The third functional part deals with dispute settlement or restitution - what a country can do when it senses that some benefits to it under the contract have been compromised.

---

[1]   This is essentially Articles I, II, III, VII, VIII, IX and X. These articles require the posting of schedules, MFN treatment, and cut off loopholes such as inflated customs valuation, excise taxes differentially imposed on imports, etc.

Studies in International Economics and Institutions
Vosgerau (Ed.) New Institutional Arrangements for the World Economy
© Springer-Verlag Berlin Heidelberg 1989

This "contract" was, and still is, called the General Agreement on Tariffs and Trade, GATT. The GATT has, in its own language, not "members" but "contracting parties". Thus the basic institutional structure of the post-World War II international trading system is not an agreed set of rules. It is a contract through which a nation party to the contract exchanges access to its domestic market for access to the domestic markets of the other parties. This exchange of market access is subject to extensive and specific reservations as to the circumstances under which (and the procedures through which) a country may reduce this access, i.e., impose import restrictions.

The same contract, when viewed from a national rather than an international perspective, becomes a statement of the circumstances in and procedures by which a nation may impose import restrictions, subject however to the reservations it has placed upon itself in the granting of access to foreigners. Taken a step further, into national laws and regulations which provide actual legal substance to a nation's perspective on this contract, the circumstances under which a country may impose import restrictions become the rights of particular interests within the country to protection from import competition.[2] The government of a GATT contracting party is then caught between this right which national law and regulation guarantee to domestic interests and the market access it has granted to foreigners through international agreement.

Within this broad view of institutional structure, this paper will review the process in the United States of deciding and imposing trade restrictions. The focus is on the implicit property-rights conception underlying the national justification for trade intervention in the trade remedy laws of the US. The reader should note that the paper is about protection and not about trade liberalization. The "GATT system" includes two distinct mechanisms. The better known of these is the tariff negotiations process, through which trade barriers can be removed, but not imposed. This paper is about the less well-known "administered protection" process, a national one, subject to international constraints.

---

[2]   The historical shift of perspective, from GATT as international agreement to maintain an open trading system to GATT as international recognition of the rights of nations to impose import restrictions, is taken up by Finger (1986).

The following section of this paper describes the formalization of the GATT contract into national law in the United States. I identify the underlying property rights conception then use this conception to explain why the VER is a popular form of import restriction. I also examine in the same context recent changes of US trade law. The argument for the validity of the model is the usual one - it helps to make sense of what we observe in the real world.

I.   The Structure of Administered Protection in the United States

Governments everywhere are subject to pressure to implement import restrictions to the benefit of particular groups. It follows that national government will have established "ways" or "tracks" to respond to or manage these pressures. Though these national tracks are, in each of the major industrial countries, more or less consistent with the GATT, their national forms tend to be quite different from one country to another. In the United States current law provides six tracks to which a domestic firm or industry may petition the US government for relief from import competition, i.e. for protection. These are:

(1) Escape clause or safeguards (201 cases);

(2) Antidumping;

(3) Antisubsidy or countervailing duty;

(4) Unfair trade practices actions (301 cases);

(5) Unfair import practices (337 cases);

(6) Market disruption (406 cases).

An escape clause or safeguards case is an investigation of injury to a US industry resulting from increased imports. Petitions are filed with and investigations are conducted by the International Trade Commission. The responsibility of the International Trade Commission is to determine whether or not injury is occurring to the named US industry. If the injury determination is affirmative, the ITC recommends a remedy to the President. This remedy might be imposition of tariffs, imposition of quantitative restrictions or other forms of import controls or it might be adjustment assistance without the imposition of any border measure to restrict imports. If the President chooses not to implement import relief different from that recommended by the ITC, his decision is subject to Congressional override.

Antidumping petitions are filed simultaneously with the ITC and with the International Trade Administration (ITA) of the Department of Commerce. An antidumping case entails two separate investigations: a material injury investigation (conducted by the ITC) and a sales at "less than fair value" investigation (conducted by the ITA). If both material injury and sales at less than fair value are found to exist, the Department of Commerce is required by law to impose antidumping duties in the amount of the dumping margin. The antidumping law provides specific opportunities for an agreement to be reached between the petitioning domestic party and the foreign party to terminate the case. Grounds for such agreed termination are almost always an enforceable and monitorable commitment by the foreign seller to eliminate the dumping practice, i.e. to raise the price it charges in the US market.

Countervailing duty cases, like dumping cases, are carried out under the authority of the Department of Commerce, the ITA. Cases involve an investigation of subsidy conducted by the ITA, and in most instances, an injury investigation conducted by the ITC. Injury investigations are carried out in all cases concerning duty-free goods and in those cases involving signatories to the GATT-subsidies code, against Taiwan and against all countries to whom the US has extended by treaty unconditional most-favored-nations status. In affirmatively determined cases, the Department of Commerce is required by law to impose a countervailing duty equal to the net foreign subsidy. As with the antidumping law, the countervailing duty law provides opportunities for a case to be terminated upon agreement between the petitioning party and exporter. Again, such agreement is conditioned upon an enforceable and monitorable commitment by the foreign party to eliminate the subsidy practice.

"Section 301" provides the President authority to act (1) to enforce US rights under a trade agreement; (2) to respond to a foreign government act or policy which is inconsistent with a trade agreement with the United States or which denies the benefits to the US interest under such an agreement; (3) on actions or policies of foreign government which are inconsistent with international obligations other than those arising under the GATT (for example, violations of a treaty of friendship, commerce and navigation) when those policies or actions oppress, restrict or burden US commerce. Under this section a complaint is brought by the US firm or industry to the Office of the US Trade Representative. The US Trade Representative investigates to determine if the alleged violation exists. Section 301 cases often involve the interests of United States exporters. For example, petitions by US insurance firms for access to the Korean insurance markets took the legal form of a 301 petition, based on a section of the US-Korea treaty of friendship and navigation. If the USTR formally determines that the alleged violation exists, then the President of the United States has the legal authority to take a variety of actions against the offending party, including the possibility of imposing import restrictions against the products of that country. This "retaliation" against the exports of the country to the United States may be applied on any product or service - it is not limited to product or service on which the foreign practice is applied.

Section 301 required the USTR to activate GATT dispute settlement procedures in parallel with its pursuit of the matter under US law, but the authority the section provides the President to retaliate is in no way conditioned on the outcome of the GATT process, though at a discretionary level, a GATT panel's decision as to the "GATT legality" of the accused foreign practice would carry great weight in the STR's determination. In practice, most cases are settled by bilateral negotiations between the US government and the country responsible for the violation. The "determination" part of the act functions primarily to force a negotiated settlement - to provide the President with the legal authority to impose sanctions on the violating country if the country does not reach agreement.

Section 337 of the Tariff Act of 1930 declares unlawful certain methods of competition in import trade, which might destroy or substantially injure a domestic industry, prevent the establishment of an industry or might restrain or monopolize trade and commerce in the United States. Most cases under this section involve patent infringement. Complaints are filed with and investigations are conducted by the International Trade Commission. The International Trade Commission might also investigate on its own initiative a suspected violation. If the ITC determines that the violation exists, it may recommend that the offending party not be allowed

to sell that particular article in the United States. As with 301 cases, implementation of this recommendation is subject to Presidential discretion.

Section 406 causes concern market disruption resulting from imports from communist countries. They are decided by the ITC and sent to the President for a decision
or final determination. The President's decision is subject to Congressional override
if he rejects or modifies the ITC recommendation.

Rights to Protection

These trade remedy laws define the *rights* of particular interests within the US
economy to import protection - or in the case of Article 301, to the use of import
restrictions as a device for enforcing the right of a US interest to export a particular product to a particular market. There is no parallel right given to buyers of
imports, no parallel right to access to imports by those interests in the US economy
which benefit from this access.

The simplest illustration is the safeguards or escape clause. This clause is concerned
only with injury to a domestic industry from import competition. It brings forward
no question of the fairness or unfairness of the foreign trade practice which
underlies these imports. The ITC investigation is aimed at and limited to whether
or not there has been or likely to be injury to the "domestic industry producing an
article like or directly competitive with the imported article".

The other five trade remedy figures all begin with the specification of a foreign
practice which is considered "unfair". The specification of what is "unfair" is
multilateral or international, in the sense that national anti-subsidy and antidumping practices are recognized under the General Agreement on Tariffs and
Trade. In similar but not identical fashion, Section 301 takes care to deal with
trade practices which are illegal under the GATT or some other international
agreement (Section 301 goes beyond antisubsidy and antidumping provisions in US
law in that they are more open-ended - relating to any form of inconsistent practice, not just a specified one). These matters are, however, unilateral in the sense
that a national authority makes the determination of whether or not the practice in
question is, in fact, dumping or some other practice proscribed by international
agreement.

The conception of fair on which each of these tracks is based relates to the effects of the trading practice on competing US producers and, like the escape clause, does not take into account possible benefits to users.

Building trade policy on a conception of when a domestic interest has a right to protection has a long history in US policymaking. Schattsneider's book on the making of the Smoot-Hawley Tariff demonstrates that the "equalization tariff" idea – that the tariff should equalize the costs of producing a good outside the United States with the costs of producing it inside the United States – dominated both government and industry thinking. Indeed the equalization formula for when and how much protection an industry "should" receive stayed in the US policymaking apparatus when the reciprocal trade agreements approach was developed. In prep-aration for early rounds of multilateral tariff negotiations under the GATT, the ITC was required to conduct "peril points" investigations, to determine the floor below which a tariff would not be cut by the President. The cost equalization idea and the contemporary unfair trade practices idea are both "institutions" in the anthropologist's sense of the term – part of the folkways of the society, something widely enough believed within the society that it is hardly ever questioned. (When such a folkway is questioned, the raising of the question brings more suspicion to bear on the person who raises the question than on the concept itself.) Though the cost equalization idea dominated the construction of the tariff before reciprocal trade agreements days, it was not legislated into a specific legal form until later, as the "peril points" idea. In the new mechanics for making trade restrictions, the unfair trade practices concept is an institution in the anthropologist's sense, and it also has a direct expression in the law, as the rules part of the trade remedies legislation.

Overriding Discretion

The idea of injury which is basic to the escape clause and a significant part of unfair trade practices tracks to import relief is in economics the mirror image of comparative advantage. Thus the rules part of the trade remedies laws makes pro-tection available or callable by virtually every part of the domestic economy which competes with imports. If this were the only part of the trade remedies laws, the outcome of the mechanism would be high levels of protection for all sectors of the domestic economy.

The offsetting factor is the discretionary authority the law provides the President of the United States to reject rules-based determinations and recommendations. The escape clause specifies that the President may set aside the recommendation for import relief based on the determination of injury to a domestic industry, if, in his opinion, such action would be contrary to "the national economic interest of the United States". The unfair trade practices tracks (excepting the antisubsidy and antidumping tracks) allow the President to set aside a recommendation for import-restricting actions if in his judgment such actions are not in the "policy interest" of the United States.

Excepting the antisubsidy and antidumping tracks from this legal generalization does not compromise the basic point that these rules tracks set out the rights of a domestic interest to protection and that the President has discretionary authority to set those rights aside. The tracks define the rights of domestic interests to protec-tion, but they do not define the *form* that protection will take. In practice, small matters are resolved by the rules, via a formal antisubsidy or antidumping or escape clause action. A large matter (measured by value of imports or of domestic production covered by the case), whether it begins as a dumping case or as an escape clause case, will usually lead to a negotiated settlement in which the con-straints on the President are political (he has to do something or he will lose sig-nificant support) rather than legal.[3]

In sum, domestic interests that would gain from import restrictions are given sub-stance and form in the trade remedies law. Conversely, the rights of domestic interests which bear the costs of import restrictions are given neither substance nor form. To the extent that there is a countervailing force to domestic protectionist interests, that force is not the domestic loss from protection. The discretion pro-vided the President is to allow him to implement the foreign policy interests of the United States and to respect the rights of access to the US market which the US

---

[3]   See Finger, Hall and Nelson (1987) on this point.

government has surrendered, through the GATT negotiations, to foreign governments.

The meaning of the phrase "policy interest of the United States" in the unfair trade practices part of the trade remedies laws has the traditional international relations meaning - that the foreign policy interest of the United States lies in "the promotion and maintenance of stability and peace through economic means". Trade is, in this conception , not a source of mutual gain but a close parallel to foreign aid - the provision of income to foreign persons by the people of the United States, admittedly a material "cost" to the people of the United States, though one defended as necessary to achieve peace and political stability. The US executive branch, in seeking Congressional support for a US leadership role in international affairs, has usually presented its case as involving economic cost to the US.[4]

The discretion given to the President to set aside a domestic claim to protection also reflects the rights to the US market that the US government has granted to foreigners. Foreign rights to the US market are institutionalized through the trade negotiations process. In the simplest sense, the foreigners *buy* access to the US market by giving similar access to the US - by making similar "GATT concessions" to the United States. This is a straightforward application of institutionalized respect or contracts - "a deal is a deal".

The idea that the foreigner has an institutionalized right to access to the US market is reinforced by the GATT conception of "enforcement" or "dispute settlement". While it is common to think of the GATT as "the law" of international trade, the GATT as an international organization has very limited enforcement authority. Being a contracting party to the GATT implies that the standard the GATT expresses will be incorporated into the contracting party's national laws and regulations. The legal force behind these standards is then national rather than international. At an international level the dispute settlement provisions of the GATT (Article 23) do not focus on correcting a possible violation of the rules. The provisions provide that an individual country may bring a matter to the attention of the entire membership for their assistance in resolving the problem or issue if that

---

4   On this point, see Nelson (1987), p. 20 and references cited there.

individual country "should consider that any benefit accruing to it directly or indirectly under this agreement is being nullified or impaired". Article 23 goes on to provide that nullification or impairment of benefits might be the result of

(1)   another country's action or policy in violation of the GATT;

(2)   another country's action or policy which does not conflict with the GATT;

(3) The "existence of any other situation".

Thus, the dispute settlement mechanism of the GATT emphasizes a basic conception on which the agreement is built - GATT membership confers benefits to a country and the substance of these benefits is access to the markets of other countries.

The legislative history of the phrase "national economic interest of the United States" (in the escape clause) demonstrates the implicit conception that foreign access to the US market is a *cost* to the US economy. During drafting of the Trade Act of 1974, the Senate Finance Committee proposed to eliminate Presidential discretion in escape clause cases - to require the President to provide import relief when the ITC returned a positive determination of injury. (The President, in setting aside ITC findings, had often cited foreign policy interests.) The executive resisted this change, the eventual compromise being introduction of the condition that the President shall follow the ITC recommendation unless he determines that to do so is "not in the national *economic* interest of the US" (emphasis added). In directing the president toward the domestic *economic* effects of the US, the Senate Finance Committee assumed they would be directing the President toward protection - implicitly, that the national economic interest of the US was correctly defined by the escape clause, i.e. by the injury concept, and that the President should be less willing to sacrifice these interests for the interest of the world.[5]

---

[5]   William Ris (1977) relates the legislative history of the 1974 changes in the escape clause.

II. Applications

The institutional framework for the management of pressures for protection in the US is based on a property rights specification not readily reconcilable with freedom of international trade. The gains from trade derive from a perception of mutual advantage to trading partners, a view that gives equal weight to consumers and the expansion of their consumption opportunities as to producers and the expansion of their production opportunities. The trade remedy laws specify property rights to domestic producers. They also provide the President with the discretion to set aside these rights when, in the President's perception, they conflict with (a) obligations created through reciprocal concessions under the GATT to allow foreign producers' access to the US market, and/or (b) the foreign policy interests of the US.

The Form of Protection

Whereas the welfare propositions of international-trade theory focus on the gains from trade to consumers, the national trade laws focus on the rights of producers. The "domestic dialogue" regarding proposed import restrictions is as a consequence one-sided. Injury to producers is emphasized with no reference to the gains to consumers. Foreigners who benefit or from access of their goods to the domestic market have rights insofar as these rights have been exchanged for rights given to domestic producers, and then only subject to final national discretion regarding what constitutes a fair international trade practice.

Viewed in this setting, recent developments in the manner of conduct of international trade policy are readily explicable. For example, voluntary export restraints provide relief from injury to domestic import-competing producers. At the same time, foreign profits are enhanced. The rents created by a VER provide a substantial transfer from the protected economy exporters. In this way the home government effectively repurchases the foreigners' right of access to the domestic market.

Evolution of US Trade Law

It follows from this institutional structure that domestic interests have an incentive to apply themselves to expanding the scope of the rules part of the law and to narrowing the degree of Presidential discretion to override the rules in the interest of foreigners. Robert Baldwin (1985) has tabulated changes in US trade law which specifically restrict the President's discretionary authority. In 1951 the Trade Act required that if the President rejected an ITC recommendation for import relief, he must submit to Congress an explanatory statement. In 1958 the Trade Act was changed to allow the Congress to override the President's rejection of an ITC recommendation by a two-thirds vote of the membership of each house of Congress. In 1962 the necessary vote was reduced to a simple majority to authorized membership of each house and in 1974 the overriding requirement was reduced to a simple majority of members present in voting. Bills currently before the Congress would eliminate the President's discretion to override a recommendation action which came from an unfair trade practices case. These bills would also make bilateral trade imbalances beyond a certain size "actionable" under trade remedies laws.

The GATT contract does not recognize the right to gain or maintain access to a foreign market through the use of unfair trade practices. Thus there has been through the 80s the sequential expansion of the unfair trade practices part of the trade remedies laws, an expansion which has increased *the range of foreign actions or policies which are grounds for relief from import competition.

The US-Canada Lumber Case

As a further example, sense is made of the manner whereby restrictions have recently come to be imposed on US imports of Canadian lumber.[6] Responding to a plea from US lumber producers, the US government imposed an antidumping tariff of 15 percent on Canadian softwood construction lumber in October 1986, but indicated that the tariff would be removed if the Canadian government were to impose an export tax of the same percentage. The Canadians complied on January 1, 1987. The US thereby transferred some estimated $220 (US) million of annual revenue from the US to Canada. The puzzle might be why the US insisted on the transfer. As Joseph Kalt (1987) has observed in his study of this protectionist episode, the US started a trade war which it then deliberately proceeded to lose by

---

[6]   I am indebted to Arye L. Hillman for this example.

insisting that its monopsonistic tariff be replaced by a Canadian monopolistic tariff. Again the sequence of events is consistent with the property rights concept of the national trade laws. Protection relieved domestic injury as a right of the domestic injured party, but foreigners were compensated for the loss of their right of US market access. Indeed, the final indication is that the revenue accruing to the Canadian federal government from the export tax was transferred to the injured parties, via redistribution to the provinces and allocation to forest improvement.[7]

III.   Conclusions, Speculations

If the economics profession was polled on the issue "Which do you see as better, free trade or protection?", it is likely that a substantial majority would vote for free trade. If the same persons were asked "Do you prefer rules or discretion?", a large majority would likely choose "rules". Free traders might be particularly favorable to rules. For example, the *Economist* describes the agreement to hold another round of GATT negotiations as follows: "They agreed to reassert GATT's authority by strengthening the rules and enforcing them better; to halt new protectionist measures and to dismantle existing barriers to trade."[8]

While it seems intuitively proper to suggest a world trading system built on rules rather than on discretion, one must recognize that the rules built into the present system are essentially protectionist, and that the continuing openness of the system depends on the discretion the system allows to put the rules aside in order to maintain a delicate balance of agreed market access. Elaborating existing rules, e.g. the "Codes" negotiated at the Tokyo Round are not an effective way to maintain the openness of the international system. The system does not need more rules, it needs better rules - rules which give the gains (and the gainers) from trade the same legal standing now provide the losses. A user of imports whose costs are increased by restrictions his government places on access to imports should be provided a way to petition for removal of those restrictions.

---

[7]   See Hillman (1987) for elaboration.

[8]   *Economist*, p. 70.

References

Baldwin, R. (1985), *The Political Economy of US Import Policy*, MIT Press, Cambridge, Mass.

Clark, L.H. Jr. (1986), "GATT Needs New Morale, Not New Rules", *Wall Street Journal*, October 21.

The Economist (1987), "GATT Negotiators Under Fire", (July 16), p.70f.

Finger, J.M. (1986), "Ideas Count, Words Inform", in R.H. Snape (ed.), *Issues in World Trade Policy*, London, MacMillan.

Finger, J.M., K. Hall and D. Nelson (1982), "The Political Economy of Administered Protection", *American Economic Review*, 72, pp. 452-466.

GATT Study Group (1986), *Trade Policies for a Better World*, Geneva, GATT, 1985; reprinted in part as "The Way Forward", in R.E. Baldwin and J.D. Richardson (eds.), *International Trade and Finance*, Little Brown and Co, Boston, pp. 199-213.

Grossman, G.M. (1986), "Imports as a Cause of Injury: The Case of the US Steel Industry", *Journal of International Economics* 20 (May), pp. 201-233.

Hillman, A.L., "The Political Economy of Protection: Comment", forthcoming in Robert Baldwin (ed.), *Trade Policy Issues and Empirical Analysis*, University of Chicago Press for NBER.

Kalt, J., "The Political Economy of Protectionism: Tariffs and Retaliation in the Timber Industry", forthcoming in Robert Baldwin (ed.), *Trade Policy Issues and Empirical Analysis*, University of Chicago Press for NBER.

Nelson, Douglas H. (1987), "The Domestic Political Preconditions of US Trade Policy: Liberal Structure and Protectionist Dynamics", Paper prepared for the World Bank Conference on "Political Economy: Theory and Policy Implications", Washington, D.C., June 17-19.

Ris, William K., Jr. (1977), "Escape Clause Relief under the Trade Act of 1974: New Standards, Some Results", *Columbus Journal of Transnational Law*, 16, pp. 297-325.

Schattsneider, F.F. (1935), *Politics, Pressures and the Tariff*, New York Prentice-Hall.

Vaubel, R. (1986), "A Public Choice Approach to International Organization", *Public Choice*, No. 1, 55, pp. 39-57.

Witzke, von, H. (1986), "Endogenous Supranational Policy Decisions: The Common Agricultural Policy of the European Community", *Public Choice*, No. 2, 48, pp. 157-174.

[13]
Trade Liberalization: A Public Choice Perspective

J. M. Finger

It is not difficult to find incidents that suggest that the trading system is becoming less liberal. In the last year the United States has unilaterally imposed quotas on imports of specialty steel products and has negotiated orderly marketing agreements with exporters of footwear and television receivers which will reduce the levels of U.S. imports of these products.

There is, of course, a general tendency for protectionist interests to dominate when trade problems are approached on an industry-by-industry or a day-to-day basis. Producer interests are concentrated in a few firms while consumer interests are divided among millions; hence, it is easier for producers than for consumers to aggregate sufficient resources to have an impact on the decision process.[1] Proponents of liberal trading regimes can hope at best to minimize the setbacks that the handling of day-to-day trade issues will bring.

Trade liberalization has a much better chance when it is approached (as at the GATT negotiations) on an economywide and reciprocal basis. Negotiations that cover many industries mute somewhat the imbalance between the concentrations of producer and of consumer interests. An exchange of concessions allows for some netting out of displaced production and places the interests of exporting producers on the side of trade liberalization.

Trade liberalization should thus be viewed in net terms. It is achieved (or a liberal trading system is maintained) when the pace of advance of general liberalization is more rapid than the tendency for protectionism to dominate day-to-day trade questions.

As often noted, general economic conditions are at present not favorable to trade liberalization. For several years, economic growth

---

I wish to thank my colleagues Stephen Golub and Joanna Shelton for fruitful discussions of many of the topics covered in this paper. I retain, however, sole responsibility for all information presented and opinions expressed here. This paper is not an expression of the official views of the U.S. Treasury Department.

[1] See Mancur Olson, Jr., *The Logic of Collective Action* (Cambridge: Harvard University Press, 1965), esp. pp. 141–48.

PART SIX: STRATEGIES

has been below desired levels, and unemployment has been a significant problem. Attempts in certain industries (notably steel) to maintain operating rates in the face of slack demand have generated charges of unfair international competition, which have, in turn, been used to justify requests for limits on imports. In addition, slow economic growth and oil import bills have intensified concerns about trade balances. Further, during the 1970s trade has increased considerably relative to GNP, leaving little "room" in the economic expansion that did take place for the increased trade that additional liberalization would bring. Given this general worsening of factors that determine the demand for, or the political will to achieve, further trade liberalization, "supply conditions" become that much more important. An important question, thus, is how institutional arrangements have evolved and whether this evolution will make additional production of a public good, trade liberalization, more or less likely.

This paper applies the analytic insights of public choice theory to that question. The record of the GATT tariff negotiations is reviewed from a public choice perspective and an attempt is made to isolate those factors that contribute to a successful outcome. The analytical apparatus thus developed is then used to examine the likelihood that the negotiating format carried over from the Kennedy Round will bring additional rounds to successful outcomes. It also serves as the basis for suggestions for format changes that might make international agreement to trade liberalizing measures more likely.

Improved Market Access as a Public Good

In form, all GATT rounds except the 1965–1967 Kennedy Round and the ongoing Tokyo Round were collections of bilateral negotiations. In pairs, countries agreed to exchanges of "concessions"—reductions of tariff rates or bindings of tariff rates at existing levels. The most-favored-nation (MFN) provision requires a GATT contracting party to grant the products of all other GATT contracting parties the same treatment on importation that it grants the products of any one of them. Because of the MFN provision, all GATT contracting parties shared in the fruits of each of the bilateral exchanges of concessions.

Under this system, trade liberalization, defined as access to export markets, displays both of the characteristic properties of a public good. First, it is *nonexclusive*. If the United States receives from Norway a pledge to allow trucks to be imported at a lowered rate of duty, the MFN provision requires that other suppliers receive access to the Norwegian market on the same terms. Second, access to the Norwegian

J. M. FINGER

market has the characteristic of *nonrivalness*. The GATT rules allow no limit to the amount of imports that enter at the agreed-upon terms. Hence, the export of trucks to Norway by one country at these terms does not affect the availability of these terms to another exporter.[2]

The nonexclusive property of market access is clearly a result of the MFN provision. If Norway were to apply the lower tariff rate only to imports from the United States, then improved market access would not be a public good. It would be available only to the country that "produced" it—in this example, the United States.

Analysis of Past GATT Negotiations

By any reasonable standard, the past performance of GATT, summarized in Table 1, must be considered a success. At the first negotiating round (Geneva, 1947), the United States exchanged concessions with twenty countries, colonies, or customs areas, which supplied 65 percent of U.S. imports.[3] At these negotiations, the United States made tariff concessions on 93 percent of (prewar) imports from the negotiating partners and tariff reductions on 74 percent of imports from participants. Relative to imports from all sources (participants and nonparticipants), U.S. tariff reductions affected 56 percent of dutiable imports, and reductions plus bindings affected 78 percent of total imports.[4] At the next round (Annecy, France, 1949), the United States negotiated with ten acceding governments. Two years later, at Torquay, England, Germany and Austria (plus Korea, Peru, and Turkey) became contracting parties to GATT, and after the accession of Japan in 1955 all of the major non-Communist developed countries were contracting parties. In this sense, the Annecy Round and the negotiations with the acceding governments at the Torquay Round can be viewed as the completion of the first round (Geneva, 1947) rather than as separate rounds.

Concessions granted at the earlier rounds were in large part bindings of tariff reductions. But by the Torquay Round, a large share of the lines in the tariffs of the GATT contracting parties had been bound, and negotiations concentrated on tariff reductions. Thus, the last three rounds have dealt almost entirely with tariff-cutting (row C, Table 1).

---

[2] The public good is represented by the terms of access to the Norwegian market, not the *size* of that market. Similarly, the playing of a radio does not diminish the signal available to another radio.

[3] Participants are listed in Table 11 at the end of this Chapter.

[4] Because the GATT procedures emphasized balanced concessions (discussed below), it is very likely that a similar volume of U.S. exports was affected. But because not all countries to whom the U.S. exports were active GATT participants, the percentage of U.S. exports affected may have been lower.

TABLE 1
INDICATORS OF THE OUTCOME FOR THE UNITED STATES OF GATT TARIFF NEGOTIATIONS

Variable (all calculated from U.S. imports and exports)	*Geneva 1947* (1939 data)	*Annecy 1949* (1948 data)	*Torquay 1951* (1949 data)	*Geneva 1956* (1954 data)	*Dillon 1960–1961* (1960 data)	*Kennedy 1964–1967* (1964 data)	
						Major participants[a]	All participants
A. Concession imports (reductions and bindings) as percent of total imports[b]	78	39	7	9	12	n.a.	46
B. Tariff reductions							
Reduction imports as percent of dutiable imports[b]	56	6	15	20	19	n.a.	64
Average depth of cut (percent reduction of ad valorem rate)	35	37	26	15	20	n.a.	44
C. Balance (affected exports less affected imports as percent of affected exports)[c]							
Overall	−27	−29	59	n.a.	n.a.	5	5
With participants							
Bilateral	n.a.	73	75	−68	18	n.a.	n.a.
Multilateral	4	76	74	n.a.	n.a.	12	5
D. Tariff reductions as percent of all concessions							
Imports from participants	32	43	91	100	95	95	93
Imports from all countries	29	20	88	100	95	93	93

E. Imports from participants as percent of imports from all countries							
Dutiable	65	6	34	67	66	68	72
Dutiable and duty free	63	5	42	52	59	58	73
F. Internalization (percent of concession imports originating in participating countries)c							
All concession							
Bilateral	n.a.	16	56	74	69	n.a.	n.a.
Multilateral	76	18	62	89	96	78	94
Tariff reductions							
Bilateral	n.a.	35	58	74	69	n.a.	n.a.
Multilateral	84	39	64	89	96	81	91

n.a.: Not available.

a EEC, Canada, Japan, United Kingdom, Austria, Denmark, Norway, Finland, Sweden, Switzerland.

b Based on figures for imports from all countries, GATT participants and nonparticipants.

c The export and import values used in the formulas for the measures of balance and of internalization are:

X = U.S. exports on which concessions were made by other countries, made up of two parts: Xa, concessions given directly to the United States; and Xb, concessions exchanged among other countries but extended to the United States according to MFN provisions. M = U.S. imports on which the United States made concessions, divided into three parts: Ma, imports from the country with whom a concession was negotiated; Mb, imports from other participating countries; Mc, imports from nonparticipating countries.

The formulas for balance are: overall, $[(X - M)/X](100)$; with participants: bilateral, $[(Xa - Ma)/Xa](100)$; multilateral, $[(Xa - (Ma + Mb))/X](100)$.

The formulas for internalization are: bilateral, $(Ma/M)(100)$; multilateral, $[(Ma + Mb)/M](100)$.

SOURCE: Calculated from data given in Table 6 below and in official U.S. reports of GATT negotiations (see Table 10 at the end of this Chapter).

PART SIX: STRATEGIES

Negotiating with countries which supplied at the time of each round approximately two-thirds of U.S. dutiable imports,[5] the United States reduced tariffs at the Geneva 1956 and Dillon rounds on over one-fourth of dutiable imports from participants, and at the Kennedy Rounds on four-fifths of such imports. As percentages of dutiable imports from all countries, the coverage of U.S. tariff reductions at the Geneva 1956, Dillon, and Kennedy rounds was 20 percent, 19 percent, and 64 percent, respectively.

The Role of Internalization. A major determinant for the success of a collective decision process is the extent to which there will be "free riders"—that is, the benefits of the public good produced will spill over to countries that do not share in the costs of producing it. The larger this spillover, the lower the benefit-cost ratio to participants and the lower the likelihood of a successful outcome.

The record of the GATT negotiations indicates a strong desire to minimize free riding or, in GATT terms, to assure reciprocity or a balance between the concessions participants made and the concessions they received. This was accomplished by concentrating concessions on those products exported only by participants—which sometimes required that new product categories be developed. For example, the United States, in negotiating with the United Kingdom, would request concessions on products for which the United States was principal, or only, supplier of exports to the United Kingdom, and would offer concessions on imports supplied principally or exclusively by the United Kingdom. In this way, the "benefits" and the "costs" tended to be internalized.

The last rows of Table 1 use data for U.S. concessions to measure the degree of internalization achieved at each GATT round. Internalization is measured bilaterally as the sum over participating countries of U.S. imports from each country of those goods on which the United States granted a concession in bilateral negotiations with that country. Multilaterally, internalization includes the spillover to other participants of the concessions granted in each bilateral session; it is the sum of all concession imports orginating in countries with whom the United States exchanged concessions, expressed as a percentage of imports from all countries, participants and nonparticipants, of concession items. The measure of bilateral internalization uses the same denominator.

The difference between the percentage of imports originating in participating countries and the percentage of internalized concessions

---

[5] For the Kennedy Round, only "major participants" are counted.

J. M. FINGER

indicates the degree to which product selection managed to internalize the benefits of U.S. concessions to countries that granted concessions to the United States in exchange. The participating countries with whom the United States exchanged concessions at the Geneva 1947, Geneva 1956, Dillon, and Kennedy rounds supplied in each case just under 70 percent of dutiable U.S. imports. At the first of these rounds, judicious selection of products managed to internalize 84 percent of U.S. concessions, and by the Dillon Round product selection had become a fine art, internalizing 96 percent of U.S. concessions.

At the Kennedy Round, the major participants adopted a multilateral, across-the-board form of negotiation rather than the bilateral form used at previous rounds. These negotiations did, however, include determination of an "exceptions list," which managed to internalize 81 percent of U.S. tariff reductions. (Because not all countries represented at the Kennedy Round participated on a fully reciprocal basis, it is not strictly appropriate to consider all of the 94 percent of U.S. concession imports as internalized, or as part of the one-for-one exchange of concessions.)

The Most Favored Nation Provision. The evidence cited above is a strong indication that the negotiators attempted to minimize spillover or free riding on the concessions. This was accomplished by judicious product selection, though it could have been achieved by eliminating the MFN provision. Without this provision, the tariff reductions agreed to could have been applied only to imports from countries that gave up concessions in return; the benefits produced could have been completely internalized. However, the trade and payments systems put together immediately after World War II tended to be bilateral arrangements, and the multilateralization as well as the expansion of trade as recovery progressed were generally accepted objectives. Thus, the multilateralization of concessions through the MFN provision should be viewed (especially at the early rounds) as an objective rather than as an instrument to help achieve the single objective of trade expansion.

General Economic Conditions. While the ability of judicious product selection to internalize the benefits of concessions contributed significantly to the success of the GATT rounds, it was certainly not the only contributing factor. As Table 2 shows, the GATT rounds began when the proportion of production entering into world trade was low by historical standards. Further, through the 1960s, covering the time span of completed GATT rounds, there was no significant increase of the ratio of trade to GNP. This was a period of almost continuous eco-

PART SIX: STRATEGIES

nomic expansion in the major industrial countries, few of which experienced significant inflation. And even with the completion from 1947 to 1967 of six GATT rounds, the ratio of trade to output did not increase over the period. It seems, thus, that trade was inelastic relative to economic expansion, that is, that economic expansion of output itself brought a less than proportional increase of international trade, leaving room for the trade-expanding effects of trade liberalization.

TABLE 2

EXPORTS PLUS IMPORTS AS A PROPORTION OF NATIONAL PRODUCTION
OF MAJOR TRADING COUNTRIES AT CURRENT PRICES:
HISTORICAL TRENDS AND RECENT YEARS
(percent)

Period[a]	United States	United Kingdom	France	Germany	Italy	Japan
Nineteenth century	13	22	18[b]	37[d]	21	10
Pre–World War I	11	44	54[d]	38[d]	28	30
1920s	11	38	51[b]	31[d]	26	36
1950s	8	30	41[b] 20[c]	35[d] 29[c]	25	19
1970s	11	38	29[c]	37[d] 36[c]	37	21
Recent						
1951	8	45	25	24	22	21[a]
1955	7	26	20	28	19	19
1960	7	23	22	30	24	20
1965	7	30	21	31	25	19
1970	9	33	23	34	28	19
1975	15	42		39		23

[a] Years for which data were used for each country are: United States, 1804–1813, 1834–1843, 1918–1928, 1954–1963, 1970–1974; United Kingdom, 1809–1813, 1837–1845, 1924–1928, 1957–1963, 1970–1974; France, 1805–1813, 1845–1854, 1920–1924, 1957–1963 and 1954–1963, 1970–1974; Germany, 1872–1879, 1919–1923, 1925–1929, 1955–1959 and 1954–1963, 1970–1974; Italy, 1861–1870, 1911–1913, 1925–1929, 1957–1963, 1970–1974; Japan, 1878–1887, 1908–1913, 1918–1927, 1950–1956, 1970–1974.

[b] Exports plus imports as a percentage of value added in agriculture and manufacturing (including mining and handicraft and some construction).

[c] Exports plus imports as a percentage of GNP.

[d] Exports plus imports as a percentage of the sums of private and government consumption and net domestic capital formation.

[e] Figures for 1952.

SOURCE: Robert Solomon and Anne Gault, "The Economic Interdependence of Nations: An Agenda for Research" (Washington, D.C.: Brookings Institution, June 1977; processed), tables 1 and 3.

J. M. FINGER

Changing "Supply Conditions" and Future Prospects

The evolution of several "supply side" factors since the GATT rounds began will have a significant influence on prospects for continuing trade liberalization through such negotiating rounds. In this section, I will attempt to analyze these changes within a framework developed for the purpose.

Number of Participants. Common sense suggests that, as the number of participants in a negotiation grows, attaining agreement will become more difficult. Table 1 indicates that at each of the first and the last three GATT rounds the United States negotiated with countries that supplied approximately two-thirds of U.S. imports. But the number of participating countries has increased from round to round. At Geneva 1947 the United States negotiated with sixteen countries, several of which negotiated for their colonies as well. Negotiating with the United States at Geneva 1956 were nineteen governments and the High Authority of the European Coal and Steel Community, and at the Dillon Round the United States negotiated with the EEC as a unit, plus eighteen country governments. By the Kennedy Round, there were, besides the United States, thirty active participants, again counting the EEC as one.

Negotiating Format Changes at the Kennedy Round. The Kennedy Round represented several significant departures from the negotiating procedure followed at previous rounds. Among major participants, the bilateral, product-specific form was replaced by multilateral, across-the-board (with exceptions) negotiations. Also, LDCs were allowed to participate on a less than fully reciprocal basis.

Bilateral versus multilateral. Comparison of the bilateral and multilateral internalization figures indicates that the switch to multilateral balancing probably took place before it was formally acknowledged at the Kennedy Round. Through the Torquay Round, the bilateral and multilateral internalization figures are quite similar, indicating that the major effort to internalize the benefits of concessions was at the bilateral level. The difference between imports from participants as a percentage of imports from all countries (row E of Table 1) and the internalization figures is between row E and the bilateral, not the multilateral, measure of internalization. At Torquay, more so at Geneva in 1956, and very markedly at the Dillon Round, the difference between row E and the internalization figures is at the multilateral, not the bilateral, level. Thus, while the *form* of negotiation remained bilateral

PART SIX: STRATEGIES

through the Dillon Round, *objectives* were obviously viewed in multilateral terms long before the Kennedy Round.

Across-the-board versus product selection. The shift at the Kennedy Round to an across-the-board approach seems to have been a significant departure from the previous format. Whereas the high degree of product selection applied at the Dillon Round achieved almost complete internalization, tariff reductions made there touched only 28 percent of dutiable U.S. imports from participants and only 19 percent of dutiable imports from all sources. Cuts at the Kennedy Round touched 64 percent of U.S. dutiable imports (from all countries), but almost 20 percent of the coverage of U.S. cuts spilled over to nonparticipants—countries that did not give concessions in exchange.

It is clear that the "exceptions list" at the Kennedy Round was clearly not the equivalent of the product selection applied at the Dillon Round. At the Dillon Round, product selection pushed the percentage of imports from participants from 66 percent (all dutiable goods) to 96 percent (goods on which tariffs were reduced). The Kennedy Round exceptions list pushed this percentage from 68 to 81 (relative to major participants).

Nonreciprocity from LDCs. The major participants in the Geneva 1956, Dillon, and Kennedy rounds were the United States, Canada, Japan, and the Western European industrial countries. There was, however, a basic difference between the position of nonmajor participants at the Kennedy Round and their position at earlier rounds. At earlier rounds, a balanced exchange of concessions among all participants was expected. At Geneva 1947, for example, the United States negotiated with seven nonmajor participants, receiving from them concessions (mostly reductions) on $135 million (1939 data) of U.S. exports. In exchange, the United States reduced tariffs on $115 million of imports from them and bound, duty free, an additional $185 million.

The Kennedy Round, however, was a balanced multilateral exchange of concessions only among the major industrial countries. Within this group, the United States "gave" concessions on $6.7 billion of imports and received concessions on $7.6 billion (1964 data). Counting only tariff reductions, the figures are $6.7 billion "received" and $6.4 billion "given." Though negotiations with other developed countries were on a bilateral basis, full reciprocity was expected from them; that is, concessions exchanged with them were expected to "balance." The United States negotiated with seven countries on this basis, granting concessions (in all negotiations) on $443 million of imports, of which $418 million were tariff reductions. Such countries made concessions on $486 million of U.S. exports, of which tariff reductions covered $112 million.

Full reciprocity was not expected from LDC participants. U.S. tariff reductions affected $546 million of imports from active LDC participants (total concessions, $571 million), while the LDC participants agreed to reduce tariffs on only $15 million of U.S. exports and to bind tariffs on an additional $190 million. The impact of this format change will be analyzed in the following section.

The Internalization-Coverage Trade-off. Since the number of commodities imported only (or in major part) from a given list of sources is limited, there is obviously a trade-off between the coverage (concessions imports as a percentage of total imports) and the degree of internalization that can be achieved. The outcomes of different GATT rounds can be viewed as movements to different positions on this trade-off. For example, product selection at the Dillon Round produced a high degree of internalization but at the cost of low coverage, while across-the-board cuts at the Kennedy Round covered a larger fraction of imports but achieved a substantially lower degree of internalization. When other conditions are favorable, negotiators can aim for high coverage; but when other conditions turn sour, they may have to emphasize internalization in order to achieve any agreement at all on concessions.

Changes in the underlying pattern of trade or in the negotiating format can be viewed as shifts of the internalization-coverage trade-off line. For example, if this curve is defined for a given list of participants, then an increase (as was observed from the earliest to the most recent GATT round) in the number of countries that provide a given percentage of U.S. imports will worsen this trade-off—shift the curve to the left. Allowing the LDCs to participate on a less than fully reciprocal basis represents a worsening of the coverage-internalization trade-off. Of a given amount of concessions, the larger the number of countries allowed to free ride, the larger the proportion of concession imports originating in countries that do not reciprocate—in other words, the larger the proportion of concessions not internalized.

This shift of the coverage-internalization trade-off obviously did not prevent agreement from being reached at the Kennedy Round. But this does not mean that under less favorable conditions than those prevailing at the time of the Kennedy Round such a shift would not be critical. Furthermore, since 1964 (the base year for the Kennedy Round), the role in world trade of Kennedy Round nonparticipants and partial participants has increased. This means that the gap has grown between the

PART SIX: STRATEGIES

coverage-internalization trade-off lines with and without a fully reciprocal role for LDCs.

Table 3 attempts to quantify this increase. In this table, manu- factured goods (Standard International Trade Classification [SITC] 5–8) is taken as an approximation of the coverage of U.S. concessions at the Kennedy Round.[6] If concessions were exchanged in 1976 among Kennedy Round participants on this basket of goods, only 74 percent of the concessions given up by the United States would be received by countries that gave up concessions in return. In 1964 this figure would have been 82 percent. The eight-percentage-point decline in the major participants' share reappears as an eight-percentage-point increase in the LDC share—almost all of which is accounted for by LDCs who were nonparticipants in the Kennedy Round.

How the Prospects for Trade Liberalization Might Be Improved

Format from the Kennedy Round. The negotiating format carried over from the Kennedy Round is not likely to produce substantial advances for trade liberalization so long as the general economic conditions that determine the "political will" for trade liberalization are not extremely favorable. An increase in the number of countries (particularly LDCs) playing a significant role in world trade, along with acceptance of a nonreciprocating role for LDCs in trade negotiations, have substantially worsened the internalization-coverage trade-off. Further, across-the- board (rather than product-specific) bargaining may not be able to achieve the degree of internalization necessary to reach agreement when other conditions are unfavorable. Ten years have passed since the com- pletion of the Kennedy Round. Previously, the longest span from com- pletion of one round to completion of the next was six years.

The Kennedy Round included, and the format of the present round includes, a provision for sectoral or industry-specific negotiations— intended to find ways to reduce such industry-specific trade restrictions as the "American selling price" system used in this country to value for

---

[6] There were, of course, exceptions across the manufactured goods list, and con- cessions were made on some materials, particularly processed materials. The coverage of Table 3 includes $9.1 billion of U.S. imports in 1964, while the Kennedy Round concessions covered $8.5 billion. The distribution of imports by country group of origin is approximately the same in Table 3 as for actual Kennedy Round concessions. According to data in Table 9 at the end of this chapter, imports of items actually reduced came 81 percent from major par- ticipants, 5 percent from other developed participants, 7 percent from active LDC participants, and 7 percent from nonparticipants. Thus, Table 3 under- states slightly the importance of nonparticipants and major participants while over- stating slightly the role of other participants.

TABLE 3

U.S. MANUFACTURED GOODS TRADE WITH VARIOUS GROUPS OF KENNEDY ROUND PARTICIPANTS, 1964 AND 1976

(values in millions of dollars)

Country Group	Imports (f.o.b.) 1964 Value	1964 Percent of total	1976 Value	1976 Percent of total	Exports (c.i.f.) 1964 Value	1964 Percent of total	1976 Value	1976 Percent of total
All countries	9,097	100.0	66,154	100.0	16,389	100.0	77,249	100.0
Major participants	7,491	82.0	49,030	74.0	8,708	53.0	40,630	53.0
Other developed participants	344	4.0	2,537	4.0	1,036	6.0	4,459	6.0
Active LDC participants	522	6.0	3,932	6.0	1,446	9.0	5,224	7.0
All participants	8,356	92.0	55,489	84.0	11,262	69.0	50,313	65.0
All LDCs	1,214	13.0	14,043	21.0	6,738	41.0	28,496	37.0
Nonparticipant LDCs	692	8.0	10,120	15.0	2,292	32.0	23,232	30.0
Nonparticipant developed countries	48	0.5	544	0.8				

SOURCE: U.S. Bureau of the Census, *Highlights of U.S. Export and Import Trade* (FT990), December 1964 and December 1976.

PART SIX: STRATEGIES

customs purposes certain chemical products. Sectoral sessions for chemicals, cotton textiles, and steel were held at the Kennedy Round, but the degree of trade liberalization agreed to was no longer than that achieved in across-the-board negotiations.

Sectoral negotiations present the potential for mutating the GATT rounds into a net protectionist rather than a trade-liberalizing influence. The tendency for producers' interests to dominate is not decreased by making *industry* discussions multicountry. The representation of each country at each sector negotiation would be tilted toward its interests as a producer, and the results of such sessions would tend toward organizing markets in ways producers find useful rather than toward trade liberalization. Given the upper hand producer interests tend to have in industry-specific negotiations, these interests will push to increase the relative importance of such sessions. Thus, as the Tokyo Round began, U.S. industry groups began to build support for the position that sectoral negotiations for an industry *automatically* put that industry on the exceptions list for the general negotiations. As the relative importance of sectoral negotiations grows, the GATT rounds will become less effective in promoting trade liberalization.

While sectoral negotiations may be the only way to "get at" industry-specific, nontariff trade restrictions, such sessions should perhaps be held separately from the general negotiations. This might make it more difficult for protectionist interests to erode the coverage of the general negotiations by expanding the list of sectoral negotiations.

A further problem is that as tariffs have been reduced the relative importance of nontariff protective measures has increased. The form such measures take varies widely, but a significant part are quantitative restrictions (import quotas). There is, however, no apparent reason why the GATT bargaining process could not be applied to liberalization of such measures. Reciprocity inherent in an exchange of quota enlargements could be measured at least as precisely as a comparison of base-year imports measures the relative increases of imports resulting from an exchange of tariff reductions. Mixed exchanges—quotas for tariffs—would require prior agreement as to what percentage change on what coverage of tariff reductions would be equivalent to a given percentage quota enlargement.

Potential for Product-Specific Negotiations. With conditions for trade liberalization generally bad, it might be a strategic move to limit negotiations to the major industrial countries and shoot for a high internalization—low coverage outcome, that is, to move down the internalization-coverage trade-off. But there are several problems with

434

J. M. FINGER

this strategy. First, high internalization at the Dillon Round (which included six developing countries) cut coverage to only 19 percent of dutiable U.S. imports, and there is considerable evidence that the coverage-internalization trade-off curve has shifted backward (worsened) since then. Hence, getting back to Geneva 1956 or Dillon Round (or perhaps even Kennedy Round) levels of internalization for this group of negotiators would probably push coverage so low that the degree of trade liberalization generated would not be sufficient to offset the tendency toward protectionism inherent in day-to-day trade issues.

Further, the negotiators would be aware of the growing importance of nonparticipants, as illustrated in Table 3. Concessions that were completely balanced and internalized in terms of 1976 trade flows would probably not be so in terms of 1980 flows. Awareness of this would be a further impediment to agreement or a further drag on coverage.

The Role of the LDCs. It is clear from the discussion that the role the LDCs play in trade negotiations will be critical. Their significance in world trade has become such that further trade liberalization depends on their active participation. Further, barriers to trade flows between developed and developing countries have been less reduced through the GATT mechanism than have barriers to trade among developed countries, and hence they are the most significant remaining impediments.

Reciprocity pays. Unfortunately, the third world and its spokespersons and institutions have taken a vocal position against a reciprocal role for the LDCs. The Kennedy Round, however, provides strong evidence that reciprocity pays. There, the United States made concessions (almost entirely tariff reductions) on $571 million or 33 percent of its (1964) imports from the nine active LDC participants (Table 4). Of some $6 billion of U.S. imports in 1964 from other LDCs, only 5 percent was subject to concessions.

TABLE 4

U.S. IMPORTS, 1964, AFFECTED BY KENNEDY ROUND CONCESSIONS (REDUCTIONS PLUS BINDINGS) AS A PERCENTAGE OF TOTAL IMPORTS

Country Group	Percentage
Major participants	70
Other developed participants	49
Active LDC participants	33
Other LDCs	5

SOURCE: Table 9.

PART SIX: STRATEGIES

The exports of the active LDC participants received this increased coverage in exchange for much less than full reciprocity. Active LDC concessions were almost entirely binding and covered only $205 million of 1964 U.S. exports to these countries. In several cases, the "concession" extended by an LDC participant was to bind under GATT tariff reforms that were implemented because of their benefit to the LDC —in other words, the LDC governments received concessions in exchange for taking actions they would have taken anyway. For example, trade reforms made by Argentina and Brazil were part of general economic policy reforms. Chilean tariff reforms bound at the Kennedy Round were not part of general economic reform but were in any case taken for their own sake rather than in exchange for benefits received.[7] Indian concessions consisted primarily of reducing "official" rates of duty to the levels actually being collected.[8] Thus, if the Kennedy Round is taken as a guide, the extension of trade liberalization to products exported by LDCs would be significantly increased by minimal acts of reciprocity by the LDCs.

But third world spokespersons often express concern that multilateral reductions of trade barriers in industrial countries would not benefit LDCs. Part of their argument is the infant-industry argument applied to exporters: if concessions are not extended *preferentially*, LDC export suppliers will be "squeezed out" by industrial country exporters to whom *multilateral* tariff reductions would also apply. The LDCs already enjoy tariff preferences on many goods imported by developing countries; hence, reducing tariffs multilaterally would erode the preference margin they presently enjoy. As to the first point, analysis of the increase of imports resulting from concessions made at the Dillon Round by the United States,[9] as well as of concessions made by the United States, the EEC, and Japan at the Kennedy Round,[10] demonstrates that imports from LDC suppliers increased by at least as large a percentage as did imports from industrial country exporters. LDC suppliers were not squeezed out. A limited number of LDCs are exporters of manufactured goods (on which the Dillon and Kennedy rounds concentrated); hence, these results do not exclude the possibility

[7] U.S. Office of the Special Representative for Trade Negotiations, *General Agreement on Tariffs and Trade, 1964–67, Tariff Conference, Geneva, Switzerland,* vol. 1, pt. 1, pp. 132–43.

[8] Ibid., p. 147.

[9] J. M. Finger, "GATT Tariff Concessions and the Exports of Developing Countries: U.S. Concessions at the Dillon Round," *Economic Journal*, vol. 84 (September 1964), pp. 566–75.

[10] J. M. Finger, "Effects of the Kennedy Round Tariff Concessions on the Exports of Developing Countries," *Economic Journal*, vol. 86 (March 1976), pp. 87–95.

that potential exports by less advanced countries have been squeezed out. They do imply that if "fourth world" countries are being squeezed out of world markets, the pressure is coming from third world as well as from developed country suppliers. If this is the case, fourth world suppliers require preferential treatment relative to third world as well as to developed country suppliers in world markets.

As to the erosion of preferences, a careful examination by Robert Baldwin and Tracy Murray indicates that the effect of multilateral tariff reductions on LDC exports would be a net increase.[11] Multilateral reductions would have broader product coverage, would apply to imports from LDCs not eligible for preferences, and would be free of the limits applied to the volume of imports that can be entered at preferential rates. The expansionary effects of these factors on LDC exports would substantially outweigh the negative impact that erosion of existing preferences would have.

Political obstacles. These factors suggest an active, reciprocal role for at least the major LDCs in multilateral tariff negotiations. Unfortunately, positions to the contrary have already solidified. The demand for "special and differential" treatment is a prominent brick in the wall of solidarity the third world is attempting to maintain. A developing country that saw the advantage of a reciprocal role in trade negotiations would come under considerable political pressure to maintain third world solidarity. And the industrial countries have publicly accepted the idea of special and differential treatment for LDCs at the Tokyo Round. Thus, progress might depend on getting away from global forums, which provide an optimal climate for posturing but are too unwieldy to allow the attention to details necessary to assure each participant that a proposed action will be to his net benefit. As indicated before, negotiations in response to industry problems will be, at best, injury minimizing; hence, what is needed is identification of manageable possibilities that are of clear mutual benefit to developed and developing countries. Several such possibilities are examined below.

Reciprocal Negotiations between the United States and Major LDCs. An approach to consider is a return to the format of the old reciprocal trade negotiations, concentrating, however, on exchanges between a major industrial country and its major LDC trading partners. The feasibility of such an approach depends on there being substantial bilateral, *principal supplier* trade flows between the proposed participants that are

---

[11] Robert E. Baldwin and Tracy Murray, "MFN Tariff Reductions and LDC Benefits under GSP," *Economic Journal*, vol. 87 (March 1977), pp. 30–46.

PART SIX: STRATEGIES

subject to negotiable trade restrictions. Gerald Lage has explored in some detail the possibility of such negotiations between the United States and ten major LDC trading partners: Mexico, Brazil, Colombia, Israel, India, Singapore, the Philippines, Korea, Hong Kong, and Taiwan.[12] In 1974, in the case of products of which one of these ten countries was the largest (principal) supplier, U.S. dutiable imports from all sources totaled approximately $4 billion, about 4 percent of total U.S. imports.[13] Of this $4 billion, 42 percent came from the principal supplier country and another 33 percent from other countries in this group. In terms of agreements reached by the United States at the Kennedy Round in bilateral negotiations with "minor" participants, this is an "acceptable" degree of internalization. As Table 5 indicates, 77 percent of U.S. concession imports from the nine active LDC participants were goods principally supplied by these countries.

Lage also identified products imported by each of the ten countries principally from the United States.[14] This list covered some $5 billion of 1974 U.S. exports. The ratio of imports for which the United States is the principal supplier to total imports from the United States exceeded 50 percent for each of the ten countries except Israel (39 percent), India (44 percent), and Taiwan (49 percent). Available figures (Table 5, last column) indicate that the United States was the principal export supplier of somewhat higher percentages of imports of products on which LDC participants granted concessions to the United States at the Kennedy Round.

The $4 billion of LDC principal supplier exports to the United States and $5 billion of U.S. principal supplier exports to these ten countries define the area for possible negotiation rather than the ultimate outcome. Of items on which LDCs finally agree to make concessions, the percentage of their imports supplied by the United States might easily equal the figure achieved at the Kennedy Round. And while the Lage study concentrated on the possibility of reciprocal tariff concessions, negotiations might focus on nontariff restrictions applied by each side to these principal supplier exports.

While the range of the internalization figures for U.S. concessions indicates that agreement might be reached, the product composition of the list of goods the United States imports principally from these ten LDCs suggests that special problems might be encountered here. Sub-

---

[12] Gerald M. Lage, "The Feasibility of Mutually Beneficial Trade Negotiations between the U.S. and Advanced LDCs" (U.S. Treasury Department, Office of Policy Research, February 1977).

[13] Based on seven-digit Schedule A classifications.

[14] Based on four-digit SITC data.

J. M. FINGER

stantial amounts are in textiles, footwear, and apparel. Even with full reciprocity from the LDCs, it might be impossible to overcome domestic resistance to reducing U.S. import restrictions on such items.

Extending Preferential Concessions. In another approach designed to get around the concentration of LDC principal supplier exports on import-sensitive goods, the United States might, as its part of the bargain, extend the present tariff preferences to other, less import-sensitive goods. If the MFN provision is not applied to U.S. concessions to LDCs—or is applied only to imports from other LDCs (or only fourth world countries)—the benefits of the concessions could be concentrated on the countries willing to make concessions in return.[15]

Objections to this approach might be raised on two grounds. First, the LDCs' comparative advantage certainly lies more in those products principally supplied by them in world markets than in other products. This increases the likelihood that these preferential tariff reductions would be more trade distorting than trade creating and hence would have undesirable efficiency effects.

Second, administering preferential tariffs involves certification of country of origin, which is not necessary when the same rate applies regardless of origin. Providing such certification might be costly and might cause administrative problems, although several years' experience with existing preferences has brought no major problems to the surface.[16]

For the United States to negotiate with one or several LDCs preferential concessions that are extended to *all* LDCs would certainly enhance the negotiating countries' positions in the third world. This would give the United States considerable influence over the makeup of third world leadership and would provide a noneconomic incentive for the LDCs to bargain seriously.

LDC Export Taxes and DC Tariff Escalation. It is often noted that developed countries protect their processors of primary materials by imposing higher import duties on processed than on raw materials. Unilateral reduction by the developed countries (DCs) of these "escalated" tariffs is often proposed as a way to improve the economic lot of the LDCs, but little has been done to implement such proposals.

---

[15] Present negotiating authority granted by the Trade Act of 1974 does not include such preference bargaining.

[16] The "competitive need" criterion in the U.S. preference scheme excludes from preferential treatment exports from any country that supplies more than 50 percent or a specified value of U.S. imports of the product in question. This criterion also serves to limit the incentive for a country to provide false certificates of origin in order to capture the preferential margin on goods produced in other countries.

TABLE 5

UNITED STATES CONCESSION TRADE WITH
SELECTED KENNEDY ROUND MINOR PARTICIPANTS
(millions of dollars, 1964 data as available)

Participant	U.S. Imports from Listed Country Affected by U.S. Concessions			Listed Country Imports from U.S. Affected by Listed Country Concessions		
	Total country exports affected (1)	Country "principal supplier" exports (2)	b as percent of a (3)	Total U.S. exports affected (4)	U.S. "principal suppliers" exports (5)	c as percent of d (6)
Greece	38.0	31.0	82.0	—	—	—
Poland	47.0	2.0	4.0			
South Africa	71.4	6.9	10.0			
Israel	44.6	0.2	0.4	40.6	34.6	85
Portugal	36.6	18.4	50.0			
Spain	71.8	39.6	55.0	47.8	34.4	72
Yugoslavia	40.8	3.2	8.0	28.4	14.0	50
Total, available data	350.2	101.3	29.0			
All LDCs	900.0					
Participating LDCs	700.0					
Nine active participants	570.0	439.0	77			
Brazil	62.5	49.5	79	31.1	28.1	90
Chile	68.5	64.4	94			

Dominican Republic	16.6	4.6	28			
India	235.4	193.0	82	18.0	17.2	96
Jamaica	95.1	83.3	88	2.8	2.3	82
Korea	12.0	3.6	30			
Peru	26.6	8.9	33	5.1	4.7	92
Trinidad and Tobago	1.7	0.8	50	0.9	0.4	50

NOTE: The countries listed are those for which data were given in the cited source.

ᵃ Poland agreed to increase its imports from GATT members by at least 7 percent a year.

SOURCE: U.S. Office of the Special Representative for Trade Negotiations, *General Agreement on Tariffs and Trade, 1964–67, Tariff Conference*, vol. 1, pp. 93–164.

PART SIX: STRATEGIES

TABLE 6

VALUES OF U.S. IMPORTS OF GOODS ON WHICH THE UNITED STATES GRANTED TARIFF CONCESSIONS AT GATT NEGOTIATIONS

(values in millions of dollars)

Round	Year for Which Data Are Given	Imports from Countries to Whom Each Concession Was Granted		Imports from Other Participants (Value)
		Value	Percent of Concession and Non-concession Imports[a]	
Geneva 1947				
All concessions	1939	n.a.	n.a.	n.a.
Tariff reductions	1939	n.a.	n.a.	n.a.
Annecy 1949				
All concessions	1948	143	37	19
Tariff reductions	1948	61	33	8
Torquay 1951				
All concessions	1949	266	10	30
Tariff reductions	1949	241	26	27
Geneva 1956				
All concessions	1954	677	13	134
Tariff reductions	1954	677	22	134
Dillon 1960–1961				
All concessions	1960	1,225	14	491
Tariff reductions	1960	1,163[a]	20	466[a]
Kennedy 1964–1967				
All concessions	1964	n.a.	n.a.	n.a.
Tariff reductions	1964	n.a.	n.a.	n.a.

n.a.: Not available.

[a] Dutiable or all imports, as appropriate.

SOURCE: Official U.S. reports of GATT negotiations (see Table 10) and Table 8.

Less often noted is the extensive use of export taxes by LDCs. These export taxes tend to be escalated in the opposite direction—that is, they are lower on processed than on primary goods. Thus, LDC export taxes tend to encourage processing in the LDCs, while DC tariffs tend to shift processing toward the DCs, offsetting one another as far as the

Total Imports from Participants		*Imports from Nonparticipants*		*Total*	
Value	Percent of Concession and Non-concession Imports[a]	Imports[a]	Percent of concession and Non-Concession Value	Value	Percent of Concession and Non-concession Imports[a]
1,337	93	430	53	1,767	78
429	74	79	24	508	56
69	42	721	38	883	39
162	38	109	4	178	6
296	11	212	6	478	7
268	29	151	8	419	15
811	15	100	2	911	9
811	26	100	7	911	20
1,715	20	71	1	1,786	12
1,629[a]	28	67[a]	2	1,696	19
8,000	n.a.	500	n.a.	8,500	46
n.a.	n.a.	n.a.	n.a.	7,900	64

division of the processing pie is concerned. But both increase the price of processed goods to DC consumers, thereby reducing the size of that pie. It should be possible to reduce LDC export taxes and DC import tariffs simultaneously in such a way that processing will expand in the LDCs but not contract in the DCs.

443

TABLE 7

VALUES OF U.S. EXPORTS OF GOODS ON WHICH OTHER PARTICIPANTS GRANTED CONCESSIONS AT GATT TARIFF NEGOTIATIONS

(values in millions of dollars)

Round	Year for Which Data are Given	Concessions granted to U.S.A.		Concessions Exchanged among Other Participants (value)	Total	
		Value	Percent of imports from United States		Value	Percent of imports from United States
Geneva 1947	1939	1,192	63	200[a]	1,392	74
Annecy 1949	1938	108	n.a.	n.a.	n.a.	n.a.
Torquay 1951	1947	537	39	100[a]	637	46
Geneva 1956	1949	1,058	19	100[a]	1,158	21
Dillon 1960–1961	1954	398	6	n.a.	n.a.	n.a.
Kennedy 1964–1967	1960	1,496	15	n.a.	n.a.	n.a.
Major participants[b]	1964	n.a.	n.a.	n.a.	7,600	70
All participants	1964	n.a.	n.a.	n.a.	8,100	42

n.a.: Not available.

[a] Bindings and reductions.

[b] EEC, Canada, Japan, United Kingdom, Austria, Denmark, Norway, Finland, Sweden, Switzerland.

SOURCE: Official U.S. reports of GATT Negotiations (see Table 10) and Table 6.

J. M. FINGER

TABLE 8

U.S. IMPORTS, DUTIABLE AND DUTY FREE, SELECTED YEARS

(millions of dollars)

Year	Duty Free	Dutiable		Total	
		All countries	Participants	All countries	Participants
1939	1,397	879	581	2,276	1,438
1948	4,175	2,918	182	7,092	382
1949	3,883	2,708	931	6,592	2,792
1954	5,668	4,572	3,078	10,240	5,332
1960	5,780	8,870	5,891	14,650	8,588
1964	7,029	11,572	n.a.	18,601	10,811

n.a.: Not available.

SOURCE: Bureau of the Census, *U.S. Historical Statistics, Colonial Times to 1970,* Series U 207–212.

In a separate study, Stephen Golub and I estimated the effects of simultaneous elimination of DC tariffs and LDC export taxes on eight commodities—copra, rubber, cocoa, cotton, wool, leather, wood, and coffee.[17] Our estimates indicate that world consumption of the eight commodities in the study would increase by 0.8 percent. Processing would increase by 8.7 percent and primary production by 4.1 percent in the LDCs. In the DCs, primary processing and production would fall by 1 percent or less.[18] For the products studied here, the 8.7 percent increase in LDC processing amounts to about $1.1 billion at 1973 prices and based on 1973 levels of activity. On the same basis, the 4.1 percent increase of production of primary products comes to a total of $0.9 billion for the eight studied here. Because world consumption increases, the corresponding declines in the DCs are about one-third as large as the volume increases in the LDCs. Over the eight commodities, the increase of LDC export earnings is about 11 percent, which, relative to trade levels in 1973, amounts to just over $1 billion. As policy alternatives go, this is a significant increase. Tariff preferences, by comparison, are estimated to have increased LDC export earnings by less than $500 million.[19]

---

[17] Stephen Golub and J. M. Finger, "The Processing of Primary Commodities: Effects of Developed Country Tariff Escalation and Developing Country Export Taxes" (U.S. Department of the Treasury, Office of Policy Research, June 1977).

[18] "Fine tuning" of the extent of concessions could theoretically keep the net change of DC processing at zero.

[19] Baldwin and Murray, "MFN Tariff Reductions and LDC Benefits," p. 37.

TABLE 9

VALUE OF 1964 U.S. IMPORTS AND EXPORTS AFFECTED BY KENNEDY ROUND CONCESSIONS

(millions of dollars, c.i.f.)

	U.S. Imports from Country Listed					
	Concession and non-concession items		Items on which U.S. made concessions			
			Bindings and tariff reductions		Tariff reductions	
Participants	Dutiable and nondutiable (1)	Dutiable (2)	Value	Percent of (1)	Value	Percent of (2)
Major participants						
EEC	2,948	2,677	2,216	75	2,170	81
Canada	3,993	1,655	1,443	36	1,257	76
Japan	1,907	1,833	1,463	77	1,458	80
United Kingdom	1,193	929	959	72	836	90
Austria	61	59	53	87	53	90
Denmark	133	110	102	77	53	48
Finland	81	35	33	41	33	94
Norway	131	108	104	79	103	95
Sweden	218	175	161	74	160	91
Switzerland	252	231	161	64	160	69
All (sums and % of sums)ᵃ	10,917	7,812	6,595	70	6,283	80
Total major participants	10,811	n.a.	6,700	n.a.	6,400	n.a.
Other DC participants						
Greece	n.a.	41.0	38.0	n.a.	38.0	n.a.
Iceland (acceded)	n.a.	15.0	12.1	n.a.	12.1	n.a.
Ireland	n.a.	n.a.	14.0	n.a.	14.0	n.a.

New Zealand (1966 data)	152.6	n.a.	12.5	n.a.	12.4	n.a.
Poland (acceded)	n.a.	n.a.	47.0	n.a.	47.0	n.a.
South Africa	n.a.	n.a.	71.4	n.a.	71.4	n.a.
Turkey	n.a.	59.0	54.0	n.a.	54.0	n.a.
Israel	53.8	n.a.	44.6	n.a.	44.6	n.a.
Portugal	56.8	40.6	36.6	n.a.	29.9	n.a.
Spain	110.6	n.a.	71.8	n.a.	58.9	n.a.
Yugoslavia (acceded)	49.5	n.a.	40.8	n.a.	36.0	n.a.
Total[a]	911.3	n.a.	442.8	n.a.	418.3	n.a.
Active LDC participants						
Argentina	105.9	n.a.	52.1	n.a.	40.7	n.a.
Brazil	533.0	87.0	62.5	n.a.	53.7	n.a.
Chile	221.6	n.a.	68.5	n.a.	67.9	n.a.
Dominican Republic	123.9	n.a.	16.6	n.a.	16.3	n.a.
India	306.4	n.a.	235.4	n.a.	233.1	n.a.
Jamaica	111.5	n.a.	95.1	n.a.	95.1	n.a.
Korea (acceded)	30.0	23.8	12.0	n.a.	12.0	n.a.
Peru	195.3	n.a.	26.6	n.a.	25.6	n.a.
Trinidad and Tobago	117.6	n.a.	1.7	n.a.	1.7	n.a.
All (sums and % of sums)	1,745.2	n.a.	570.5	33	546.1	n.a.
Total[a]	1,769	n.a.	n.a.	n.a.	n.a.	n.a.
All participating LDCs[a]	2,200	1,000	700	33	n.a.	n.a.
All LDCs[a]	5,800	3,140	900	16	n.a.	n.a.
All participating countries (sums above)	n.a.	n.a.	7,738	n.a.	7,176	n.a.
All participating countries[a]	n.a.	n.a.	8,000	n.a.	n.a.	n.a.
All countries, participating and nonparticipating[a]	18,601	11,572	8,500	n.a.	7,900	n.a.

TABLE 9 (continued)

VALUE OF 1964 U.S. IMPORTS AND EXPORTS AFFECTED BY KENNEDY ROUND CONCESSIONS
(millions of dollars, c.i.f.)

	Concession and non-concession items		Listed Country Imports from U.S.			
			Items on which listed country made concessions			
			Bindings and tariff reductions		Tariff reductions	
Participants	Dutiable and nondutiable (3)	Dutiable (4)	Value	Percent of (3)	Value	Percent of (4)
Major participants						
EEC	4,616	3,150	3,029	66	2,724	86
Canada	4,744	2,346	1,405	30	1,403	69
Japan	2,334	1,265	1,177	50	886	70
United Kingdom	1,562	1,161	981	63	889	77
Austria	98	57	49	50	31	54
Denmark	195	80	118	61	73	91
Finland	88	65	70	80	59	91
Norway	124	58	72	58	48	83
Sweden	364	227	303	83	211	93
Switzerland	305	287	263	86	228	79
All (sums and % of sums)	14,430	8,696	7,467	52	6,552	75
Total major participants[a]	14,617	n.a.	7,600	n.a.	6,700	n.a.

Other DC participants						
Greece	150.0	n.a.	50.0	n.a.	n.a.	n.a.
Iceland (acceded)	n.a.	n.a.	5.2	n.a.	1.4	n.a.
Ireland	65.0	n.a.	27.0	n.a.	10.0	n.a.
New Zealand (1966 data)	117.5	11.8	16.4	n.a.	11.8	n.a.
Poland (acceded)	n.a.	n.a.	0.0	n.a.	0.0	n.a.
South Africa	n.a.	n.a.	6.3	n.a.	6.3	n.a.
Turkey	155.9	n.a.	155.9	n.a.	0.7	n.a.
Israel	212.2	n.a.	40.6	n.a.	11.2	n.a.
Portugal	80.6	n.a.	8.8	n.a.	8.6	n.a.
Spain	526.7	n.a.	47.8	n.a.	47.4	n.a.
Yugoslavia (acceded)	173.0	n.a.	28.4	n.a.	14.6	n.a.
Total[a]	1,902.4	n.a.	486.4	n.a.	112.0	n.a.
Active LDC participants						
Argentina	n.a.	n.a.	88.3	n.a.	0.0	n.a.
Brazil	n.a.	n.a.	31.1	n.a.	0.0	n.a.
Chile	n.a.	n.a.	6.1	n.a.	5.0	n.a.
Dominican Republic	n.a.	n.a.	6.3	n.a.	0.0	n.a.
India	n.a.	n.a.	18.0	n.a.	0.0	n.a.
Jamaica	n.a.	n.a.	2.8	n.a.	2.5	n.a.
Korea (acceded)	n.a.	n.a.	46.6	n.a.	2.0	n.a.
Peru	n.a.	n.a.	5.1	n.a.	5.0	n.a.
Trinidad and Tobago	n.a.	n.a.	0.9	n.a.	0.0	n.a.
All (sums and % of sums)	n.a.	n.a.	205.2	n.a.	14.5	n.a.
Total[a]	2,546	n.a.	n.a.	n.a.	n.a.	n.a.

(continued on next page)

449

TABLE 9 (continued)

VALUE OF 1964 U.S. IMPORTS AND EXPORTS AFFECTED BY KENNEDY ROUND CONCESSIONS
(millions of dollars, c.i.f.)

	Listed Country Imports from U.S.					
	Concession and non-concession items		Items on which listed country made concessions			
			Bindings and tariff reductions		Tariff reductions	
Participants	Dutiable and nondutiable (3)	Dutiable (4)	Value	Percent of (3)	Value	Percent of (4)
All participating LDCs[a]	n.a.	n.a.	n.a.	n.a.	n.a.	n.a.
All LDCs[a]	n.a.	n.a.	n.a.	n.a.	n.a.	n.a.
All participating countries (sums above)	n.a.	n.a.	8,159	n.a.	n.a.	n.a.
All participating countries[a]	n.a.	n.a.	8,100	n.a.	n.a.	n.a.
All countries, participating and nonparticipating[a]	n.a.	n.a.	8,100	n.a.	n.a.	n.a.

n.a.: Not available.
NOTE: This table is the result of an attempt to consolidate into a common format information presented (in the cited source) in various tables (not numbered) with different formats. A good deal of numerical information was also taken from the text of the report. The overall results given in the text often do not equal the sums built up from the available country-by-country figures. Giving the page on which each figure was found would require as many footnotes as there are figures.
[a] These "total" figures were found in the text of the source and are not sums of the column.

SOURCE: U.S. Office of the Special Representative for Trade Negotiations, *General Agreement on Tariffs and Trade, 1964–67, Trade Conference*, vol. I, pt. 1.

TABLE 10

OFFICIAL REPORTS ON U.S. PARTICIPATION IN MAJOR GATT ROUNDS

Round	*Report*
Geneva 1947	U.S. Department of State, *Analysis of General Agreement on Tariffs and Trade, Signed at Geneva, October 30, 1947.* Pub. 2983, Commercial Policy Series, no. 109, November 1974.
Annecy 1949	U.S. Department of State. *Analysis of Protocol of Accession and Schedules to the General Agreement on Tariffs and Trade, Negotiated at Annecy, France, April-August 1949.* Pub. 3651, Commercial Policy Series, no. 120, October 1949.
Torquay 1951	U.S. Department of State. *Analysis of Torquay Protocol of Accession, Schedules, and Related Documents, General Agreement on Tariffs and Trade, Negotiated at Torquay, England, September 1950–April 1951.* Pub. 4209, Commercial Policy Series, no. 135, May 1951.
Geneva 1956	U.S. Department of State. *General Agreement on Tariffs and Trade, Analysis of United States Negotiations, Sixth Protocol (Including Schedules) of Supplementary Concessions Negotiated at Geneva, Switzerland, January-May 1956.* Pub. 6348, Commercial Policy Series, no. 158, June 1956.
Dillon 1960–1961	U.S. Department of State. *General Agreement on Tariffs and Trade, Analysis of United States Negotiations, 1960–61, Tariff Conference, Geneva, Switzerland.* 4 vols. Pub. 7349, Commercial Policy Series, no. 186, March 1962 (vols. 1 and 2), June 1967 (vol. 3), May 1963 (vol. 4).
Kennedy 1964–1967	U.S. Office of the Special Representative for Trade Negotiations. *General Agreement on Tariffs and Trade, 1964–67, Tariff Conference, Geneva, Switzerland.* Vol. 1 (General Summary), pts. 1 (Concessions by Country) and 2 (Special Multilateral Negotiations); vol. 2, pts. 1 and 2 (List of Tariff Concessions Granted by the United States), 1967.

TABLE 11

COUNTRIES WITH WHOM THE UNITED STATES EXCHANGED CONCESSIONS AT GATT NEGOTIATIONS

Geneva 1947	Annecy 1949	Torquay 1951	Geneva 1956	Dillon 1960–1961	Kennedy 1964–1967
Australia	*Acceding countries*	*Acceding at Torquay*	Australia	EEC	*Major participants*
Belgium and colonies	Denmark	Austria	Austria	Austria	EEC
Brazil	Dominican Republic	Germany	Benelux	Cambodia	Canada
Canada	Finland	Korea	Canada	Canada	Japan
Chile	Greece	Peru	Chile	Denmark	United Kingdom
China (Hong Kong and Kwantung)	Haiti	Turkey	Cuba	Finland	Austria
Cuba	Italy		Denmark	Haiti	Denmark
Czechoslovakia	Liberia	*Acceding before Torquay*	Dominican Republic	India	Finland
France and colonies	Nicaragua	Benelux	Federal Republic of Germany	Israel	Norway
India	Sweden	Brazil	Finland	Japan	Sweden
Lebanon (Syro-Lebanese Union)	Uruguay	Canada	France	New Zealand	Switzerland
Netherlands and colonies		Denmark	Haiti	Norway	
		Dominican Republic	Italy	Pakistan	*Other DC participants*
		France	Japan	Peru	Greece
		Indonesia	Norway	Portugal	Iceland
		Italy	Peru	Sweden	Ireland
			Sweden	Switzerland	New Zealand
				United Kingdom	Poland

New Zealand
Norway
Union of South
Africa
United Kingdom
and colonies

Burma
Ceylon
Newfoundland

Norway
Sweden

Turkey
United Kingdom
Hong Kong
Bahamas
High Authority of
the European
Coal and Steel
Community

South Africa
Turkey
Israel
Portugal
Spain
Yugoslavia

*Active LDC
participants*
Argentina
Brazil
Chile
Dominican
Republic
India
Jamaica
Korea
Peru
Trinidad and
Tobago

453

The Meaning of "Unfair" in United States Import Policy

J. Michael Finger*

Unfair trade cases are where the action is. According to two of Washington's top trade lawyers, these cases "have become the usual first choice for industries seeking protection from imports into the U.S."[1] There are indeed a lot of cases. From 1975 to 1979, the U.S. government processed 245 antidumping and countervailing duty (antisubsidy) cases, or around fifty cases a year.[2] In the 1980s, the caseload rose even higher, to eighty-six cases a year.[3] By comparison, there have been only four escape clause cases a year;[4] cases in which an industry sought protection from import competition without accusing the foreign seller of employing or benefiting from unfair practices.[5]

Several features stand out from the pattern of U.S. antidumping and countervailing duty cases from 1980 through 1988 (see Tables 1 and 2):[6]

■ The number of antidumping and countervailing duty cases

* J. Michael Finger is Lead Economist, Trade Policy, at the World Bank. University of Texas, B.A.; University of North Carolina, Ph.D. The author wishes to thank Gary N. Horlick and Robert E. Hudec for their thoughtful comments on an earlier version, and Ms. Nellie T. Artis for administrative and editorial assistance that has been invaluable. But the author alone is responsible for opinions and interpretations expressed here, and for remaining errors.

1. Gary N. Horlick & Geoffrey D. Oliver, *Antidumping and Countervailing Duty Law Provisions for the Omnibus Trade and Competitiveness Act of 1988*, 23 J. WORLD TRADE 5, 5 (1989).

2. J.M. Finger et al., *The Political Economy of Administered Protection.* 72 AM. ECON. REV. 452, 463 (1982) (Table 4).

3. Table 1.

4. N. David Palmeter, *The Antidumping Emperor*, 22 J. WORLD TRADE 5, 5 (1988).

5. The United States is not alone. Since 1980, the three other major users of GATT-based import screens — Australia, Canada, and the European Community (EC) — have processed over a thousand antidumping and countervailing duty cases, but only seventeen escape clause cases. J. MICHAEL FINGER, ANTIDUMPING: HOW IT WORKS AND WHO GETS HURT, Table 1.1 (forthcoming Oct. 1992 from U. Michigan Press).

6. The data for Tables 1 and 2 are from J. Michael Finger & Tracy Murray, *Policing Unfair Imports: The United States Example*, 24 J. WORLD TRADE 39, 43, 45 (1990).

directed at developed and developing countries is roughly proportional to their exports to the United States.[7] Within these groups, however, there are large differences.

TABLE 1

U.S. antidumping and countervailing duty cases and U.S. merchandise import shares, by country or trading bloc, 1980-88.

Country or Group	Number of cases[a]	Cases as a percentage of total cases	Percentage 1987 U.S. merchandise imports	Percentage cases with restrictive outcomes[b]
All countries	774	100	100	70
Developed countries	450	58	63	65
Developing countries	286	37	36	75
Eastern European countries	38	5	0.5	87
European Community	304	40	20	64
Brazil	56	7	2	79
South Africa	20	2.6	0.3	100
Korea	36	4.7	4.2	86
Mexico	35	4.5	4.9	91
Taiwan, China	29	3.7	6.1	62
Hong Kong	1	0.1	2.4	100
Singapore	6	0.8	1.5	67
Canada	35	5	18	54
Japan	49	6	21	69

[a] Antidumping and countervailing duty cases completed during 1980-88.
[b] Negotiated export restraints are counted as restrictive outcomes.

Japan and the EC each supply about 20% of U.S. imports, but the EC has been the object of 40% of U.S. antidumping and countervailing duty cases, while Japan has been the object of only 6%.[8] Among developing countries, imports from Brazil generate a disproportionately high number of cases, and imports from Taiwan, Hong Kong, and Singapore, a disproportionately low number.[9]

■   Negotiated export restraints have superseded almost half the cases (348 of 774).[10]

■   Three-fourths of the cases against developing countries resulted in restrictive outcomes while only two-thirds of cases against developed countries produced restrictive outcomes.[11]

---

7.   Table 1.
8.   *Id.*
9.   *Id.*
10.   Table 2.
11.   *Id.* Cases categorized as having restrictive outcomes include those that reached an affirmative final determination and those that were superseded by a restrictive agreement with the exporter.

Negotiated export restraints, however, were much more often used against *developed* countries — the outcome in 36% of cases compared with 15% for developing countries.[12] A country that possesses the countervailing power to retaliate is accorded the courtesy of a negotiated settlement. Others are restricted to the normal course of administrative procedures.

TABLE 2

Antidumping and countervailing duty case outcomes compared, 1980-88.

Country or Group	Antidumping as a percentage of total number	Restrictive outcomes as a percentage of total cases			Negotiated export restraints as a percentage of restrictive outcomes		
		Anti-dumping	Counter-vailing	Both	Anti-dumping	Counter-vailing	Both
All countries	50	72	67	70	63	66	64
Developed countries	49	69	61	65	65	82	74
Developing countries	46	73	77	75	55	46	49
Eastern European countries	87	91	60	87	77	100	78

■   The U.S. government almost always finds that the foreign exporter is unfair or is benefiting from the unfair actions of its government. Only 11% of dumping and subsidy determinations result in negative determinations.[13]

■   Finally, when the United States does not take action against the accused exporter, more than six times in seven it is because no competing U.S. producer has been harmed. Based on percentages of affirmative and negative determinations at each stage (preliminary injury, preliminary dumping or subsidy, final dumping or subsidy, and final injury) over the 1980-88 period, a "typical" one hundred cases that go through the process to a formal ending will produce the following outcomes: forty-four affirmative determinations (affirmative final determinations on

---

12. *Id.*
13. Finger & Murray, *supra* note 6, at 46 (Table 5). This figure can be derived in two ways. If withdrawn cases or terminated proceedings are not considered, but instead only those cases that resulted in formal determinations are considered, there were 11.0% negative and 89.0% affirmative determinations. If, on the other hand, cases withdrawn or terminated by the Commerce Department are added to the cases having formal "negative" determinations and cases that resulted in successful negotiation of a restrictive agreement are added to the cases having formal "affirmative" determinations, the split is then 11.5% , 88.5%. *Id.*

injury and on dumping-subsidy), and fifty-six negative
determinations. Of the fifty-six cases that end with a negative
determination, eight will end with a negative dumping or
subsidy determination, forty-eight with a negative injury
determination.[14]

This Article examines the patterns of unfair trade cases in
the United States and how these patterns fit into or are shaped
by the politics of U.S. trade policy. It argues that an objective
definition of "unfair" neither is nor ever has been the basis for
determining when the U.S. government will act against imports.
The unfair trade laws provide the political rhetoric for
restricting imports, and the unfair trade procedures provide the
podium from which an import-competing U.S. firm or industry
can take its case to the public. However, injury to domestic
producers drives U.S. trade politics, and the mark an instance of
import competition receives on the *political* barometer of injury
determines when the power of the state will be used against
imports. Current U.S. import policy is a matter of pasting the
label "unfair" on a bottle that was filled from the spring of
domestic politics. It is not a matter of putting into the bottle
only what a studied prescription demands.

I. DID ANYBODY EVER CARE IF FOREIGNERS
ARE FAIR?

Suppose a car mechanic examines your car and concludes
that it will not run because the spark plug gaps are too wide. He
adjusts the spark plug gaps to the proper setting. Will your car
run now? It will if his diagnosis was correct; it will not if his
diagnosis was wrong.

Suppose the government examines your business and concludes that you are losing money because your competitors are
pricing unfairly. The government orders them to set higher
prices. Will your business now improve? It very likely will, but
that improvement will not depend on whether the government's
diagnosis was correct. Regardless of whether your competitors
are pricing fairly or unfairly in some legal or philosophical
sense, simply forcing them to set higher prices will improve your
business. Thus, your interests lie in creating a broad and encom-
passing definition of what will cause the government to act in
your favor, not a definition in accord with an abstract concept

---

14. *Id.* at 47.

that *may* have an indirect bearing on the economic and financial health of your business.

Any business beset by import competition will attempt to explain its circumstances as those that the law can remedy and, when the occasion presents itself, will attempt to change the law so that it offers a remedy for its particular circumstances.[15] The role of the law is to extract legitimate claims from this universe of requests for import restrictions. This role suggests a *public* goal different in some cases from the private goal;[16] only when the two are in accord would public means be used to satisfy the private motive.

The public motive that built U.S. trade policy after World War II was not fueled by the economic factors that motivate private requests for import restrictions. The U.S. leadership considered freedom of commerce an important instrument for building international stability and maintaining world peace.[17] To Cordell Hull, Secretary of State for President Franklin D. Roosevelt, the link was straightforward: "unhampered trade dovetailed with peace; high tariffs, trade barriers, and unfair economic competition, with war."[18] The Cold War allowed a vulgar version of this idea to generate wide public support for the government's trade policy — if the United States did not provide markets for these countries, they would be taken over by the communist bloc.

Within this strategy, trade remedies provided protection for Congress against the wrath of special interests that pressured members of Congress sympathetic to the general thrust of U.S. trade policy.[19] The 1950s and 1960s were generally prosperous times during which the United States enjoyed substantial trade surpluses. Directing a protection-seeking industry into a maze

---

15. It is, of course, neither illegal nor immoral to act from such motives. Congress decides what the law will be, and every person has a right to attempt to influence Congress' decision. The administering agencies, instructed by the law and overseen by the courts, decide which petitions do in fact meet the criteria established by the law. Any person may attempt to show that his or her circumstances fit the prerequisites for the remedy that the law provides. Honest enforcement of a policy, however, does not guarantee it will be a good policy.

16. I do not suggest that the public motive is "higher" on some moral scale than private motives. This Article addresses requests that *will* be honored, not those that *should* be honored.

17. R.N. Cooper, *Trade Policy as Foreign Policy*, in U.S. TRADE POLICIES IN A CHANGING WORLD ECONOMY 291, 300 (Robert M. Stern ed., 1987).

18. CORDELL HULL, THE MEMOIRS OF CORDELL HULL 81 (1948).

19. I.M. DESTLER, AMERICAN TRADE POLITICS: SYSTEM UNDER STRESS 12-13 (1986).

of administrative procedures bought time. By the time the industry eventually emerged from the end of the maze without a prize, business had improved and it pressed its case no further. Besides, the system satisfied the American sense of fairness. It provided a place to complain where officials listened, investigated, and held hearings. One had one's day in court. To complain further would be un-American, and maybe even procommunist if the closing of the U.S. market tipped a country over to the Soviet side in the Cold War.

On trade issues, two objectives came into play. One, which I characterize as "internationalist," was to restore global stability and to preserve world peace. The other, which I characterize as "protectionist," was to preserve American profits and jobs in import competing industries. And, as the above quote from Cordell Hull dramatizes,[20] on trade issues the two objectives were in direct conflict. While internationalists wanted lower U.S. trade barriers,[21] protectionists sought to bolster them. But neither side — not the "profits and jobs and save our communities" calculus of import competing industries nor the "restore global stability and preserve world peace" calculus of the internationalists — had a direct interest in seeing that the term "fair" was defined in some moral, economic, or otherwise objective sense. For each, such a standard would limit rather than complement its primary objective.

As for trade policy, the conflict between the two objectives was more versus fewer trade restrictions, and those who favored fewer carried the day. They won by emphasizing export politics[22] and playing on the citizenry's sympathy for their strategic and diplomatic concerns. They left the "fair versus unfair" issue aside by making the trade negotiations the major thrust of U.S. trade policy, not by demonstrating that everything exporters did was fair. The politics of the day allowed the government to calibrate trade remedy law to produce trade restrictions at a slower pace than the trade agreements removed them.

In the 1980s, the issue was still more versus fewer trade restrictions. Fairness continued to be the *rhetoric* of the matter, but not the substance. Instead, injury has been the focus of U.S. trade remedy law. However, determining gradations that distin-

---

20. *See* text accompanying note 18.
21. Stephen D. Krasner, *U.S. Commercial and Monetary Policy: Unraveling the Paradox of External Strength and Internal Weakness*, 31 INT'L ORG. 635 (1977).
22. DESTLER, *supra* note 19, provides the best discussion of export politics.

guish an affirmative injury determination from a negative one, such as the difference between "serious injury" and "material injury," have been so difficult to define that the results tend to be arbitrary.[23]

II.   FREE TRADE, NOT PROTECTION, DEPENDS ON LOOPHOLES

The American obsession with regulation through formalized rules combined with economists' abhorrence of import restrictions fuel the belief that those seeking import restrictions must be winning by deceit and trickery, cynically exploiting loopholes in the law and pressing vulnerable members of Congress to insert new ones. But two related arguments suggest that this is not true:

■   In the past, the executive branch depended on loopholes and convenient details to control trade remedies, and

■   Congress has expanded the trade power and the scope of trade remedies primarily by eliminating the details on which the executive branch used to depend.

The loopholes on which the executive branch depended to keep trade remedies under control were not subtle. Before 1974, there was no time limit for completing a countervailing duty investigation. The Treasury Department[24] often used this loophole, defeating complaints against alleged foreign subsidies by choosing not to complete an investigation. This loophole has not been available since 1974 because Congress imposed deadlines on countervailing duty cases.[25] Also, in 1980 the ITC determined there to be "no injury" in an escape-clause petition filed by the

---

23.   For example, the Antidumping Authority Act of 1988 required the Australian Antidumping Authority to investigate how "material injury" could be defined in practice. ANTIDUMPING AUTHORITY, ADA PUB. NO. 4, INQUIRY INTO MATERIAL INJURY, PROFIT IN NORMAL VALUES AND EXTENDED PERIOD OF TIME 27 (Australian Gov't Pub. Serv., Mar. 1989). Some submissions to the Authority argued that even the slightest injury should be taken to be material, others said that material injury should mean that the Australian industry was at the point of extinction. *Id.* The Authority, however, could find no operational guidelines to separate one degree of injury from another, and in the end recommended that "material injury" be taken to mean injury which is *"not immaterial,* insubstantial or insignificant." *Id.* (emphasis added).

24.   At that time, the Treasury Department was the administering agency. Gary N. Horlick, THE UNITED STATES ANTIDUMPING SYSTEM, *in* ANTIDUMPING LAW AND PRACTICE 99, 105 (John H. Jackson & Edwin A. Vermulst eds., 1989).

25.   Robert E. Baldwin & Michael O. Moore, *Political Aspects of the Administration of the Trade Remedy Laws, in* DOWN IN THE DUMPS: ADMINISTRATION OF THE UNFAIR TRADE LAWS 253, 256-57 (Richard Boltuck & Robert E. Litan eds., 1991).

automobile industry.[26] Commissioners who voted against injury did so not because the industry had not lost *any* money and jobs to import competition, but because a recession and a shift of consumer tastes away from larger cars had caused a *greater* loss of money and jobs.[27] This loophole was closed by the 1988 trade bill. As the law was revised, the International Trade Commission (ITC) "may not aggregate the causes of declining demand associated with a recession or economic downturn in the United States economy into a single cause of serious injury. . . ."[28]

The same argument applies for "cumulation."[29] If a domestic industry is beset by competition from fifty different countries, it may be difficult to show that the domestic industry is seriously injured by imports from any one of them. Yet combined imports from the fifty might have a significant effect. Prior to the trade bill of 1984, the ITC had discretion to consider cumulated imports, but sometimes did not. The 1984 Act, at the behest of domestic textile and steel companies, made cumulation mandatory.[30] The 1988 trade bill restored to the ITC the authority to eliminate minimal suppliers at the preliminary stage. However, the legislative history of the bill makes clear that Congress expects the ITC to "apply the exception narrowly and [not use it] to subvert the purpose and general application of the [cumulation] requirement."[31]

By closing loopholes that allowed negative determinations, legislative modification and court review have pushed the meanings of "subsidy," "dumping," and "injury" toward their meanings in common usage. Cumulation of injury illustrates the point. Would it be reasonable to grant relief to an industry that was losing its U.S. market to a vigorous Korean industry, yet deny it to an industry that was being nibbled to death by fifty competitors? Consider downstream dumping. If the Canadian

---

26. Certain Motor Vehicles and Certain Chassis and Bodies Therefor, Determination of No Serious Injury Thereof, 45 Fed. Reg. 85,194 (1980) (U.S. Int'l Trade Comm.).

27. *See* Gordon I. Endow, Recent Development, *Car Wars: Auto Imports and the Escape Clause*, 13 LAW & POL'Y INT'L BUS. 591, 603 (1981).

28. Omnibus Trade and Competitiveness Act of 1988, Pub. L. No. 100-418, § 1401(a), 102 Stat. 1107, 1228 (codified at 19 U.S.C. § 2252(c)(2)(A) (1988)).

29. For a discussion of how cumulation serves protectionist interests, see *infra* notes 66-67 and accompanying text.

30. Horlick & Oliver, *supra* note 1, at 35. The Court of International Trade later ruled that the 1984 act requires cumulation across antidumping and countervailing duty cases. Bingham & Taylor Div., Virginia Indus., Inc. v. United States, 627 F. Supp. 793 (Ct. Int'l Trade 1986), *aff'd*, 815 F.2d 1482 (Fed. Cir. 1987).

31. H.R. CONF. REP. NO. 576, 100th Cong., 2d Sess. 621 (1988).

government subsidizes the production of logs or sells them to Canadian mills at one-tenth of their market value, it also subsidizes or dumps the lumber. Therefore, protecting U.S. lumber mills from Canadian competition seems reasonable. If the basic concept of the law is implemented "reasonably," the result is increased protection.

III. POWER POLITICS

Not all of the expansion of unfair trade law has been a matter of filling in loopholes. Some of it has been straightforward power politics.[32] For example, Senator Russell B. Long of Louisiana[33] successfully sponsored an amendment to the 1974 trade bill to rescue a local sulfur producer in that state whose antidumping petition had been turned down under existing law.[34] Long's amendment required investigators to screen their observations of the exporter's home market price against their estimate of the exporter's fully-allocated production costs.[35]

Under this provision, even if export and home market prices are identical, the exporter violates U.S. dumping law if the cost estimated for the product by the Commerce Department exceeds the price charged. Generally, when the Commerce Department finds that "below cost" sales are more than 10% of home market transactions (by volume), it will base its dumping calculations on the remaining "above cost" sales. When more than 90% of home market transactions are at "below cost" prices, *all* information on home market prices is discarded. Foreign market value is then based on the Commerce Department's estimate of the exporter's costs.[36]

In short, this provision requires the U.S. government to sys-

---

32. *See generally* Pietro S. Nivola, *Trade Policy: Refereeing the Playing Field, in* A QUESTION OF BALANCE: THE PRESIDENT, THE CONGRESS, AND FOREIGN POLICY 201-53 (Thomas E. Mann, ed. 1990) (providing examples of how constituent pressures have expanded U.S. unfair trade laws).

33. Senator Long, as chairman of the Senate Finance Committee, probably had more power over trade legislation than any other member of Congress.

34. Nivola, *supra* note 32, at 229-30.

35. 19 U.S.C. § 1677 (1988) (amended version of the Tariff Act of 1930 § 773(b)).

36. *See* Harvey M. Applebaum & David R. Grace, *U.S. Antitrust Law and Antidumping Actions Under Title VII of the Trade Agreements Act of 1979*, 56 ANTITRUST L.J. 497 (1987). Along these lines another commentator adds that a 50% benchmark is sometimes used in cases involving fresh agricultural products. N. David Palmeter, *The Antidumping Law: A Legal and Administrative Nontariff Barrier, in* DOWN IN THE DUMPS: ADMINISTRATION OF THE UNFAIR TRADE LAWS, 64, 74 n.26, 85 (Richard Boltuck & Robert E. Litan eds., 1991).

tematically throw out the price information that is most favorable to the exporter's case.[37] Thus, foreigners (exporters) whose prices in the U.S. market are below fully-allocated costs are dumping and will be restrained, even though such pricing is common practice in competitive markets and domestic firms that follow the same pricing strategy are not in violation of U.S. antitrust laws.

IV. CONGRESS INTENDS THE LAW TO PROTECT

Intent is important. Because Congress cannot anticipate the details of every potential case, antidumping and countervailing duty laws must provide administrative agencies with somewhat general instructions.[38] Therefore, legal remedies primarily depend on administrators' understanding of the laws' objectives.

Congress probably revealed implicit support for fewer trade restrictions when it winked at the loopholes that allowed the executive branch to maintain the openness of the U.S. economy. However, Congress has since vigorously moved to close those loopholes, signaling that the antidumping and countervailing duty procedures should not overlook any import competition that injures a U.S. interest. The low standard of proof required for an affirmative preliminary injury determination confirms that Congress favors the domestic petitioner. Congress does not presume that the U.S. market should be open to international competition.

While trade bills are celebrated for the authority they give the president to negotiate tariff reductions, expansion of the circumstances under which imports can be restricted has been a quiet part of many of them. Through a sequence of changes Congress has reduced the president's discretionary authority to refuse to impose import restrictions when the International Trade Commission makes affirmative decisions in escape clause cases.[39] Various drafts of the 1988 trade law contained provisions in seemingly generic language which entitled the titanium, ammonia, cement, and aircraft industries to antidumping and countervailing duty protection.[40] Not every such proposal earns

---

37. Horlick, *supra* note 24, at 137. Horlick reports that this provision has been applied in sixty percent of investigations performed in the 1980s. *Id.* at 136.

38. "General" laws may nonetheless dictate the factors which will influence their administration. This matter is taken up later in this Article.

39. *See generally* ROBERT E. BALDWIN, THE POLITICAL ECONOMY OF U.S. IMPORT POLICY 33-78 (1985).

40. Gary C. Hufbauer, *Comments on 'Protectionist Rules and Internation-*

legal enactment, but many of them do. Thus, protection of domestic industry has expanded gradually, but considerably.

V.   CONGRESS DOES NOT INTEND TO POLITICIZE

Those who consider rules and free trade "good" tend to associate "bad" results with politics: if trade policy is deteriorating, it must be because politics has been allowed to creep in. Again, preconceptions can be misleading. While Congress is clearly moving to expand the availability of import relief, Congress is *not* moving to loosen the criteria for import relief so that administrators' determinations can bend with the political breezes blowing that day. The text of the law has grown longer and more detailed, and the administrative regulations have become thicker. Perhaps the strongest indication that Congress does not want to politicize the administration of trade law is that it has made that administration subject to judicial review.[41] Judicial review helps to provide predictable outcomes based on systematic interpretations of the legal criteria.

Shortly after administrative authority shifted from the Treasury Department to the Commerce Department, critics in Washington argued that the Commerce Department had, in a matter of months, overthrown sixty years of consistent enforcement of the antidumping and countervailing duty laws. These accusations were probably valid: Congress probably intended changes in enforcement practice. The Treasury Department's tradition of enforcement had evolved during a period of time when international considerations and the public interest were supposed to be taken into account. By 1980, however, Congress wanted to break away from this mold. A total break with the past, however, was not intended: throwing out sixty years of consistent enforcement does not necessarily mean replacing it with haphazard enforcement. Congress wanted a different mold, not no mold at all.

The thrust of the enforcement and judicial traditions in the United States is toward a consistent and systematic practice. This does not mean that each individual will interpret the law in the same way. In a study of injury determinations in antidumping cases adjudicated between 1980 and 1986, Michael Moore found that the percentage of affirmative votes for each of the

---

alist Discretion in the Making of National Trade Policy', in NEW INSTITU-
TIONAL ARRANGEMENTS FOR THE WORLD ECONOMY (Hans-Jurgen Vosgerau ed.,
1989).
    41.   19 U.S.C. § 1516(e)-(f) (1988).

twelve people serving on the International Trade Commission ranged from 21% to 100%.[42] Yet, when Moore analyzed the factors on which the decisions were based, he found that each commissioner systematically based his or her decision on the factors that the law identifies with injury and that factors not specified in the law had minimal influence.[43] He found that each individual assigned different weights to the various factors, but that each systematically applied these weighted factors to the reviewed cases.

However, this tendency to systematize the interpretation of the law and to make it objective is not a limit on the frequency of restrictive actions. Every new dimension of unfairness allows interest groups to argue for a new import restriction and allows Congress eventually to add to the law a new, more restrictive interpretation of that dimension. "For every unfair practice that is attacked, several new ones pop up, summoning amendments as the definition of unfairness expands."[44]

VI. THE PRESIDENTIAL POLITICS OF UNFAIR TRADE

The failure of the "protectionist" message in the presidential campaigns of Walter Mondale, John Connolly, and Richard Gephardt is evidence that blatant protectionism is still a loser in U.S. politics. The regulation of unfair foreign trade practices, however, is surely a political winner. The rhetoric of unfair trade provides the president the same opportunity it provides the Congress — to have one's cake and eat it too.[45] The president can collect his political rewards and honor his political commitments by enforcing the law and by negotiating voluntary export restraints.

For example, in response to a growing number of congressional initiatives on trade policy, President Reagan took a giant step toward re-establishing the Executive's leadership by announcing a two-pronged policy plan in a speech given on September 23, 1987: to work with the leadership of other countries to lower the value of the dollar and to aggressively attack for-

---

42. *See generally* Michael E. Moore, *Rules or Politics? An Empirical Analysis of International Trade Commission Antidumping Decisions*, 30 ECON. INQUIRY (forthcoming, 1992).

43. *Id.* A similar analysis in dumping and subsidy determinations likewise found that influences not expressed in the law did not effect the determinations. Finger et al., *supra* note 2, at 452.

44. Nivola, *supra* note 32, at 247.

45. *Id.* at 223-24 (arguing that the rhetoric of unfair trade provides an effective means to avoid blame for the executive branch and for Congress).

eign unfair trade practices. The first draft of the trade speech was a free trade speech; the draft he delivered was a fair trade speech. Officials in the White House did not make the change for any principled legal or economic reason, but rather because the officials considered fair trade rhetoric more politically salient than free trade rhetoric.[46]

While this fair trade speech marked a significant shift in President Reagan's rhetoric on the matter, it did not mark his administration's discovery of unfair trade politics. Two weeks before, in defending the administration's international economic policy, Treasury Secretary James A. Baker III pointed out, "We have not neglected our responsibilities to fair trade . . . . President Reagan, in fact, has granted more import relief to U.S. industry than any of his predecessors in more than half a century."[47] Half a century covers every president since Herbert Hoover, the president who signed the Smoot-Hawley tariff.

VII. THE GATT DOES NOT RESTRICT TRADE ACTIONS

John H. Jackson expressed a long-standing concern of the Contracting Parties to the GATT as follows: "[T]he mere initiation of a dumping procedure . . . is often so costly to the importer that [the initiation], on the threat of such procedure, inhibits imports even if the procedure ultimately establishes that no dumping occurred . . ."[48] Jackson quotes a 1959 GATT Working Group on the intent of the GATT: "[I]t was essential that countries should avoid immoderate use of anti-dumping and countervailing duties, since this would reduce the value of the efforts that had been made since the war to remove barriers to trade."[49]

The GATT, however, has proven to be a minimal limit to the expanding use of unfair trade laws. Firstly, because the GATT's language on what is permissible is very broad, the explosion of cases in the 1980s has triggered only a handful of ap-

---

46. A perceptive *Wall Street Journal* story documents the transformation that took place from first draft to last: "One business lobbyist called to say 'free-trade rhetoric is a loser politically; fair-trade rhetoric is a winner.'" Robert W. Merry, *Reagan's Aides Split over His Trade Speech and Altered It Sharply*, WALL ST. J., Sept. 24, 1985, at A12. White House Chief of Staff Don Regan met with a group of outside advisers, including long time Reagan strategists Stuart Spencer and Lyn Nofziger, who echoed that view. *Id.*
47. James A. Baker III, Remarks before a Conference Sponsored by the Institute for International Economics (Sept. 14, 1987), *in* TREASURY NEWS, 1988, at 4.
48. JOHN H. JACKSON, WORLD TRADE AND THE LAW OF GATT 407 (1969).
49. *Id.* at 409.

peals to the GATT. Moreover, countries against which GATT panels have ruled continue to rely on their own interpretations of GATT provisions.

The United States is the only country that makes extensive use of countervailing duties to control imports.[50] Though such U.S. actions often raise the ire of exporting countries, that ire has usually been political rather than legal.[51] India, in 1980, was the first country to ask for a GATT panel on a U.S. countervailing duty action. After the United States and India reached a satisfactory bilateral resolution, India requested that the panel be terminated.[52] Five other countervailing actions by the United States have been taken to GATT panels. Three of the actions are very recent and panel investigations are still under way. The panel report from one of the other two cases has not (yet) been adopted.[53]

---

50. Of some 370 countervailing duty investigations by industrial countries in the 1980s, 316 were initiated by the United States. Finger, *supra* note 5, at Table 1.1.

51. J. Michael Finger & Julio Nogues, *International Control of Subsidies and Countervailing Duties*, 1 WORLD BANK ECON. REV. 707-25 (1987).

52. *United States — Imposition of Countervailing Duty without Injury Criterion*, BISD 28th Supp. 113 at ¶ 5 (1982) (GATT panel report adopted Nov. 3, 1981). Horlick and Oliver describe the outcome as a "soft deal," in which the United States agreed to include India among the countries for which the U.S. countervailing duty procedure would include an injury test, in exchange for soft discipline on Indian export subsidies. Horlick & Oliver, *supra* note 1, at 12.

53. Panels appointed by the Committee on Subsidies and Countervailing Measures are presently investigating the following matters: Countervailing measures on salmon from Norway (GATT Doc. SCM/M/57), Measures affecting the export of pure and alloy magnesium from Canada (GATT Docs. SCM/130 and SCM/M/57), and Measures affecting the export of softwood lumber from Canada (GATT Docs. SCM/133 and SCM/M/57). The U.S.-Canada dispute over softwood lumber was reopened when Canada terminated a bilateral memorandum of understanding that had ended an earlier dispute, the earlier dispute having also gone to a GATT panel. *United States — Initiation of a CVD Investigation into Softwood Lumber Products from Canada*, BISD 34th Supp. 194 (1988) (Subsidies Code panel report adopted June 3, 1987, providing terms of the memorandum of understanding). In 1988, Brazil requested a panel (under the Subsidies Code) to investigate U.S. failure to automatically backdate the revocation of a countervailing duty order on Brazilian exports of non-rubber footwear. When this panel did not find in Brazil's favor, *United States — Countervailing Duties on Non-Rubber Footwear from Brazil*, GATT.Doc. SCM/94 (Oct. 4, 1989) (Subsidies Code panel report), Brazil brought the matter to the GATT Council, and a panel appointed by the Council found in Brazil's favor. *United States — Denial of Most-Favored-Nation Treatment as to Non-Rubber Footwear from Brazil*, GATT Doc. DS/18/R (Jan. 10, 1992) (GATT panel report). As of June 1992, neither panel report on non-rubber footwear had been adopted. The other U.S. countervailing action taken to a GATT panel (under the Subsidies Code) involved an EC complaint concerning wine and grape products. A panel report delivered in 1986 was finally adopted on April 28, 1992. *United States — Defini-*

The first GATT case against a U.S. antidumping action was filed by Sweden in 1988. In August 1990, the GATT panel that investigated the case returned a finding in favor of Sweden,[54] but as of this writing (October 1992) the United States has not allowed the panel's report to be adopted.[55] A few months earlier, a GATT panel that looked into a Japanese complaint about an EC antidumping action found against the European Community,[56] and the panel's report was adopted by the GATT Council. The European Community has announced, however, that it will neither lift the action that was contested nor change its antidumping policy, pending the outcome of the Uruguay Round negotiations.[57]

---

tion of Industry Concerning Wine and Grape Products, GATT Doc. SCM/71 (Mar. 24, 1986) (Subsidies Code panel report).

54.   *United States — Imposition of Antidumping Duties on Imports of Stainless Seamless Steel Hollow Products from Sweden*, GATT Doc. ADP/47 (Aug. 20, 1990) (Antidumping Code panel report).

55.   The panel chose not to consider the substance of the Swedish complaint, instead basing its finding on a procedural technicality — that in the U.S. antidumping proceeding, the U.S. International Trade Commission (ITC) did not determine *at the appropriate stage of its proceedings* that the petitioner was representative of the U.S. industry. *Id.*, ¶ 5.18-19. If the ITC chose to treat this finding as it would a remand from the U.S. Court of International Trade, it could go through its proceedings in the sequence the panel considers proper and shortly return the same affirmative injury finding.

The ITC, in the original case, had determined that Swedish welded stainless steel tubes caused *no injury* to the U.S. welded stainless tubes industry, *but* that Swedish seamless stainless steel tubes did cause injury. Reg. 45,265 (1987). The action Sweden brought to GATT concerned the antidumping measure imposed on seamless tubes as a result of the "seamless half" of the ITC case. *USA — Anti-dumping Duty in the United States on Stainless Seamless Pipes and Tubes from Sweden*, ADP/40, (Jan. 4, 1989) (communication from Sweden). Meanwhile, the petitioner appealed the welded tubes determination to the U.S. Court of International Trade. That court remanded the case to the ITC for reconsideration. Trent Tube Div., Crucible Materials Corp. v. United States, 741 F. Supp. 227 (Ct. Int'l Trade 1990), *modified*, 741 F. Supp. 921 (1990). On remand, the ITC determined that the petitioner was in fact injured by the Swedish welded tubes. Trent Tube Div., Crucible Materials Corp. v. United States, 752 F. Supp. 468. Thus, while Sweden has attempted — so far unsuccessfully — to enlist the GATT's help to remove the U.S. antidumping order on seamless tubes, the U.S. government reversed itself on the other half of the case and imposed antidumping duties on welded tubes. 55 Fed. Reg. 51,745 (1990). *See* J. Michael Finger, *Bad Law Begets Embarrassing Diplomacy: An Example of How U.S. Trade Law Really Works*, ECONOMISK DEBATT (forthcoming) (providing a detailed analysis of this case).

56.   *European Economic Community — Regulation on Imports of Parts and Components*, BISD 37th Supp. 132 (1991) (GATT panel report adopted May 16, 1990), *reprinted in* 30 INT'L LEGAL MATERIALS 1081 (1991).

57.   *EEC Comments on the Panel Report on EEC — Regulation on Imports of Parts and Components*, GATT Doc. L/6676 (May 16, 1990).

More than 170 pages of proposals have been submitted at the Uruguay Round to modify the antidumping code. The proposals are almost evenly split between expanding and limiting the circumstances which allow an antidumping action.[58] Meanwhile, the permissive U.S. and EC interpretations of GATT have been used as ammunition *against* reform in Australia and Canada.[59] As the Uruguay Round moves toward final agreement, GATT's broad language will not significantly inhibit the increasing use of antidumping and countervailing duty regulations.

Even where there are clear limits in GATT, they do not necessarily restrict the U.S. government from acting against imports. Sometimes GATT's restrictions do not carry over into U.S. law. Robert Hudec sums up the relation between GATT and U.S. trade law in these words:

> The general structure of U.S. foreign trade law exhibits a reasonable degree of consistency with the main policy lines set down in GATT. . . . In a number of these laws, the Congress has provided as much or more substantive detail as the GATT itself contains. . . . At the other extreme, the number of laws openly violating GATT remain reasonably few. *The main body of U.S. trade law occupies a middle position between these extremes of compliance and direct violation, a middle position in which the Executive has discretionary power which allows him to comply with GATT or not*, according to policy decisions that are largely unreviewable . . . . Wherever U.S. foreign trade law takes this discretionary middle position, there is in fact no meaningful legal requirement that GATT rules be observed. There may, of course, be a reasonable level of GATT compliance in fact, but if so, it is a matter of day-to-day Executive policy, and not law.[60]

Even when there are limits in U.S. unfair trade law, these limits do not prevent the government from restricting imports politically perceived as unfair. I turn again to Hudec:

> Trade barriers are fungible, and they overlap. Legal controls on one type of trade barrier, like an escape clause, will not be fully effective if those seeking protection can achieve the escape clause result by other means that are not controlled. . . . A classic example occurred in late 1983 when certain U.S. textile producers, seeking additional barriers to restrict textile imports, brought a countervailing duty action alleging

58. *See* J. Michael Finger & S. Dhar, *Do Rules Control Power? GATT Articles and Agreements in the Uruguay Round, in* THE GLOBAL TRADING SYSTEM: ANALYTICAL AND NEGOTIATING ISSUES (Allan W. Deardorff & Robert M. Stern eds., forthcoming from U. Michigan Press).

59. *See* M. Dutz, Enforcement of Canadian 'Unfair' Trade Laws, PRE Working Paper, WPS 776 World Bank (1991) (discussing Canada); G. Banks, Australia's Antidumping Experience, PRE Working Paper, WPS 551 World Bank (1990) (discussing Australia).

60. Robert E. Hudec, *The Legal Status of GATT in the Domestic Law of the United States, in* THE EUROPEAN COMMUNITY AND GATT 187, 238-39, 248 (Meinhard Hilf et al. eds., 1986) (emphasis added).

that the Chinese government was subsidizing the export of such products. The legal theory of the complaint was novel and unlikely to be approved by the courts; it was in fact disapproved by the Commerce Department in a similar case several months later. In this case, however, the expected legal response was not allowed to be controlling because the Executive Branch agreed to use its discretionary powers under the textile agreements law to achieve an equivalent degree of trade restriction by other means, by changing a "rules of origin" requirement.[61]

Rules of origin are only one of several possible ways to restrict imports. GATT itself lists eight categories of forbidden protectionist measures, and eleven categories of measures permitted in specified circumstances. Such options provide a complete menu for a country seeking alternative means to restrict imports.[62]

In sum, this section has advanced two points. First, GATT provisions for antidumping and countervailing duties have proven to be broad enough to allow an explosion of such actions in the 1980s. Second, the limits in GATT do not prevent U.S. government actions. When the politics of an unfair trade case are compelling, but an affirmative legal determination is not possible, the United States often can find an alternative legal basis for restricting trade. Making U.S. antidumping and countervailing duty laws consistent with GATT introduces procedural complications, but it does not severely limit trade-restricting actions by the U.S. government.

VIII. ECONOMIC NONSENSE

Increasingly, the focus of the unfair trade laws is on protecting *any* U.S. production that might be displaced by import competition, even if the proposed remedy would have a negative effect on U.S. production on the whole. This point is sometimes difficult for economists to accept, but it seems generally accepted by the legal community. "Under the GATT, under current U.S. law and under other countries' antidumping statutes, dumping is not considered to be criminal or immoral, but rather a business practice; the remedy, which is only necessary if injury is caused to a domestic industry, is to force the companies engaged in dumping to raise their prices, *usually a net negative*

---

61. This paragraph was included in the 1984 draft of Professor Hudec's study, but omitted from the published 1986 draft, *id.* I quote it here with the permission of the author.

62. John H. Jackson, THE WORLD TRADING SYSTEM: LAW AND POLICY OF INTERNATIONAL ECONOMIC RELATIONS 40-43 (1989).

effect on the country imposing the duty."[63]

The change in drawback regulations further illustrates trade remedy law's disregard of issues of broader economy-wide concern. Prior to 1988, U.S. exporters could draw back, i.e. be reimbursed for, any antidumping or countervailing duties they paid on a product that they re-exported or incorporated into a product that was exported.[64] In the 1988 trade act, Congress excluded antidumping and countervailing duties from eligibility for drawback.[65] Any U.S. exporter's interest in access to lower-priced inputs was thus made secondary to the U.S. input producer's interest in protection from import competition.

Many of the above reviewed changes in U.S. unfair trade law demonstrate that its dominant concern is avoiding injury to U.S. producers, rather than preserving competition in the U.S. market. For example, cumulation of injury tests over imports of steel sheets from various sources seems reasonable *if* the objective is only to protect the interests of U.S. *producers* of steel sheets. Because import competition arising from many sources is not predatory, it will not leave U.S. users of products such as steel sheets exposed to exploitation by foreign monopoly sellers.[66] Cumulation, in effect, extends the scope of regulation from what the antitrust laws attempt to isolate as bad competition to what economic theory would describe as normal competition. If applied to domestic commerce, cumulation would require intervention to protect any firm that could not keep up with its competitors. To believe in the cumulation principle is to believe that competition normally does not serve society's interests.[67]

---

63. Horlick & Oliver, *supra* note 1, at 23 (emphasis added).

64. *Id.* at 42.

65. Omnibus Trade and Competitiveness Act of 1988, Pub. L. No. 100–418, § 1334(a), 102 Stat. 1107, 1209 (1988).

66. Proof of predatory effects or intent is not required in an unfair trade case. "We . . . should put to rest the media concept that predatory dumping exists. It may exist, but none of the trade laws require any showing of predatory intent whatsoever." Harvey M. Applebaum, *The Interface of Trade/Competition Law and Policy: An Antitrust Perspective*, 56 ANTITRUST L.J. 409, 412 (1987). "[N]o less a body than the United States Supreme Court has observed that 'predatory pricing schemes are rarely tried and [are] even more rarely successful.' It probably is safe to predict that in none of the 767 affirmative antidumping determinations reached by Australia, Canada, the EC and the US between 1980 and 1986 was predatory pricing remotely present." Palmeter, *The Antidumping Emperor, supra* note 4, at 6 (quoting Matsushita Elec. Indus. Co. v. Zenith Radio Corp., 475 U.S. 574, 589 (1986)).

67. The fully-allocated-costs pricing standard and cumulation of injury are only two of many ways in which the unfair trade laws impose much more strin-

CONCLUSION

It seems clear that the unfair trade laws do not embody any moral, economic, or philosophical definition of "unfair." Why should they? None of the political pressures and economic interests that have propelled the laws' passage or molded their enforcement would measure their effectiveness by how accurately these laws approximate such standards.

Antidumping and countervailing duty laws aim to protect U.S. production threatened by import competition. Unfair trade procedures neither focus on what foreign sellers do, nor ask whether what they do is fair or unfair. The legal definitions of unfairness offer so many possibilities that any U.S. producer who would be better off if imports were restricted can find a way to qualify — if not now, then after the next trade bill.

This does not mean that just *any* briefcase full of information from a U.S. industry will be sufficient to win an affirmative determination. However, a domestic interest stopped by a mere detail of the law need only prepare a new petition, or wait for a revision of the administrative regulations or amendment of the law — as did the Louisiana sulfur company whose problem was fixed by adding "constructed value" to the law.[68]

In the long run, a winning portfolio *can* be pulled together by any industry that experiences substantive competition from imports. The cost of putting that portfolio together and the tedium of negotiating a voluntary export restraint that will give the exporters enough extra profit to buy off their sovereign right to retaliate are the major limits on the protection the system provides. Domestic politics impose only the necessity of explaining that foreigners are unfair, while the trade laws provide the podium from which to do so.

Almost all of the procedural changes (but not the substantive changes) that have been made are commendable. Standards are stated with increased precision, objective application is guarded by court review, and interested parties have the right to review the evidence and to comment on its accuracy and interpretation. Transparency, openness, and objectivity are important parts of the American 'rule of law' ideal. Yet these procedural refinements seem to contribute more to the problem than to a solution. The emphasis on doing things the right way

---

gent limits on what foreign sellers can do in the U.S. market than the U.S. antitrust laws impose on domestic sellers. *See supra* text accompanying note 37; Palmeter, *The Antidumping Emperor, supra* note 4, at 6-7.

68. *See supra* notes 32-34 and accompanying text.

distracts us from seeing that we are doing the wrong thing. The unfair trade laws, with their broad definitions of what is unfair, recall a cynical characterization of American justice: we give every horse thief a fair trial, then we hang him.

The GATT expresses the best intentions and highest aspirations of international leadership since the end of World War II. However, its provisions have been proven too general to provide effective limits on trade restrictions. Robert Hudec's point that trade restrictions are fungible is important. The limits on authority provided in one section of the law can be evaded by using the discretion provided in another section.

The unfair trade laws — as Congress has expanded them and as the president has enforced them — provide protection for every American industry that faces import competition. An earlier analysis of the expansion of the protective system explains:

> One of the great defects of the protective system is that it provides no clear basis for discrimination, and that, since discrimination is politically difficult, Congress destroys the essential character of the policy in order to make it politically strong.[69]

The analyst I am quoting is E.E. Schattschneider (1935), and the passage comes from his celebrated analysis of the politics of the Smoot-Hawley tariff. "The history of the American tariff," argues Schattschneider, "is the story of a dubious economic policy turned into a great political success."[70]

There is further parallel between 1930's politics of the tariff and today's politics of unfair trade. The "principle" behind the Smoot-Hawley tariff was that it should offset the difference between the cost of an article outside and inside the United States. But, as Schattschneider saw things:

> [T]alk of tariffs written on the costs formula is no more than an elaborate sham and a bluff . . . . The [congressional] committees did not generally determine rates according to the formula advertised and they did not do so for the conclusive reason that they could not.[71]
>
> [T]he difference of costs formula is to be classified more properly as a slogan belonging to the politics of gaining acceptance of the legislation than as a method of determining rates. It is an argument rather than a formula.[72]

U.S. commercial policy has gone full circle. The fairness-equalization policy of the 1980s enforced through antidumping and countervailing duty orders is the same as the cost-equaliza-

---

69. E.E. Schattschneider, POLITICS, PRESSURES AND THE TARIFF 85 (Archon Books 1963) (1935).
70. *Id.* at 283.
71. *Id.* at 84.
72. *Id.* at 284.

tion policy of 1930 enforced through the tariff. I do not point out this parallel to predict that unfair trade regulations will go the way of the Smoot-Hawley tariff, but to predict that when a new wind in trade policy thought blows aside the unfair trade rules, future policy makers will regard the current unfair trade rules to be as absurd as we now consider the Smoot-Hawley cost-equalization formula.

HOW DO WE GET TO CINCINNATI?
SOME POLICY ADVICE

What we are doing now is worse than doing nothing at all: therefore, we should not do it. But how do we change course?

A city slicker, driving through the countryside on his way to Cincinnati, realized that he had lost his way. He stopped and asked a farmer, "How do I get to Cincinnati?"

The farmer responded, "Well, you go down the road, take the second fork to the left. Eventually you'll come to a crossroads where you'll see a sign directing you to Wilson's Store. Go toward Wilson's Store, but before you get there . . . now wait a minute. It might be better if you go *up* this road, then after you cross a bridge . . . . No, I don't believe that will get you there either. You know, mister, I don't think you can get to Cincinnati from here."

To this the city slicker responded, "What? You've lived here all your life and you don't know the way to Cincinnati? You must be pretty stupid."

The farmer replies, "Maybe so, but I'm not lost."

This old story usually ends here, but in my version the city slicker has the last word: "That's only because you don't want to go to Cincinnati. If you knew how much nicer it is in Cincinnati than it is here, then you'd be lost, too."

Perhaps the United States has never been to Cincinnati, but it has been closer than it is now. Indeed, the U.S. administration and Congress of the 1980s might paraphrase Pogo: "We have met Smoot, Hawley, and Hoover, and they are us."

How do we get to Cincinnati? Perhaps we start by changing the law so that it explains how nice it is in Cincinnati as well as how nice it is here. Anyone should be able to petition for an import restriction, as is now the case. However, trade regulation should focus on both those who would benefit and those who would suffer from a proposed trade restriction, and should consider how much will be gained or lost. Because the domestic economic costs of a trade-restricting action can be as substantial as its gain, a domestic entity which is hurt economically by an impediment to imports should have the same standing in law and in administrative procedures as someone who profits from the impediment. This should include the administrative mechanics to petition for removal of an impediment to imports when that impediment compromises an entity's economic interests.[73] This is hardly a new notion. The idea that the gains from free trade are usually greater than the costs has been around since Adam Smith; it just has never been recognized in U.S. law.

---

73. J. Michael Finger, *Incorporating the Gains from Trade into Policy*, 5 THE WORLD ECONOMY 367-77 (1982).

PART FIVE

DEVELOPING COUNTRIES IN THE GATT/WTO

[15]

Development Economics and the
General Agreement on Tariffs and Trade

J. Michael Finger

What trade policies best support economic development? Over the past forty years, developing countries have tried many different approaches and recorded many different outcomes. Their experiences have been analyzed for policy lessons by many scholars, among whom Béla Balassa has been one of the leaders. Also, the international community has developed a system of rules, the General Agreement on Tariffs and Trade (the GATT) that attempts to guide countries toward certain policy choices and away from others. One might presume that the parts of the GATT relating to developing countries reflect the knowledge these scholars have sorted out of experience. That presumption would be incorrect, however. The process of rules making or institution building, it seems, has a momentum quite separate from the emergence of knowledge about what works. Nobel laureate James M. Buchanan (1984, 5) makes the point as follows: "Institutions do matter — over the long run perhaps far more than the adoption of this or that policy option or the election of this or that politician or party."

In this essay, I compare the evolution of GATT rules about what policy choices a developing country should take with the growth of knowledge about what trade policies are effective. The first section, which reviews this growth of knowledge, is brief because its content is familiar. Balassa's and others' studies of developing countries' actual experiences tended to show that countries did well when they followed what classical economics would prescribe as reasonable trade and exchange rate policies. The thrust of the GATT toward developing countries, a less familiar matter, occupies the next three sections. In these sections, I explain how the GATT has come to institutionalize a set of economic presumptions shown to be inappropriate by the work reviewed in the first section.

The institutional structure, having been established without incorporating the "new" ideas and facts about trade and development, now serves to keep these concepts out. Developing countries, although very active at the Uruguay Round, have been reluctant to bring forward proposals based on economic concepts other than those embodied in the present rules. Thus proposals based on the experiences of the successful developing countries are excluded from consideration. This neglect is a significant loss to the international community. The experiences of successful developing countries have considerable potential to guide the improvement of international rules — rules that could not only pass the lessons of experience from one developing country to another but could also help *developed* country governments resist growing internal pressures for import restrictions. Such matters are taken up in the fifth section of this essay.

The Growth of Knowledge: Developing Countries' Experiences as Validation of Classical Economics

Perhaps the problem was a simple matter of timing. The important decisions that determined the economics of the GATT were made in the 1950s and 1960s, whereas the "new" research on the role of trade in development gained momentum later — its arrival perhaps best signaled by the almost simultaneous publication in 1970-71 of Balassa's *The Structure of Protection in Developing Countries* and of Little, Scitovsky, and Scott's *Industry and Trade in Some Developing Countries.*

I have put the word "new" in quotation marks because even in the 1950s there were strong and clear applications of classical economics to the problems of development, particularly by Jacob Viner (1953) and Gottfried Haberler (1959)[1] — applications arguing that developing countries should avoid direct trade controls and impose at most a modest tariff. Although the "new" economics came wrapped in a new technology, these ideas are close to its central policy conclusions. In essence, what Viner and Haberler took as postulates the new research formulated and tested as hypotheses, then presented as conclusions.

Such thinking was, however, a long way from mainstream development thinking in the 1950s. Ian Little refers to Haberler and Viner as "rebels," and adds that "their opponents would have referred to them as orthodox neoclassicists" (Little 1982, 75). But, Little explains, they were not "orthodox" in the sense that their views coincided with those of policymakers or even with those of economists who wrote mostly about development. "Certainly, United Nations officials were not in this camp, and almost no developing country policymakers would have endorsed such views" (p. 75).

It is interesting to see the orthodox view of development through the eyes of one of the rebels. Viner, in the third of his National University of Brazil lectures of 1950, stated:

> All that I find in Prebisch's study and in the other literature along similar lines emanating from the United Nations and elsewhere is the dogmatic identification of agriculture with poverty, and the explanation of agricultural poverty by inherent natural historical laws by virtue of which agricultural products tend to exchange on ever-deteriorating terms for manufactures, technological progress tends to confine its blessings to manufacturing industry, and agricultural populations do not get the benefit of technological progress in manufactures even as purchasers, because the prices of manufactured products do not fall with the decline in their real costs (1953, 44).

Popular development thinking separated itself not only from conventional economic thinking but from conventional economic history as well. Compare, for example, the following two statements. The first is from Viner:

No country except the United States has attained a high level of per capita income which has not maintained a high ratio of imports to total national product, and no country, except possibly Russia, can in this respect make the United States its model without courting perpetual poverty. The high degree of self-sufficiency of the United States was due in part to a deliberate national policy of high tariff protection. But it was the continental character of the United States ... as well as the technical skills of its people, which enabled the American [economy] to dispense with foreign products ... [and] to achieve economic prosperity despite its commercial policy and its low ratio of foreign to domestic trade (1953, 116-17).

The second is from Prebisch:

Development [in the nineteenth century and the initial decades of the twentieth] in the periphery was a spontaneous phenomenon of limited scope and social depth; it came about under the dynamic influence of a unique combination of external factors which have since ceased to exist (1964, 6).

History and economic theory were irrelevant, and thus everything had to be *planned* anew. Little (1982, chapters 3 and 4) explains that "planning" was an important element of popular development thinking in the 1950s. This belief was complementary to several other precepts. One was the presumption that "industrialization" and "development" were the same thing. Manufacturing made for good jobs and rich countries; agriculture provided bad jobs and kept countries poor. To raise wages, a less developed country had to establish the industries that had the higher wages in the industrial countries. And, because commodity earnings would inexorably decline and capital goods imports would inexorably be required, less developed countries would have a persistent tendency toward balance of payments problems. There was "the absolute necessity of building up trade in industrial exports" (Prebisch 1964, 20).

Every industrial sector was presumed to be linked to every other one in an "external" way — thus, for example, the ceramics industry could not be world class unless the steel industry was likewise world class. But nothing was linked through profits or prices. Price movements created "monopoly" if prices went up and "poverty" if they went down, but they did not provide "resource allocation" or "efficiency." Efficiency had to be planned in, and because industrialization had to change everything simultaneously if it were to succeed, planning, particularly investment planning, had to be based on the shadow prices that would prevail *after* the plan was achieved. The importance of "structural" rather than price links meant that all-at-one-time or "big bang" changes were necessary. A less developed country could be competitive in manufactured goods *across the board* or not at all. The planned-for big bang would transform a country from an exporter of materials and importer of manufactures to the opposite.

What changed? First Japan changed into an industrial power. Then other Asian-Pacific countries that followed Japan's policy experience began to register similar successes. At the level of public perception, this was the beginning of what Staffan Burenstam Linder calls the "demonstration effect," which eventually engendered among the Asian newly industrialized countries a rising regional confidence in their own development model. A scholarly look could perceive across countries varying degrees of mix of import-substitution versus open trade policies, and for a trained observer, the existence of "varying degrees of" allows identification of "the effects of." In 1970-71 came the Little, Scitovsky, and Scott study and the initial World Bank studies, in which Béla Balassa was the leading researcher (Balassa and associates 1971). These were followed by studies at the Kiel Institute led by Jurgen Donges (1976); the 1978 Bhagwati and Krueger studies for the National Bureau of Economic Research; and, eventually, many others.[2]

Balassa also played a leading role in two related lines of research. For one, his research on the European Economic Community showed that the effects of removing trade barriers was to a large degree an expansion of *intraindustry* trade. There were no major displacements of industries in one country by exports from another. Comparative costs, in general, were not so different, and competition tended to be on a product-variety rather than industry basis. This work (Balassa 1963, 1966) helped to put aside the "big bang" presumption of the 1950s that trade in industrial goods was an "all or nothing" proposition.

Second, Balassa initiated work after the 1974 oil shock to investigate how well developing countries had coped with such external shocks.[3] This work compared again the performances of countries with import-substitution strategies and countries that had export-oriented or open-trade strategies or had shifted significantly toward open-trade strategies when hit by severe external shocks. Balassa found that countries that continued or shifted to open-trade strategies were significantly more successful in maintaining investment and growth. The popular presumption that less developed countries are hit by relatively large terms of trade shocks was found to be correct. But the research showed that forced import substitution was not the best policy response. The absence of policies to *force* import substitution did not mean that there would be no import substitution, however. Balassa's work showed that neutral policies that allowed relative price changes to work through the economy would induce significant substitution of domestic production for imports of products whose relative prices had increased.

Perhaps the key shift in development thinking came with the realization that less developed countries *could* export manufactured goods and that they could move into such export production a bit at a time. At the level of the mechanics of development thinking, this change involved (or allowed) two significant simplifications. First, observable world prices, not almost-impossible-to-calculate shadow prices, are the relevant measure of alternatives. "For the individual country, world prices are the pivot on which all scarcities turn" (Bell 1987, 824). Second, the project replaces the plan as the intrinsic unit of analysis. These changes did not make enemies of the technocrats. Indeed, the technocrats saw them as a new challenge: finding ways to see, through the mess of country policies, incentives, and disincentives, how far the signals that influenced domestic decisions were from the real scarcities that lay below.

The content of this change of thinking is well-reviewed elsewhere (see, especially, Little 1982), so I will not extend this discussion. In closing this section, however, I want to note the timing of that change. Almost all the rest of the "new" empirical research on trade and development was published in 1970 or later. As I explain below, the economics of the GATT was mostly in place by 1970.

The Initial GATT Negotiations

Kenneth W. Dam, in his well-known study on the GATT, describes it as "a product of U.S. planning and a reflection of certain views that dominated the thinking on trade matters of U.S. diplomats in the 1940s" (1970, 11). Freedom of international commerce had been the third of President Woodrow Wilson's Fourteen Points. To Cordell Hull, Secretary of State for President Franklin D. Roosevelt, the link was straightforward: "[U]nhampered trade dovetailed with peace; high tariffs, trade barriers and unfair economic competition with war."[4] Keeping trade unrestricted was, in the bigger scheme of things, a means to maintain global peace and stability.

As to *how*, the U.S. proposal came down to asking each member country to accept three basic obligations: that it use only approved instruments of trade control, that is, tariffs only; that it apply these instruments in a nondiscriminatory way; and that it submit them to a long-term process of binding and reduction through multilateral negotiation (Hudec 1987, 133).

The mechanics were drawn from the U.S. Reciprocal Trade Agreements Program. Under the Reciprocal Trade Agreements Act of 1934 and its extensions, the United States by 1947 had negotiated and implemented thirty trade-liberalizing agreements, sixteen of them with a developing country. Each agreement contained a provision for a reciprocal exchange of tariff reductions and a framework of other obligations to protect the commercial value of the tariff reductions. There were some specific exceptions from the general framework of obligations, but there was no pattern of special exceptions for developing countries. Indeed, Hudec reports, "the sixteen developing country agreements ... tended to contain fewer special derogations than did the agreements with developed countries" (1987, 7). The United States, in its presentations to the International Trade Organization negotiations in 1946-47, actively opposed special commercial policy conditions for developing countries. The United States held that development was primarily a matter of private capital investment and that special measures to deal with this belonged elsewhere, not in the commercial policy rules of the international system.

Neither the United Kingdom nor France fully supported this position. Both wanted to retain preferential tariff regimes of the traditional "metropol versus former colony" sort, and both wanted to retain the power to protect their own economies from imports in order to promote the reconstruction and eventual growth of their economies. Also behind their reluctance to accept nondiscrimination as a universal principle was the worry that they would never catch up to the United States as exporters of industrial goods. And both of these countries accepted to a much greater degree than did the United States that infant industry protection was an effective way to promote industrialization.

Developing countries argued that import quotas were essential to implementation of other development plans and that preferences for developing countries (that is, discrimination against imports from developed countries) were necessary to promote their own industrialization. At the level of principle, they wanted the international community to recognize explicitly that protection in developing countries would, in the long run, increase trade (Little 1982, 60, 61). Developing country proposals at the International Trade Organization negotiations displayed two major concerns: the desire for a commitment from the developed countries to provide significant resource transfers and the desire for freedom from the general idea of discipline that the arrangement was trying to impose among the other members. Behind developing countries' unwillingness to accept any international discipline over their trade policies, Little sees the following presumptions:

- *First, and this was a grave mistake, they never expected to be able to export manufactures to the industrialized countries; but they might export a little to their [ethnic and geographic] neighbors....*
- *Second, they assumed that the industrialized countries would not protect against raw materials.*
- *Third, on competing farm products (sugar being the most important) the case was probably lost anyway, for the United States itself proposed to exempt farm products from the ban on quotas (1982, 61).*

At a more direct level of concern, developing countries wanted to preserve the manufacturing firms that had grown up during World War II.

As no doubt the reader knows, agreement was never reached on the International Trade Organization. The international rules for commercial policy that were agreed are contained in the GATT. The International Trade Organization draft charter had more tightly circumscribed exceptions for developing than for developed countries. In the GATT, the opposite is true. The draft International Trade Organization charter recognized the right of a country to provide infant industry protection by raising bound tariffs or imposing quotas, but prior approval of the organization was necessary (Hudec 1987, 14). In contrast, no prior approval was required for what might be described as developed country exceptions, such as import restrictions for balance of payments or safeguards reasons.

Article XVIII was the principal provision of the original GATT dealing with the trade problems of developing countries. According to Dam, "The theory of the article is quite simply that less developed countries should be freer than developed countries to impose quantitative and other restrictions in order to protect infant industries and to combat payments imbalances" (1970, 227). Section A of Article XVIII allows protection "to promote the establishment of a particular industry" (para. 7a). Section B allows a developing country to establish restrictions "to safeguard its external financial position and to ensure a level of reserves adequate for ... development" (para. 9). Section B of Article XVIII parallels Article XII, which allows balance of payments restrictions by developed countries, but the Article XVIII criteria are less stringent. For example, consultations are required of developing countries only every second year rather than every year.[5] In sum, the GATT exceptions for developing countries were circumscribed by procedural requirements, but the international community, in ratifying the GATT, explicitly acknowledged that the special position of developing countries justified some dispensation from the legal discipline other countries must accept (Hudec 1987, 15).

Why, at the time of organizing the GATT, did the United States allow the position it had negotiated into the draft International Trade Organization charter to be significantly compromised? A major reason seems to be the nature of the negotiations themselves. The overall structure of the negotiations was that the community of nations would agree to a program of discipline on the behavior of individual countries. The underlying conceptualization recognized this discipline as a "cost" to an individual country, but a cost that would be borne in pursuit of a common good. So the acceptance of *individual costs* for the *common good* was the basic trade-off each participant was asked to make — the basic form of the negotiations. In such a context, it is very difficult to ask the weaker members of the community to make the same sacrifice as the stronger. Protestations that commercial policy rules are not the appropriate way to provide for the less fortunate sound like excuses for greed.

Hudec, in his interpretation of the role of developing countries in the GATT, brings out this factor — what one might describe as the influence of Max Corden's conservative social welfare function on relations between rich and poor states. "It is very difficult to convene an enterprise involving rich and poor without having some welfare dimension to the work.... [The] inability to resist this need to give 'something' has been a constant factor in the dynamics of GATT legal policy" (1987, 16).

A second factor pushing toward U.S. agreement on exceptions for developing countries was its desire for some exceptions of its own: for its restrictions on agriculture, its existing safeguards, and antidumping and countervailing duty laws. A third reason was that the United States had no clearly articulated economic argument for the economic benefits each country would receive by participating in an open economic system.[6] The articulated "pro" arguments tended to be political arguments based on strategic considerations and the idea of building a political relationship among the free world countries.

Another point against imposing equal discipline on developing countries was that once these countries had taken a position of asking for this kind of "benefit," granting it began to have immediate political value but no immediate economic or budgetary cost. And finally, the GATT itself was not the forum in which the rules of the international trading game were negotiated. The initial GATT was merely the paperwork used to quickly put in place an already agreed round of tariff cuts. If the agreed tariff cuts were not implemented quickly, pressures to renegotiate would build. Besides, everything but the tariff cuts was considered "provisional" and was expected to be superseded by the International Trade Organization. From the U.S. perspective, the GATT was the bird in the hand of trade liberalization for which it might perhaps be worth letting go a few birds in the bush of exceptions — compromises to the idea of discipline. A nice pragmatic solution — get what you most want now and fix the problems that come with it later.

In the conclusion to the first chapter, Hudec provides a less pragmatic interpretation — indeed, an ominous one:

> Once it had been conceded, as a matter of principle, that legal freedom constitutes "help" to developing countries, the future was virtually fixed.... When other kinds of "help" were not enough there was always the possibility of doing something more on the legal side. Granting legal freedom to other countries is an easy concession to give, for it requires neither domestic legislation nor the use of other legal powers by the grantor countries. It is possible to "give" merely by doing nothing (1987, 18).

The Haberler Report and the GATT Action Program

For the first seven or eight years, the GATT system operated more or less by the book.[7] The GATT became, in use, the legal code that the International Trade Organization charter had been intended (at least by the United States) to be. The "contracting parties" (the official GATT language for "member" is "contracting party") overcame the absence of an institutional existence by referring to themselves as the CONTRACTING PARTIES (in all capital letters) when they acted collectively and officially — for example, to determine whether the agreed code had been violated. There were tight reviews of exceptions to the general idea of discipline against import restrictions. "Resort to the infant industry exception in Article XVIII was limited, but what activity there was was treated with some importance.... Balance of payments reviews were carried out with careful scrutiny" (Hudec 1987, 26). In practice, conditions were imposed on the development exceptions, and when developing countries acceded to the GATT they were required to make substantial tariff concessions.

The period 1954-60 saw a considerable shift in the momentum of the GATT. Developing countries pressed for more freedom for infant industry measures and for less reciprocity in the trade-liberalization negotiations. The United States became more concerned with strategic-block issues: the Cold War made the building of a political relationship more important and the United States therefore more willing to give ground on the details of the economic relationship. Consequently, at the 1954-55 review, the GATT was modified to include in its text a statement that the infant industry argument was consistent with its principles.

From that point, the infant industry justification for protection was written in as consistent with the GATT rather than being treated as an excuse for an exception to the GATT. "In the same spirit, the draftsmen deleted a tough-minded sentence in the original text warning that unwise use of such measures would harm both the applicant country and others" (Hudec 1987, 27). In sum, the review session presented an almost enthusiastic endorsement of the principle that freedom from the sort of constraints that the GATT attempted to impose on individual country behavior *helped* the developing countries. So the GATT in the late 1950s was rapidly losing interest in the enforcement of legal discipline on developing countries (although a formalistic compliance was maintained) and was developing an enthusiasm for an infant industry ideology of growth.

At the same time, the trade performance of developing countries began to worry the international community. The trade of developing countries was expanding less rapidly than the trade of the industrial countries, and the industrial countries were also posting better overall economic growth rates. This lagging economic performance of the developing countries spurred the CONTRACTING PARTIES in November 1957 to ask a Panel of Experts to study the matter. The panel was made up of Roberto de Oliveira Campos, Gottfried Haberler (Chairman), James Meade, and Jan Tinbergen. The panel's report, commonly called "the Haberler Report," is described by Kenneth Dam as "perhaps the turning point in the GATT's relations with less-developed countries" (1970, 228).

The terms of reference of the panel begins with an expression of concern "regarding certain trends in international trade, in particular the failure of the trade of less developed countries to develop as rapidly as that of industrialized countries, excessive short-term fluctuations in prices of primary products, and widespread resort to agricultural protection." The panel is charged to provide "an expert examination of past and current international trade trends and their implications, with special reference to the factors referred to above; [and] an assessment of medium-term prospects for international trade in the light of the facts and trends as [the panel] sees them" (Campos et al. 1958, 1).

The report is concerned mostly with trade in primary products and with policies relating to this trade. Of the fifty-seven summary points listed in the first chapter, only one is about manufactured exports. Some twenty concern fluctuations in export earnings or commodity stabilization policies; some twenty more are about the agricultural policies of the industrial countries, including the formation of the European Economic Community (EEC). If the reader interprets as realities the concerns the report expresses about what EEC agricultural policies might become, the discussion of agricultural policies sounds very much like a 1989, rather than a 1957, review.[8]

The report provides a comprehensive response to its terms of reference and does so mostly within the (then) mainstream of development thinking implicit in the terms of reference. For example (the numbers preceding these statements are the paragraph numbers in the report):

22.   *It is impossible, upon the evidence now available, to conclude whether or not there has been an increase in agricultural protection in industrial countries in recent years.*

24.   *The terms of trade in the post-war period were more favorable to non-industrial countries than in 1938, but recently turned against them ....*

25.   *The import requirements of the non-industrial countries are likely to increase more quickly than the rest of world trade....*

26.   *The exports of the non-industrial countries are very sensitive to internal policies of industrial countries....*

44. *A number of underdeveloped countries are now exporting low-priced manufactures, the markets for which depend upon moderation in industrial protectionism in the highly industrialized countries.*

The report's conclusions, however, as summarized in the first chapter, demonstrate much broader thinking:

61. *The issues which we have considered in detail in our report affect primarily the policies of the highly industrialized countries; but we consider that they, as well as the primary producing countries, would gain by the proposed changes.*

62. *We think that there is some substance in the feeling of disquiet among primary producing countries that the present rules and conventions about commercial policies are relatively unfavorable to them.*

63. *While the underdeveloped primary producing countries have valid reasons for making a rather freer use of trade controls than the highly industrialized countries, in a number of cases protective policies have been carried too far by these countries; and these countries also have used for the protection of their industries a number of special weapons which are not normally the subject of negotiation with other countries. We have not examined in any detail these problems of protectionism in the non-industrial countries.*

64. *Further progress depends upon the willingness of the industrial and the non-industrial countries to negotiate on a wide range of their economic and financial policies.*

Thus the report concludes that existing arrangements are relatively unfavorable to primary producing countries. While it also concludes that there are valid economic reasons for a developing country to restrict imports, it points out that they have done so to excess and that progress depends on both developed and developing countries reducing their restrictions.[9] The conclusion the report puts first is the crux of the classical economic view of trade policy: a country's import policy reform will have a positive effect on its own economy, not just on the economies of exporting trade partners.

To the diplomatic community, the Haberler report made one point: it verified that developing countries were losing ground under the GATT. Hudec (1975, 209) captures the tone well: "[T]he Haberler Report exploded a good deal of the developed country righteousness by showing that the developing country trade was actually losing ground under GATT." Kenneth Dam, another legal scholar not known for taking a soft line on the matter of GATT discipline for developing countries, argues that "The substance of the report was that the predicament of the underdeveloped countries was due in no small measure to the trade policies of the developed countries" (1970, 229). Thus, in the political world the report's warning about developing countries' own policies was ignored.[10] In effect, the international community overlooked the report's analysis and conclusions.

The thinking implicit in the reports' terms of reference, not the thinking explicit in its conclusions, became the basis for policy actions. The CONTRACTING PARTIES responded with a resolution "to initiate immediate consideration of a coordinated program of action" to embrace three topics: a new tariff round, nontariff protection of agriculture, and other obstacles, particularly to the expansion of developing country exports. "Committee III," which was created to take up the third topic, prepared a number of tabulations of developed countries' import restrictions on a long list of "products of export interest" to developing countries. Later, the CONTRACTING PARTIES created an Action Committee to examine submissions by developed countries of such information and to consult the developed countries "with a view to removing" these trade barriers.

The international community saw the matter as a direct one: developing country exports are lagging; therefore, developed country restrictions are the cause.[11] Only a few maverick intellectuals considered the possibility that the lagging trade performance of developing countries might be explained in significant part by their own policies.

The Haberler Report, the Action Program, and the Action Committee added a new *affirmative action* dimension to the developed-developing country relationship within the GATT. Beyond the developed countries' obligation to exempt developing countries from GATT's normal discipline — that is, to allow them to impose trade restrictions — the developed countries also had an obligation to unilaterally remove their import restrictions on products of export interest to the developing countries. In other words, developed countries were to extend the concessions they agreed to at any further tariff rounds beyond the scope of products traded principally among themselves.

Several other factors also contributed to the changes within the GATT that weakened the belief in the need for policy discipline for developing countries and strengthened the belief that developed countries had an obligation to do something for them. One was a simple matter of numbers. From 1960 until 1970, GATT membership increased from twenty-one developed and sixteen developing countries to twenty-five developed and fifty-two developing countries. Twenty-eight of the thirty-six new developing country members came in under special procedures for newly independent territories; only eight got in by negotiating tariff concessions (Hudec 1987, 24).

Another factor was the competition between the U.N. Conference on Trade and Development (UNCTAD) and GATT to be the institution through which relations between developing and developed countries were managed. That rivalry is the topic of the next section.

The GATT-UNCTAD Rivalry

What is the best trade policy for development? One alternative is the harsh "tariffs only" conclusion derived from classical economics, as explained, say, in Haberler's Cairo Lectures (Haberler 1959). The idea of "GATT discipline" as it prevailed in the period 1947-54 is the institutional representation of this viewpoint. But the alternative to which the international community turned in the late 1950s and in the 1960s suggested a kinder, gentler attitude toward developing countries. As the poorer members of the trading community, developing countries ought not to be asked to assume the same burden of discipline as the richer members. And, since the facts showed that they were slipping further behind, a kinder, gentler attitude should include an affirmative action program by the richer members, to create new opportunities for the poorer countries to export to the richer. The rivalry between GATT and UNCTAD to "staff out" this concern to promote developing country exports became, in the 1960s, an important influence on the economics of the GATT. Within this rivalry, UNCTAD achieved three significant victories.

First, the UNCTAD view captured the facts: not only the lagging trade performance of developing countries, but also the growing awareness that all was not well with import-substitution policies. As Prebisch phrased it, "Industrialization encounters growing difficulties in the countries where it is pursued furthest" (1964, 9). Extreme capital intensity and very high costs were becoming apparent. The problem, Prebisch explained, is another "vicious circle."[12] Costs are high because exports are low (economies of scale are not achieved), and exports are low because costs are high (1964, 22). Developed countries must therefore provide the needed export opportunities — the developing world requires affirmative action from the developed. UNCTAD's particular twist on the matter was that this access should be preferential, that developing country exporters should not be required to compete with, say, established German exporters for sales in the United States.

The political attractiveness of preferences for developing countries acted synergistically with two technical victories for UNCTAD. These technical victories allowed UNCTAD's concepts rather than the GATT's to provide the scale used by the international community to "keep score" on the amount of affirmative action provided.

One of these victories concerned the attachment of negative connotations to the way in which the normal GATT mode of reducing trade barriers would provide improved access for developing country exporters — even when the improved access was granted unilaterally. Let me give an example. In negotiations with each other through the GATT, Australia and New Zealand agree that each will reduce its tariff on $1000 of imports from the other and that each will also reduce its tariff on $500 of imports from a developing country. The latter action is obviously a unilateral extension of access to the developing country.[13] The case is much the same if Australia and New Zealand exchange concessions on products that each imports two-thirds from the other, one-third from a developing country. In both cases each developed country (Australia and New Zealand) has reduced its tariff on $500 of imports from a developing country, and has done so without receiving a reciprocal concession.

Yet, as UNCTAD taught the world to keep score, Australia and New Zealand would receive no credit for affirmative action. UNCTAD'S calculations compared the amount of developed country exports covered by the agreed concessions ($2000 in the example) with the amount of developing country exports covered ($1000 in the example).

Are Australia and New Zealand therefore "good citizens" because the $1000 is something, or "bad citizens" because the $1000 is less than the $2000? UNCTAD's evaluation of the Kennedy Round used the second standard; for example, "the products in which the developing countries had expressed particular interest, and in which they have already established some trade, received on average significantly smaller tariff reductions than did other products. This result reflects the fact that those product groups for which industrialized countries are the main suppliers received deeper and more widespread cuts" (UNCTAD 1968, 4).

By emphasizing that developed countries reduced tariffs on a larger share of their imports from each other than from developing countries, UNCTAD suppressed the idea that such tariff cuts provided a unilateral concession and assigned guilt to the developed countries because the concessions they exchanged among themselves were larger than those they provided without compensation to the developing countries. In so doing, UNCTAD detached the traditional GATT mode of going at trade liberalization — reciprocal most-favored nation concessions — from the earning of any affirmative action credits.[14] The international community (even the GATT, as the following paragraphs show) accepted the UNCTAD way of evaluating the morality of tariff reductions.

The other UNCTAD tactical victory was to build up the idea that tariff preferences (particularly the Generalized System of Preferences, which UNCTAD administered) were the only true indicator of a country's affirmative action.

A concern for expressing the growing belief that developed countries had positive obligations toward the developing countries led also to the adoption in 1965 of Part IV of the GATT. Part IV uses the "shall" language of legal obligation but then adds other specific language that undercuts the sense of *legal* obligation. For example, Article XXXVII, titled "Commitments," begins: "The developed contracting parties shall to the fullest extent possible — that is, except when compelling reasons, which may include legal reasons, make it impossible...."

The strength of the old test of good faith — exempting developing countries from normal GATT discipline — did not wane as that of the new test — affirmative action — ascended. Consider, for example, a pamphlet published in 1964 by the GATT Secretariat titled *The Role of GATT in Relation to Trade and Development*. According to Hudec's review, the pamphlet accurately described the GATT's legal discipline for developing countries. "What was interesting was its effort to portray the absence of legal obligations as a virtue. This is perhaps the clearest demonstration ... of the link during this time between the GATT legal policy towards developing countries and its very strong desire to attract and hold developing country members" (1987, 60).

As this analysis implies, the GATT rules were being shaped by an our-organization-versus-their-organization competition for membership, and not by any concern to guide or push countries to choose the most effective trade policies. UNCTAD for its part was doing the same. Raul Prebisch, UNCTAD's first Secretary-General in 1961, actively recruited developed and developing countries' loyalty to UNCTAD:

> [GATT represents] *the classic pattern of exchanging manufactured goods for primary commodities (Prebisch 1964, 7).*
> *GATT has brought about considerable reductions in ... tariffs and other restrictions [but they] ... have been of benefit mainly to the industrial countries (p. 27).*

[In GATT,] problems of international trade are dealt with in a fragmentary fashion, and not as part of a general problem of development.... GATT has not proved effective in coping with trade between the developing and the industrial countries nor has it promoted trade relations among the developing countries themselves (p. 99).

By the time of the Tokyo Round of negotiations, the developed countries had returned (at least in form) to the idea of discipline. The focus was shifting from tariffs to nontariff trade restrictions, and the Tokyo Round codes attempted to expand and interpret agreed rules about the use of such restrictions. However, each code included a provision for special and differential treatment of developing countries. Only the United States went so far as to threaten to limit extension of the codes' privileges to developing countries that accepted the codes' disciplines, although it pulled back from its threat whenever practical politics intervened.[15]

At the end of the Tokyo Round, the GATT Secretariat prepared a report on the outcome of the round. Hudec interprets the report as follows:

It was written quickly (but very thoroughly) in order to preempt the kind of negative evaluation that UNCTAD had made after the Kennedy Round .... It celebrated all the "victories" achieved by the Group of 77.... [A] central element of the "victories" was all the new legal freedoms developing countries had won, especially those which involved discriminatory special and differential treatment.... The year was 1979. Here was the GATT, still thoroughly preoccupied with holding the allegiance of developing countries and still making a virtue of the fact that GATT rules do not apply to developing countries (1987, 91).

If the Kennedy and Tokyo Rounds were the two halves of a GATT-UNCTAD soccer match, we would say that the score was UNCTAD 2, GATT 0, the second goal being an "own-goal." Put another way, the GATT church pretty much took on the theological position of UNCTAD concerning developing-developed country relations and the role of trade in economic development.

Neither the score nor the theology has changed. The subtitle of Hudec's chapter on developments in the 1980s is "form without substance," and this seems to be the mainstream interpretation of developing countries' obligations under the GATT. Another noted legal scholar, John H. Jackson, concludes that "many developing countries are able to take advantage of either explicit or implicit exceptions in the GATT so as to pursue almost at will any form of trade policy they wish" (1989, 277).

If "individual sacrifice for the common good" accurately reflected the economics of the GATT and if the GATT were supposed to serve a social welfare function, then the position of developing countries in GATT might be considered appropriate. But if we look at GATT from a public choice perspective — as an institution designed to nudge countries toward the best choice of trade policy — then we would give it a lower score.

The Uruguay Round

That things in the GATT have not changed in the 1980s does not mean that things have not changed. Concern is growing about the increased use of trade restrictions by developed countries. While some of these restrictions are GATT-questionable, a significant fraction of them, including antidumping and counter-vailing duty measures, are arguably GATT-legal.[16] Another matter of concern is that major movements by the developed countries to remove trade restrictions have been bilateral or regional, for example, the Australia-New Zealand and Canada-United States trade agreements and the European Community's "1992" program.

Trade policy changes in developing countries have been equally significant. There have been major reforms in some countries — Chile and Mexico are examples — and continuing liberalization in many others, particularly Korea and other newly industrialized countries in Asia. There have been some new restrictions as well.[17]

Several developing countries took an active role in getting the Uruguay Round under way. In early 1986, achieving agreement to undertake the round seemed impossible. Preparations were stuck, and agendas for the Punta del Este meeting were reviewed several times without progress. Quietly, however, officials from a group of middle-size developing and developed countries began to discuss matters among themselves. They shaped perspectives, forged operational ideas, and calculated relevant balances. Much more, they discussed ideas with other delegations, patiently modifying and extending their proposals as they went along. One of the positive effects of this behind-the-scenes leadership was the sense of the value of the GATT system that it conveyed to smaller countries and the development of a perspective that gave expression to their concerns.

The contribution of the developing countries to the politics of getting the new GATT round under way raised hopes that these countries would make an equally important contribution to GATT's economics. Most decisions by developing countries to remove trade restrictions have been unilateral decisions, based on an appreciation of the own-country benefits of such reforms versus the costs.

For developed countries, the removal of trade restrictions has been shaped by a strong vision of an open international trading system and of that system's collective benefits to the community of nations. A concern to promote and maintain peace and stability through economic means has perhaps been a clearer objective than have the economic benefits likely to accrue to a particular nation. The focus has been systemic and the approach multilateral. This systemic focus has characterized not just the GATT, but other important vehicles for the reduction of developed countries' trade barriers as well, such as negotiations to remove trade and exchange restrictions in Europe and to form the European Economic Community and the European Free Trade Association. Within the multilateral approach, trade liberalization means an exchange of concessions. Reductions of import restrictions increase the imports of the country granting the concessions and are viewed as a cost. But in the multilateral process, such costs buy increased exports and help build the system from which all will benefit.

For developing countries, the perspective on trade policy reform has been different. The focus has been national and the approach unilateral. This perspective may underestimate the value and fragility of a coherent international trading system, but it includes a fuller appreciation of the classical perspective, particularly of benefits that openness to international competition can convey to an individual economy. Like the multilateral decisions of the developed countries, unilateral decisions for reform reflect an appreciation of the economic benefits that export expansion allows. High-cost inputs are a burden to exports, and lower restrictions on imported inputs are a stimulus to export expansion.

Export expansion is a valid reason for import liberalization, but not the only one. Many developing countries have built on the other reasons. They recognize that economic development requires the improvement of human resources and the acquisition of modern technology. They also recognize that close communication with other economies, through the competitive process, is an important stimulus to the upgrading of domestic resources and domestic forms of economic organization.[18] The experience of these countries provides many lessons on how an individual economy can benefit from the removal of restrictions that isolate it from the international economy.

Looking at increased international trade from the perspective of the gains to an individual economy offers many possibilities, particularly for controlling the spread of new trade restrictions. The current GATT technology attempts to limit the use of import restrictions by specifying when a country may impose them. A country is not asked to weigh the domestic gains from an instance of import competition against the domestic costs. The GATT technology looks only at the domestic costs and authorizes import restrictions when these costs take a certain form or reach a certain degree. By so doing, the GATT system reinforces the idea that the importer bears the costs of trade while the exporter enjoys the gains.

Despite the promise of a new perspective on the benefits of trade, things seem to have gone the wrong way. The urge to get more exports and suffer fewer imports has dulled the developed countries' sense of the value of the system. Asking developing countries to examine trade liberalization in a multilateral context brings them to the instinctive view that exports are the gains from trade and imports the costs. At GATT, things are done the GATT way.

My pessimism that the potential discussed above will not be realized is based on two observations. The first concerns the developing countries' positions and proposals at the Uruguay Round. At the highest level of visibility, the developing country position is the Brazil-India position, which is the traditional GATT position of developing countries: against any compromise of developing country freedom from stated GATT obligations and for unilateral affirmative actions by the developed countries to help the developing countries. The implicit definition of what will "help" is (as always) the mercantilist one. At a lower level of visibility, developing countries have offered technical suggestions to limit the scope of allowable trade restrictions, for example, on the determination of "dumping" or "injury." These are, *in the traditional GATT sense*, good and responsible proposals. But (and I have emphasized "in the traditional GATT sense" for this reason) the traditional GATT sense of how to discipline the use of trade restrictions no longer works very well.

The other reason for my pessimism comes from the responses I have received when I have challenged researchers and academics on these matters. For example, at a symposium in South America I suggested that the developing countries had missed a chance to contribute to the international community from their own experiences. I asked: What did the government of Mexico or Chile take into account when it decided on its own trade reforms? What is there in such thought processes that might contribute to the Uruguay Round?

I offered two suggestions: (1) a proposal in the safeguards negotiations to give the costs of protection equal standing with the gains; perhaps even introduction of a "reverse safeguards" procedure through which a domestic interest could petition for removal of a trade restriction that caused it harm (for example, machinery producers for removal of restrictions on steel imports); and (2) a proposal to make the "protection balance sheet" (a concept elaborated in the GATT "Wise Men's Report" of 1985) the focus of the trade policy review mechanism.

There were three responses to my suggestion that developing countries prepare and present nonmercantilist proposals: (1) the United States would not accept nonmercantilist proposals, so it would be futile to make them; (2) the current GATT builds on mercantilist economics, and since developing countries want to improve the GATT not overthrow it, they must work within its mercantilist confines; (3) within the mercantilist conception of access to foreign markets as a country's right and discipline over its own use of import restrictions as the obligation, it is easy to define special and differential treatment for developing countries — unrequited access and less discipline. If this perception of costs and benefits is put aside, it is not immediately clear how special and differential treatment for developing countries might be defined.

There is perhaps a reply to each of these objections, but a reply is not my point. My point is this: We think about the GATT only in the GATT way.

Conclusions

At the beginning of this essay, I posited rhetorically that the institutionalized bad economics of the GATT might be just a matter of bad timing: the rules were written one day, but the appropriate economics were not uncovered until the next. It is time to take the question on directly: Is the problem simply a matter of unfortunate timing?

The answer is "no."

The work of Haberler and Viner shows that the "new" ideas about trade and development were around from the beginning. The supporting evidence reviewed at the beginning of this essay came later, but its emergence did overlap some of the events that shaped the GATT's perspective on trade and development, such as the UNCTAD-GATT rivalry throughout the 1970s and the GATT's Tokyo Round report, which was published in 1979. Finally, at no time did more of the evidence favor the economics that was built into the GATT than favored the economics that was left out.

In any case, given the way the choices were made, such evidence was irrelevant. The formative decisions came out of an adversarial process that focused first the emotions and then the intellect on the issue of more versus less of whatever sense of discipline the rules happened to contain.[19] The evidence is relevant mostly to the issue of determining what is the most effective form of discipline. But as the decision process came into being, that was not the focal issue.

As the Uruguay Round unfolds, it is becoming even clearer that the institutional structure of the GATT, having initially left out the "new" ideas and evidence about trade and development, now serves to keep them out. Building the "old" economics into the institutional decision structure of the GATT preserved a developed-developing country division that would have disappeared had the only influence been a strictly intellectual one.

In summary, my conclusions are these three:
- There is a GATT way of thinking about the role of trade in development.
- The economics of the GATT way is different from what is considered good economics by much of the profession.
- When we — policymakers and academics alike — put on our "GATT hats," we tend to put on our "GATT minds" as well.

Notes

1. Both Viner and Haberler refer to their work as applications of "classical" economics. Haberler, in his exposition, often talks about what the "old-fashioned economist" would conclude.
2. The World Bank's *World Development Report* 1987 reviews and extends what has been learned about the topic "industrialization and foreign trade." It also provides an extensive bibliography.
3. See, for example, Balassa (1981, 1985, part II). Balassa's method became the basis for a significant part of the World Bank's *World Development Report 1981*.
4. Quoted by Cooper (1987, 299) from Cordell Hull's *Memoirs*. Cooper provides similar quotations from Presidents Franklin D. Roosevelt and Harry S. Truman.
5. Dam (1970, 227ff) provides a more extensive comparison.
6. As explained in the first section above, there was no trade and development literature on which to draw.
7. Hudec (1975) provides a useful history and analysis.
8. The other summary points concern capital flows, monetary reserves, and macro-economic stabilization policies.
9. The statement quoted above includes the words "to negotiate" but the text of the report (p. 127) is more specific: "a negotiated settlement involving a gradual shift away from undesirable policies on both sides."

10. Less than a year later, Haberler (1959), in his Fiftieth Anniversary Commemoration Lectures at the National Bank of Egypt, elaborated on these points: "My overall conclusion is that international trade has made a tremendous contribution to the development of less-developed countries in the 19th and 20th centuries and can be expected to make an equally big contribution in the future, if it is allowed to proceed freely" (p. 5). "[D]evelopment policies should be such as to work through and with the help of the powerful forces of the price mechanism instead of opposing and counteracting the market forces" (p. 36). Haberler accepted the infant industry argument and suggested a uniform tariff of 20-30 percent as the only allowable interference with free trade. But he added, "I am fully aware of the fact that practically all underdeveloped countries (and developed countries for that matter) pursue policies that are almost the exact opposite of those sketched above [highly differentiated tariffs, exchange controls, and the like]. It is my contention that this type of policy hurts the underdeveloped countries" (p. 36).

11. Had the community been trained to see the matter as an application of effective protection or domestic resource cost concepts, things might have been different. But such concepts were yet to come in popular usage.

12. Little (1982, chapters 3 and 4) points out that during the period 1943-60, "vicious circles" were a popular form of explanation among development theories of why poverty persists. "Big push" was the complementary concept in policy advice.

13. The concessions are extended on a most-favored nation basis. We assume, for simplicity, that each good is imported only from the country with which the concession was negotiated or only from the developing country.

14. My own work contributed a footnote on this matter. In 1971, while on the UNCTAD staff, I set out to examine the effect of the GATT rounds on developing country exports. My intent was to demonstrate the need for preferences. My hypothesis was that with most-favored nation tariff cuts, even when they covered developing country exports, developing country exporters were left at the starting gate. I found the opposite to be the case. Where the Dillon and Kennedy Round cuts had touched developing country exports, the response was much faster growth of developing than of developed country exports. These findings are published in Finger (1974 and 1976). Like many of the relevant facts, these were dug out long after decisions had institutionalized the wrong economics.

15. In the 1980s, Section 301 of the U.S. Trade Act has emerged as an important policy instrument of the United States. Section 301 borrows some of the external features of legalism, but its application of a unilateral interpretation of what is legal and its availability to any U.S. interest that argues that its foreign competition is "unreasonable" (though not necessarily "illegal") suggest that it is grounded not in "legalism" but in old-fashioned mercantilism. Section 301 is not reviewed here.

16. Finger and Messerlin (1989) provide a review of these restrictions.

17. World Bank (1988) and Whalley (1989) provide lists of countries in both categories — those implementing new trade restrictions and those removing old ones.

18. The "old-fashioned" or classical view of Viner (1953), Haberler (1959), and Keesing (1976) emphasized the importance of the market process as communication.

19. I have taken this idea so much to heart that I am no longer willing to ask if it is Robert Hudec's idea or mine.

References

Balassa, B. 1963. "European Integration: Problems and Issues." *American Economic Review Papers and Proceedings* 53 (May): 175-84.

Balassa, B. 1966. "Tariff Reductions and Trade in Manufactures Among Industrial Countries." *American Economic Review Papers and Proceedings* 56 (June): 466-73.

Balassa, B. 1981. "Policy Response to External Shocks in Selected Latin American Countries." In M. Gillis and W. Baer, eds, *Export Diversification and the New Protectionism.* Urbana: University of Illinois Press for the National Bureau of Economic Research.

Balassa, B. 1985. *Change and Challenge in the World Economy.* London: Macmillan.

Balassa, B., and associates. 1971. *The Structure of Protection in Developing Countries.* Baltimore, Md.: Johns Hopkins University Press.

Balassa, B., and associates. 1982. *Development Strategies in Semi-Industrial Economies.* Baltimore, Md.: Johns Hopkins University Press.

Bell, C. 1987. "Development Economics." In J. Eatwell, M. Milgate, and P. Newman, eds, *The New Palgrave, A Dictionary of Economics.* London: Macmillan; New York: Stockton; Tokyo: Maruzen.

Bhagwati, J. 1978. *Anatomy and Consequences of Exchange Control Regimes.* Cambridge, Mass.: Ballinger.

Buchanan, J. M. 1984. "Alternative Perspectives on Economics and Public Policy." (Cato Institute) *Policy Report* 6: 1-5.

Burenstam Linder, S. 1986. *The Pacific Century: Economic and Political Consequences of Asia-Pacific Dynamism.* Stanford, Calif.: Stanford University Press.

Campos, R. de Oliveira, G. Haberler, J. Meade, and J. Tinbergen. 1958. *Trends in International Trade.* Geneva: GATT.

Cooper, R.N. 1987. "Trade Policy as Foreign Policy." In Robert M. Stern. ed., *U.S. Trade Policies in a Changing World Economy.* Cambridge, Mass.: MIT Press.

Dam, K. 1970. *The GATT: Law and International Economic Organization.* Chicago: University of Chicago Press. (Midway Reprint 1977).

Donges, J. B. 1976. "A Comparative Survey of Industrialization Policies in Fifteen Semi-Industrial Countries." *Weltwirtschaftliches Archiv.* Band 112 (Heft 4): 626-59.

Finger, J.M. 1974. "GATT Tariff Concessions and the Exports of Developing Countries." *Economic Journal* 84 (September): 566-75.

Finger, J.M. 1976. "Effects of the Kennedy Round Tariff Concessions on the Exports of Developing Countries." *Economic Journal* 86 (March): 87-95.

Finger, J.M., and P.A. Messerlin. 1989. *The Effects of Industrial Countries' Policies on Developing Countries.* Policy and Research Series No. 3. Washington, D.C.: World Bank.

GATT. 1979. *The Tokyo Round of Multilateral Trade Negotiations.* Geneva.

GATT. 1985. *Trade Policies for a Better Future.* (The Leutwiler Report). Geneva.

Haberler, G. 1959. *International Trade and Economic Development.* Cairo: National Bank of Egypt.

Hudec, R.E. 1975. *The GATT Legal System and World Trade Diplomacy.* New York: Praeger.

Hudec, R.E. 1987. *Developing Countries in the GATT Legal System.* London: Gower, for the Trade Policy Research Center.

Jackson, J. H. 1989. *The World Trading System: Law and Policy of International Economic Relations.* Cambridge, Mass., and London: MIT Press.

Keesing, D. B. 1976. "Outward Looking Policies and Economic Development." *Economic Journal* 77 (June): 303-20.

Krueger, A. O. 1978. *Liberalization Attempts and Consequences.* Cambridge, Mass.: Ballinger.

Little, I.M.D. 1982. *Economic Development: Theory, Policy and International Relations.* New York: Basic Books.

Little, I.M.D., T. Scitovsky, and M. F. Scott. 1970. *Industry and Trade in Some Developing Countries: A Comparative Study.* London and New York: Oxford University Press for the Development Centre of the Organization for Economic Cooperation and Development.

Prebisch, R. 1964. *Towards a New Trade Policy for Development.* New York: United Nations.

United Nations Conference on Trade and Development. 1968. *The Kennedy Round: Estimated Effects on Tariff Barriers.* New York: United Nations.

Viner, J. 1953. *International Trade and Economic Development.* London: Oxford University Press.

Whalley, J., coordinator. 1989. *The Uruguay Round and Beyond.* London: Macmillan.

World Bank. 1988. *Adjustment Lending: An Evaluation of Ten Years of Experience.* Policy and Research Series No. 1. Washington, D.C.

[16]

What Can the WTO Do for Developing Countries?

J. Michael Finger and L. Alan Winters

We begin from the widely accepted premise that the integration of many developing countries into the world economy has been an important source of their recent success. This integration has ensued from two factors: (1) the access to international markets that was available to them, and (2) reforms of developing countries' policies that integrated their industries into international markets. The criterion then for answering the question that is the title of our paper is obvious: how can the WTO continue to help developing countries to integrate themselves into the international economy? We deal minimally with access to international markets for products of export interest to developing countries, however, and focus instead on how the WTO supports reform of developing countries' own policies. Given that access to major markets does not vary substantially across developing countries, while trade performance and integration do, we infer that the latter plays a fundamental if not a predominant role.

The WTO assists the process of reform of developing countries' policies in several ways. GATT/WTO sponsors multilateral negotiations through which countries agree to reduce and to bind their restrictions, particularly tariffs, against unilateral increases. It provides rules that specify what restrictions are not allowed, what restrictions a country may retain or newly put in place (safeguards, antidumping, etc.), and how trade restrictions are to be administered (e.g., customs valuation).

J. Michael Finger is a lead economist in the International Trade Division, International Economics Department of the World Bank. L. Alan Winters is division chief of the same division.

The authors are grateful to Alan Hirsch, their official discussant, conference participants, and some anonymous referees for comments on an earlier draft of this paper. The authors gratefully acknowledge skillful assistance from Ulrich Reincke and Francis Ng. The views expressed here are those of the authors alone. They do not necessarily represent those of the World Bank or any of its member governments.

Our emphasis is on the WTO and GATT rules, particularly on how these rules influence *unilateral* trade policy decisions by developing countries. While post–World War II liberalization among the industrialized countries has been mostly reciprocal, liberalization by the developing countries has been much more a matter of unilateral decisions by individual countries.

In the context of multilateral, reciprocal liberalization, GATT rules such as those that condition when a safeguard, antidumping, or other trade-remedy decision can be applied can be reasonably viewed as pressure valves designed to let off a bit of protectionist steam from time to time, while the engine of reciprocal liberalization keeps rolling on. In the context of unilateral liberalization, however, the GATT's policy rules have a different meaning. They become guidelines for determining which trade restrictions to impose or retain, and which to avoid. Particularly for countries whose small economies make it impossible for them to integrate the domestic politics of liberalization into the reciprocal GATT process,[1] GATT rules that relate to unilateral actions are the most influential part of the agreement. Governments will interpret these rules as guidelines for good policy.[2] Perhaps more important, international rules provide a basis for a government to resist domestic pressures for protection, and in this way what the GATT/WTO rules allow or disallow serves as a mold for unilateral policy choices.

Section 14.1 reviews developing-country participation in the reciprocal tariff negotiations of the Uruguay Round. We go on in later sections to examine three important sets of GATT/WTO rules. We argue that antidumping and other rules that specify when a country may unilaterally restrict troublesome imports are not good policy advice—they do not separate those interventions that will augment the national economic interest of the country that intervenes from those that will not. In the case of regional arrangements—currently popular among developing countries—we argue that the GATT/WTO requirements are less incorrect than incomplete. We also examine the good deal of special and differential treatment that remains in the GATT/WTO system. On market access, GATT/WTO rules ask the developing countries to meet the same standards as the industrialized countries—reciprocity in the tariff negotiations and the elimination of quantitative restrictions to defend the balance of payments are examples. In other areas such as customs valuation procedures or technical standards, areas shaded by their technical nature from the spotlight of political accountability, special and differential treatment remains substantive. Section 14.4 presents our conclusions and recommendations.

1. In a negotiation in which all foreign liberalization is most-favored-nation (MFN), the government of a small country will have trouble convincing exporters that their access to foreign markets depends on their convincing local producers to allow foreign access to the domestic market.
2. In governments' dealings with other multilateral institutions, e.g., the World Bank and the International Monetary Fund (IMF), the objective, if not always the result, of the relationship is to determine policies that best serve the national economic interest of the country.

367   What Can the WTO Do for Developing Countries?

14.1 Tariff Negotiations and the Developing Countries

From the perspective of an individual country, the multilateral negotiation of tariff reductions provides opportunities of different sorts:

- to bargain for lower tariffs in markets of interest,
- to use the multilateral negotiation as leverage against domestic interests that resist tariff reductions, and
- to negotiate bindings that will provide defenses against future domestic pressures to increase rates or to provide protection by other means.

Binding has the effect not only of putting a cap on unilateral increases of tariffs; it also restrains a government from providing protection through other means that could be interpreted as nullification or impairment of that tariff binding.

In this section we examine how extensively developing countries agreed at the Uruguay Round to reduce their tariffs. We also examine how extensively they agreed to bind their tariffs, and to what extent those bound rates are above presently applied rates. Finally, for a sample of developing countries that introduced extensive unilateral tariff reductions during the 1980s and early 1990s, we examine the extent to which they have bound these unilateral reductions at the Uruguay Round.

Table 14.1 provides summary results from a tabulation of the concessions agreed on at the Uruguay Round. This tabulation covers only those countries that have supplied data to the WTO Integrated Data Base (IDB).[3] According to the WTO Secretariat, the IDB covers all industrial and transition economies that participated in the Uruguay Round, plus twenty-six of ninety-four developing-economy participants. The countries covered are listed in the notes to table 14.1. This data base provides post– and pre–Uruguay Round bound rates, as reported by the member countries.

Measuring applied rates was more complicated. From several alternative measures[4] we chose the best proxy for the applied rate that reflected unilateral changes made just before or during the Uruguay Round, but excluded any

3. The IDB includes countries that account for 100 percent of nonpetroleum imports of North America, western Europe, and WTO members (at the time of the Uruguay Round) in central and eastern Europe. The IDB covers 90 percent of Asia's nonpetroleum imports, 80 percent of Latin America's nonpetroleum imports, but only two sub-Saharan African countries (Senegal and Zimbabwe), which together account for 30 percent of sub-Saharan Africa's nonpetroleum imports.

4. Various of the countries whose applied rates are below their bound rates provided different measures of applied rates. Some of these are labeled in the IDB as the "MFN applied rate," the "MFN Uruguay Round base rate," or the "MFN statutory rate." As our proxy for MFN applied rates before the Uruguay Round cuts, we used the MFN applied rate whenever it was available. If the MFN applied rate was not available, we used the lower of the MFN base rate and the MFN statutory rate. A number of countries, particularly in Latin America, introduced substantial unilateral reductions of their tariff rates before or during the years of the Uruguay Round. These unilateral changes were in some cases not reflected in the MFN applied rate. In those cases we updated

368   **J. Michael Finger and L. Alan Winters**

Table 14.1   **Bindings of MFN Tariff Rates before and after the Uruguay Round, and Uruguay Round Tariff Reductions for Selected Countries and Country Groups**

	Percentage of Imports GATT Bound				Average Uruguay Round Tariff Reduction[a]	
			Post–Uruguay Round			
Country or Group	Pre–Uruguay Round	Total	At Applied Rate	Below Applied Rate	Across Reduced Items Only	Across All Imports
High-income countries[b]	80	89	38	30	3.2	1.0
European Union	98	100	43	39	3.1	1.5
Japan	73	83	42	38	2.7	1.0
United States	92	93	41	37	2.9	1.4
Hong Kong	1	28	28	0	—	—
Lower- and middle-income countries[c]	31	81	13	29	8.1	2.3
South Asia[d]	11	52	10	23	16.5	3.9
East Asia[e]	16	77	14	40	9.4	3.8
Korea	21	83	13	64	8.5	5.5
Philippines	9	61	27	17	7.9	1.3
Eastern Europe[f]	55	96	28	41	2.4	1.00
Latin America[g]	50	100	3	1	2.4	0.02
Argentina	17	100	0.2	0	4.2	0.001
Brazil	16	100	6.0	1	1.1	0.007
Mexico	100	100	2.0	0	0.9	0.004
Senegal and Zimbabwe[h]	26	40	22.0	1	5.8	0.05

Source: Finger, Ingco, and Reincke 1996.
[a]Weights are based on 1988 import values.
[b]Australia, Austria, Canada, European Union, Finland, Hong Kong, Ireland, Japan, New Zealand, Norway, Singapore, Sweden, Switzerland, and the United States.
[c]All countries covered below plus Tunisia and Turkey.
[d]India and Sri Lanka.
[e]Indonesia, Korea, Macao, Malaysia, Philippines, and Thailand.
[f]Czech and Slovak Customs Union, Hungary, Poland, and Romania.
[g]Argentina, Brazil, Chile, Colombia, El Salvador, Jamaica, Mexico, Peru, Uruguay, and Venezuela.
[h]Senegal and Zimbabwe are the only sub-Saharan African countries that have submitted tariff data to the WTO IDB.

changes that were the results of the round. We then measured the post–Uruguay Round applied rate (tariff line by tariff line) as the lower of this applied rate and the Uruguay Round bound rate. The figures provided in the tables are averages across all merchandise imports, including agricultural prod-

---

the MFN applied rate with data from the United Nations Conference on Trade and Development (UNCTAD) TRAINS data base.

ucts. For all sectors, including agriculture, where the Uruguay Round requires the conversion of all nontariff barriers (NTBs) to tariffs, our data do not include tariff equivalents of NTBs.[5]

14.1.1 Tariff Reductions

The right-hand columns in table 14.1 report the degree of tariff reduction agreed on at the Uruguay Round. In interpreting these numbers, the reader should be aware that we have measured tariff change as the reduction of the ad valorem rate (or ad valorem equivalent rate) divided by unity plus the ad valorem rate, as $dT/(1 + T)$, expressed as a percentage. For a country whose imports do not affect world prices, $dT/(1 + T)$ measures the percentage by which the domestic price of imports will fall as a result of the tariff cut. In this way, we take into account that halving a 20 percent rate will have a larger effect on imports, other things given, than halving a 2 percent rate. The second-to-last column in table 14.1 provides an average over only those tariff lines on which the tariff was reduced. The last column measures the overall tariff cut, an average cut across all tariff lines. Zero reductions are included in the second average, but not in the first.[6]

Our tabulations of Uruguay Round tariff reductions and bindings are presented in detail in Finger, Ingco, and Reincke 1996. Here we highlight only a few of our findings.

Looking first at the amounts by which tariffs were reduced, the table reports that the developing and transition economies agreed at the Uruguay Round to reduce their tariffs by an average 8 percent on 29 percent of their imports. These reductions come to a 2.3 percent reduction of their overall tariff. By comparison the industrial and other high-income countries agreed to reduce their tariffs by an average 3.2 percent on 30 percent of their imports, for an average reduction of 1 percent across all tariff lines. Among developing countries, the Asian countries agreed to relatively large reductions. Tariff reductions agreed on at the Uruguay Round by Latin American countries were quite small, but as we shall see below, the Latin American countries introduced large unilateral reductions in the 1980s and 1990s. For them, the relevant issue is the extent to which they bound these reductions at the round.

14.1.2 Tariff Bindings

Until the Uruguay Round, insistence on special and differential treatment was an important part of many developing countries' policy toward the multilateral negotiations. One result was that few developing-country tariffs were

---

5. We measure a reduction of tariffs on agricultural products only when the post–Uruguay Round bound rate is below the pre–Uruguay Round applied tariff rate. Likewise, elimination of voluntary export restraints under the safeguards and clothing-textiles agreements are not taken into account by these figures.

6. The last column is arithmetically the product of the two immediately preceding, divided by 100.

Table 14.2   **Average Tariffs, Post–Uruguay Round Applied and Bound Rates for Selected Countries and Country Groups**

Country or Group	Applied Rates	Bound Rates
High-income countries*	2.6	3.7
European Union	2.8	3.2
Japan	2.8	3.7
United States	2.8	3.3
Hong Kong	0.0	0.0
Lower- and middle-income countries[b]	13.3	25.2
South Asia[c]	30.4	50.8
East Asia[d]	11.9	21.0
Korea	7.7	16.4
Philippines	19.0	21.9
Eastern Europe[e]	6.7	13.3
Latin America[f]	11.7	32.7
Argentina	10.3	31.0
Brazil	11.7	29.0
Mexico	10.4	34.1
Senegal and Zimbabwe[g]	9.0	19.4

Source: Authors' calculations based on UNCTAD TRAINS data base.

Note: Weights are based on 1988 import values.

[a]Australia, Austria, Canada, European Union, Finland, Hong Kong, Ireland, Japan, New Zealand, Norway, Singapore, Sweden, Switzerland, and the United States.

[b]All countries covered below plus Tunisia and Turkey.

[c]India and Sri Lanka.

[d]Indonesia, Korea, Macao, Malaysia, Philippines, and Thailand.

[e]Czech and Slovak Customs Union, Hungary, Poland, and Romania.

[f]Argentina, Brazil, Chile, Colombia, El Salvador, Jamaica, Mexico, Peru, Uruguay, and Venezuela.

[g]Senegal and Zimbabwe are the only sub-Saharan African countries that have submitted tariff data to the WTO IDB.

---

bound—in table 14.1, less than one-third of imports were under bound rates. Note, however, that at the Uruguay Round the developing and transition economies agreed to significant bindings. The major Latin American countries have agreed to bind all of their tariffs; the extent of bindings is as high now in many developing and transition economies as in the industrialized countries.

Table 14.2, which compares post–Uruguay Round applied and bound rates, focuses on this point.[7] While developing countries' tariff reductions, as we have measured them, have been rather large, their tariff rates are still high, as compared with those of the industrialized countries. Many developing-country bindings are at ceiling rates, above applied rates. India's post–Uruguay Round

7. Generally, Uruguay Round agreed rates will be effective no later than 1 January 1999, but some countries have, for some commodities, negotiated later deadlines. The bound rates we report are final rates, after all stages are completed. We measure the post–Uruguay Round applied rate, tariff line by tariff line, as the lower of the current applied rate and the post–Uruguay Round bound rate. Average applied rates cover all tariff lines, but average bound rates cover only those tariff lines that are bound.

average bound rate is 52 percent; its average applied rate is 31 percent. Latin American countries' bound rates average around 30 percent (with minimal dispersion, most rates are near 30 percent); their applied rates average 10 to 12 percent.

As noted above, a ceiling binding provided a government a basis for resisting pressures to backslide on the liberalizations it had already made. Nontariff measures other than the kind of restrictions allowed under the "rules" part of the GATT would likely be considered nullification or impairment of the tariff binding. Any restriction other than a tariff increase or a GATT-legal "trade remedy" would open the possibility of complaints through GATT enforcement processes from trading partners.

14.1.3   Binding of Unilateral Concessions

The Uruguay Round also provided countries that had unilaterally liberalized the opportunity to bind these concessions. Such binding might be useful in two ways: as "coin" for buying concessions from trading partners and as a basis for resisting domestic pressures to raise the rates again.

Table 14.3 reports calculations for selected countries of the percentage of recent tariff reductions that have been bound. (The sample is limited to the countries for which suitable data are available.) In these calculations we used the IDB "Uruguay Round base rate"—as of 1986—as our measure of tariff

Table 14.3   **Percentages of Unilateral Tariff Reductions by Selected Countries That Were Bound at the Uruguay Round**

Country	Total Reduction[a]	Bound Reduction[b]	Percentage of Total Reduction Bound[c]
Argentina	16	9	57
Brazil	25	12	47
Chile	19	8	39
Mexico	27	8	30
Peru	20	9	46
Uruguay	6	3	41
Venezuela	19	2	12
India	27	22	82
Average, weighted by import value			39

Source: Authors' calculations based on the WTO's Integrated Database.

[a]Import weighted average of changes calculated by tariff line. The change is from the rate before unilateral reductions and before reciprocal (Uruguay Round) reductions to the rate after both. Reduction is defined as $dT/(1 + T)$.

[b]Import weighted average of changes calculated by tariff line from the rate before unilateral reductions and before reciprocal reductions to the post–Uruguay Round bound rate. Reduction is defined as $dT/(1 + T)$. In calculating the averages, in those tariff lines for which the bound rate was above the initial rate, the bound reduction was set equal to zero.

[c]Bound reduction as a percentage of total reduction.

rates pre–Uruguay Round and pre–unilateral concessions. We measured the "total reduction" as the change from this base rate to the lower of the 1992 applied rate[8] or the IDB post–Uruguay Round bound rate. The "bound reduction" is the change from the base rate to the post–Uruguay Round bound rate.

Overall, our calculations indicate that the countries in the group have bound somewhat less than half of the unilateral concessions that they have implemented since 1986. Measured as we have measured tariff cuts, that comes to a bound cut of 8 to 12 percent for a number of Latin American countries and 22 percent for India. Comparing these figures with those in the last two columns of table 14.1, we find that, except for India, these countries have added little to their tariff reductions through the reciprocal negotiations. At the Uruguay Round Latin American countries agreed to reciprocal reductions that averaged only 0.02 percent across all of their imports.[9] Even so, the 5 to 6 percent bound cut compares favorably with the 1 to 2 percent reduction agreed to by the higher-income countries at the round.[10]

14.2 GATT Rules

Some eleven of the GATT's twenty-five functional articles provide rules about what trade restrictions a country can and cannot impose—nine of the eleven providing for the application of certain kinds of measures—safeguards, antidumping, general exceptions, national security exceptions, and so forth.[11]

The historical reason that the many provisions allowing trade restrictions are in the GATT is most likely that protectionist interests have been strong enough to insist that such restrictions be provided for. To those seeking to create an open international trading system, the provisions are part of their losses, not of their victories. The familiar rationale for the provisions is that, had they not been included, protectionist interests would have prevented the tariff reductions that have been the core of the GATT. In figurative language, allowing for a possible step backward was part of the price of achieving two steps forward. A related and more forward-looking version of the latter rationale is that any government that maintains a liberal trade policy must have ways to deal with constituent pressures for exceptions—pressures for protection of particular domestic sectors. We build our evaluation of such provisions on that view.

8. These data were taken from the UNCTAD TRAINS data base.

9. It is tempting to think that the bound reduction plus the reciprocal reduction equal the total reduction, but they do not. The bound reduction plus the "unbound reduction" (not presented) would equal the total reduction; the reciprocal reduction is a part of the bound reduction.

10. The results indicate that on the whole these countries' bound rates are about halfway between their initial applied rates and the rates to which their unilateral reforms have brought them. For only a few tariff lines is the Uruguay Round bound rate below this unilateral rate. Since the Latin American countries' bindings are more or less uniform at 30 percent, these few tariff lines are likely the ones for which the unilateral rates are relatively high, above 30 percent.

11. Finger (1996) lists these articles and reports the frequency with which GATT members have used them.

14.2.1   GATT Pressure-Valve Provisions

Any government that strives to maintain an open trade regime must have mechanisms for managing domestic pressures for protection. In a system such as the GATT/WTO system, part of the discipline built into such domestic mechanisms is the international commitment not to impose new trade restrictions. Within the international system, the latitude the domestic mechanisms have to acquiesce to domestic pressures are in the rules the GATT/WTO provides as to when new restrictions may be imposed.

In reviewing the criteria that underlie the pressure valve provided by the GATT, we will evaluate them against two standards. (1) Good trade restrictions versus bad: Do the criteria make economic sense? Do they isolate actions that have greater economic benefits than costs for the country that takes the action, or for the world economy? Do these rules provide a basis for a developing-country government to resist domestic pressures for actions that would not serve the national economic interest? (2) Less trade restrictions versus more: Do the criteria provide an objective basis for saying no? On the presumption that most trade restrictions would not pass the economic sense criteria, fewer trade restrictions would make more economic sense than more.

Emergency Actions under Article XIX

GATT article XIX begins: "If, as a result of unforeseen developments and of the effect of the obligations incurred . . . under this Agreement, including tariff concessions, any product is being imported . . . as to cause or threaten serious injury to domestic producers . . . of like or directly competitive products . . . the contracting party shall be free . . . to suspend the obligation . . . or to withdraw or modify the concession." This sentence obviously authorizes import-restricting actions, but what limits are there on such actions? The following two subsections discuss two possible sources of constraint: the article's statement of the conditions under which pressure-valve actions can be taken, and the relation between this article and the notion of reciprocity that underlies the GATT tariff-cutting process.

Conditions. As the quoted sentence states, emergency action is conditioned on (1) injury from imports that results from (2) a concession (liberalization) *and* from (3) "unforeseen developments." The intent of conditioning import relief on "unforeseen developments" seems obvious: without this qualification relief would be available each time a liberalization had its probable effect—to increase imports—and the emergency-action provision would provide for the undoing of all the liberalization negotiated.

Early on in the GATT's history, in the hatters' fur case of 1950, a GATT working party interpreted "unforeseen developments" in a way that eliminated it as a constraint on emergency actions. As Gary Sampson concludes (1987, 143): "What this [interpretation] meant in practical terms was that any increase in imports, even if through normal changes in international competitiveness, could therefore be considered actionable under Article XIX."

Other interpretations further weakened article XIX as discipline against emergency actions. The hatters' fur working party also concluded that the country taking emergency action is entitled to the benefit of the doubt in determining injury: the exporting country has to actively disprove injury (to importing country producers) in order to overturn an action. Near the same time as the hatters' fur case, another working party concluded that a determination of serious injury from imports does not require even that imports be *increasing* before injury can be determined (Sampson 1987, 143).

The import of these decisions is that the condition "unforeseen developments" was nullified as a constraint on article XIX actions to restrict imports. At the same time, the capacity of the condition "injury" to constrain was weakened by allowing the importing country the benefit of the doubt in determining its operational meaning.

Reciprocity. While article XIX's conditionality has not restrained its use, the other constraint, reciprocity, has provided discipline. Article XIX explicitly calls for consultations with exporters and explicitly provides for retaliation— suspension of "substantially equivalent concessions or other obligations." Compensation (to buy off retaliation) is implicit in these provisions.

In the early years of its application, most invocations of article XIX were accompanied by either mutually agreed compensation or retaliation. Of the twenty-five actions taken under the escape clause between 1948 and 1962, compensation was offered in fourteen cases and retaliation took place four times, including three cases in which compensation had been offered (GATT 1994, 500–516).

The Uruguay Round Safeguard Agreement. The major elements of the Uruguay Round on an agreement on safeguards are described below.

Phase out of voluntary export restraints (VERs) must be completed within four years, with the exception that each member may retain one VER until 31 December 1999. Only the European Union has notified an exception, its VER on Japanese cars and trucks. Likewise, existing article XIX measures (GATT-legal measures) must be phased out eight years after application or by 31 December 1999, whichever comes later. Quantitative restrictions are explicitly recognized, however, and after a formal determination of injury, an import quota applied as a safeguard measure may, by mutual agreement, be administered by the exporting country.

Actions under article XIX are subject to several limits. The key ones are progressive liberalization and limits on the duration of safeguard measures.

Two major changes that make article XIX more usable by interests seeking protection are the explicit allowance of discriminatory quantitative restrictions and the removal of the exporting country's right to retaliate against a safeguard

measure for the first three years. The latter change removes the burden to negotiated compensation, that is, it allows an article XIX action to be unilateral,
disciplined only by the condition that injury must be determined.

The 1994 agreement contains many explicit procedural requirements for
transparency and openness that were not in the original article XIX. First, a
member may apply a safeguard measure only after an investigation and a determination of injury.[12] The investigation must be carried out according to procedures previously established and made public; it must include public notices
to all interested parties and public hearings for the presentation of evidence,
views, and comments from all sides.[13] The determination must demonstrate a
causal link between imports and injury.[14] The agency that conducts the investigation and makes the determination must publish a detailed analysis, setting
out its findings and conclusions, and how these relate to the facts developed
and to the applicable law.[15]

The economic criteria that conditions when an import restriction may be
imposed is *serious injury* to domestic producers of like or competing products.
Injury is more or less a translation into administrative terms of the economic
concept of comparative disadvantage; hence it is not a criteria that will isolate
those restrictions that serve the national economic interest. Indeed, the gains
from trade are likely to be larger when the cost advantage of imports over
domestic production is large, and injury is of significant magnitude. Injury,
simple or serious, fails the economic sense criterion.

Likewise, unless there is injury (i.e., displaced domestic production) from
imports, there will be little motive for petitions for import restrictions. Hence
"injury" will not provide a basis for rejecting a significant share of petitions
for relief. For the criterion to provide a basis to reject some petitions (i.e.,
provide less import restrictions rather than more) will depend on there being a
politically convincing basis for separating serious injury from less serious. In
practice, this has not been the case.[16]

The public notice and transparency requirements the Uruguay Round safeguards agreement adds to article XIX procedures—like similar requirements
for antidumping procedures—are laudable on their own terms, but they do not
correct the bad economics of article XIX. To do the wrong thing the right way
is still to do the wrong thing. Because the requirements do nothing to bring
out the costs of protection or to enfranchise those interests that will bear these
costs, they are not likely to change the domestic political balance in favor of
fewer restrictions.

12. The familiar details of article XIX are retained, e.g., "serious" injury, "cause or threaten."
13. Information and views may be presented to show the safeguards measure is in the public interest.
14. The "unforeseen circumstances" requirement of article XIX has been removed.
15. Extension of a safeguard measure has the same requirements as the initial action.
16. Administratively operational criteria for distinguishing degree of injury have often been
arbitrary. Finger (1992) examines the issue. Note that a negative finding is described in news
releases and in political rhetoric as a finding of "no injury," not as a finding of "not serious" injury.

Restrictions to Protect the Balance of Payments. GATT article XVIII permits developing countries to introduce trade restrictions either to support infant industries or to protect their balance of payments. Neither makes economic sense. In practice, developing countries' use of the balance-of-payments exception has far exceeded their use of the infant-industry exception. Table 14.4 reports almost 3,500 restrictions declared under the balance-of-payments exception, less than 100 under the infant-industry exception.[17]

Why have there been so few actions under the infant-industry provision? The procedural requirements of the balance-of-payments provision are easier—developing countries find it easier to obtain GATT "cover" for infant-industry protection under the guise of "balance-of-payments" reasons.

The facts of usage bear out this interpretation. Anjaria (1987, 680) reports that in almost three-fourths of the developing countries that declared article XVIII:B measures, the measures covered less than half of import categories. If these restrictions were truly for balance-of-payments purposes, they would cover all import categories.

Before the Uruguay Round began, the increased commercial presence of developing countries had provoked industrial countries to press for market-opening actions by the developing countries. The industrial countries applied this pressure both through the GATT Committee on Balance-of-Payments Restrictions and the Trade Committee of the Organization for Economic Cooperation and Development (OECD). One of its focal points was reduced use by developing countries of article XVIII:B restrictions.

At the same time, the demonstration effect of the Asian model of export-led development changed developing countries' view of trade policy. Realistic exchange rates had been an important element in this experience, and there was a growing realization that an unrealistic exchange rate buttressed by trade control was bad development policy. Hence developing countries were more willing to give in on use of article XVIII:B. As of June 1996, only three developing countries (Tunisia, India, and Pakistan) maintained import restrictions declared under GATT article XVIII:B that are of major concern to potential exporters.

Uruguay Round Balance-of-Payments Understanding. During the Uruguay Round, OECD countries—the United States and Canada in particular—were strong proponents of strengthening GATT balance-of-payments provisions to more accurately reflect changes in economic ideas about the interrelation of trade and development. The Uruguay Round understanding has added statements to encourage use of price-based measures rather than quantitative restrictions, and to encourage phasing-out of balance-of-payments measures.

---

17. Article XVIII:A and D also provide in slightly different ways for import restrictions to support industry development. As of March 1994, article XVIII:A had been invoked nine times, while section D had not been invoked at all. For details on the use of section A, see GATT 1994, 465.

Table 14.4   **Number of Customs Cooperation Council Nomenclature Items on Which Developing Countries Notified Quantitative Restrictions under Different GATT Articles, 1974–87**

GATT Article Cited as Justification		Number
VIII	Fees and formalities connected with importation and exportation	316
XI:2	Restrictions in order to apply standards or classifications, to manage short supplies, or to complement agricultural or fisheries support programs	108
XVII	State trading enterprises	15
XVIII:B	Balance-of-payments measures for developing countries	3,437
XVIII:C	Industrial development	91
XX	General exceptions	131
XXI	National security	4

Source: OECD 1992, 100.

The understanding also adds detailed documentation requirements.

The Uruguay Round understanding thus earns high marks as a guide to sensible economic policy—it reflects the growing realization that an unrealistic exchange rate that must be buttressed by trade control is bad development policy.

Antidumping

Antidumping was a minor instrument when the GATT was negotiated, and provision for antidumping regulations was included with little controversy. Since then, antidumping has become the industrial countries' major safeguard instrument, and is gaining increasing popularity among developing countries. As of July 1996, fifty-eight developing and transition-economy countries have notified antidumping laws or regulations to the WTO, and sixteen had notified antidumping actions to the WTO.[18]

Several features of antidumping explain its popularity.

- Discriminatory action is permitted.

- In national practice, the injury test for antidumping action tends to be softer than the injury test for action under article XIX.

- The rhetoric of foreign unfairness provides a vehicle for building a political case for protection.

- Antidumping and VERs have proved to be effective complements; that is, the threat of formal action under the antidumping law provides leverage to force an exporter to accept a VER.[19]

18. Since 1985, GATT member countries have notified over 150 antidumping cases per year. Article XIX notifications have been less than 3 per year.

19. Finger and Murray 1993 report that over 1980–88, 348 of 774 U.S. antidumping cases were superseded by VERs.

- Suspension agreements are provided for in the 1989 Tokyo Round antidumping code and in the Uruguay Round agreement.[20]
- The investigation process itself tends to curb imports. This is because exporters bear significant legal and administrative costs, importers face the uncertainty of having to pay, once an investigation is completed, backdated antidumping duties (Finger 1981; Staiger and Wolak 1994).

The Uruguay Round Agreement. The negotiations were a pitched battle between victims and users of antidumping. The only clear victory for the victims was the introduction of a sunset clause requiring that all antidumping actions be terminated after no more than five years—unless a review determines that termination would lead to continuation of recurrence of dumping and injury. The agreement considerably increases documentation requirements, but they do not change its economics.[21]

The Economics of Antidumping. National regulations allow antidumping action in a broad range of circumstances. This point, supported by considerable research, is stated by different authors in different ways, for example, that such regulations are biased toward finding dumping and toward overstating dumping margins (Bierwagen 1991; Litan and Boltuck 1991) or that antidumping is ordinary protection with a good public relations program (Finger 1993a).

An important detail of these findings is that, in practice, the criteria of what constitutes dumping are so broad that the dumping standard is met in virtually every case.[22] Without the injury standard, all antidumping cases would reach affirmative outcomes; that is, the criterion that distinguishes an affirmative antidumping finding from a negative one is the same as the criterion of an article XIX safeguard action: injury to competing domestic producers.

Its rhetoric aside, neither legal nor economic analysis finds a link between antidumping investigations and the detection of anticompetitive practices. An OECD study, for example, has found that imports posed no threat to the existence competition in more than 90 percent of the cases in which the U.S. and EU imposed antidumping duties in the 1980s (de Jonquieres 1995, 5).

As economics, antidumping is an injury test, nothing more. Thus the eco-

20. Stegemann (1992, 8) reports that from July 1980 through June 1989, of 384 antidumping actions taken by the European Community, 184 were price undertakings. Though the Tokyo Round code does not explicitly provide for such settlement, both U.S. and EC antidumping regulations allow for suspension through acceptance by the exporter of a quantity limit (Jackson and Vermulst 1989, 52, 116).

21. The agreement is examined in some detail by Finger (1996), who points out that the victims were in large part successful only in adding documentation requirements to the practices that they wanted removed.

22. Quantitative evidence for this conclusion is based on U.S. experience only, the United States being the only country that separately publishes outcomes of dumping and of injury determinations. Finger 1993a, chap. 3, reviews the evidence.

nomic evaluation presented above of article XIX actions as a pressure valve applies equally to antidumping. Its sorting of restrictions that are authorized from those that are not makes no economic sense, and it serves minimally as an influence for fewer restrictions than for more. While antidumping may not score a zero by the criterion "fewer restrictions rather than more," the inflammatory rhetoric that antidumping supports and the weaker injury test that it embodies suggest that it should receive a lower score than article XIX. This, as noted above, is why the protectionists prefer it.

14.2.2 Conclusions about GATT Pressure Valves

This brief review of pressure valves allowed by the GATT leads to the following conclusions.

1. GATT pressure valves make no economic sense. The conditions under which the GATT allows a country to take emergency actions or antidumping actions, or to impose trade restrictions to protect the balance of payments are not the conditions under which such action would serve the national economic interest of the country. In economics, pressure valves are just ordinary protection, with sufficient political influence that antiprotection forces cannot overcome it.

The rationale for these mechanisms remains political. Their nonsense economics raises the following question, however: might there be processes that served as a pressure valve for protectionist pressures and at the same time make economic sense? One of the major disappointments of the Uruguay Round is that this question was never addressed.

2. GATT rules provide little discipline over use of pressure valves. This proposition follows from the following two.

3. Trade restrictions are fungible. The GATT provides a long list of apparently special-purpose restrictions, but the type of restriction that a country imposes is not determined by the nature of the "problem" that the country faces. It is determined by the relative ease of qualifying for one or another type of GATT coverage for the restriction. In the GATT's first decade, article XIX actions, renegotiations, and negotiations were impossible to distinguish from each other. At present, antidumping is the instrument of choice of protection-seeking interests. In the 1970s and 1980s, VERs were the favorite form of protection of the industrial countries, article XVIII:B balance-of-payments actions the favorite GATT cover for developing countries' import restrictions.

4. Safeguard action is always possible under the rules. "Injury" is the economic concept that underlies article XIX actions and antidumping. Each of these pressure valves includes a second factor, "dumping" for antidumping and "unforeseen developments" for article XIX action. But in practice, the meaning of "dumping" is so broad that the injury test is the only constraint on antidumping action. And the "unforeseen developments" condition on article XIX action was rendered ineffective the first time it was challenged. Thus, "injury"

is the sole condition that restrains article XIX or antidumping action, and "injury," as economics, is identical with comparative disadvantage. Any time imports displace or threaten to displace domestic production, pressure-valve action is GATT-legal. The GATT chain is as strong as its weakest link, and antidumping is at present the protectionists' favorite means.

5. GATT pressure-valve processes make little political sense. Only in the cheap sense of bowing to political reality are the GATT's pressure valves defensible. They do nothing, however, to empower the good guys—the interests that would be hurt by the imposition of an import restriction.

Worse, the GATT's pressure valves empower the bad guys. An investigation of injury—on which pressure-valve actions are premised—provides a tribune from which the interests that will benefit from an import restriction can make their case. An antidumping investigation adds the opportunity to accuse exporters of unfairness. Given the proprotection logic and structure of the pressure-valve process, reasons to refuse protection are arbitrary[23]—free trade, not protection, depends on exploiting the loopholes in trade law.

14.2.3   Customs Unions and Free Trade Areas

Article XXIV of the GATT seeks to specify circumstances under which countries may violate the most-favored-nation (MFN) clause by forming free trade areas or custom unions. It imposes three principal restrictions, that the free trade area or customs union (1) cover "substantially all trade" (par. 8); (2) reduce internal tariffs to zero and remove internal quantitative restrictions other than those justified by other GATT articles (par. 8); and (3) not raise the average level of protection against excluded countries (par. 5).

Mercantilist Sense. These provisions were written in a pre-Vinerian world which did not recognize the concepts of trade diversion and trade creation, and which held that liberalizing trade with a subset of partners was a good thing.[24] They are also, of course, part of a document whose primary focus is the mercantilist one on the rights of trading partners rather than the economist's one on the benefits of policy for the member country itself. From these perspectives there is some logic to conditions 2 and 3. Condition 3 may be viewed as preserving the sanctity of tariff bindings by ensuring that forming a customs union does not provide a wholesale way of dissolving previous bindings. There is also a convention that compensation is due to individual partners (in terms of other tariff reductions) for increases induced by the customs union if the

23. For example, antiprotectionists oppose "cumulation," the adding-up of injury from each of many exporters, no one of which is large enough to cause "serious" injury. But is it reasonable to provide protection to an industry that has been devoured by a shark, while denying protection to an industry nibbled to death by piranhas? Finger (1992) takes up in detail the point that the constraints on safeguards actions are arbitrary.

24. In fact, Viner first defined the concepts in 1931—in Swedish—but they were not widely known. We are grateful to Richard Snape for this observation.

corresponding reductions to keep the average constant are not adequate. Together, these provisions offer reasonable assurances about the barriers facing nonmembers.

Condition 2 is best seen as a means of defending the MFN clause by making it subject to an "all-or-nothing" exception. If countries were free to negotiate different levels of preference with each trading partner, binding and nondiscrimination would be fatally undermined—no member could be sure that it was receiving the benefits it expected from a bound tariff negotiation. Moreover, one might view customs unions as a first step toward deeper integration— ultimately nation building—and feel it inappropriate that an international trade treaty should stand in the way of such progress. If so, internal free trade, such as one (usually) achieves within a single country, would be an acceptable derogation of MFN, whereas preferences would not be. Condition 1 does not lie within the GATT tradition of tariff-line by tariff-line negotiation, but does reinforce 2 by requiring a serious degree of commitment to a free trade area or customs union before sanctioning it under the GATT.

Economic Sense. The conditions of article XXIV also make some, albeit incomplete, sense when viewed from a more modern and economic perspective. The requirement not to raise barriers against nonmembers not only honors the latters' market-access rights under the GATT but also heads off one otherwise available route to increased protectionism. This is desirable on any account, but in the context of free trade areas and customs unions the danger and costs of trade diversion will be greater if the members can increase their external tariffs. It is also useful that the Uruguay Round Understanding on the Interpretation of Article XXIV offers instruction on how to assess whether this condition has been met.[25]

Condition 2 is, from an economic point of view, unnecessary. Trade theory is now quite clear that, from the point of view of the free trade area or customs union, a small tariff on trade between members is better than free trade if there are positive tariffs on nonmember countries (Ethier and Horn 1984). However, its rationale in defending MFN seems sufficiently strong both systemically and individually to create a net benefit overall. The benefit to an individual country of preserving the condition is that, if partial preferences are permissible, governments may come under increased pressure internally or externally to use them, and could have to expend considerable effort resisting proposals for degrees of preference that did not generate Ethier-Horn-type benefits.

---

25. It is worth noting that this instruction refers to the applied rates of duty, not the bound rates. The exact impact of this is not clear yet. On the one hand it may be seen as effectively binding an average of the previously applied rates—at least for so long as the conditions applicable to the *creation*, as opposed to the operation, of a customs union remain in force. On the other hand, it may imply a lack of discipline on the relationship between the preintegration bound rates of the members and those of the customs union.

Political Sense. Condition 1 does have an important role from a welfare point of view. Recent advances in political-economy modeling—for example, Grossman and Helpman 1995—have suggested that, if governments are susceptible to lobbying by sectoral producer groups, political pressures will tend to favor trade-diverting regional arrangements. Trade diversion unambiguously generates gains for partner exporters, so when two countries swap trade-diverting concessions, both sets of producers gain. On the other hand, if they swap trade-creating concessions, producers lose some sales in their home markets and may or may not gain overall. Lobbies increase the weight of producer gains and losses in overall decision making, so that it is perfectly possible that trade diversion is politically more powerful than trade creation and that the option of regional liberalization undermines the incentives for first-best nondiscriminatory liberalization (Krishna 1994; Levy 1994). Condition 1 means that governments cannot select only commodities that are likely to feature trade diversion, and this in turn seems likely to encourage more efficient free trade areas and customs unions.

This argument makes obvious the case that the GATT/WTO generates welfare less through disciplining a country's trading partners than through bolstering the country's government against pressures to pursue inappropriate policies at home. Not only does condition 1 constrain the government's response to such pressures, but it also, one hopes, reduces the frequency with which such pressure is applied.

Does Article XXIV Ensure Good Policy?

The previous paragraphs suggest that article XXIV is generally an aid to rational policymaking. However, they do not suggest that it is sufficient for good policy. The rules prevent a given group of countries from limiting a free trade agreement to those products on which trade will be diverted, but they do not prevent a free trade agreement among countries for which elimination of internal barriers will be entirely or predominantly trade-diverting.

In fact, article XXIV has not provided as much discipline as it might have, for it has been notoriously weakly enforced. WTO (1995) reports that of sixty-nine working parties reporting up to and including 1994, only six had been able to agree that a free trade area or customs union met the requirements of article XXIV. However, the remainder did not conclude that the agreement under review was not in conformity, but merely left the matter undetermined.

The reluctance of the GATT as an institution to decide on the consistency of regional agreements with the rules does not mean that the rules have had no effect—we do not know which potential arrangements they discouraged—but it is not an encouraging record. There have been clear breaches of condition 1 (e.g., the European Coal and Steel Community), breaches of condition 2 (e.g., the European Economic Cooperation's monetary compensatory amounts on intra-EEC agricultural trade), and, on some interpretations, breaches of condition 3 (e.g., the EEC, of which the GATT executive secretary[26] expressed "the view, with which he thought there was no disagreement, that the incidence of the Common Tariff was higher than that of the rates actually applied by the Member States at the time of entry into force of the Treaty of Rome" [GATT Document C/M/8, 6; cited in GATT 1994, 750]).

The Enabling Clause

A further complication for developing countries is the enabling clause—the Decision on Differential and More Favorable Treatment, Reciprocity, and Fuller Participation of Developing Countries of 1979 (see GATT 1994). This significantly relaxes the conditions for creating free trade areas or customs unions that include only developing countries. It drops condition 1, on the coverage of trade, and dramatically relaxes condition 2, allowing developing countries to reduce tariffs on mutual trade in any way they wish and NTBs "in accordance with criteria which may be prescribed by the CONTRACTING PARTIES." It then supplements condition 3 by requiring that the arrangement not constitute a barrier to MFN tariff reductions or cause "undue difficulties" for other contracting parties.

In practice, developing countries have had virtual carte blanche. Twelve preferential arrangements have been notified under the enabling clause, including the Latin American Integration Association (LAIA), the Association of Southeast Asian Nations (ASEAN), and the Gulf Cooperation Council (GCC). These have made liberal use of the scope allowed by the enabling clause. Internal preferences of 25 percent and 50 percent figured in ASEAN's trading plans and in many of the arrangements concluded in the LAIA and the GCC. There is little sign that internal preferences have undermined MFN agreements with other trading partners in the sense of causing a reversal of previous conditions. Until the late 1980s, however, the Latin American countries' frequent use of regional arrangements and weak participation in the multilateral rounds might suggest a substitution of one form of liberalization for the other. Probably more pernicious have been the sectoral agreements that have abounded in Latin America. For example, Argentina and Brazil signed seventeen such agreements in 1986; there was little doubt that they generated a fair measure of trade diversion (Nogués and Quintanilla 1993). Similarly, ASEAN's trading arrangements were, for some time, partial in their coverage of products, although they are probably better categorized as ineffective than as harmful (DeRosa 1995).

Overall, the enabling clause serves to dilute even the weak discipline that article XXIV imposes. Even if article XXIV does not actually stop many harmful practices, at least it does not give them the respectability of legal cover as a matter of course. Thus, as Finger (1993b) notes, while the GATT knowingly

---

26. Before 1965, the director general of the GATT was called the executive secretary.

and willingly permitted the earlier manifestations of the LAIA (the Latin American Free Trade Agreement, 1960) and the initial notification of ASEAN (in 1977) to violate article XXIV, it at least left open the possibility of challenge in the dispute settlement process.

14.3   Special and Differential Treatment

One of the most profound institutional changes that the conclusion of the Uruguay Round induced in the world trading system was the advent of the so-called single undertaking. This entailed that all members of the WTO should adhere to nearly the same set of agreements on trading rules, in contrast to the situation prior to the round, in which members adhered to the GATT plus whatever subset of codes on trading rules that they chose. However, while the Uruguay Round agreements reduced the scope of the special and differential treatment that the GATT system had offered the developing countries, they did not eliminate such treatment completely. In many instances, the agreements common to all members permit or prescribe different treatment for developing countries. This section considers how much special and differential treatment has slipped through into the post–Uruguay Round trading system.

Hindley (1987) suggests five areas in which developing countries received special and differential treatment prior to the Uruguay Round: one from the 1947 GATT (article XVIII, the right to infant-industry and balance-of-payments trade restrictions); one from part IV of the 1964 GATT (exemption from making reciprocal tariff concessions); and three stemming from the enabling clause (the right not to sign the Tokyo Round codes, exemption from article XXIV, and the legitimization of the Generalized System of Preferences [GSP]). We have already dealt with articles XVIII and XXIV above. The remainder of this section comprises subsections on special and differential treatment for developing countries as victims of trade policy, special and differential treatment for developing countries as perpetrators of trade policy, and some conclusions.

14.3.1   Special and Differential Treatment for "Victims"

The Generalized System of Preferences

Perhaps the developing countries' most significant exceptions from other countries' trade policy arise from the GSP, which permits industrial countries to exempt some of their exports from MFN duties. These exemptions are autonomous policies (i.e., granted unilaterally by the industrial countries), which continue quite independently of the outcome of the Uruguay Round, under the cover of the enabling clause. The reductions in tariffs in the Uruguay Round agreements eroded GSP margins of preference, but, with a few exceptions, not very significantly. For example, the average reduction in margin was below two percentage points for sub-Saharan Africa (Amjadi, Reincke, and Yeats 1996).

At first sight, there seems little to object to in the notion that industrial countries should exempt imports from developing countries from tariffs. Even if the exceptions are not much of a basis for industrial development—because many are subject to quantitative limits and all are unbound and hence reversible—at least they transfer some tariff revenue to developing-country producers. Moreover, it might be argued that, since developing countries have little bargaining power in reciprocal negotiations, this is the only way that they will obtain relatively free access to the world's major markets.

There are four problems with these arguments. First, preferences essentially transmit to developing countries the production distortions inherent in developed countries' tariff structures. That is, they permit—perhaps encourage—producers to have costs above those in nonpreferred countries. Second, and closely related, current GSP schemes are so hedged with exclusions, quantitative limits, and rules of origin that they have only limited coverage.[27] The excluded imports are typically the most important from the point of view of development (e.g., clothing, footwear, leather) and the effect of the scheme is to divert resources away from them.

Third, the fact that the preferences might be withdrawn at any time encourages a degree of short-termism on the part of entrepreneurs. Their decisions are likely to be biased toward the quick fix rather than the long haul. Fourth, both for entrepreneurs and for their governments the desire to keep and exploit the rents inherent in preferences distract from longer-term and ultimately more productive activities. For example, the wish to maintain preferences could undermine developing countries' willingness to invest in rounds of negotiated trade liberalization, or even devalue their stake in the world trading system itself.

Special Treatment under the Rules

Developing countries also formally receive a measure of special and differential treatment in the ways in which they are treated by other countries' trading rules. In the case of countervailing duties and safeguards this is explicit and mandated. A developing country's exports to a market cannot be countervailed if its share of total imports of the product is 4 percent or less and if the sum of all such small suppliers' shares is 9 percent or less. Similarly, developing countries are exempt from safeguards actions if their share is 3 percent or less. There are no such limits for developed suppliers. Also, in the countervailing-duty agreement, whereas the *de minimis* limit is 1 percent for developed suppliers, it is 2 percent for developing countries (and 3 percent for least-developed countries until 2003).

In addition to these concessions, the WTO texts are handsomely endowed with exhortatory rather than mandated suggestions of special and differential

---

27. UNCTAD (1994) reports that in the European Union only 68 percent of dutiable imports from beneficiary countries qualify for preferences under the Generalized System of Preferences, of which only 33 percent (slightly below half) actually take them up. The corresponding figures for Japan are 35 percent and 16 percent and for the United States 36 percent and 18 percent.

treatment. For example, for antidumping, active countries are urged to seek "constructive remedies" when "essential interests of developing countries" are at stake and generally to pay regard to the "special situation" of the developing countries. In import licensing, members are asked to give "special consideration to . . . developing country members" in allocating new licenses. The Agreement on Technical Barriers to Trade (TBT) and the Agreement on the Application of Sanitary and Phytosanitary Measures have several special and differential treatment clauses urging, inter alia, special recognition of the needs of developing countries and their difficulties in formulating, implementing, and testing standards. Whether such exhortations amount to anything concrete remains to be seen.

14.3.2   Special and Differential Treatment for Perpetrators

Of much greater significance to their economic performance is the special and differential treatment that developing countries receive as perpetrators of trade policy. While the advent of the single understanding removes some aspects of special treatment, several instances remain in which general obligations under the GATT are relaxed for developing countries. If the relaxed obligations are constraining and harmful, this is indeed the "more favorable treatment" that the formal terminology for special and differential treatment implies, but if the obligations have the effect of encouraging countries' progress toward better economic policy, the exemptions are harmful. We quote those specific examples here.

Part IV

Superficially among the most important aspects of special and differential treatment is part IV of the GATT. Its article XXXVI:8 states baldly that the developed countries do not expect reciprocity from the developing countries. This exemption took quite concrete form for the former colonies of member countries, which could use it to avoid providing schedules of tariff concessions (bindings) when they assumed membership (see Hoekman and Kostecki 1995). This privilege no longer pertains: every WTO member has to submit schedules of bindings in goods and services.

The broader form of nonreciprocity embodied in part IV—the absence of need to negotiate and offer concessions in order to win them—was modified but not revoked by the Uruguay Round. Part IV was exhortatory rather than binding and has been replaced by equally nonoperational language. The Punta del Este declaration stated that developing countries were not expected to make concessions inconsistent with their "development, financial and trade needs" and the Marrakesh Decision on Measures in Favor of Least-Developed Countries continued this for least-developed countries.

Practice was quite different from these exhortations. In the Uruguay Round, developing and industrialized countries each agreed to cut their tariffs on about 30 percent of their imports. The cuts by the industrialized countries will reduce the prices of those imports by an average of 3 percent, those by the developing countries by an average 8 percent.[28] Thus, many developing countries made significant concessions. But the Marrakesh agreement provides at least legal cover for those who wish to be left out as a matter of principle.

Technical Barriers to Trade

The TBT agreement offers special and differential treatment to developing countries on both their exports and their imports. On the latter, they are not expected to "use international standards as a basis for technical regulations or standards, including test methods, which are not appropriate to their . . . needs." This concession is intended to allow the preservation of indigenous technology and technologies appropriate to countries' development needs. While the general terms of the TBT agreement restrict the use of standards for protectionist purposes, and developing countries are not exempt from its provisions, this particular piece of language seems to grant the right to use idiosyncratic standards. If so, it could put a substantial brake on the modernization and competitiveness of developing-country industry.

Subsidy/Countervailing Measures

The Uruguay Round Agreement on Subsidies and Countervailing Measures substantially revised the corresponding Tokyo Round code, linking together for the first time the concepts used in the two parts of the agreement. The agreement imposes significant discipline on specific subsidies, identifying prohibited, actionable, and nonactionable classes and providing far readier action against the first class than against the second. Unfortunately it then goes on to use special and differential treatment to dilute the disciplines significantly for developing countries and even further for least-developed countries (defined as the UN list plus countries with per capita income below $1,000). For example, whereas export subsidies are banned almost immediately for developed countries, they are banned in eight years for developing countries and never (subject to a condition on quantities) for least-developed countries. Similar differentials impose tighter conditions on WTO members before they can take action against developing-country exports, and give more generous definitions of "de minimis" for the latter. The overall impression is that subsidies do not matter much for least-developed countries so long as they do not disrupt other countries' markets, and this view is significantly enhanced by the statement that "subsidies may play an important role in the economic development programs of developing country members" (article XXVII:1 of the Agreement on Subsidies and Countervailing Measures). In sum, the agreement offers governments of least-developed countries virtually no cover against lobbies seeking subsidies (Winters 1994).

---

28. Abreu (1996) and Finger, Ingco, and Reincke (1996) provide details of developing country concessions.

Among other areas in which special and differential treatment dilutes developing countries' obligations to liberalize are customs valuation (longer transition periods), agriculture (smaller tariff cuts), safeguards (longer-lasting restrictions), trade-related investment measures (restrictions available for balance-of-payments purposes), and services (similar special and differential rules as for goods).

14.3.3   Conclusions on Special and Differential Treatment

It is impossible to make a simple quantitative assessment of the extent of special and differential treatment, but some qualitative conclusions are possible. In terms of market access for developing countries' exports, special and differential treatment is quite extensive—if not very effective economically—in offering tariff reductions on a wide variety of exports. In terms of market access to their own markets, developing countries have successfully managed to avoid the obligation to make tariff concessions, but have, at least in industrial products, frequently made them anyway. In the area of rules, special and differential treatment is de facto no longer very extensive in the visible high-profile cases. Thus, for example, balance-of-payments restrictions are coming under increasing pressure in the WTO Balance of Payments Committee and are fading away quite rapidly, and antidumping and countervailing-duty rules are the same for developed and developing countries. In the lower visibility areas, however, shrouded in technicality, special and differential treatment appears to continue unchecked. Least-developed countries have virtually free rein to subsidize exports, and, apparently, a great deal of latitude in both standards and, for several years, in customs valuation. Arguably, the least-developed countries need the most, not the least, support of the multilateral system in devising satisfactory policies.

14.4   What the WTO Can Do for Developing Countries

We second, but have not repeated, important points about market access, such as assuring that liberalization of agricultural trade and trade in clothing and textiles and other products of export interest maintain the schedules agreed on at the Uruguay Round.

Our focus instead has been on the GATT/WTO system as a guide for unilateral decisions. From this perspective we offer two broad guidelines: Pay attention that its guidelines make economic sense; they often do not.[29] Avoid the temptation to view immunity from rules that make sense as a benefit.[30]

We provide below more specific recommendations in three issue areas.

29. "But our policies are GATT-legal" is an argument we often hear against our recommendations for reform.
30. Hudec (1987) shows why this view is a snare and a delusion.

14.4.1 A Better Pressure Valve

Some may comment that a pressure valve cannot make economic and political sense at the same time. Not true. A pressure valve or trade-remedy process that truly enfranchised all the economic interests affected by a proposed import restriction would be more honest and more transparent politics than the obfuscation and misdirection politics of the present antidumping system.

Here are some of the general guidelines on how a government might meet its need for a means to evaluate requests for exceptions to a basically liberal trade policy.

Identify the costs and the losers. Procedures should bring out the costs of the requested exception, and the identities of the persons or groups who will bear these costs. More expensive imports will cost somebody money and—if the imports are needed materials—eliminate somebody's job. These costs, and the people in the domestic economy who will bear them, should have the same standing in law and in administrative practice as the other side already enjoys. The process of considering the request for an exception should be used to help fortify the politics of not granting it.

Be clear that the action is an exception. Procedures should establish that the requested action would be an exception to the principles that underlie the liberalization program. Admitting to political weakness is better than admitting that the exception is a good idea.

Don't sanctify the criteria for the action. Procedures should not presume that there is some good reason for granting an exception—procedures that compare the situations of the petitioner with preestablished criteria for granting an exception should be avoided. Procedures should stress that the function of the review is to identify the benefits and the costs—and the domestic winners and domestic losers—for the requested action.

The last guideline is more important than it might seem. The history of antidumping and other trade remedies shows that clever people will always be able to present their situation exactly as the criteria describe. If you start out to find just the few exporters who are being unfair to Australia or the United States or Mexico, you will soon be swamped by evidence that everyone is.

At the technical level, useful concepts for review procedures—such as transparency and automatic expiration for any exception that is granted (a sunset clause)—can be gleaned from procedural changes made at the safeguards negotiations of the Uruguay Round.

14.4.2 Regional Arrangements

The guidelines presently provided suffer more from incompleteness than from error. Indeed, given their necessarily sui generis nature, it may be impossible to write GATT-style rules to cover all of the dimensions that distinguish an economically beneficial regional arrangement from a bad one. The WTO and, perhaps, other international organizations should sponsor economic analyses of regional arrangements—as was done by the European Commission for the European Union's Single Market initiative—but taking pains *not* to limit the review to criteria provided in article XXIV. As we have pointed out, the latter was written even before the basic concepts of trade creation and trade diversion were widely available to guide thinking.

Such reviews should be useful for the partners to a potential regional arrangement to identify their own interests. They should also identify effects on excluded countries—an obvious area of concern to the WTO—but not just in terms of the potential changes in their exports to the integrating countries. As we have argued elsewhere (Winters 1997), this is an inappropriate yardstick and must be supplemented at least by information on excluded countries' imports and their terms of trade. Moreover, such reviews should be done ex ante and used as a guide to the renegotiation of the free trade area's or customs union's instruments of trade policy. There is no virtue to McMillan's suggestion (1993) that ex post adjustments be made to maintain excluded countries' exports at preintegration levels: this is both the wrong criterion and redolent of managed trade.

14.4.3   Special and Differential Treatment

Special and differential treatment as commonly interpreted in the WTO agreements does not do much for developing countries. Special access to developed-country markets transfers revenue to them but at the expense of discouraging effective efforts to integrate into the world economy. Exemptions from WTO rules—inadequate as some of these are—and exemption from the need for reciprocal trade liberalization merely exacerbate the difficulties of pursuing satisfactory policies at home. They should be phased out as soon as possible.

The one element of special and differential treatment that does seem to us potentially beneficial is to offer assistance in the business of being a WTO member. Meeting the full procedural requirements of the WTO is very burdensome and can absorb disproportionate amounts of human capital. To the extent that they can be implemented without compromising substance or transparency, the elements of special and differential treatment that permit developing countries to use streamlined procedures and/or lighter notification burdens seem, to us, desirable. By the same token, the actual delivery of the technical assistance referred to so frequently in the Uruguay Round agreements would be beneficial, especially if it can be devoted to training and capacity building rather than just to producing a product.

References

Abreu, M. 1996. Trade in Manufactures: The Outcome of the Uruguay Round and Developing Country Interests. In *The Uruguay Round and the Developing Countries,* ed. W. Martin and L. A. Winters, chap. 3. Cambridge: Cambridge University Press.

Amjadi, A., U. Reincke, and A. Yeats. 1996. Did External Barriers Cause the Marginalization of Sub-Saharan Africa in World Trade? Policy Research Working Paper no. 1586. Washington, DC: World Bank.

Anjaria, S. J. 1987. Balance of Payments and Related Issues in the Uruguay Round of Trade Negotiations. *World Bank Economic Review* 1, no. 4: 669–88.

Bierwagen, R. M. 1991. *GATT Article VI and the Protectionist Bias in Antidumping Law.* Kluwer Studies in Transnational Law, vol. 7. Deventer: Kluwer.

de Jonquiers, Guy. 1995. Report Counts Cost of Antidumping. *Financial Times,* 2 September, p. 5.

DeRosa, Dean A. 1995. Regional Trading Arrangements among Developing Countries: The ASEAN Example. Research Report no. 103. Washington, DC: International Food Policy Research Institute.

Ethier, W. J., and H. Horn. 1984. A New Look at Economic Integration. In *Monopolistic Competition and International Trade,* ed. H. Kierzkowski, 207–29. Oxford: Clarendon Press.

Finger, J. M. 1981. Policy Research. *Journal of Political Economy* 89:1270–71.

———. 1992. The Meaning of "Unfair" in United States Import Policy. *Minnesota Journal of Global Trade* 1, no. 1: 35–56.

———, ed. 1993a. *Antidumping: How It Works and Who Gets Hurt.* Ann Arbor: University of Michigan Press.

———. 1993b. GATT's Influence on Regional Arrangements. In *New Dimensions in Regional Integration,* ed. J. de Melo, and A. Panagariya, 128–48. Cambridge: Cambridge University Press.

———. 1996. Legalized Backsliding: Safeguard Provisions in the GATT. In *The Uruguay Round and the Developing Countries,* ed. W. Martin and L. A. Winters, chap. 8. Cambridge: Cambridge University Press.

Finger, J. M., M. D. Ingco, and U. Reincke. 1996. *The Uruguay Round: Statistics on Tariff Concessions Given and Received.* Washington, DC: World Bank.

Finger, J. M., and T. Murray. 1993. Antidumping and Countervailing Duty Enforcement in the United States. In *Antidumping: How It Works and Who Gets Hurt,* ed. J. M. Finger, 241–54. Ann Arbor: University of Michigan Press.

General Agreement on Tariffs and Trade. 1994. *Analytical Index: Guide to GATT Law and Practice.* 6th edition. Geneva: GATT.

Grossman, G., and E. Helpman. 1995. The Politics of Free-Trade Agreements. *American Economic Review* 85:667–90.

Hindley, B. 1987. Different and More Favorable Treatment—and Graduation. In *The Uruguay Round,* ed. J. M. Finger and A. Olechowski, 67–74. Washington, DC: World Bank.

Hoekman, B., and M. Kostecki. 1995. *The Political Economy of the World Trading System: From GATT to WTO.* Oxford: Oxford University Press.

Hudec, R. E. 1987. *Developing Countries in the GATT Legal System.* Aldershot: Gower.

Jackson, J. H., and E. A. Vermulst. 1989. *Antidumping Law and Practice: A Comparative Study.* Ann Arbor: University of Michigan Press.

Krishna, P. 1994. Regionalism and Multilateralism: A Political Economy Approach. Brown University. Photocopy.

Levy, P. I. 1994. A Political Economy Analysis of Free Trade Agreements. Economic Growth Centre Discussion Paper no. 718. New Haven: Yale University.

Litan, R. E., and R. Boltuck, eds. 1991. *Down in the Dumps: Administration of the Unfair Trade Laws.* Washington, DC: Brookings Institution.

McMillan, J. 1993. Does Regional Integration Foster Open Trade? Economic Theory and GATT's Article XXIV. In *Regional Integration and the Global Trading System,* ed. K. Anderson and R. Blackhurst, 292–309. New York: Harvester Wheatsheaf.

Nogués, J., and R. Quintanilla. 1993. Latin America's Integration and the Multilateral Trading System. In *New Dimensions in Regional Integration,* ed. J. de Melo and A. Panagariya, 278–313. Cambridge: Cambridge University Press.

Organization for Economic Cooperation and Development. 1992. *Integration of the Developing Countries into the International Trading System.* Paris: OECD.

Sampson, G. 1987. Safeguards. In *The Uruguay Round,* ed. J. M. Finger and A. Olechowski, 143–52. Washington, DC: World Bank.

Staiger, R. W., and F. Wolak. 1994. The Trade Effects of Antidumping Investigations: Theory and Evidence. In *Analytical and Negotiating Issues in the Global Trading System,* ed. A. V. Deardorff and R. M. Stern, 231–61. Ann Arbor: University of Michigan Press.

Stegemann, K. 1992. *Price Undertakings to Settle Antidumping Cases.* Ottawa: Institute for Research on Public Policy.

United Nations Conference on Trade and Development. 1994. *Review of the Implementation, Maintenance, Improvement, and Utilization of the Generalized System of Preferences.* Geneva: UNCTAD.

Winters, L. A. 1994. Subsidies. In Organization for Economic Cooperation and Development, *The New World Trading System,* 129–34. Paris: OECD.

———. 1997. Regionalism and the Rest of the World: The Irrelevance of the Kemp-Wan Theorem. Oxford Economic Papers.

World Trade Organization. 1995. *Regionalism and the World Trading System.* Geneva: WTO.

Comment on the Paper by J. Michael Finger and L. Alan Winters   Alan Hirsch

This is an intellectually stimulating paper, addressing first principles and conventional thought about the role of multilateral trade rules. It has the deceptive simplicity and clarity of thought that has often characterized previous works by the same two authors. However, does it address the whole question as posed? The question appears to ask about the role of the WTO, which is an organization, not simply about the rule environment for multilateral trade agreements. But the authors say early on that their "emphasis is on the WTO and GATT rules, particularly on how these rules influence *unilateral* trade policy decisions by developing countries."

If I had been asked the question posed, I would have attempted to answer it not only by looking at the rules of the GATT, but also by looking at the *functioning* of the WTO in relation to developing countries.

Alan Hirsch is chief director for industrial and technology policy in the Department of Trade and Industry in Pretoria, Cape Town, South Africa.

Implementation of Uruguay Round Commitments: The Development Challenge

J. Michael Finger and Philip Schuler

1. INTRODUCTION

𝕬 T the Uruguay Round, developing countries took on unprecedented obligations not only to reduce trade barriers, but to implement significant reforms both on trade procedures (e.g., import licensing procedures, customs valuation) and on many areas of regulation that establish the basic business environment in the domestic economy (e.g., technical, sanitary and phytosanitary standards, intellectual property law).

This paper is about the latter commitments. They are more than policy commitments, they are investment decisions. Implementation will require purchasing of equipment, training of people, establishment of systems of checks and balances, etc. This will cost money and the amounts of money involved are substantial. Based on Bank project experience in the areas covered by the agreements, an entire year's development budget is at stake in many of the least developed countries.

Would such money be well spent? Least developed country institutions in these areas are weak, and might benefit from strengthening and reform. However, our analysis indicates that WTO regulations reflect little awareness of development problems and little appreciation of the capacities of the least developed countries to carry out the functions that SPS, customs valuation, intellectual property, etc. regulations address. For most of the developing and transition economies – some 100 countries – money spent to implement the WTO rules in these areas would be money unproductively invested.

We touch also on another point. Because of their limited capacity to participate in the Uruguay Round negotiations, the WTO process has generated no sense of

---

J. MICHAEL FINGER is from the World Bank. PHILIP SCHULER is from the University of Maryland. This research was supported by the Global and Regional Trust Fund Component of the Bank/Netherlands Partnership Programme. The views expressed are personal and should not be attributed to the World Bank.

512   J. MICHAEL FINGER AND PHILIP SCHULER

'ownership' of the reforms to which WTO membership obligates them. From their perspective, the implementation exercise has been imposed in an imperial way, with little concern for what it will cost, how it will be done, or if it will support their development efforts. Thus the developing countries have neither economic incentive nor political will to implement these obligations.

Our analysis is based on World Bank project experience in customs reform, SPS, and intellectual property regulation. In each of these areas we reviewed Bank experience with four questions in mind:

1. How much will implementation cost?
2. What are the development problems in this area?
3. Does the WTO agreement correctly diagnose the development problems?
4. Does the WTO agreement prescribe an appropriate remedy?

'Appropriate' in the fourth question refers both to correct identification of the problem and to recognition of the capacities (resource constraints) of the least developed countries. To provide specificity to the scope and cost of investments that may be involved in implementing Uruguay Round commitments, the core of this paper is a review of (primarily) World Bank experience with customs reform, with application of sanitary and phytosanitary standards, and with installation of systems of intellectual property rights. In each area we outline basic WTO obligations and we examine how implementation might be managed so that it best helps the least developed countries to use trade as a vehicle for development. We start with a brief look at least developed countries' participation in the Uruguay Round negotiations. This participation, or lack thereof, has left these countries with no sense of ownership of the commitments they have undertaken.

2. NO LEAST DEVELOPED COUNTRY 'OWNERSHIP' OF THE RULES

'Ownership' of the rules is an important element in the functioning of any system of rules; particularly important in systems such as the WTO, where the central organisation has limited power to enforce. Building among members a solid sense of ownership of such rules begins with participation in establishing them – for WTO rules, with effective participation in the WTO negotiations in which the rules were agreed.

The African Economic Research Consortium's (AERC) evaluation of sub-Saharan African countries' participation in the Uruguay Round found that it had been minimal. These countries lacked the capacity to engage substantively on the wide range of issues that the Uruguay Round embraced. An indicator: of all the written proposals, comments, etc. circulated at the WTO during the Uruguay Round negotiations, less than three per cent were submitted by sub-Saharan

IMPLEMENTATION OF URUGUAY ROUND COMMITMENTS   513

countries (Ogunkola, 1999, p. 3). The AERC evaluation identified weaknesses at three levels:

1. Geneva delegations were small and lacked persons with the technical backgrounds needed to participate effectively. A competent diplomat without the backing of a technical staff was not an effective delegation.[1]
2. Links between WTO delegations and the government at home were not developed. There was a lack of established process to involve the relevant ministries with issues that were being negotiated in Geneva, e.g., health and agriculture ministries with negotiations on sanitary and phytosanitary standards, the customs agency with the customs valuation negotiations.
3. Stakeholders, e.g., the business community, were minimally involved.

But all of the African members of the GATT chose to accept the new obligations of the WTO. Ogunkola (1999) concludes that

> [w]hile the participation of Africa has been limited by the capacity to negotiate, the ratification of the agreement and the single undertaking clause made the implementation of the agreement almost non-negotiable.[2]

Result: there came forward in these countries no sense of ownership of the implied reforms. To them, the reforms were imposed by the major trading countries.[3] Given these attitudes, it is difficult to rally support for implementation, and attempts to force implementation through the WTO dispute settlement mechanism would likely reinforce the impression that the WTO rules are imperially imposed from the outside, for the benefit of the outside.

---

[1] Of 65 developing country GATT/WTO members when the Uruguay Round began, 20 did not have delegations in Geneva. Of the 20, 15 were represented from embassies in other European cities, and 5 by delegations based in their national capitals. Furthermore, developing country delegations were notably smaller than those of the industrial countries. In 1987, when the Uruguay Round began, the EU had in Geneva a delegation of 10, EU Member States' delegations included an additional 57 persons. The US delegation numbered 10, the Japanese, 15. Only 12 developing countries had delegations of more than three persons. The larger ones: Korea, Mexico and Tanzania, 7 each; Brazil and Indonesia, 6 each; Thailand, Hong Kong and Egypt, 5 each. Of the 48 least developed countries, 29 are WTO members, but only 11 of these maintain delegations in Geneva. As of January 1999, 6 least developed countries were negotiating accession to the WTO, another 6 were observers, not negotiating accession. Data are from Michalopoulos (1998).

[2] 'Single undertaking' here means that each member was expected to take on all obligations, that the codes approach of the Tokyo Round, in which each member could opt to sign some codes and not sign others, was not available. John Croome, who served in the GATT/WTO Secretariat throughout the Tokyo and Uruguay Rounds, has pointed out in correspondence that 'single undertaking' initially referred to the members voting on all parts of the agreement as a whole, i.e., that the outcome of the tariff negotiations would not be put up for approval separately from the outcome of the subsidies negotiations. As the negotiations progressed, the meaning of 'single undertaking' expanded to include the 'no country can opt out of any part' meaning.

[3] An African food scientist remarked to us in conversation, 'They want us to adopt the SPS agreement so that we will import more chickens from them.'

TRIPS, the customs valuation agreement, the SPS agreement and several others suggest that developed country members furnish technical assistance to developing country members that so request it. This provision however is not a binding commitment. Thus, the developing countries took on *bound* commitments to implement in exchange for *unbound* commitments of assistance.

3. CUSTOMS VALUATION

The WTO agreement addresses only customs *valuation* – only one part of the customs process. In addition to providing information on how much customs reform might cost, we will argue in this section that given the initial situation in many developing countries (which we will briefly characterise) changing the valuation process without overall customs reform is not likely to improve the predictability of the customs process. Likewise, changing the customs valuation process would not lessen significantly the possibility of using the customs process as a non-tariff barrier.

Scope and content of the Customs Valuation Agreement. The Uruguay Round Customs Valuation Agreement establishes the *transactions value* of the shipment in question as the primary basis for customs value and prescribes a hierarchy of methods for determining that value. The first, and basic, option is that customs value will be the transaction value of *the* imported merchandise – the price actually paid or payable for *the* specific shipment. The agreement provides a list of items (add-ins) that must be included in the price actually paid or payable, e.g., packing costs, cost of tools, dies and moulds provided by the buyer. The second alternative is the transaction value of *identical* merchandise – sold for export to the same country of importation at or about the same time – for which a transaction value can be determined. The third, fourth and fifth are likewise attempts to come as close as operationally possible to the transactions value of the specific shipment. The agreement also provides a rogue's gallery of methods that *may not* be used, such as the selling price of competing domestic products, or the selling price on the market of the exporting country or on another export market.

Presumed administrative environment. The valuation process the Uruguay Round agreement imposes is one that complements customs systems in place in most of the advanced trading nations (including both developing and industrial countries). That system is based on generalised use of electronic information management and built-in incentives for self-compliance. Trade in these countries takes place in large-scale lots and duty rates are generally low. In this context, departure from routine business practice is costly, e.g., retrieving additional information in response to a valuation inquiry. Importers normally conduct the valuation process themselves, including application of the add-ins and take-outs needed to comply with the rules. In Norway, a paperless customs declaration system operates around-the-clock, average clearance takes 15 minutes and is almost always completed well before the goods arrive. About 85 per cent of declarations pass through the system without being stopped for further investigation (WCO, 1999). Questioning and verification of the importer-submitted customs value does not normally cause physical delay of the shipment. Instead, the importer posts a customs bond sufficient to cover the amount in question. Financial institutions in many least developed countries do not offer such bonds.

a. Developing Countries' Customs Practices and Problems

Customs practices in many least developed countries differ significantly from those in place in the more advanced trading nations. The differences are often differences in basic concept, not just differences of detail or efficiency.

Physical control. Effective customs administration has both *physical* and *administrative* dimensions. Physical control is about keeping track of what passes into and out of the country. In many poorer countries, traditional smuggling – goods sneaked across the border away from recognised ports – is a significant problem. At a duty rate of 50 per cent, the duty on the number of televisions one person can transport on a bicycle-jitney can come, in a poor country, to a year's wages. Where physical control systems are poor, smuggling need not involve clandestine overland trails or secret moonlit beaches. Goods often move through ports without coming under the supervision of customs authorities.

Administrative processes. Customs processes in poorer countries exhibit many interacting weaknesses – excessive procedures that are not codified – often not even a published schedule of current tariff rates is available – poorly trained officials, a civil service system that does not pay a living wage and depends on officials receiving side-payments for performing their functions, and ineffective provision for appeal. Cunningham (1996), in an assessment of several least developed countries considering customs reform, observed that systems and procedures appeared to have evolved to maximise the number of steps and approvals – to create as many opportunities as possible for negotiation between traders and customs officials. It should be evident from this introduction to customs problems in poorer countries that valuation is only an inch in the whole yard of customs operations that need improvement.

b. Reform Experience in Developing and Transition Economies

We present in this section a brief digest of our review of customs reform projects in several countries. A brief tabulation of the cost of customs reform projects in several countries is reported in Table 1.

516   J. MICHAEL FINGER AND PHILIP SCHULER

TABLE 1
Costs of Customs Reform Projects, Selected Countries

Country	Major Elements	Cost
Armenia, 1993–1997	Draft new customs law, train staff, and computerise procedures – component of an institution building project	$1.604 million
Lebanon, 1994–2001	Train staff, introduce new tariff classification, computerise procedures – component of a revenue enhancement and fiscal management project	$3.82 million
Tunisia, 1999–2004	Computerise and simplify procedures	$16.21 million
Tanzania	Buildings, equipment, new processes, training	$10 million

Scope.   Reform projects have included the following elements, few projects covered all the elements.

- *Computerisation* – including computerised customs systems, systems for warehouse inventory control and for statistical reporting.
- *Valuation procedures.*
- *Cargo controls* – speed up processing and eliminate fraudulent or incorrect valuation.
- *Building refurbishment* – refurbish customs buildings necessary to house ASYCUDA.
- *Administrative reforms* – establish a new division responsible for customs valuation and tariff classification, recruit and train staff, establish appeals tribunal, reduce discretion exercised by customs officers.
- *Anti-smuggling equipment* – provide laboratory and detection equipment for drug interdiction and other anti-smuggling efforts. Equipment ranges from x-ray equipment and gas chromatographs to communications equipment.
- *Management and staff training* – train staff in basic management, customs procedures and computer operations; establish staff training schools.
- *Screenings for drug interdiction.*
- *Legislative reforms* – rewrite laws, formally accede to the Harmonised System Convention, increase transparency.

To sum up this section, the reforms we have reviewed cover some 16 major categories of activities ranging from rewriting legislation through training in auditing procedures, physical security in customs warehouses, to policing of smuggling and of traffic in illicit drugs. Various of these components involve a cost in the neighbourhood of $10 million per country.

4. SANITARY AND PHYTOSANITARY STANDARDS

The SPS agreement recognises the right of governments to restrict trade when necessary to protect human, animal or plant life or health, but limits exercise of that right to the measures that do not unjustifiably discriminate between countries with the same conditions and are not disguised restrictions on trade. The SPS agreement further constrains a Member to impose such restrictions:

- only to the extent necessary to protect life or health,
- based on scientific principles,
- not maintained if scientific evidence is lacking.

The latter bullet implies that SPS measures can be put in place only on the basis of careful laboratory testing and analysis and if science-based concerns about food safety or serious threats to animal or plant health have been identified.

The WTO SPS agreement requires that the process of developing and enforcing SPS regulations be transparent. Governments must publish proposed regulations in advance and allow public comment, including from foreign exporters. Governments must notify the relevant international body of any changes to SPS rules and must establish Enquiry Points so that traders can determine a country's present and planned SPS regulations and processes.

Clout for exporters. Before the SPS agreement was in force, an exporter had, in effect, to comply with the importing country's SPS measures. With the agreement in force, the exporter must still comply with the importing country's SPS measures, but the importing country is, by the agreement, required to demonstrate that its SPS measures are in fact based on science and are applied equally to domestic and foreign producers. The Uruguay Round agreement puts the WTO on the side of those exporters who do comply – the exporter now has clearer grounds for challenging an import restriction.

In use, a heavier burden for developing countries. While the SPS agreement does not require that a country's *domestic* standards meet the agreement's requirements, it does require that the standards the country applies *at the border* meet those requirements. In this regard, the agreement likely places a heavier burden on developing than on industrial countries – this resulting from the standards already in place in the industrial countries more-or-less being established as the standard to which the developing countries must comply.

Article 3 of the SPS agreement specifies that SPS measures in conformity with relevant international conventions are to be *deemed* necessary to protect human, animal or plant health, and *presumed* consistent with the agreement. A country may adopt other standards or methods, but to apply them at the border the WTO agreement places on the country the burden of demonstrating their scientific merit and appropriateness. Industrial countries have been leaders in establishing these international conventions, the resulting conventions being in significant part

J. MICHAEL FINGER AND PHILIP SCHULER

generalisations of industrial country practices and standards. This does not imply that such standards are bad standards in a scientific sense, it does however imply that the SPS agreement provides for a more effective assault against current developing countries' use of SPS measures against imports than against industrial countries' use.

Application requires investment. For a developing country to effectively use the WTO agreement to defend its export rights or to justify its import restrictions, it will have to upgrade its SPS system to international standards. Effective use of the WTO agreement depends on extensive investments, it is not a matter of applying *existing systems* of standards to international trade, it is a much broader matter of installing world-class systems.

a. Lessons Learned from World Bank Experience

The World Bank has assisted several countries to implement sanitary and phytosanitary regulations. Bank projects supporting SPS systems have typically placed these measures in a general development context of ensuring food security, increasing agricultural productivity and protecting health, rather than focusing on the narrower objective of meeting stringent requirements in export markets.

Scope. One SPS-related project that the Bank has supported, an export reform project in Argentina, did however have as its objective to improve trade performance. The principal objective of the programme was to gain international recognition of certain zones as disease free or pest free. Argentina's meat, fruit and vegetable exports have been limited by other countries' concerns over the presence particularly of foot and mouth disease and citrus canker. In addition, the programme recognised that diversification into higher value-added exports such as processed meats, seeds, and horticultural products required producers to meet more stringent quality control standards. Some of the components of the programme that related directly to implementation of SPS standards were: upgrading veterinary services, central and field; laboratories; quarantine stations; disease and pest eradication programmes; certification of disease-free and pest-free zones; training, facilities and equipment for seed certification and registration, for quality control, and for certification to ensure the absence of chemical residues in exported meat; a laboratory to bring wool certification up to international standards; and staff and equipment for research aimed at reducing chemical residues.

Cost. The costs of several SPS-related projects that the World Bank has supported are reported in Table 2. In addition to such costs to the government, producers in the private sector bear other costs of complying with SPS regulations: vaccinating livestock, eliminating pesticide residues, guaranteeing sanitary food processing conditions, etc.

IMPLEMENTATION OF URUGUAY ROUND COMMITMENTS   519

TABLE 2
Costs of SPS-related World Bank Projects

Country	Project Description	Cost
Argentina, 1991–1996	General agricultural export reform project	$82.7 million
Brazil, 1987–1994	Livestock disease control project	$108 million
Algeria, 1988–1990	Locust Control project	$112 million
Vietnam, 1994–1997	Pest management component of Agricultural Rehabilitation project	$3.5 million
Madagascar, 1980–1988	Livestock vaccination component of Rural Development project	$11.8 million
Hungary, 1985–1991	Slaughterhouse modernisation component of Integrated Livestock Industry project	$41.2 million
Russia, 1992–1995	Improve food processing facilities, disease control – component of Rehabilitation Loan	$150 million
Poland, 1990–1995	Food processing facilities modernisation component of Agro-industries Export Development project	$71 million
China, 1993–2000	Animal and plant quarantine component of Agricultural Support Service project	$10 million
Turkey, 1992–1999	Modernise laboratories for residue control – component of Agricultural Research project	$3.3 million

5. INTELLECTUAL PROPERTY RIGHTS

The WTO TRIPs agreement covers the *seven* main areas of intellectual property: copyright, trademarks, geographical indications, industrial designs, patents, layout designs of integrated circuits, and undisclosed information including trade secrets. In each area, the agreement specifies minimum standards of protection that governments must provide,[4] requires governments to provide procedures to enforce, and provides means of dispute settlement. The minimum standards are similar for each of the seven areas; they cover, in the instance of patents (WTO, 1999, pp. 214f):

---

[4] One critic however argues that 'these [are] not "minimum" standards of intellectual property protection in the classical sense of the term; rather, they collectively expressed most of the standards of protection on which the developed countries could agree among themselves' (Reichman, 1998, p. 586).

J. MICHAEL FINGER AND PHILIP SCHULER

- What is patentable.
- What rights flow to the owner of a patent – government is obligated to prevent unauthorised persons from using, selling or importing the patent, the patented process, the patented product or the product or products directly made from the patented process.
- What exceptions to those rights are permissible – e.g., compulsory licensing may be required.
- How long the protection lasts.[5]

The TRIPs agreement, like the SPS agreement, builds on standards expressed in relevant international conventions such as the Paris Convention for the Protection of Industrial Property (1967) and the Washington Treaty – the Treaty on Intellectual Property in Respect of Integrated Circuits, sometimes labelled the ICIP Treaty (1989).

Extension of IPR obligations. The TRIPS Agreement requires each WTO member to adhere to the provisions (with a few provisions excepted) of these international IPR conventions, whether or not the member is party to those conventions. This, of itself, is a major extension for many countries. For example, the coverage of integrated circuits is an extension for many countries, including industrial countries.[6] Under TRIPs, WTO members must consider unlawful – if not authorised by the right-holder – the import, sale, or other commercial distribution of the integrated circuit design, of integrated circuits containing that design, and of articles that contain such integrated circuits.

Another example, the Rome Convention that establishes rights of performers, producers of sound recordings, and broadcasters has few signatories, particularly among developing countries. The TRIPs agreement creates the obligations on governments that allow recording companies from one country to attack unauthorised reproduction and sale of its products within another country. In addition, the TRIPs agreement in some areas has broader coverage than the relevant international convention. It goes beyond, for example, the Berne Convention to obligate copyright protection for certain computer programs and computerised data bases, and it provides the first multilateral obligations on industrial designs (e.g., textile designs).

---

[5] The TRIPs agreement provided the following transition periods: developed countries, until 1 January, 1996; developing countries and transition economies, up to 1 January, 2000; least developed countries, up to 1 January, 2006 – and may be extended on 'duly motivated' request by a least developed country. Developing countries that at present provide patent protection to processes and not to products, for example in the food, chemical and pharmaceutical sectors, can delay up to 1 January, 2005, the application of the obligation to protect products. Even here, governments must provide that inventions made between 1995 and 2004 will be able to gain patent protection after 1 January, 2005.

[6] This treaty is not yet in force; having thus far only nine signatories, of which only one has ratified.

The enforcement provisions of TRIPs require that a member provide civil as well as criminal remedies for infringement of intellectual property rights. They also obligate members to provide means by which right-holders can obtain the cooperation of customs authorities to prevent imports of infringing goods.

Wiggle room. While it is impossible to predict how the process of application and interpretation through the WTO dispute settlement mechanism will play out, a number of legal experts[7] see sufficient 'wiggle room' in the agreement so that developing countries could – within a good faith implementation of their obligations – strike a balance between the interests of second-comers and the need to promote innovation and investment. This would however require a considerable departure from the balance that has been institutionalised in the industrial countries' intellectual property rights law. That balance, many experts argue, is tipped toward the interests of commercialised producers of knowledge – tipped past the point of optimality even for the community of interests that make up industrial country societies.[8]

The tendency of the WTO is however to give the benefit of the doubt to established standards. Finding grounds for moving away from established standards is particularly difficult in the area of intellectual property rights. They are, after all, an existential matter of legal definition, not a scientific matter of empirical estimation.

How to do it. Even for an individual country, it would be nigh on impossible to provide objective guidelines as to how to strike the optimal balance between legal incentives to create, and the costs that are thereby incurred by users and potential second-comers. Systems in place must be defended as the outcome of accepted (e.g., democratic) political processes, not of scientific calibration. It would be even more difficult to scale this balance to different levels of economic development. Analysts have so far built up little knowledge of the impacts of various forms of intellectual property rights on economic development, even less about different degrees of any form.[9]

Our review of case studies in support of IPR again shows a considerable range of needed reforms; drafting new legislation (e.g., to extend IPR protection to plant varieties), augmenting administrative structures (e.g., capacity to review applications, including computerised information systems and extensive training for staff) and buttressing enforcement. Some information on costs is reported in Table 3.

---

[7] Reichman (1998), and references cited there.

[8] Reichman (1998, p. 589) for example urges that 'the logical course of action for the developing countries in implementing their obligations under the TRIPs Agreement is to shoulder the pro-competitive mantle that the developed countries have increasingly abandoned. Templeman (1998) argues that there is no public justification for the level of intellectual property rights defined by industrial countries' laws.'

[9] Abbott (1998, p. 501) in his introduction and summing-up to an issue of the *Journal of International Economic Law* devoted to TRIPs, notes this lack of understanding of the impact of IPR on economic development.

J. MICHAEL FINGER AND PHILIP SCHULER

TABLE 3
World Bank Projects Related to Intellectual Property Rights

Country	Project Description	Cost
Brazil, 1997–2002	Train staff administering IPR laws – component of Science and Technology Reform project	$4.0 million
Indonesia, 1997–2003	Improve IPR regulatory framework – component of Information Infrastructure Development project	$14.7 million
Mexico, 1992–1996	Established agency to implement industrial property laws – component of Science and Technology Infrastructure project	$32.1 million

6. CONCLUSIONS

We draw the following major lessons from our review.

Reform is needed. In the areas we have covered, customs administration, sanitary and phytosanitary standards and intellectual property rights, we found no shortage of projects to review. Developing countries are willing to borrow money to finance improvements in these areas; hence it is evident that they, themselves, see a need for reform.

Delay is not an asset. We should be careful not to be lulled into the mercantilist ethic of a reciprocal negotiation in which delay, of itself, is a victory. Where reform is needed, to delay the improvements is to lengthen the time that the people in these countries remain poor. Time will, of course, be needed for implementation, but implementation periods should be based on the engineering requirements to accomplish the required construction, not handed out as second prize in a tough negotiation.

Do it my way. The content of the obligations imposed by the WTO agreements on customs valuation, intellectual property rights and SPS can be characterised as the advanced countries saying to the others, *Do it my way!* The customs valuation agreement imposes a system in use in the leading industrial countries on all TRIPS and the SPS agreement is explicit in establishing international conventions developed in large part by the industrial countries as the WTO standard.

While the SPS agreement appears to allow the retention of an indigenous system, doing so is not a real alternative. In defending trade-related actions, the systems recognised by international conventions have the legal benefit of the doubt, an indigenous system must prove itself. The least developed countries do not have the resources needed to do that; hence the only effective option for a country that retains an indigenous system of standards is *not to apply* standards at the border.[10] The WTO's *free* rider problem has not gone away, it has been swapped for a *forced* rider problem, its burden shifted from the industrial countries to the least developed countries.

Heavier obligations on developing countries.   For the advanced countries whose systems are compatible with international conventions (or vice versa) the WTO brings no more than an obligation to apply their *domestic regulations* fairly at the border. This includes not discriminating among transactions involving different countries and not unnecessarily impeding international transactions. Countries that at present apply their own indigenous standards, have the additional – and far larger – obligation to apply the internationally sanctioned standards in their domestic economies. Though new WTO areas, e.g., SPS, intellectual property rights, aim at the trade-related aspects of their subject matter, for the least developed countries they require first the establishment of such systems, or the conversion of indigenous systems to the system recognised by international conventions.

A related lesson is that the scope of what the WTO regulates is narrower than the scope of what must be done to make development sense out of implementation. For example, customs valuation versus customs reform – it helps little to change customs *valuation* procedures if containers still stay on the dock for 60 days.

Inappropriate diagnosis and inappropriate remedy.   One effect of this 'Do it my way!' nature of the agreements is to intensify the ownership problem, discussed below. In addition, this characteristic brings back our initial questions. From a development perspective:

- Do the WTO agreements appropriately identify the problems faced by developing countries?
- Given the least developed countries' needs and their resource bases, do the agreements provide the most effective remedy?

The customs valuation agreement, we have argued above, provides neither appropriate diagnosis nor appropriate remedy. It addresses only a small part of least developed countries' problems with customs administration and of course provides no remedy over other parts. Over the small part of the problem it covers, it provides an inappropriate remedy, one incompatible with the resources they have at their disposal.

Our conclusions on the intellectual property rights agreement are similar. As to diagnosis, its focus is not on encouraging innovation or protecting endogenous technology in developing countries, it is on industrial country enterprises' collecting for intellectual property on which least developed countries now

---

[10] We are not arguing here that the iron fist imposes the wrong standards. Our concern is to remove the velvet glove of comforting rhetoric from that fist.

recognise no obligation to pay. The default remedy is to copy industrial country intellectual property law. While legal scholars point out that the intellectual property agreement allows for the possibility of adopting intellectual property law that is friendly to users and to second-comers, they point out that the benefit of the doubt is on the side of copying present industrial country approaches. A major cost of standardising on the current industrial country example is to cut off experimentation – the process of developing more appropriate legal approaches in developing countries.[11]

Effective implementation and compliance involves investment-development projects, but WTO negotiations have not supported examination from this perspective. The dynamic behind the WTO process has been the export interests of major enterprises in the advanced trading countries. Development ministries in the advanced countries frequently complain how hard it is to get their trade ministries to pay attention to development issues. In the advanced countries, development ministries are junior partners in making trade policy; at the WTO, the least developed countries have little capacity to organise and to advance their own interests.

No ownership of the reforms in least developed countries. The lack of instinctive ownership of the reforms needed to comply with WTO obligations will make implementation very difficult, and will likely push governments to superficial adjustments aimed at avoiding clashes with trading partners. Private and social sector shareholders were not involved in the creation of these obligations – nor even the government agencies that will ultimately be responsible for implementation. How the least developed countries organise their participation in WTO affairs needs modification; perhaps the WTO process also.

Allowing for alternatives vs. providing alternatives. Each of the three Uruguay Round agreements we have reviewed includes a promise of assistance to implement. In addition, each provides for delayed implementation, and provides also a way for a least developed country to request an extension beyond the agreement's deadlines. The latter provision might be interpreted as recognition that the prescribed or default technology included in the agreements might not be the most suitable for the least developed countries. Though the agreements allow for the possibility that alternative approaches might be developed and recognised, they provide no such alternative. As to developing alternatives, the WTO negotiations are a self-interest propelled process. Narrowly interpreted, that places the burden of developing alternatives that are appropriate to least developed countries' needs and their resources on the least developed countries themselves.

---

[11] Matthew Stillwell of the Centre for International Environmental Law pointed this out to us.

It costs money. The project costs we have presented here provide a first approximation to the investments needed to implement WTO obligations on SPS, IPR and customs reform. To gain acceptance for its meat, vegetables and fruits in industrial country markets, Argentina spent over $80 million to achieve higher levels of plant and animal sanitation. Hungary spent over $40 million to upgrade the level of sanitation of its slaughterhouses alone. Mexico spent over $30 million to upgrade intellectual property laws and enforcement that began at a higher level than are in place in most least developed countries. We identified some 16 elements, in customs reform, each of which can cost more than $2.5 million to implement. The figures, for just three of the six Uruguay Round Agreements that involve restructuring of domestic regulations, come to $150 million.[12] One hundred and fifty million dollars is more than the annual development budget for eight of the twelve least developed countries for which we could find a figure for that part of the budget.

REFERENCES

Abbott, F.M. (1998), 'The Enduring Enigma of TRIPS: A Challenge for the World Economic System', *Journal of International Economic Law*, 1, 4 (Oxford: Oxford University Press), 497–52.

Cunningham, B. (1996), *Tanzania: Strategy and Action Plan to Reform Customs Administration* (Tanzania Revenue Authority, June).

Michalopoulos, C. (1998), *Developing Countries' Participation in the World Trade Organization*, Policy Research Working Paper No. 1906 (Washington DC: The World Bank, March).

Ogunkola, E.O. (1999), 'African Capacity for Compliance and Defense of WTO Rights', Conference Paper for AERC Sponsored Africa and the World Trading System (Yaounde, Cameroon, 17–18 April).

Reichman, J.H. (1998), 'Securing Compliance with the TRIPS Agreement After US v India', *Journal of International Economic Law*, 1, 4 (Oxford: Oxford University Press), 603–6.

Templeman, L.S. (1998), 'Intellectual Property', *Journal of International Economic Law*, 1, 4 (Oxford: Oxford University Press), 585–602.

World Customs Organisation (1999), 'Survey of Customs Reform and Modernization: Trends and Best Practices', on WCO Website at www.wcoomd.org/frmpublic.htm.

WTO Secretariat (1999), *Guide to the Uruguay Round Agreements* (The Hague, Kluwer Law International).

---

[12] The experiences we have reviewed were in the more advanced developing countries, the costs could be higher in the least developed countries who will begin further from the required standards.

PART SIX

CONCLUSION

[18]

Policy Research

The title of this discourse is "Policy Research," a contradiction in terms. Its purpose is to explain that the demise of this once proud office was not an accident of circumstance but an inexorable consequence of a tendency which has been at the heart of political systems since the Middle Ages.

The elements which come together to explain this phenomenon were collected in various places.

The first element appeared at the International Trade Commission, where for a year I was privileged to observe both the deliberations of the commission to reach decisions and the diligent efforts of their staff to produce a staff report. But there was no relationship of one to the other. Indeed, the place where the commission's decision and the staff report came together was always the printshop. I notice that though its purpose was obscure, the staff report did serve a function—to misdirect and to obfuscate. Having been exposed to the institutionalist tradition, I was confident that this function served some purpose, but I was unable to determine what that purpose was.

Years passed, and I observed that in nearly every town and city of Europe, there was a "Jews quarter" or *Ruelle des Juifs* in the old commercial part of town. This treasure, too, I stored in the backyard of my mind.

Finally, a book by Lester Thurow reminded us that zero-sum decisions are *very* difficult for a democratic political process to make. Then things began to fall into place. The purpose of misdirection and obfuscation became obvious. By making the decision process difficult to understand, they discourage those with a diffuse or marginal interest from participating in the decision; that is, they tend to disenfranchise the opponents to a petition for protection and hence transform a zero-sum *situation* into a positive-sum *decision*—a decision from which all the *effective* participants will gain.

This, then, is the essence of the decision process. Unless the great clamor of procedure confuses one side about what is going on, there can be no decision, that is, no policy.

Presented September 4, 1980, at the U.S. Treasury Department, on the occasion of the departure of Finger and the dissolution of the Office of Trade Research, of which Finger was the director.

[*Journal of Political Economy*, 1981, vol. 89, no. 6]

Of course, if procedure confuses both sides, the government is in the ideal situation of not having to make a decision at all. This occurs with some frequency.

But if one side sees through the obfuscation and the other does not (the result which the system seems designed to produce), then the aware side's interests will be disproportionately weighted in the decision process, and equilibrium will be "too far" in their direction. In summary, the policy process in an open political system

       (1) does not do a lot of things it should do,

       (2) appears to do a lot of things it does not do, and

       (3) overdoes everything it does do.

Good research which accurately identifies the costs and benefits of a course of action is, in any of these avenues, more likely to be embarrassing than welcome. It returns attention to the direct conflict which had to be *avoided* before a course of action—a policy—could be set. This means that a person who delivers a novel piece of analytical work to his Political Master will be made to feel like a woman who brings a new child to her husband—who had a vasectomy 5 years before. The Master is less likely to share her joy in the birth of a new thing than to decry this evidence of her having conspired with mean spirits. Political responsibility is, you see, the ultimate intellectual vasectomy.

The history of research in government agencies is like the history of Jews in pre–Industrial Revolution Europe. The Gentiles of a town would decide that they wanted to establish their town as a center of commerce. They would then invite the practitioners of this science into their town and set aside a place where they might live and practice. But, the Jews would practice their trade by rules so basic that they would not allow their gentlemen competitors, to whom commerce was a diversion and a livelihood but not a life-style, to turn a profit. So, slowly the number of streets open to the Jews would be restricted and the number of products they were allowed to trade reduced. Or, they would be limited to the wholesale trade, in the hope that gentlemen could turn a profit retailing the merchandise the Jews gathered.

But their numbers would dwindle, not so much because they had been sent away but because other Gentiles in other towns had decided that they should establish centers of commerce and had lured them away, to begin the process again.

As we see across Europe the signs announcing the former presence of Jews, we see across organization charts of government agencies the street signs of research. But the original citizens of these quarters have usually gone, and their places have been taken by reform congregations, or even Gentiles. Thus, we, the researchers, like the Jews of the Middle Ages, are cursed to wander from agency to agency, deprived of home and property by our inability to lose track of what we do.[1]

J. MICHAEL FINGER

World Bank

[1] The mortal remains (former employees) of the dissolved Office of Trade Research were sent away with a memento inscribed "There are no Statesmen in this business. Trade theory is about whose hand is in whose pocket and trade policy is about who should take it out." It was noted gratefully that as they departed, their temple would be dismantled and the signs in their quarter taken down. Thus they would be spared the indignity of seeing a reform congregation move in and eat pork and write briefing papers where once they followed the old law. The spirit of the office was also dispatched. It was represented by a full frontal picture of a charging infantry brigade, inscribed, "We owe our success to a simple underlying philosophy."

Name index